A MAN OF SUCCESS IN THE LAND OF SUCCESS

The Biography of Marcel Goldman, a Kracovian in Tel Aviv

Jews of Poland

Series Editor
Antony Polonsky (Brandeis University, Waltham, Massachusetts)

A MAN OF SUCCESS IN THE LAND OF SUCCESS

The Biography of Marcel Goldman, a Kracovian in Tel Aviv

Łukasz Tomasz Sroka

Translated by
Katarzyna Rogalska-Chodecka

BOSTON
2022

Library of Congress Control Number: 2022934568

ISBN 9781644699119 (paperback)
ISBN 9781644698730 (adobe pdf)
ISBN 9781644698747 (epub)

Copyright © 2022 Academic Studies Press
All rights reserved

Reviewers: Prof. Antony Polonsky, Prof. Sławomir Jacek Żurek

Book design by Tatiana Vernikov
Cover design by Ivan Grave

Published by Academic Studies Press
1577 Beacon Street
Brookline, MA 02446, USA
press@academicstudiespress.com
www.academicstudiespress.com

Book was financed with funds from the National Science Center (Poland), granted under contract number UMO-2015/19/B/HS3/02116

Contents

Preface by Aleksander B. Skotnicki	8
Introduction	11
1. Mythical Krakow—Childhood (1926–1939)	36
2. The Hell of Extermination—Youth, Part One (1939–1945)	75
3. The Aliyah Time—Youth, Part Two (1945–1954)	123
4. In the Land of Success—The Mature Age (1954–2019)	238
Conclusion	390
Afterword by Leopold "Poldek" Wasserman, or Yehuda Maimon	403
Bibliography	409
Index	424

People in Israel are a record of history, history is so strong in people that it is impossible to tear it away from human stories, it is impossible not to talk about the history of the nation talking about the history of a single man, and this is one more peculiarity of Israel

—*Aleksander Rozenfeld*
Podanie o prawo powrotu

Preface

As a postwar Krakovian, walking the streets of our city, to which I owe so much, for seventy years, I have always been interested in its history and its inhabitants.

Knowledge about the past can be increased using archival resources, documents, published monographs, but also postcards, photos, or other so-called leaflets. You can also look back and learn history thanks to eyewitnesses, especially those who have lived before us, and look through their eyes at the reality of that time unknown to us.

About twenty years ago, I was lucky and honoured to meet many prewar Krakovians who, born in the 1920s and 1930s, remembered or remember that world unknown to me, with its many colours, climate, people living at that time, customs and atmosphere of schools that they went to. Their prewar history, then the tragic period of the German occupation of Krakow during World War II, and the postwar time spent in Poland, as well as in the United States and Israel, were the subject of several studies that I dedicated to them and their families. One of those people was Marcel Goldman and his wife Bianka.[1] Describing their biographies, as well as stories of other people from those times, I tried to learn about interpersonal relations in the multicultural prewar Krakow, living conditions, social and political organizations, education and earning opportunities, taking into account their role in the economic, social, and cultural development of the city.

I am very happy that Prof. Łukasz Tomasz Sroka from the Pedagogical University of Krakow has made the effort to study the history of Jewish people living at that time to a much greater extent than I did. Writing about the life of Marcel Goldman, he also presented his role in the construction of the new Jewish state, in which he has actively participated since 1949.

Marcel Goldman is an extraordinary person in many ways—charming as a man, full of kindness to others, making friends in Poland, Israel, and in Switzerland, where he lived and worked for ten years. Wherever he is, his interest in

---

1 *Marcel Goldman. Krakowian i Izraelczyk*, ed. A. B. Skotnicki with M. Ostoja-Wilamowska, [s.l.] 2008. This book was published by Stradomskie Centrum Dialogu.

local community affairs, history, and achievements arouses sympathy, and his extraordinary clarity of mind, great memory, and knowledge of modern means of communication create a space of mutual relations that gives both sides a lot of satisfaction.

Over the past dozen or so years, despite the passing time, he has visited Poland, and especially Krakow, many times, he was here two or even three times a year. He came here for the need of his heart, a noble memory for Holocaust victims, to take part in the annual Remembrance March, as well as in meetings and lectures in high school and academic circles to which he was invited.

As a member of the Polish-Israeli Friendship Society, he builds bridges between both of his homelands, although today he rather considers himself an Israeli visiting his old homeland.

When I was hosted by him in Israel, I could explore the beautiful spots of the country including Jerusalem, Haifa, Eilat, and the Dead Sea. His knowledge of history, ease of making contacts, and the anecdotes he told added colour to those visits and meetings and made them memorable for many years. He is an extraordinary erudite who attracts the attention of listeners, and the content transmitted by him is well-thought-out and deep in its philosophical, social, and political layer. He has a strong opinion in many matters, which proves his strong character, rich personality, and fidelity to the principles he adheres to.

He started his career from the lowest levels, gaining more and more banking skills, until he reached a position that allowed him to manage banks in Israel and Switzerland. His opinions and consultations in this field count to this day. It confirms that he has consistently pursued his goals in his life path, which also brought him recognition, acceptance and respect in the new environment of the Israeli community.

Despite his preoccupation with professional and social life, he also showed literary and poetic talents, publishing volumes of poetry and stories about past and modern times. I had the honour to organise and participate in the promotion of Marcel Goldman's works in Krakow. I undertook this task not only because of many years of friendship, but also because of genuine admiration for his need and determination in sharing his thoughts and life experience with others.

I have been to his hospitable home in Tel Aviv many times, meeting eminent personalities from the world of culture, art, and politics. Marcel Goldman also helped me in research and publishing activity, making it easier for me to reach many prewar Jews of Krakow. Among them, there were Tulo Schenirer, Poldek Wasserman, and Rena Wohlfeiler from Haifa.

I am convinced that the present book by Prof. Łukasz Tomasz Sroka will deepen the knowledge about this extraordinary man, his achievements, and intellectual and cultural wealth. I hope that this book will be interesting not only for researchers, but also for people for whom Krakow's past and present, Polish-Jewish relations, as well as the present of Israel are areas of interest and deep reflection.

Prof. Aleksander B. Skotnicki
Jagiellonian University

Introduction

Israel is a state that, being firmly rooted in history, actively participates in the discourse about the future. The joy of considerable successes is intertwined with the reflection on tragic events from the near and distant past. Futuristic ideas and technologies grow there in a reality full of still unsolved problems, sometimes prosaic, sometimes more serious. The keyword accompanying the description of Israel should be "diversity" because it concerns nature, architecture, monuments, culture, society, cuisine, political attitudes, and many other areas.

The phenomenon of Israel has been the subject of research and analysis of scholars and experts representing various fields. Representatives of the business world are fascinated by how this small country has achieved international success at a pace and to the extent of which even the most developed countries can be envious. Foreign scientists associated with practically all scientific disciplines, including medicine, computer science, cybernetics, biology, biotechnology, and biochemistry want to draw on the rich treasury of Israeli scientists' experience. Military and intelligence agents from various countries are interested not only in the armament, but also in the achievements, working methods, and solutions used by the Israeli army and special services. Information about the progress recorded in Israel in the work on artificial intelligence, genetics, renewable energy sources, care for the natural environment, and the development of modern techniques used in industry, construction, and agriculture are not out of the forefront of global media. Journalist programs, as well as popular science and scientific works on this subject are being constantly created.

It is impossible to list here all the important scientific positions in the field of interest to us. The first successful attempts to explain Israel's economic success include books by David Horowitz.[1] The book by Dan Senor and Saul Singer

---

1   See D. Horowitz, *The Economics of Israel*, Oxford 1967; idem, *The Enigma of Economic Growth. A Case Study of Israel*, New York 1972. David Horowitz, born in 1899 in Drohobych, died in 1979. He had an economics background. He was involved in the HaShomer HaTzair movement. In 1920 he emigrated to Eretz Yisrael, worked in a kibbutz, later also as a laborer in Jerusalem. In 1932 he became an economic advisor to the American Economic Committee for Eretz Yisrael. In the years 1935–1948 he worked for the Institute of Economic Research of the Jewish Agency and the Department of Economic Affairs of Israel. Those institutions preceded the later Ministries of Finance and Economy of the State of Israel. In 1947, he

entitled *Start-up Nation: The Story of Israel's Economic Miracle*[2] gained wide publicity and became a world bestseller (listed, among others, by the *New York Times*).

Among historical syntheses, Anita Shapira's work *The History of Israel*[3] has a canonical character—it is a well-documented book full of brilliant theses. The more frequently cited publications also include the monograph by Colin Shindler, *A History of Modern Israel*. It was created using memoirs, press (in particular Israeli, American, and British), and international literature (including Hebrew). The work of Michael Bar-Zohar *Kitzur toldot Yisrael* (Brief history of Israel)[4] is also noteworthy. The author, a historian, writer, politician, and Israeli intelligence specialist, created a picture of Israel that is colourful, easily written, and at the same time abundant in deep political reflection. The classics of the genre also include the work of Polish historians, Andrzej Chojnowski and Jerzy Tomaszewski, entitled *Izrael*.[5]

In 2018, the first interdisciplinary academic textbook on contemporary Israel, *Demokracja izraelska* (Israeli democracy), was written by Krzysztof Chaczko, Artur Skorek, and the author of these words.[6] Tom Segev described the influence of the Shoah on shaping social and political relations within Israel and its relations with Western countries (especially Germany). He is the author of an extremely efficiently written and richly documented book, *The Seventh Million: The Israelis and the Holocaust*.[7] In many countries of the world, authors explaining the specificity of Israel and discussing, and sometimes even co-shaping their relations with Israel, are very popular. In Poland, Shevah Weiss is a well-known and respected connector with Israel and a commentator on current affairs of this country.[8]

---

co-created the delegation of the Jewish Agency for Israel. He was the first general director of the Israeli Ministry of Finance. In 1954 he became the first governor, initiator of the creation and the actual organiser of the Bank of Israel. In 1970 he published an autobiography entitled *My Yesterday*.

2   D. Senor, S. Singer, *Naród start-upów. Historia cudu gospodarczego Izraela*, preface Shimon Peres, trans. A. Wojtaszczyk and O. Wojtaszczyk, Warsaw 2013.
3   A. Shapira, *Historia Izraela*, trans. A. D. Kamińska, Warsaw 2018.
4   M. Bar-Zohar, *Kitzur toldot Yisrael*, Rishon LeZion 2018.
5   A. Chojnowski, J. Tomaszewski, *Izrael*, Warsaw 2001.
6   K. Chaczko, A. Skorek, Ł.T. Sroka, *Demokracja izraelska*, preface S. Weiss, Warsaw 2018.
7   T. Segev, *Siódmy million. Izrael—piętno Zagłady*, trans. B. Gadomska, Warsaw 2012.
8   Shevah Weiss, born in 1935 in Borysław, professor of political science, Israeli politician and diplomat, MP of the Knesset (1981–1999) and its chairman (1992–1996), in 2001–2003

I find the book by Yehuda Avner (who died in 2015 in Jerusalem) *The Prime Ministers: An Intimate Narratives of Israeli Leadership*[9] to be very valuable and original, as it reveals to the reader what was behind the scenes of the functioning of the highest circles of power in Israel. Avner publishes first-hand information because he was a high-ranking diplomat, the author of texts for, and secretary of, the prime ministers Levi Eshkol and Golda Meir, and adviser to Yitzhak Rabin, Menachem Begin, and Shimon Peres. Earlier (1982), his other publication *The Young Inheritors: A Portrait of Israel's Children* (with photos by G. Levine) was released and welcomed by readers in Israel, the United States and many other countries.[10] Yehuda Avner's son-in-law, David Sable, called him "Begin's Shakespeare,"[11] emphasising that: "His legacy is the State of Israel, the state to which he devoted his life. His gift to us: his words that will live and continue to inspire future generations around the world."[12]

Of course, historiography does not lack biographies describing the life and work of the leading figures of Zionism, the founding fathers of the State of Israel and its greatest political leaders.[13] The two-volume work of Henry Near

---

the Israeli ambassador in Poland. In our country, he received the highest awards and distinctions, including the Grand Cordon of the Order of Merit of the Republic of Poland (2004) and the Order of the White Eagle (2017). To date, he has been awarded the title of doctor honoris causa by the University of Wrocław (2006), the University of Warsaw (2011), the Medical University of Lodz (2011), the Academy of Special Education (2012) and the University of Economics in Katowice (2013). He made himself known to Poles as a frequent guest of television and radio programs, author of texts published in the press (including right-wing press), and books. See S. Weiss, E. Czerezińska, *Z jednej strony, z drugiej strony*, Warsaw 2005; S. Weiss, *Czas ambasadora*, ed. and comp. J. Szwedowska, Krakow 2003; idem, *Ludzie i miejsca*, Krakow 2013; idem, *Pamiętam...*, interview by K. Drecka, Krakow 2018.

9 Y. Avner, *The Prime Ministers: An Intimate Narrative of Israeli Leadership*, 2nd ed., Jerusalem 2017.

10 Idem, *The Young Inheritors: A Portrait of Israel's Children*, photographs G. Levine, introduction H. Wouk, New York 1982.

11 A. Lewis, "Yehuda Avner, Diplomat and Political Icon, Dies at 86," https://www.timesofisrael.com/yehuda-avner-diplomat-and-political-icon-dies-at-86/, accessed February 12, 2018.

12 Ibid.

13 In this trend, the most original and important works include Sh. Avineri, *Herzl's Vision. Theodor Herzl and the Foundation of the Jewish State*, transl. H. Watzman, New York 2014; M. Bar-Zohar, *Ben Gurion: Biografia*, Jerusalem 1980; idem, *Ben Gurion: Ha-yish me-achorei ha-agadah*, Tel Aviv 1987; D. Gordis, *Menachem Begin: Ha-maabak al nishmatah shel Yisrael*, Jerusalem 2015; O. Grosbard, *Menachem Begin: Diyukano shel manhyig—Biografia*, Tel Aviv 2006; M. Medzini, *Ha-yehudiah ha-geah: Golda Meir ve-chazon Yisrael. Biografia politit*, Tel Aviv 1990.

The Kibbutz Movement. A History[14] is considered the leading position regarding the movement in question. The city of Tel Aviv also became the subject of research. In this regard, I especially recommend the book by Ilan Schori, whose title, *Tel-Aviv: The Dynamics of a Dream*,[15] is itself very thought-provoking. The unique status of Jerusalem was accurately analyzed by, among others, Simon Sebag Montefiore in the book *Jerusalem. The Biography*[16] and Karen Armstrong in the publication *Jerusalem: One City, Three Faiths*.[17]

Among the books on Israeli intelligence, I particularly recommend *Mossad: The Greatest Missions of the Israeli Secret Service*, written in an accessible and passionate way by Michael Bar-Zohar and Nissim Mishal.[18] Ronen Bergman's *Rise and Kill First: The Secret History of Israel's Targeted Assassinations*[19] is also noteworthy. Its strength are several hundred conversations that the author conducted with people associated with the Israeli defense sector, often with high-ranking intelligence officers. Israel's achievements in military technology were described in an interesting and reliable way in the volume by Yaakov Katz and Amir Bohbot, *The Weapon Wizards: How Israel Became a High-Tech Military Superpower*.[20]

There is a long list of publications describing Israel in the context of international relations. Topics that bother researchers most often include Israel's relations with Western countries, primarily with the United States.[21] It is worth noting several well-documented works, often cited in international literature,

---

14 H. Near, *The Kibbutz Movement. A History*, vol. 1: *Origins and Growth, 1909–1939*, vol. 2: *Crisis and Achievement, 1939–1995*, Oxford 2008.

15 I. Shori, *Chalom she-hafakh li-khrakh. Tel Aviv, leda u-tzemicha: Ha-ir she-holida medina*, Tel Aviv 1990.

16 S. Sebag Montefiore, *Jerozolima. Biografia*, transl. M. Antosiewicz, W. Jeżewski, Warsaw 2011.

17 K. Armstrong, *Jerozolima: miasto trzech religii*, transl. B. Cendrowska, Warsaw 2000.

18 M. Bar-Zohar, N. Mishal, *Mossad. Najważniejsze misje izraelskich tajnych służb*, transl. K. Bażyńska-Chojnacka, P. Chojnacki, Poznań 2013.

19 R. Bergman, *Powstań i zabij pierwszy. Tajna historia skrytobójczych akcji izraelskich służb specjalnych*, trans. P. Grzegorzewski and J. Wołk-Łaniewski, Katowice 2019/

20 Y. Katz, A. Bohbot, *Czarodzieje broni. Izrael—tajne laboratorium technologii militarnych*, trans. N. Radomski, Poznań 2018.

21 As a side note, let me point out that one of the most famous Israeli writers in the world, Amos Oz (died in December 2018) warned the Israelis: "David Ben Gurion taught us that the State of Israel would not be able to survive without support from at least one power. Whose? It changes. Once, Great Britain, at other times even Stalinist Russia, once, for a short period of time, it was England and France, and in recent decades, America. But the alliance with America does not belong to the laws of nature. It is a variable, not a constant factor," A. Oz, *Do fanatyków. Trzy refleksje*, trans. L. Kwiatkowski, Poznań 2018, 119–120.

on the contribution of the United States to the creation and development of Israel.²² In 2018, Justyna Podemska's book *Amerykańska krucjata. USA wobec powstania Państwa Izrael* (The American crusade. USA and the creation of the State of Israel)²³ was published. Thanks to her advanced studies and meticulous work with reference literature, she wrote a book full of original thoughts as well as detailed and important information.²⁴ Further, Artur Patek is the author of the reliable monograph *Wielka Brytania wobec Izraela w okresie pierwszej wojny arabsko-izraelskiej, maj 1948–styczeń 1949* (Great Britain's relations with Israel during the First Arab-Israeli War, May 1948–January 1949), based on a large selection of primary sources.²⁵

The concept of this book is that the State of Israel has been portrayed from the perspective of one man's life and accomplishments. Methodologically, I assumed the parallelity of the narrative. On the one hand, I am telling the story of the rise of the state and the people who created it in a chronological and geopolitical order: Poland, emigration, Israel. On the other hand, I describe the life of a specific person in a chronological and biographical order: childhood, youth, adulthood. The work does not aspire to the role of a full synthesis, which explains all issues related to the history of Israel, but it is a pretext biography. I defined two main research goals. The first one is to familiarize the reader with the figure of Marcel Goldman, while on the basis of his life and achievements I tried to portray the social and economic development of Israel and explain why this development has been successful. In my opinion, the life path and professional profile of Marcel Goldman make it possible to broaden the scope of knowledge about the social and economic circumstances of building and developing the State of Israel, which is so often admired because of the successes associated with it. The Israeli economy, which stands out globally, along with science representing

---

22 See M. T. Benson, *Harry S. Truman and the Founding of Israel*, foreword S. A. Taylor, Westport, CT 1997; A. Radosh, R. Radosh, *A Safe Haven. Harry S. Truman and Founding of Israel*, New York 2009; D. Schoenbaum, *The United States and the State of Israel*, New York 1993.

23 J. Podemska, *Amerykańska krucjata. USA wobec powstania Państwa Izrael*, Warsaw 2018.

24 This book appeared, to a large extent, thanks to the author's year-and-a-half-long stay in the United States, during which she researched archival materials collected in Harry S. Truman Presidential Library in Independence, MO. She also conducted research at the University of Notre Dame in Indiana (Hesburgh Library).

25 A. Patek, *Wielka Brytania wobec Izraela w okresie pierwszej wojny arabsko-izraelskiej maj 1948–styczeń 1949*, Krakow 2002.

a high level, innovative medicine and agriculture as well as the legendary army and intelligence, are in a way Israel's trademarks.

The book's title requires a brief commentary, being marketing-friendly, and at the same time having solid substantive justification. I wanted it to convey the message that the book is about two phenomena: the life of a single man and the history of the country he co-created. I tried to emphasise the existing relationship between them, showing that Israel's success was possible thanks to the life attitude of people such as Marcel Goldman, and they in turn gained unique development conditions in that country. The subtitle *Krakovian in Tel Aviv* also needs clarification. For some readers, it may turn out to be misleading, as the protagonist, after arriving in Israel, lived in Haifa for many years, and the Tel Aviv period of his life was interrupted with a long stay in Zurich. The term "Krakovian" is to emphasise Marcel Goldman's lasting relationship with the city where he was born and spent the first twenty years of his life. He himself

The history of Israel is inseparably connected with the multitude of names used to designate its territory. The name "Israel" comes from the Hebrew Bible (Tanakh)—this is the name that Patriarch Jacob received as "one who fights victoriously with God" (Genesis 32:25–33). The biblical nation grew from the descendants of Jacob, commonly called "Children of Israel" or "Israelites." The modern state, whose independence was proclaimed on May 14, 1948, is called in Hebrew Medinat Yisrael, which translates into English as "the State of Israel." The correct translation should be "Land of Israel," but the name "State of Israel" has become common, which is why I use it in the book. For Jews, Israel is also the Promised Land—the biblical Canaan. For Christians, this is the Holy Land related to the life and teaching of Jesus Christ. In the second century CE, the term "Palestine" appeared. After the suppression of the Bar Kokhba revolt, which broke out in 135, the Romans changed the name of the province of Judea to Palestine, which comes from the name of the Philistines—one of the non-Semitic so-called "peoples of the sea." This name was popularized by Christian literature. By 1922, no state organism had been, for a long time, known as Palestine. Indeed, the territory stretching from the Mediterranean coast to the mountainous area east of the Jordan River was constantly being conquered. after the Romans came the Byzantines, who were followed by the Arabs, the Muslim Seljuk dynasty, the Christian crusaders, the Muslim Mameluks, and the Ottoman Turks. In 1917, during World War I, the British took over that territory. In

declares that despite decades of separation from Poland, he never stopped feeling a Krakovian. In contrast, Tel Aviv, which is commonly identified with success in Israel, and Israelis consider it a proper place to crown their professional careers, is to draw readers' attention to the incredible professional success of the book's protagonist and to let them realise that this success, achieved in Tel Aviv, is much more important than a success in other cities of this country. In this respect, only Jerusalem can be competitive, while Haifa, in which Marcel lived for years, cannot.

I would also like to add that the book was created for an international reader—the Polish edition was the basis for the translation into English—which is why I tried to make it understandable for those interested in the topic in Poland, Israel, and in every other country in the world. When I started writing the book, I assumed that it would allow readers to get to know the background of the State of Israel. Traditional monographs on the history of a (specific) state most often

> 1922, the international community of the League of Nations sanctioned the then-current state of affairs, entrusting the British with a mandate over Palestine. The British Mandate for Palestine existed until 1948. At that time, the name "Palestine" was propagated even more, but it did not mean an autonomous state, let alone a Palestinian nation. The term "Palestine" was also used by Zionist activists—a large part of the institutions they founded included the name "Palestine" in various ways (for example, the Anglo-Palestine Bank). With the development of the Zionist movement, Jews increasingly used the name Eretz Yisrael (Hebrew: Land of Israel). It was only after the creation of the State of Israel that international public opinion began to use the term "Palestinians" to distinguish the Arab population (living in the same territory) from the Jewish one. Currently, when talking about the territory of Israel in the period before the proclamation of independence of that state, the names "Eretz Yisrael" and "Palestine" are used interchangeably. Both terms have their political overtones. It is worth noting that at the beginning of the twentieth century "Palestine" meant a territory much larger than it is today. In 1923, with the consent of the League of Nations, the British Mandate for Palestine was divided into Palestine and the Emirate of Transjordan, which took over the lands east of Jordan (on May 25, 1946, the Emirate declared independence as the Kingdom of Transjordan).

focus on issues related to politics, social and economic relations, diplomacy, and wars. This type of books is undoubtedly needed, as they enlarge and systematize our knowledge. However, when this stage of getting to know something is already behind us, the bar is raised. Readers have the right to expect more than a repetition of the same facts, even if it would be done in a different (more attractive) form. This possibility is provided by the history of the state seen through the lens of one person and his family. This choice results in certain restrictions. We will not include those events in which they did not participate (even indirectly) or which they did not observe. At the same time, we will learn about the processes and events in which they took part in a deepened way, from the inside. We will learn about the details that have no chance of "breaking through" in the pages of more general syntheses and monographs. With this convention, we do not limit ourselves to official documents or normative acts. After all, we know that the course of events and people's lives are outside the official limits. We will extract the depth of the picture only by combining theory with practice. It is worth trying to achieve this depth even though the resulting image will necessarily have a narrow range.

I wrote this book thinking about business people seeking inspiration, diplomats, politicians, and students in fields such as history, political science, economics, international relations, and Jewish studies.

Works written by locals are usually (and it is not surprising) Israeli-centric, while the visions of foreign and external authors can be superficial and simplified. Anyway, both can think in stereotypes. Before I wrote this book, I had followed the path of its protagonist—a Polish Jew, my countryman, a Krakovian. I describe and evaluate his life and achievements objectively, in accordance with facts, but I do not intend to hide my sincere sympathy and admiration.

Marcel Goldman was born in 1926 in Krakow, and his story begins here. It could be a quiet narrative about the life of a Jewish child coming from a merchant family, who, thanks to his diligence and hard work, multiplied the modest assets of his parents running a clothing shop in the city center. However, the outbreak of World War II introduced new aspects into the story: the darkness of occupation, the chaos of the escape from the ghetto, the uncertainty of life on Aryan papers, then, the difficult acclimatization to the conditions of communist Poland, and, finally, what is worth paying attention to, another escape in the life of the only twenty-three-year-old Marcel. This time, he had to leave his homeland permanently. He had yet to face a long and not easy road, which included even a two-week detention on the Czechoslovak side of the border. Theoretically, this story could end when the ship on which Marcel Goldman travelled reached the shores of Haifa. In practice, the story described in this book gains another, no less important momentum after my protagonist arrives in Israel. Since then, we are dealing not with one but with two equally interesting stories. Assuming that life is a kind of theater (Latin: *theatrum vitae*), for Marcel Goldman and his wife Bianka (née Ebersohn) the scenery is changed to the State of Israel, whose independence was announced just a year before Marcel's arrival.

I also tried to devote as much space as possible to Bianka Goldman. Marcel became the undisputed head of the family, he gained higher education, brilliantly developed his professional career, and earned a good living for his wife and children. However, reducing Bianka's role to "her husband's brave companion" or "home carer" would be a misunderstanding. Bianka's biography opens a new road for us and encourages us to ask at least a few important questions. She survived the hell of World War II, not under Nazi occupation, but in exile in the depths of the Soviet Union. We are used to assessing the nightmarish situation of the Jews during World War II mainly through the lens of their lives under the Nazi rule. Indeed, living first in Krakow and later in Radom, Marcel and his family were in mortal threat every day. At any time, they were at risk of being exposed and then shot on the spot or taken to one of the extermination camps, where there was only death, immediate or slow and painful. The point is that the lives of Bianka and her relatives were also threatened every day. Indeed, in Russia under Stalin's rule, before the so-called Kremlin Doctors' plot,[26] no one persecuted Jews because of their nationality. The Ebersohn family was on the "wrong list" not because of their nation but because of belonging to the "hostile" bourgeoisie—in prewar Poland, Bianka's father was an attorney. However, when a man is declared the enemy of the dictator, his life is in real danger, and that is all that matters. Many other families in a similar situation died of hunger, severe illnesses, and slave labour. Today, their graves are scattered throughout the territory of Russia, Kazakhstan, Kyrgyzstan, and other countries. We know

---

26 Shortly after Israel proclaimed its independence, the authorities of that country clearly took a pro-Western course in foreign policy. This provoked Stalin's anger, who, unable to immediately apply a proper retort to Israel, turned against the Jews living in the USSR. An action allegedly aimed at the "Zionists," and, in fact, an anti-Jewish campaign, was unleashed. Its key link was the so-called Doctors' plot, the case of the Kremlin doctors, against whom the most serious accusations were made (including an attempt to kill the leaders of the state). See J. Rapoport, *Sprawa lekarzy kremlowskich. 1953—ostatni akt terroru Stalina*, trans. Z. Błaszczyk, Warsaw 1990; S. Sebag Montefiore, *Stalin. Dwór czerwonego cara*, trans. M. Antosiewicz, Warsaw 2008, 617–630.

much less about their tragic fate than about Jews living under Nazi occupation. I hope that the story of Bianka Goldman incorporated into this book will at least partially fill the evident gap existing in current historiography. A closer look at her life also creates an opportunity to wonder why we know so little about Israeli women. Many names of Jewish statesmen broke through to the general consciousness, just to mention: David Ben-Gurion, Moshe Dayan, Menachem Begin, Shimon Peres, Yitzhak Rabin, and Ariel Sharon. In this group of men, we can mention only one woman equal to them in terms of popularity—Golda Meir. This is surprisingly little for a country that was largely built by women (serving in the army, working in kibbutzim, being successful in science, and so forth). Women got involved in the work of building Israel long before the proclamation of its independence. They worked hand in hand with men, while historians immortalized mainly men.

The choice of Marcel Goldman as the guide to the history of Israel brings the added value outlined above, as it allows the reader to learn more about the community of Polish Jews in Israel. This is important because their contribution to the construction of this country is really significant.[27] The problem is that the history of Israel resembles a painting standing in the studio, which is approached by subsequent painters who draw new lines and apply new layers of paint, covering some or all of the old ones. The migration waves of Polish Jews were among the first and most important ones in terms of quantity and quality—there were numerous young and well-educated people. For some time, they formed a separate and distinctive group; however, their education, skills, mobility, and determination meant that they relatively quickly (in the second generation at the latest) merged with the general public and began to co-create its mainstream. Later, numerous groups of Oriental Jews arrived in Israel—mainly from the Middle East and Africa—and in the 1980s and the 1990s more than a million Jews emigrated there from the areas of the former Soviet Union. Today, there is a real threat of forgetting or diminishing the merits of Polish Jews who served Israel. Similarly, their distinctness ceases to be visible, replaced by the "otherness" of the above-mentioned Russian-speaking and Oriental Jews (Hebrew: *mizrachi*—"Eastern"). It is possible that in the future their history will be overshadowed by waves of other large groups of emigrants, or, using Israeli terminology, *olim chadashim* (Hebrew: "newcomers"). Therefore, the

---

27 See Ł.T. Sroka, M. Sroka, *Polskie korzenie Izraela. Wprowadzenie do tematu. Wybór źródeł*, Krakow–Budapest 2015.

additional task of this book is to present the forgotten or quite unknown elements of the history of lives of Polish Jews in Eretz Yisrael and finally in independent Israel.

The chronological framework of this book is structured by the years of its main protagonist's life, so it spans from 1926 to the newest times. Naturally, this book is not only about Marcel Goldman and the history of Israel. There are also side threads related to Krakow, World War II, and Polish-Jewish and Polish-Israeli relations. During this time, several historical periods can be distinguished. Taking into account the Polish historical perspective, this book covers the interwar period, World War II, the postwar years and the communist years, the democratic changes at the turn of the 1980s and the 1990s, as well as Poland's accession to NATO and the European Union. Bearing in mind the Israeli point of view, the following periods must be noted: the time of intensive settlement in Eretz Yisrael at the beginning of the twentieth century, the last years of the European diaspora in its centuries-old shape, the Holocaust, the postwar period, the proclamation of Israel's independence, the absorption of subsequent migration waves, shaping diplomatic relations with various countries of the world (including such strategic partners as Germany or the United States), the phenomenal development of economy, science, culture, and settlement (construction of new kibbutzim, moshavim, and cities). During this period, the first Arab-Israeli war took place (1948–1949), the Suez crisis (1956), the Six-Day War (1967), armed clashes on the Israeli-Egyptian border, also called the "War of Attrition" (1967–1970), the Yom Kippur War (1973), the Lebanon War (1982–1985), the First Intifada (1987–1991), the Second Lebanon War (2006), the Second Intifada (also called the Al-Aqsa Intifada, 2000–2002), and a number of terrorist attacks and special operations of the Israeli army and special services on the territory of the Palestinian Authority, the Gaza Strip, in some neighboring countries (mainly in Syria) and in various parts of the world. Therefore, it is not surprising that for a today's Pole the term "postwar" means rather unequivocally the time after World War II, while an Israeli needs clarification: "after which war?"

The wide chronological framework of the book allows us to see the continuity of various events and phenomena, many of which can be put together as a whole. An example of this is the migration of Polish Jews to Israel. Most of the works that have appeared in Poland so far describe their lives only until they left Poland. Later the trail breaks off and we do not know how they lived after that . . . The exceptions include a great monograph by Ewa Węgrzyn entitled *Wyjeżdżamy! Wyjeżdżamy?! Alija Gomułkowska*

1956–1960[28] (English: We're leaving! We're leaving?! The Gomulka Aliyah 1956–1960). In Israel, in turn, researchers have not yet shown due interest in the past of the citizens of this country, who spent the first years of their lives in the diaspora. An important purpose of the book is to fill this gap. Previously, such attempts were made only by Polish Jews living in Israel, wanting to save the memory of their lives after leaving Poland. This is evidenced by numerous publications of remembrance nature, published by Polish Jews, mainly in Israel. Their effort, however, brought an extremely modest effect, and it was determined by two main issues. First of all, the vast majority of these works were published only in Polish, hence they had no chance to interest a wider group of readers in Israel. Secondly, the authors most often relied on the services of small Israeli publishing houses, which did not guarantee distribution, either on the local book market or in Poland. Independent and full funding of books was also disastrous—as the publishers had a full refund, they were no longer interested in advertising and distributing the publications. In addition, a large proportion of writers was not a part of professional science and culture institutions, and therefore did not have the tools or opportunity to interest researchers in this field. The publication of this type of books was often an event not even of community significance (let's say it could be the community of Polish Jews), but rather a family one with some extension to a group of friends. The most valuable, and at the same time forgotten one, of these books is the memoir of Dr. Heshel Klepfish entitled *Przedwojenny świat przez pryzmat młodego Żyda polskiego. Eseje 1931–1937*[29] (English: The prewar world from the point of view of a young Polish Jew. Essays 1931–1937).

After 1989, some Polish Jews living in Israel began publishing in Poland. However, many valuable items appeared in publishing houses that (mainly for economic reasons) could not guarantee their proper promotion. Among the

---

28   E. Węgrzyn, *Wyjeżdżamy! Wyjeżdżamy?! Alija Gomułkowska 1956–1960*, Krakow–Budapest 2016.

29   H. Klepfish, *Przedwojenny świat przez pryzmat młodego Żyda polskiego. Eseje 1931–1937*, Tel Aviv 1999. Heshel Klepfish, born in 1910 in Żyrardów in a rabbinical family, died in 2004 in Jerusalem. Until 1939 he lived and worked in Warsaw. He dealt with social, scientific and literary activities. During World War II he was a rabbi in the rank of major in the Polish Armed Forces in the West. After the war, he worked as a rabbi in Panama, and lectured in Jewish studies at the local university. Then he settled in Jerusalem, where he continued his scientific and writing work. H. Klepfish's publication cited here did not meet with much response from Polish readers. The exceptions include T. J. Żółciński's article entitled "Dobrze, że przypomniane," *Słowo żydowskie* 4 (2001): 15, 26.

examples, there are excellent autobiographical novels by Józef Kornblum *Ziemia przeobiecana*[30] (English: The So-Promised Land) and *Miłość i szarańcza na tle Ziemi Obiecanej*[31] (English: Love and locusts against the background of the Promised Land; the publication of the book was financed by the author), as well as Henryk Palmon's *Powroty i wyjazdy Natana*[32] (English: Returns and departures of Nathan).

Of course, there are also authors whose works have met with a wide social response. Such phenomena include: Ida Fink, Irit Amiel and Leo Lipski,[33] who have developed a well-established position in the world of literature. Their works have numerous translations and received prestigious awards. Miriam Akavia, known and appreciated in the world, can serve as an example of success.[34] The publications of Maria Lewińska, based on personal experience, also gained much publicity.[35] The latest book by Ilona Dworak-Cousin[36] met with great interest of journalists and friendly reception from readers. Exceptions also include

---

30 J. Kornblum, *Ziemia przeobiecana*, Krakow 1993.

31 Idem, *Miłość i szarańcza na tle Ziemi Obiecanej*, Bielsko-Biała 1999.

32 H. Palmon, *Powroty i wyjazdy Natana*, Łódź 2000.

33 Ida Fink, born in 1921 in Zbaraż, died in 2011 in Tel Aviv. See K. Famulska-Ciesielska, "Ida Fink (1921–2011)," *Archiwum Emigracji. Studia—Szkice—Dokumenty* 1/2 (2011): 369–371; K. Famulska-Ciesielska, S. J. Żurek, *Literatura polska w Izraelu. Leksykon*, Krakow–Budapest 2012, 52–54. Irit Amiel was born in 1931 in Częstochowa. See Famulska-Ciesielska, Żurek, *Literatura polska w Izraelu*, 17–19; K. Hoffmann, "Rana i staranność. Wokół 'Spóźnionej' Irit Amiel," *Miasteczko Poznań* 2 (2016): 150–155; J. Waligóra, "Nikomu się nie udało... O prozie Irit Amiel," in *Lęk, ból, cierpienie. Analizy i interpretacje*, ed. G. Różańska, Słupsk 2015, 17–27. Leo Lipski, born in 1917 in Zurich, died in 1997 in Tel Aviv. See M. Cuber, "Uwagi do monografii twórczości Leo Lipskiego," in *Literatura polsko-żydowska. Studia i szkice*, ed. E. Prokop-Janiec, S. J. Żurek, Krakow 2011, 253–259; A. Nowak, "Wędrowiec: Leo Lipski (1917–1997)," *Archiwum Emigracji. Studia—Szkice—Dokumenty* 1 (1998): 195–197; Famulska-Ciesielska, Żurek, *Literatura polska w Izraelu*, 104–106.

34 Miriam Akavia, born in 1927 in Krakow, died in 2015 in Tel Aviv. She started publishing quite late, only in 1975, thirty years aftr she moved to Israel. She wanted to testify of her own experiences related to her childhood and World War II. It soon turned out that she had extraordinary literary talent, her books began to be translated into foreign languages (including Hebrew, English, German, French, Danish, and Hungarian). She has received numerous literary awards and distinctions, both in Israel and in Europe.

35 See M. Lewińska, *Emigracji dzień pierwszy*, Warsaw 1999; idem, *Przechowane słowa*, Tel Aviv 2008; idem, *Analfabeci z wyższym wykształceniem*, Krakow–Budapest 2016.

36 Ilona Dworak-Cousin, born in 1949 in Wrocław, is a pharmacist by profession. She obtained a PhD in pharmacy at the University of Bologna in Italy. She combines her professional work with social activity (she is the head of the Israel-Poland Friendship Association) and a passion for writing. She publishes in Polish and Hebrew. See I. Dworak-Cousin, *Podróż do krainy cieni*, trans. H. Szafir, Krakow–Budapest–Syracuse 2018.

Ryszard Löw (born in 1931 in Krakow), a respected Polish and Israeli propagator of culture, bibliographer, literary critic, researcher of Polish-Hebrew literary relationships and the history of Jewish antiquarians in Poland.[37] He was distinguished due to his talent for popularising the results of his research, thanks to which his texts can be found in niche publications and magazines, but also in those definitely better known ones.[38] Beginning with the fourth issue, he was responsible for the publication of the literary and historical literary yearbook *Kontury*, published in Polish in 1988–2006 in Tel Aviv (a total of sixteen issues).[39] He was also active in Polish and Israeli scientific and cultural institutions. From 1957 to 1981 he worked as a correspondent for the Bibliographic Laboratory of the Literary Research Institute in Poznań. In 1987–1988, and later from 1990, he was the president of the Union of Polish Writers in Israel.

Among writers, Henryk Ritterman-Abir, born in 1906 in a wealthy and assimilated family, took an important position.[40] In 1949 he co-founded the weekly *Przegląd* (English: Review), and later also *Nowiny Poranne* (English: Morning News). He wrote texts for cabarets popular in Israel: Li La Lo and Matate (the

---

37 See R. Löw, *Literackie podsumowania, polsko-hebrajskie, polsko-izraelskie*, ed. M. Siedlecki and J. Ławski, afterword B. Olech, Białystok 2014; and Ł. T. Sroka's review of this book, *Scripta Judaica Cracoviensia* 14 (2016): 177–179; Famulska-Ciesielska, Żurek, *Literatura polska w Izraelu*, 107–108.

38 He published, among others, in London's *Wiadomości*, Israeli magazines *Nowiny Kurier* and *Od Nowa*, *Tygodnik Powszechny* and *Kraków. Magazyn Kulturalny*, *Ruch Literacki*, *Lithuani*, and in the Parisian magazines *Zeszyty Historyczne* and *Kultura*. His writings include, among others: "Mickiewicz w kręgu hebrajskim," *Więź* 1 (1999); "Trylogia w oczach krytyki hebrajskiej," *Pamiętnik Literacki* 4 (2000); "'Chłopi' Raymont w literaturze hebrajskiej," *Teksty Drugie* 7 (2000); "Brzozowski wśród lektur syjonistycznych," *Teksty Drugie* 7 (2003); "Jerozolimski przyjaciel Tuwima. Leib Jaffe w kręgu polskim. Spotkanie z Tuwimem," *Zeszyty Literackie* 38 (1992): 108–115; "Adolf Rudnicki w literaturze hebrajskiej," *Ruch Literacki* 30, no. 3 (1989): 251–255; *Pod znakiem starych foliantów. Cztery szkice o sprawach żydowskich i książkowych*, Krakow 1993.

39 Famulska-Ciesielska, Żurek, *Literatura polska w Izraelu*, 107; Interview with Ryszard Löw, in Lewińska, *Analfabeci*, 25; P. Tański, "'Kontury'—Izraelskie pismo literackie," *Archiwum Emigracji. Studia—Szkice—Dokumenty* 3 (2000): 301–307.

40 Henryk Ritterman-Abir completed legal studies at the Jagiellonian University, where in 1929 he obtained the degree of doctor of law. Before 1939, he worked at the General Prosecutor's Office. He published texts on commercial and criminal law. He collaborated with the Zionist *Nowy Dziennik*. In the early 1940s, he came to Eretz Yisrael with the army of General Anders with his wife and two daughters. He was a lawyer in the British Army. After Israel's proclamation of independence, he worked briefly in diplomacy. At that time, urged by the Foreign Affairs Minister, Moshe Sharett, he made his name sound Hebrew and began acting as Chaim Abir (Abir is the Hebrew translation of the German *Ritter*, or "knight"). He returned to the legal profession, but he devoted most of his time to publishing and literary work.

Qui Pro Quo cabaret operating in Poland in the years 1919–1931 was an inspiration for the creators of Li La Lo). In 1951, in Tel Aviv, he published a volume of satirical works *Pan Tuwia i inne parafrazy literackie. Fraszki, humoreski, felietony* (English: Mr. Tuwia and Other Literary Paraphrases. Epigrams, humoresques, columns).[41] In 1984, a volume of his memories entitled *Nie od razu Kraków zapomniano* (English: Krakow was not immediately forgotten)[42] appeared in Tel Aviv. This book received an award at the memoir competition of the Association of Krakovians in Israel. However, this did not help in its adequate publicity. The book did not hit the masses, but it was noticed by literary scholars and historians.[43] Our knowledge of Polish-language literature and magazines in Israel is definitely facilitated by the work of Karolina Famulska-Ciesielska and Sławomir Jacek Żurek.[44]

The material on which my book is based are sources related to the life of its main character. The most important role in this case is played by an electronic recording lasting several dozen hours and notes from the conversations that I had with Marcel and Bianka Goldman in the years 2014–2019. For me, an excellent and irreplaceable source of knowledge were the works written by Marcel Goldman. A special place in this regard is occupied by his autobiographical book entitled *Iskierki życia* (English: *Sparkles of life*),[45] which, published in 2002, met with such a lively and friendly reception from readers that there was a demand for its next editions—a total of three were published by 2014, and each of them quickly disappeared from book shelves.[46] The majority of *Iskierki życia* are poignant memories of World War II. First of all, it is a very valuable testimony regarding life on Aryan papers outside the ghetto. Thanks to the book *Iskierki*

---

41 Interview with Ryszard Löw, 136–137.
42 H. Ritterman-Abir, *Nie od razu Kraków zapomniano*, [Tel Aviv] 1984.
43 See E. Prokop-Janiec, "Literatura polska w Izraelu: pomiędzy pamięcią Europy a nowym życiem," *Roczniki Humanistyczne* 64, no. 1 (2016): 63–74.
44 See Famulska-Ciesielska, Żurek, *Literatura polska w Izraelu*; K. Famulska-Ciesielska, *Polacy, Żydzi, Izraelczycy. Tożsamość w literaturze polskiej w Izraelu*, Toruń 2008; S. J. Żurek, "Krytyka literacka na łamach izraelskiego dziennika "Nowiny-Kurier" po roku 1968: wyimki z dyskursu," in *Prasa Żydów polskich: od przeszłości do teraźniejszości*, ed. A. Karczewska, S. J. Żurek, Lublin 2016, 139–159; idem, "Polish literature in Israel: a reconnaissance," *Roczniki Humanistyczne* 64, no. 1 (2016): 125–137; idem, "Polska i Polacy w poezji autorów piszących po polsku w Izraelu," *Postscriptum Polonistyczne: pismo krajowych i zagranicznych polonistów poświęcone zagadnieniom związanych z nauczaniem kultury polskiej i języka polskiego jako obcego* 2 (2016): 59–75.
45 M. Goldman, *Iskierki życia*, Krakow 2002.
46 In this book I am using the 2014 edition.

życia, we have a unique testimony to the Jewish perspective, but not the one from the ghetto or the hidden one. This is a record of the observations made by a Polish Jew who had Germans and Poles among his neighbours and colleagues. There are also memories related to the postwar period—regarding emigration to Israel and the private and professional life there. A bit incompatible with the whole, but valuable in cognitive terms, is the last chapter entitled "Powrót do Jalal-Abadu" (English: Return to Jalal-Abad, 143–155). It was devoted to the journey of Marcel and his wife Bianka to Kyrgyzstan, where she lived with her family for about five years during World War II.

I also repeatedly consulted another work of Marcel Goldman entitled *A w nocy przychodzą myśli* (English: And thoughts come at night).[47] It has a complex structure: next to memories, it contains mainly occasional poems. The main value of these works, however, lies not in their literary form, but in the depth of the thoughts hidden in them, even when they are expressed in a light and playful way. Attempts at self-reflection and retrospection can be noticed. The author shares with the reader his achievements, worries and fears. Above all, it is a kind of a social chronicle covering the community of Polish Jews who came to Israel after World War II, mainly as part of the Gomulka Aliyah (1956–1960).

Both of these works, *Iskierki życia* and *A w nocy przychodzą myśli* were written in Polish. Their intertextuality within Polish and Jewish culture impresses. The texts of Marcel Goldman clearly show the influence of the Polish poet and national bard Adam Mickiewicz (1798–1855) and the leading Polish novelist and publicist, Nobel Prize winner Henryk Sienkiewicz (1846–1916). Even Goldman's works written originally in Hebrew are immersed in Polish culture, such as two previously unpublished stories used in this book: "Spowiedź starego człowieka" (English: Confession of an old man)[48] and "W małym pokoju w Ramat Ha-Szaron" (English: In a small room in Ramat HaSharon),[49] published in the supplement to the most influential Israeli daily *Haaretz, Culture and Literature*.

I highly value the credibility of testimonies written by Marcel Goldman, and the same applies to his oral relations. I verified the information they contained with accounts of other witnesses of history and with sources from that period;

---

47 M. Goldman, *A w nocy przychodzą myśli*, foreword A. B. Skotnicki, Krakow 2012.

48 Idem, "Spowiedź starego człowieka," *Haaretz*, February 21, 2014, supplement: *Culture and Literature*. Goldman translated this story into Polish himself.

49 Idem, "W małym pokoju w Ramat Ha-Szaron," Tel Aviv 2018, typescript, Family collection of Marcel and Bianka Goldman (Tel Aviv).

I mean here, among others, press and legal acts. In addition, the circumstances of their creation are important. He published his memories on his own initiative after the end of his professional career. Consequently, he did not create them in order to become known in any circle or for honors, as the previously achieved social and professional position allows him to remain independent. This is reflected in the content of his printed works and statements—they often undermine current political trends in Poland or Israel, being full of criticism and cynicism.

Documents, photos, and keepsakes collected by the Goldman family, which were made available to me for the book, are also of great importance. A natural complement to this database is my correspondence with people who knew Marcel Goldman in person.[50] I also used documents, film materials, and information posted on the websites of such institutions as the Yad Vashem Institute and the Israeli Central Bureau of Statistics (Hebrew: HaLishka HaMerkazit LiStatistika).

As Marcel Goldman's life and activities were a starting point for me to prepare a book on socio-economic history of Israel, I used a wide set of materials that allowed me to thoroughly explore the atmosphere of this country in recent years. I aimed, among others, to determine the conditions in which Israelis lived, what caught their daily attention, how their public discourse developed. In order to learn that, I queried and researched the three largest newspapers in Israel: *Haaretz* (the oldest Israeli newspaper, founded in 1918), *Yedioth Achronoth* (published since 1939), and *Yisrael Hayom* (appearing since 2007). I was interested in the full content of these titles, starting with informational and journalistic texts and ending with ads and announcements. I also read the texts published by the Jewish Telegraphic Agency, established in 1917. In addition, I looked at the rich collection of Israeli posters, leaflets (advertising and electoral), postcards, occasional envelopes, cards, and stamps, which can be found in the collections of public institutions (including the libraries of: Ariel University, Beit Berl College, Levinsky College of Education and Tel Aviv University) and in private hands. I am grateful to Mr. Prof. Aleksander B. Skotnicki, who was willing to share his collections of postcards, cards and postage stamps with me. I remember with gratitude the meetings in Ryszard Löw's apartment in Tel Aviv, who shared with me his collection of manuscripts, typescripts, prints, books and

---

50   The most valuable is my correspondence with Peter von Muralt (July 2018) and Shalom Singer (November 16, 2017).

magazines. I also used my own collection of Israeli keepsakes, which consists of several hundred artifacts, including maps, posters, postcards, occasional envelopes, and postage stamps. I evaluated their practical function and substantive content, as well as symbolic value and ideological message. At present, in the era of the Internet and mobile communication devices, it is easy to lose sight of sources such as posters, occasional envelopes, and postage stamps, for example. In the last century, posters, letters, and postal items belonged to the basic tools of communication.[51]

For a thorough understanding of the way in which the foundations of Israeli statehood were built, I searched the Central Zionist Archives in Jerusalem, the Tel Aviv-Yafo Municipal Historical Archives, and the Central State Historical Archives of Ukraine in Lviv. In the first of these institutions, I examined the documents of Zionist organizations, including Keren Hayesod and Keren Kayemet LeYisrael.[52] Valuable documents are kept in the Tel Aviv-Yafo Municipal Historical Archives, including documents created in the course of the work of the local government and statistics on the absorption of immigrants settling there.[53] The materials stored in the Central State Historical Archives of Ukraine in Lviv are of great importance. I mean here, among others, correspondence and information bulletins sent to Lviv (as an important center of the Zionist movement in Europe) from Eretz Yisrael.[54]

Although this is the first biography of Marcel Goldman, he is not an anonymous figure, neither in Poland nor in Israel. In Israel, he created his own brand

---

51 See A. Essen, "Znaczek pocztowy jako źródło ikonograficzne," *Studia Środkowoeuropejskie i Bałkanistyczne* 25 (2017): 191–206.

52 Central Zionist Archives in Jerusalem [hereinafter: CZA], Keren Hayesod documents, reference number KH4/10023; Documents regarding Keren Kayemet LeYisrael and other Zionist organizations, reference number S6/2937.

53 Tel Aviv-Yafo Municipal Historical Archives [hereinafter: TAYMHA], collection 5132, file number 08–233, Letters and documents 1926; collection 5132, file number 08–230, Resolutions of the City Council 1938–1939; collection 5132, file number 8–231, Letters and documents, document number 1929; Collection 5136, file number 08–254, Reports on groupings and communities 1926–1935.

54 Central State Historical Archives of Ukraine in Lviv [hereinafter: CSHAU], fond 335, description 1, Society for the Reconstruction of Palestine Keren Hayesod [1921–1939]: case 36: Information of the Central Office in Jerusalem regarding the publication of propaganda literature, case 177: Correspondence with the Central Office in Jerusalem, regarding organisational matters [1927]; fond 338, description 1, National Zionist Organisation in Lviv: case 736: Lectures on Zionism and Palestine, the first lecture: Palestine's absorption capacity, Lviv–Warsaw 1939, case 759: Report on the activities of the Polish-Palestinian Chamber of Commerce for 1935, Warsaw 1936.

as an efficient and thoroughly honest banker and economic advisor. With his retirement, he made himself known to readers of the *Haaretz* daily as the author of moving stories, mainly about World War II, and letters in which he comments on the current social, political, and economic situation of Israel. However, it seems that Marcel Goldman is most popular in Poland. In 2003 a film about him, *Zrabowana młodość* (English: Robbed youth, 25 minutes, script and production Teresa Olearczyk) was prepared there. Thanks to the efforts of Professor Aleksander B. Skotnicki, the book entitled *Marcel Goldman. Krakowianin and Izraelczyk* (English: Marcel Goldman. A Krakovian and Israeli),[55] which consists of short notes about Marcel and Bianka Goldman and fragments of other works about them, was published. The transcript of a conversation with Marcel Goldman was published in the book by Irek Grin, *Ich miasto. Wspomnienia Izraelczyków, przedwojennych mieszkańców Krakowa* (English: Their city. Memories of Israelis, prewar residents of Krakow).[56] A biographical entry about him can be found in the work of Karolina Famulska-Ciesielska and Sławomir Jacek Żurek, *Literatura Polska w Izraelu. Leksykon* (English: *Polish literature in Israel. A lexicon*).[57] A text about him can be found in the publication *Świadkowie polsko-żydowskiej historii* (English: *Witnesses of the Polish-Jewish history*), published thanks to the efforts of the Galicia Jewish Museum.[58] The website www.sztetl.org.pl contains a summary of two interviews he gave in Israel in 2007 in Hebrew as part of the "Polish Roots in Israel" project, entitled *Marcel Goldman-Galas (ur. 1926)—o swoim życiu w Krakowie, Radomiu, Europie i Izraelu i korzeniach jego rodziny* (English: Marcel Goldman-Galas (born in 1926)—on his life in Krakow, Radom, Europe, and Israel, and the roots of his family).[59] The author of this book had the opportunity to publish in the Konspekt magazine the article entitled "Gdy nadmiar myśli nie pozwala zasnąć... Kilka refleksji na temat literatury polskiej w Izraelu na przykładzie twórczości Marcela Goldmana" (English: When the excess of thoughts does not allow to fall asleep... A few

---

55 *Marcel Goldman Krakowian i Izraelczyk*, ed. A. B. Skotnicki with M. Ostoja-Wilamowska, [s.l.] 2008.
56 I. Grin, *Ich miasto. Wspomnienia Izraelczyków, przedwojennych mieszkańców Krakowa*, Warsaw 2004, 145–156.
57 Famulska-Ciesielska, Żurek, *Polska literatura w Izraelu*..., 61–62.
58 *Świadkowie polsko-żydowskiej historii*, ed. M. Stępień, L. Michalska, Krakow 2016, 28–31.
59 "Marcel Goldman-Galas (ur. 1926)—o swoim życiu w Krakowie, Radomiu, Europie i Izraelu i korzeniach jego rodziny," http://www.sztetl.org.pl/pl/article/krakow/16,relacje-wspomnienia/11084,marcel-goldman-galas-ur-1926-o-swoim-zyciu-w-krakowie-radomiu-europie-i-izraelu-i-korzeniach-jego-rodziny/, accessed March 11, 2017.

reflections on the Polish literature in Israel on the example of Marcel Goldman's works).[60]

In addition to sources, when writing this book, I also used rich literature on Polish-Jewish and Polish-Israeli relations. Interesting topics include the exchange between the markets of Poland and the British Mandate for Palestine described by Jerzy Łazor.[61] Innovative works by Bożena Szaynok[62] and Joanna Dyduch[63] also deserve recognition. An important place in historiography is occupied by the work *Stosunki polsko-izraelskie (1945–1967). Wybór dokumentów* (English: Polish-Israeli relations [1945–1967]. Selection of documents) prepared by Szymon Rudnicki and Marcos Silber.[64] I also analyzed works on the first migration waves after World War II, followed by the Gomulka Aliyah and post-March emigration. In this regard, we have, among others, works highly rated in the scientific community and written by Natalia Aleksiun,[65] Grzegorz

---

60 Ł. T. Sroka, "Gdy nadmiar myśli nie pozwala zasnąć . . . Kilka refleksji na temat literatury polskiej w Izraelu na przykładzie twórczości Marcela Goldmana," *Konspekt* 2 (2016): 53–60.

61 J. Łazor, *Brama na Bliski Wschód.Polsko-palestyńskie stosunki gospodarcze w okresie międzywojennym*, Warsaw 2016.

62 B. Szaynok, *Ludność żydowska na Dolnym Śląsku 1945–1950*, Wrocław 2000; idem, *Pogrom Żydów w Kielcach 4 lipca 1946*, intro. K. Kersten, Warsaw 1992; idem, "Stosunki polsko-żydowskie w latach 1948–1967," in *Państwo Izrael. Analiza politologiczno-prawna*, ed. E. Rudnik, Warsaw 2006, 101–111; idem, *Z historią i Moskwą w tle. Polska a Izrael 1944–1968*, Warsaw–Wrocław 2007.

63 J. Dyduch, "Dyplomacja kulturalna w służbie polityki zagranicznej państwa. Nowe formy promocji kraju za granicą na przykładzie 'Roku polskiego w Izraelu,'" in *Historia—polityka—dyplomacja. Studia z nauk społecznych i humanistycznych. Księga pamiątkowa dedykowana Profesorowi Marianowi S. Wolańskiemu w siedemdziesiątą rocznicę urodzin*, ed. M. Mróz and E. Stadtmüller, Toruń 2010, 605–619; idem, "Percepcja Polski i Polaków przez Izraelczyków," in *Uwarunkowania i kierunki polskiej polityki zagranicznej w pierwszej dekadzie XXI wieku*, ed. M. S. Wolański, Wrocław 2004, 364–393; idem, *Stosunki polsko-izraelskie. Próba analizy czynników je kształtujących*, https://www.academia.edu/5193057/Joanna_Dyduch_Stosunki_polsko-izraelskie._Pr%C3%B3ba_analizy_czynnik%C3%B3w_kszta%C5%82tuj%C4%85cych?fbclid=IwAR0vp-maJtd0oBE2sc9SLc6KTXQfQg9hzIRmhSUHy-7FObjYL0AINqm80Pjk, accessed August 8, 2014; idem, *Stosunki polsko-izraelskie w latach 1990–2009. Od normalizacji do strategicznego partnerstwa*, Warsaw 2010.

64 *Stosunki polsko-izraelskie (1945–1967). Wybór dokumentów*, comp. Sz. Rudnicki, M. Silber, Warsaw 2009.

65 N. Aleksiun, *Dokąd dalej? Ruch syjonistyczny w Polsce (1944–1950)*, Warsaw 2002; idem, "Stosunki polsko-żydowskie w piśmiennictwie historyków żydowskich w Polsce w latach trzydziestych XX wieku," *Studia Judaica* 1 (2006): 47–67; idem, "Nielegalna emigracja Żydów z Polski w latach 1945–1947," part 1, *Biuletyn Żydowskiego Instytutu Historycznego* 3/2 (1995/96): 67–99; part 2, *Biuletyn Żydowskiego Instytutu Historycznego* 3 (1996): 33–49; part 3, *Biuletyn Żydowskiego Instytutu Historycznego* 4 (1996): 35–48; idem,

Berendt,[66] Marcos Silber,[67] Dariusz Stola,[68] and the already mentioned Ewa Węgrzyn.[69]

The process of cultural integration of Polish Jews in Israel has become the subject of Elżbieta Kossewska's scientific research, to whom we owe a series of richly documented works full of interesting insights.[70] The crowning achievement of the author's many years of interest in this issue is the extensive monograph entitled *"Ona jeszcze mówi po polsku, ale śmieje się po hebrajsku." Partyjna prasa polskojęzyczna i integracja kulturowa polskich Żydów w Izraelu (1948–1970)* (English: She still speaks Polish, but laughs in Hebrew. Polish-language political press and cultural integration of Polish Jews in Israel [1948–1970]).[71]

Among many valuable works on the situation of Polish Jews during World War II, the books by Katarzyna Zimmerer should be mentioned: *Zamordowany*

"Stosunek żydowskich partii politycznych w Polsce do emigracji," *Polska 1944/45–1989. Studia i materiały* 2 (1996): 123–150.

66 G. Berendt, *Między emigracją a trwaniem. Syjoniści i komuniści żydowscy w Polsce po Holokauście*, Warsaw 2003. See also idem, "Emigracja Żydów z Polski w latach 1960–1967," in *Z przeszłości Żydów polskich. Polityka—gospodarka—kultura—społeczeństwo*, ed. J. Wijaczki and G. Miernik, Kraków 2005, 297–309.

67 M. Silber, "'Immigrants from Poland Want to Go Back.' The Politics of Return Migration and Nation Building in 1950s Israel," *Journal of Israeli History* 27 (2008): 201–219. See also idem, "Swoi i obcy—Izrael, Polska i Żydzi w Polsce (1948–1967): zwięzłe prolegomena do stałego problemu," in *Brzemię pamięci. Współczesne stosunki polsko-izraelskie*, ed. E. Kossewska, Warsaw 2009, 31–53.

68 D. Stola, *Emigracja pomarcowa*, Warsaw 2000; idem, *Kampania antysyjonistyczna w Polsce 1967–1968*, Warsaw 2000; idem, *Kraj bez wyjścia? Migracje z Polski 1949–1989*, Warsaw 2012.

69 Węgrzyn, *Wyjeżdżamy!*; idem, "Emigracja ludności żydowskiej z Polski do Izraela w latach 1956–1959. Przyczyny, przebieg wyjazdu, proces adaptacji w nowej ojczyźnie," *Zeszyty Naukowe Uniwersytetu Jagiellońskiego* 1312, *Prace Historyczne* 137 (2010): 137–151.

70 Including E. Kossewska, "Absorpcja polityczna polskich Żydów, byłych komunistów w Izraelu—'Od Nowa' (1958–1965)," *Zeszyty Prasoznawcze. Kwartalnik Ośrodka Badań Prasoznawczych* 54, nos. 3–4 (2011): 179–196; idem, "Adaptacja alii gomułkowskiej w Izraelu (1955–1960)," *Przegląd Humanistyczny* 57, no. 6 (2013): 97–118; idem, "Izraelski 'Kurier'—okoliczności powstania," *Media Studies* 2 (2009): 121–138; idem, "'Nowiny'—prasa polskojęzyczna Partii Postępowej w Izraelu," *Kwartalnik Historii Żydów* 4 (2009): 426–447; idem, "Od politycznej koalicji do prasowej opozycji: „Nowiny i Kurier" w latach 1959-1961," *Kwartalnik Historii Żydów* 2 (2012): 207–232; idem, "'Zużyty komunizm i apostaci'—Ignacy Iserles i jego izraelska odnowa," *Dzieje Najnowsze. Kwartalnik Poświęcony Historii XX wieku* 44, no. 2 (2012): 125–152.

71 Idem, *"Ona jeszcze mówi po polsku, ale śmieje się po hebrajsku." Partyjna prasa polskojęzyczna i integracja kulturowa polskich Żydów w Izraelu (1948–1970)*, Warsaw 2015.

świat. Losy Żydów w Krakowie 1939–1945 (English: Murdered world. The history of Jews in Krakow 1939–1945)[72] and *Kronika zamordowanego świata. Żydzi w Krakowie w czasie niemieckiej okupacji* (English: Chronicle of the murdered world. Jews in Krakow during the German occupation),[73] as well as the book by Szlomo (Szloyme) Mendelsohn *Polscy Żydzi za murami nazistowskich gett* (English: Polish Jews behind the walls of the Nazi ghettos) with an extensive introduction and comments by Marek Skwara.[74] Reading Janka Goldstein's diary edited by Katarzyna Zimmerer and Ewa Czekaj was also extremely informative.[75]

A great contribution to learning about the lives of Polish Jews in Israel is made by subsequent editions of the already mentioned magazine, *Kontury* (English: Contours), where memories, essays, poems, and stories were published and the social life of Polish-language writers was reported in the form of a chronicle. It is difficult to overestimate the works of Aleksander Klugman, some of which are scientific, other journalistic, but all retain the value of originality, which is a result, among other factors, of the fact that their author, a popular journalist, participated himself in some of the events he described or reported.[76] The correspondence from Israel, which Alexander Klugman published years ago in the magazine *Midrasz* published in Poland, was also instructive for me.

In my scientific research, I also took into account the achievements of foreign scholars, which were published in foreign languages or in translations into Polish.[77] In resolving methodological dilemmas, Moshe Rosman's book, *How Jewish is Jewish History*, has often been helpful.[78] I took a whole series of practical workshop tips from the work *Biografie nieoczywiste. Przełom, kryzys,*

---

72 K. Zimmerer, *Zamordowany świat. Losy Żydów w Krakowie 1939–1945*, Krakow 2004.

73 Idem, *Kronika zamordowanego świata. Żydzi w Krakowie w czasie niemieckiej okupacji*, Krakow 2017.

74 The basis for the publication of this book was a paper read by Mendelsohn during the sixteenth annual conference of the Jewish Scientific Institute in New York on January 11, 1942 (Yiddish Scientific Institute—YIVO).

75 J. Goldstein, *Dziennik*, ed. K. Zimmerer and E. Czekaj, Krakow 2018.

76 See A. Klugman, *Izrael. Ziemia świecka*, Warsaw 2001; idem, *Polonica w Ziemi Świętej*, Krakow 1994; idem, "Pomoc Polski dla żydowskiego ruchu narodowego w Palestynie," *Więź* 5 (1997): 133–151; idem, *Żyd—co to znaczy?*, Warsaw 2003.

77 First of all: Y. Bauer, *Flight and Rescue: Brichah, the Organized Escape of Jewish Survivors of Eastern Europe 1944–1948*, New York 1970; D. Bensimon, E. Errera, *Żydzi i Arabowie. Historia współczesnego Izraela*, trans. R. Gromacka, K. Pruski, Warsaw 2000.

78 M. Rosman, *Jak pisać historię żydowską?*, trans. and ed. A. Jagodzińska, Wrocław 2011.

transgresja w perspektywie interdyscyplinarnej (English: Non-obvious biographies. A breakthrough, a crisis, a transgression in an interdisciplinary perspective).[79] The methodological tips and recommendations contained in the work titled *Biografistyka we współczesnych badaniach historycznych. Teoria i praktyka* (English: Biography in contemporary historical research. Theory and practice) are also very important.[80] I consider the monographic editions of *Teksty Drugie* to be valuable: *Autobiografie* (English: Autobiographies 6 [2018]) and *Biografie* (English: Biographies 1 [2019]).[81] Philippe Lejeune is one of the greatest researchers and interpreters of autobiographies.[82] On the Polish publishing market, there is one of his most important works *Napisać swoje życie. Droga od paktu autobiograficznego do dziedzictwa autobiograficznego* (English: Write your life. The road from the autobiographical pact to the autobiographical heritage).[83] All doubts related to the translation of Hebrew-language texts were resolved with the help of the three-volume Polish-Hebrew dictionary by Miriam Szir (Wolman-Sieraczkowa) and Dawid Szir.[84] A complete list of sources and literature used can be found in the bibliography to this volume.

The creation of this book required several years of intensive work, which consisted of conversations, archival, and library research, analysis of the source database, as well as field research regarding places related to the life and work of Marcel and Bianka Goldman. The successful culmination of my efforts was possible thanks to the trust, help, and kindness of the Goldmans, to whom I would like to express my warmest thanks.

I would like to thank everyone who supported me at various stages of writing this book. I want to thank everyone who encouraged me years ago to extend

---

79 *Biografie nieoczywiste. Przełom, kryzys, transgresja w perspektywie interdyscyplinarnej*, ed. M. Karkowska, Łódź 2018. The following texts in this volume were extremely inspiring to me: Zofia Okraj's "Dlaczego działania transgresyjne intrygują i inspirują do badań (także) autobiograficznych" (99–111) and Magda Karkowska's "Tajemnice i ich biograficzne znaczenia a proces kształtowania tożsamości" (113–137).

80 Ed. J. Kolbuszewska, R. Stobiecki, Łódź 2017.

81 The most important for me are the texts by Sidonie Smith, Julia Watson, "Archiwa zapisów życia: czym i gdzie są?," trans. D. Boni Menezes, *Teksty Drugie* 6 (2018): 174–199; Anna Legeżyńska, "Wystarczy mocno i wytrwale zastanawiać się nad jednym życiem . . . Biografistyka jako hermeneutyczne wyzwanie," *Teksty Drugie* 1 (2019): 13–27.

82 See P. Rodak, "Od biblioteki do archiwów. Droga badawcza 'papieża autobiografii,'" *Teksty Drugie* 1 (2019): 128–137.

83 P. Lejeune, *Napisać swoje życie. Droga od paktu autobiograficznego do dziedzictwa autobiograficznego*, trans. A. Słowik, M. Sakwerda, Wrocław 2017.

84 M. Szir and D. Szir, *Słownik polsko-hebrajski*, Tel Aviv 1976.

my research on the history and culture of Jews in Galicia to the history of Israel. In the literature on the subject, the former Galicia is referred to as "the Jewish heartland"[85] or "the mother of Israel."[86] Jews coming from there contributed significantly to the creation and development of the State of Israel. I would like to thank the management of the Pedagogical University in Krakow for providing me with excellent working conditions. With gratitude and warm feelings I remember all the meetings and conversations with Lili Haber, the president of the Association of Cracowians in Israel, who has helped me many times and in various ways. Many thanks to Ryszard Löw for support and informative conversations. I remember with gratitude all conversations with Nili Amit, who was so kind as to share with me her rich knowledge about the history and contemporary reality of Israel. I thank Professor Aleksander B. Skotnicki for inspiration for research and many valuable suggestions. I would also like him to accept my thanks for writing the preface to this book and for sharing with me his wonderful collections of Israeli stamps and postcards. I am extremely grateful to Leopold "Poldek" Wasserman for preparing the afterword and for the conversation that allowed me to significantly broaden my knowledge about the history of Polish Jews before World War II and the history of Israel.

I would like to thank the following people for their help in gathering information about Marcel Goldman: Bianka Goldman, Gabriela Haratyk, Ryszard Löw, Peter von Muralt, Shalom Singer.

I would like to thank Dr Kamila Follprecht, deputy director of the National Archives in Krakow, for valuable help in carrying out archival queries. I would also like to thank Dr Anna Jakimyszyn-Gadocha for familiarising herself with the general concept of the book and for expressing a number of inspiring comments in this regard. I would like to thank my friend, Prof. Grzegorz Nieć, for a thorough reading of the typescript and giving valuable comments that have significantly influenced the final shape of the work. I thank the editor, Zofia Wyżlińska, for her support in working on the book. Dr. Ewa Węgrzyn, thank you for the language consultation in reference to the Hebrew philology.

As beautifully as I can, I thank Professors Antony Polonsky and Sławomir Jacek Żurek. It is an honour that such distinguished scholars agreed to review

---

85 See T. Gąsowski, "Galicja—'żydowski matecznik,'" in *Galicja i jej dziedzictwo*, vol. 2: *Społeczeństwo i gospodarka*, ed. J. Chłopecki, H. Madurowicz-Urbańska, Rzeszów 1995, 125–135.

86 E. Gawron, "Matka Izraela," trans. I. Reichardt, *Herito. Dziedzictwo, Kultura, Współczesność* 4 (2015): 48–57.

my book. The comments contained in the reviews of both professors helped me improve the final shape of the publication.

For valuable support, I thank my irreplaceable friend Dr Konrad Meus. I thank my brother Mateusz for help in resolving many dilemmas related to the translation of Hebrew texts. Last but not least, thank you to my wife Anna and my son Joachim for their help and understanding.

The honorary patronage over the book was taken by the Polish-Israeli Chamber of Commerce, the Association of Cracowians in Israel, the JCC Krakow Jewish Community Center, and the Galicia Jewish Museum, for which I express my deep gratitude. It is extremely honourable for me to include the book in the Krakow UNESCO City of Literature program, I would like to thank the Krakow authorities and the Krakow Festival Office for this. I would also like to thank the media patrons of the book: the Jewish Magazine *Chidusz*, *Słowo Żydowskie*, the *Krakow* monthly, and the *Wielka HISTORIA.pl* magazine.

1

Mythical Krakow—Childhood (1926–1939)

Marcel Goldman was born on November 7, 1926 in Krakow to the merchant family of Maksymilian (Mordechaj) Goldman (born 1901) and Sara née Goldberger (born 1903). Since then, the city has changed its face several times, the Krakow that our protagonist knew and loved no longer exists... In fact, damages here were not as serious as those that occurred in Warsaw during World War II; monuments, old tenements, and even the house with the flat once occupied by the Goldman family survived. However, while the spatial arrangement of the city survived, the social and national structure underwent profound changes. First of all, in 1926, Krakow was a bipolar city, co-created by Poles and Jews, who constituted a quarter of the total population. According to the census carried out on September 30, 1921, 14.7% of Krakow residents declared their Jewish nationality. However, the total number of Jews in Krakow must have been more than that, because 24.6% of the city's residents declared themselves as belonging to the Jewish religion.[1] This difference proves the far-reaching assimilation of some Jews, who often referred to themselves as "Poles of the Jewish religion."

The Goldman family is not easy to define. Up to the outbreak of World War II they had not been hiding the fact that they were Jews, but, as Marcel recalls, "they ran a Polish home."[2] Why does he say so? To fully understand the cultural profile of his father, it must be remembered that he came from Silesia, so it is not surprising that he was fluent in German and had a very good understanding of that country's culture. Until the Nazis invaded Poland, he had constantly been subscribing to the German press, thanks to which he knew the intentions of the Nazis well. When he and his family found themselves in the ghetto, he knew that they had to escape from it, thanks to which they survived. However,

---

1 L. Mroczka, *Krakowianie. Szkice do portretu zbiorowego w dobie industrialnej transformacji 1890–1939*, Krakow 1999, 45.
2 Interview with Marcel Goldman carried out on March 25, 2017.

Fig. 1. The Old Synagogue in Krakow, the beginning of the twentieth century, photo: Ignacy Krieger, collections of the Krakow Museum

the relevance of Mordechaj's, called Maksymilian, Silesian origin still does not explain everything.

He was born in Rajcza, a small town in the Żywiec region, geographically in the Żywiec Beskids, which does not belong to the industrial part of Silesia. Orphaned at a young age,[3] he lived with his uncle (father's brother) in Żywiec. The uncle enjoyed a high economic status, so he could send Maks to a renowned technical school in Cieszyn, where lessons were conducted in German, which probably determined his excellent knowledge of the language.[4] As an orphan, he did not take the final exams and had to go to work to cover at least a part of his living expenses.[5] We should notice that, before the war, someone who completed secondary education was considered a very well-educated person. It is also worth remembering that he grew up surrounded by mountains, which had to make a big impression on him, because he considered himself a highlander until the end of his life. He served in the First Regiment of Podhale Rifles. In

---

3   Marcel Goldman's paternal grandparents were buried in the cemetery in Milówka.
4   Goldman family documents.
5   Ibid.

that unit, he never encountered any manifestations of antisemitism, on the contrary, Marcel remembered from his father's story that he could always count on the kindness of his colleagues. For example, when celebrating Yom Kippur he fasted during the day, and his colleagues took a meal for him for the evening so that he would not have to go hungry to sleep. After leaving military service, he felt strongly associated with his unit and took part in all reservist exercises. He treated the hat and cape worn by the Podhale Rifles, referring to highlander folklore, with reverence. Little Marcel sometimes managed to sneak out of the house in that outfit, thanks to which he could become "the king of the yard."[6] In *Iskierki życia* he wrote:

> I remember I was six or seven years old when my father got a pass and came home from exercises for a few days. It was a great event for me. I put on my head a hat with seashells and an eagle feather, threw a cape over my shoulders, put on a belt and paraded proudly like a peacock in our yard. My legs were tangling in the cape, the hat fell on my eyes, but what did it matter considering the fact that I could impress my peers.[7]

Fig. 2. A march of the Podhale Riflemen, led by the orchestra, before the King of Romania Charles II in Pole Mokotowskie in Warsaw, June 27, 1937, photo: Narcyz Witczak-Witaczyński, public domain

---

6   Interview with Marcel Goldman carried out on March 25, 2017.
7   M. Goldman, *Iskierki życia*, 3rd edition, Krakow 2014, 7–8.

In the illustration (Fig. 2) presenting the Podhale Riflemen during one of the march parades it can be seen what the uniform described by Marcel looked like before World War II.

Marcel's father always expressed his attachment to Podhale folklore, for example, he liked highlander music and often listened to it. In the whole, he was a rather complicated personality type: he read the German press daily, with often a dose of highlander music, but he kept his distance to the Jewish community. He attended the synagogue only twice a year: at Rosh Hashanah (Jewish New Year) and Yom Kippur (the Day of Atonement, also called the Judgment Day). Jewish matters, however, had to be important to him, since he also subscribed to *Nowy Dziennik*, a leading newspaper of Polish Zionists, which was published in Krakow in Polish. For the full picture, his intellectual ambitions, his expressed passion for books, theater, and opera must not be overlooked.

The image of Maks reading a book or newspaper must have been typical. Therefore, his marriage with Sara may come as a surprise. She came from the village and represented the language and style characteristic of its inhabitants. She only graduated from elementary school, throughout her youth she spoke only in Polish. It was a unique relationship from the very beginning. At the time, Jews usually got married with the help of matchmakers, while Sara and Maks met without intermediaries—in the dentist's waiting room. Maks was on a business trip in Krakow and came with a sore tooth, while Sara accompanied her mother. They got married in 1925.[8]

The social origin of Sara and her family should be considered unusual for Polish Jews, who mostly lived in cities or shtetls at that time. Her parents, Chana née Wichner and Jakub Goldberger, ran a farm inherited by her mother in Zbydniowice near Krakow (currently within Krakow), located near Swoszowice in a hamlet called Pokrzywki. Another Jewish family, the Szajns, who ran an inn, lived next to them. Sara remembered the years spent in Zbydniowice with nostalgia, although her family, like most Polish peasants, struggled with poverty. It is enough to note that the Goldbergers had five children (in addition to Sara: Isaac, Moniek, Frania, and Janek).[9] Sara, living in Krakow after her marriage, continued to use the dialect from her homeland, she also did not show much interest in science or culture, Marcel never saw her with a book in hand. Perhaps

---

8   Interview with Marcel Goldman carried out on February 8, 2017.
9   Goldman, *Iskierki życia*, 15; conversation with Marcel Goldman carried out on March 25, 2017.

she would sporadically read the press, and apart from that, she did not have this type of intellectual needs. When she saw her husband with a book in his hand, she would say ironically: "father walks like a fortune-teller with a book under his arm."[10]

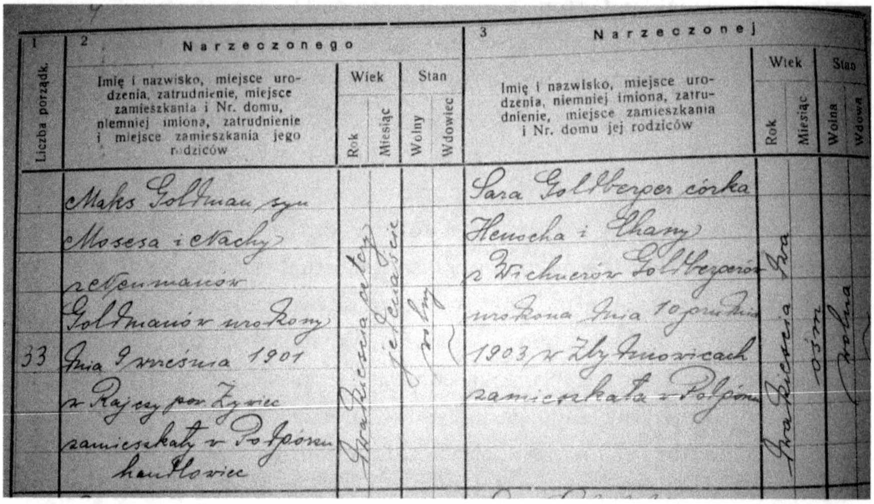

1 Liczba porządk.	2 Narzeczonego: Imię i nazwisko, miejsce urodzenia, zatrudnienie, miejsce zamieszkania i Nr. domu, niemniej imiona, zatrudnienie i miejsce zamieszkania jego rodziców	Wiek: Rok	Wiek: Miesiąc	Stan: Wolny	Stan: Wdowiec	3 Narzeczonej: Imię i nazwisko, miejsce urodzenia, niemniej imiona, zatrudnienie, miejsce zamieszkania i Nr. domu jej rodziców	Wiek: Rok	Wiek: Miesiąc	Stan: Wolna	Stan: Wdowa
33	Maks Goldman, syn Mosesa i Nachy [illegible] Goldmanów urodzony dnia 9 września 1901 w Rajczy pow. Żywiec zamieszkały w Podgórzu handlowiec	[illegible]	[illegible]	wolny		Sara Goldberger córka Henocha i Chany z Wichnerów Goldbergerów urodzona dnia 10 grudnia 1903 w Zbydniowicach zamieszkała w Podgórzu	[illegible]	ośm	wolna	

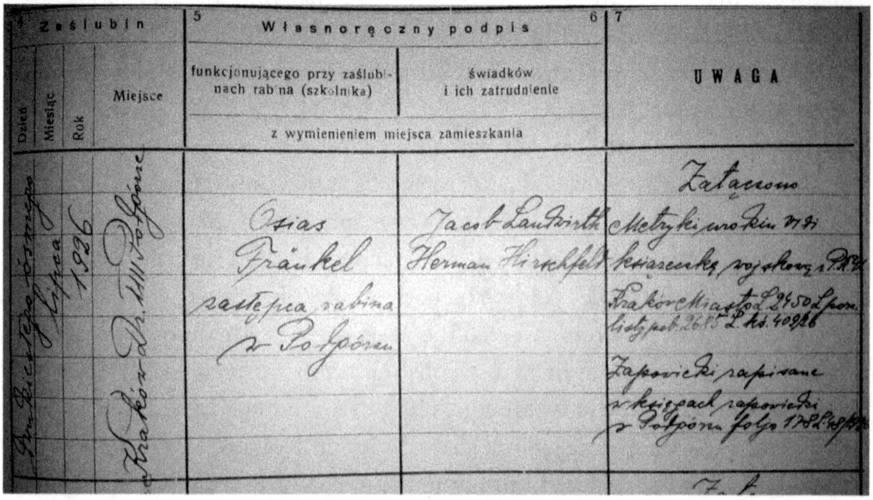

4 Zaślubin: Dzień	Miesiąc	Rok	Miejsce	5 Własnoręczny podpis funkcjonującego przy zaślubinach rabina (szkolnika)	świadków i ich zatrudnienie z wymienieniem miejsca zamieszkania	6	7 UWAGA
Dwudziestego ósmego	lipca	1926	Kraków Nr. [illegible] Podgórze	Osias Fränkel zastępca rabina w Podgórzu	Jacob Landwirth, Herman Hirschfeld		Załączono metryki [illegible] Zapowiedzi zapisane w księgach zapowiedzi w Podgórzu [illegible]

Figs. 3 and 4. The wedding certificate of Marcel Goldman's parents, Maks Goldman and Sara née Goldberger, signed on July 28, 1926. National Archives in Krakow [hereinafter: NAK], Civil registry files of the Klasno-Podgórze Israeli Metrical District, reference number 29/1473/110

10 Interview with Marcel Goldman carried out on February 8, 2017.

After many years, Marcel came to the conclusion that he took a passion for books and for learning as such after his father.[11] Thanks to the well-stocked home library, Marcel started his literary pilgrimages very early. He also reached for books that were certainly not intended for children: at about nine years old he read *Father Goriot* by Honoré de Balzac and *The Peasants* by Władysław Reymont. He was very attentive to *Pan Tadeusz* by Adam Mickiewicz, Henryk Sienkiewicz belonged to his favorite authors, while he was less interested in Słowacki, who was too abstract according to him.[12] School also played a big role in his intellectual development and stimulation of literary passions, which will be discussed later.

Marcel remembers his mother as a woman full of natural grace and elegance, which is confirmed by photographs from that period. Despite her rural origin, she attached great importance to good manners, which she also instilled in her children. In the childhood photos, Marcel and his sister are always neat and tastefully dressed. Their mother devoted all her free time to them. She combined her household responsibilities with running a shop, and the effort to manage it lay mainly with her. Usually, she would stand behind the shop counter, and mainly behind the cash register. The material well-being of her family depended on her discernment in the clients' needs and good contact with them. The family did not decide to entrust the management of the shop to someone else, believing, not without reason, that in this case no one would show as much commitment as they themselves. For other tasks in the shop, they had two full-time employees, which proves the scale of turnover. In addition, on Saturdays or during the holidays, when there was a lot of business, there were also occasional helpers, most often family members (such as the daughter of Marcel's father's cousin). Sara showed the so-called common sense, associated with her rural origin; during the war this feature was to save the life of her loved ones.

The spouses complemented each other very well: he was characterised by an intellectual, while she, by a practical approach to life. Maks took on the responsibility of settling accounting matters and contacts with the tax office. He also bought goods. Marcel believed that running the shop did not really interest his father, and certainly did not suit his intellectual aspirations. He expected much more from life, although he did not show a sense of disappointment or dissatisfaction. He fulfilled his ambitions by reading inspirational texts or going

---

11   Ibid.
12   Interview with Marcel Goldman carried out on December 22, 2016.

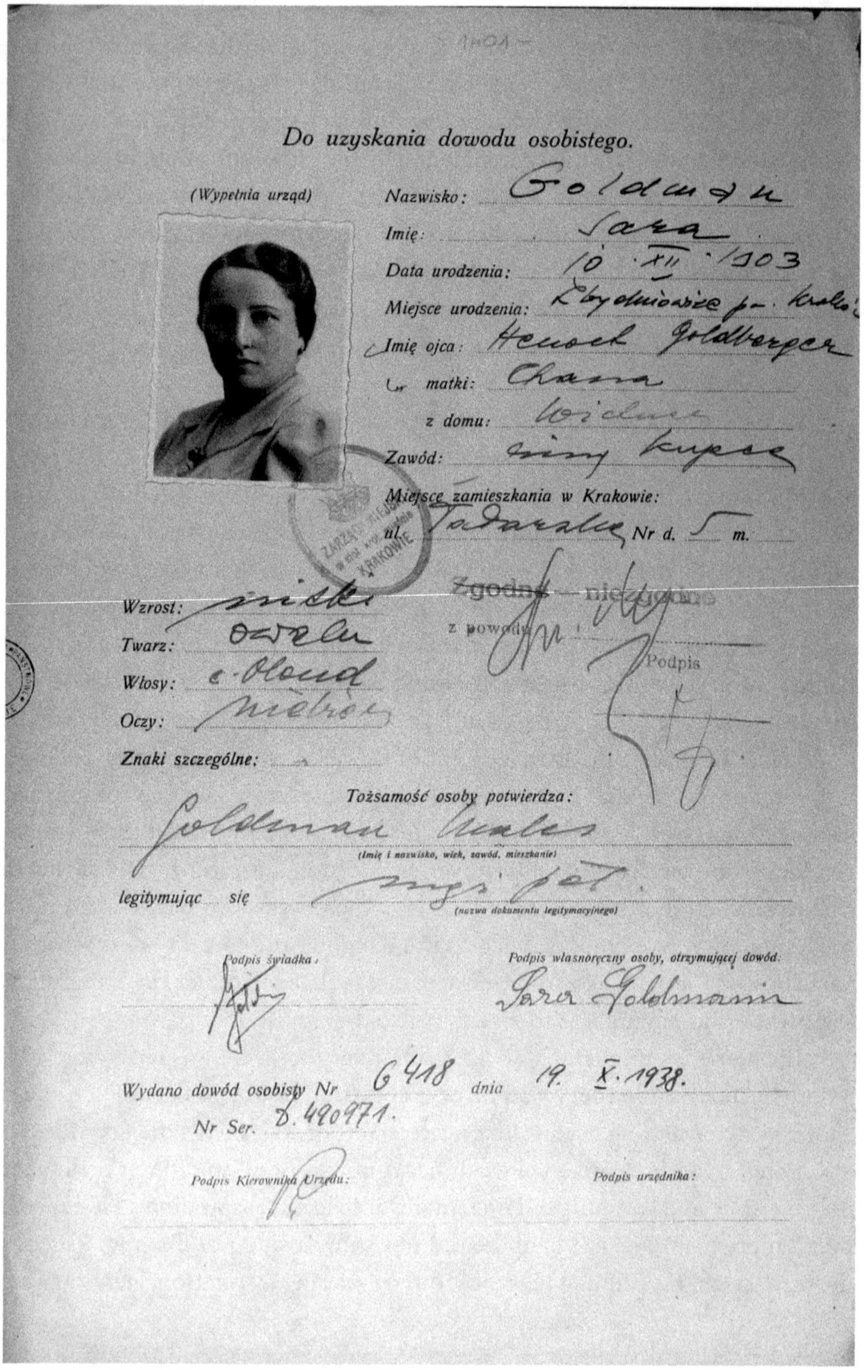

Figs. 5 and 6. Application for an ID card: Sara Goldman, NAK,
Krakow District Office, reference number 29/218/867;

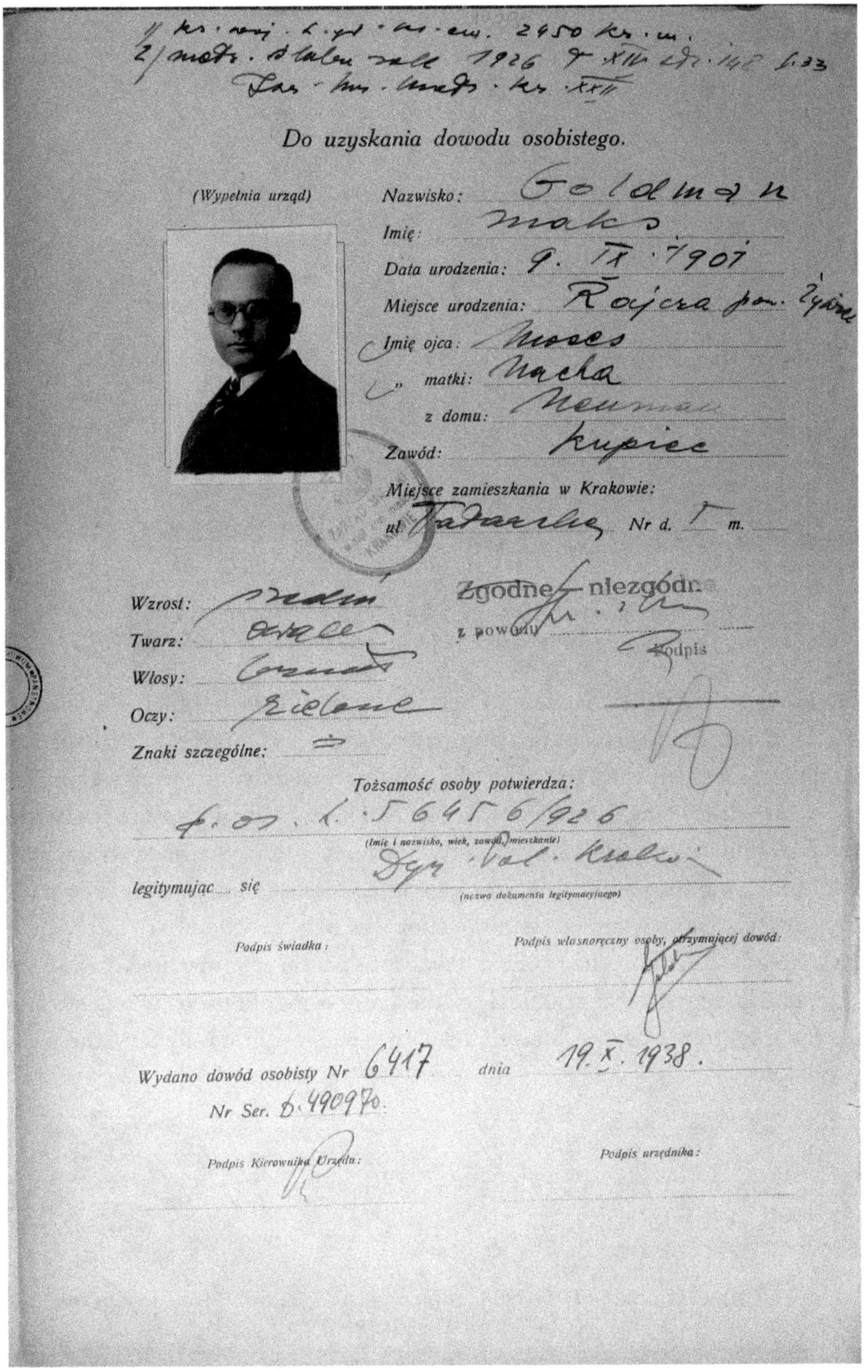

Do uzyskania dowodu osobistego.

(Wypełnia urząd)

Nazwisko: Goldman
Imię: maks
Data urodzenia: 9. II. 1907
Miejsce urodzenia: Rajcza pow. Żywiec
Imię ojca: Moses
  „ matki: Nacha
  z domu: Neuman
Zawód: kupiec

Miejsce zamieszkania w Krakowie:
ul. Tatarska Nr d. 5 m. ___

Wzrost: średni
Twarz: owalna
Włosy: ciemne
Oczy: zielone
Znaki szczególne: —

Tożsamość osoby potwierdza:
ł. os. L. 5456/926
(Imię i nazwisko, wiek, zawód, mieszkanie)

legitymując się Dyr. Pol. Kraków
(nazwa dokumentu legitymacyjnego)

Wydano dowód osobisty Nr 6417 dnia 19.X.1938.
Nr Ser. D. 490970

Application for an ID card: Maks Goldman,
NAK, Krakow District Office, reference number 29/218/867

Fig. 7. Maks and Sara Goldman—Marcel's parents, 1948, family collections of Marcel and Bianka Goldman (Tel Aviv)

to the theater and opera. He taught his children to set the bar high, but also to be able to appreciate present achievements. In turn, his mother felt satisfied at work, it was her element. First of all, she was impressed that the shop was profitable because she came from a poor family, and it was a great pleasure for her to keep the family at a relatively high level.[13] Marcel mentions that such an arrangement, satisfying his parents, did not guarantee him due interest on their part. His mother was preoccupied with the shop, his father with books, and Marcel was left alone. Therefore, he reached for various readings or invented games. He also had to learn self-reliance quickly, at the age of eight or nine he would already take the tram to the dentist himself, his father paid for him only after the visit, by the way.[14]

Fig. 8. Birth certificate of Marcel Goldman, NAK, Health Office in Krakow, reference number 29/83/393

---

13   Interview with Marcel Goldman carried out on December 22, 2016.
14   Ibid.

Marcel's parents were respectful but also distant to the Jewish community and to the Jewish religion. We are talking about distance in both intellectual and geographical terms. Krakow Jews lived in the Kazimierz District (once a separate city).[15] They felt safe there, they had synagogues, Jewish schools, and kosher food shops nearby. The equality of Jews, introduced in the second half of the nineteenth century, enabled them to purchase and rent fixed property also outside that district. Although the majority decided to stay in Kazimierz, many took the opportunity to settle in Stradom, and they also arrived in Śródmieście (the city center).[16] Many Jews moved to Grodzka Street (36.9%), the satirical press even proposed renaming it to Jewish Street![17] The choice was not accidental, the former royal road was an extension of the streets leading from Kazimierz to Krakowska and Stradom streets, which, due to high traffic, were suitable for running shops, cafés, restaurants, service points, as well as law and notary offices.

Jews running a business in the very center of Krakow often kept their houses in Kazimierz, where they returned after work. The Goldmans apparently did not feel such a need as they lived in the Kleparz district, numerically and culturally dominated by Poles. There, in a tenement house at the corner of Krowoderska Street and Słowiański Square, they ran a haberdashery shop, the assortment of which included shirts, ties, socks, underwear, belts, handbags, sewing supplies, buttons, and threads.[18] Articles of this type were popular at the time, because clothes were generally not bought, but made to measure. Clothing was expensive, so it was often changed and repaired. In the same tenement, the Goldmans lived in a rent apartment: "it was not comfortable, without a bathroom, with an outside toilet in the yard."[19] Although they cherished some Sabbath-related traditions, they did not observe the religious rigors that followed: "Our Mom did light shabbat candles on Friday, but [as it was often said in Poland] 'Saturday rituals were not observed.' My father did not say the Sabbath prayer, and my

---

15 In 1910, 21,711 Jews lived there, who constituted 75.2% of the total population. See K. Karolczak, *Ludność żydowska w Krakowie na przełomie XIX i XX wieku*, in *Żydzi w Małopolsce. Studia z dziejów osadnictwa i życia społecznego*, ed. F. Kiryk, Przemyśl 1991, 253.
16 In 1910, 4042 Jews settled in Stradom, constituting 57.1% of all residents, and their number increased in Śródmieście as well (11.6%), ibid.
17 Ibid.
18 A. D. Pordes, I. Grin, "Wywiad przeprowadzony w maju 2001 r. w mieszkaniu Marcela Goldmana w Tel Awiwie," in *Ich miasto. Wspomnienia Izraelczyków, przedwojennych mieszkańców Krakowa*, Warsaw 2004, 145.
19 Ibid., 146.

mother came home, lit candles and returned to the shop, because it was open late. But on the Sabbath evening there were always *challot* at home."[20]

Fig. 9. Krakow, Sukiennice (the Cloth Hall), early twentieth century, public domain

On Saturday, despite the Jewish holiday, they opened the shop because it was located in the Christian quarter, and besides, they achieved high profits at that time, as paid employees received weekly salaries on Saturdays. They only closed the shop on Sundays. However, this did not mean a full day of rest. Maks most often obtained supplies from manufacturers in Łódź,[21] but he often made purchases from Jewish wholesalers in Kazimierz, and he could also do so on Sundays, which for Jews are not a holiday, but a normal day of the week. During that period, non-Jewish merchants in Kazimierz, losing competition with Jews, tried to obtain a legal advantage over them—they led the so-called fight for Sunday rest. They put pressure on subsequent governments and legislators to introduce the obligation to celebrate Sundays. They argued that such a provision would protect the rights of Christian workers employed by Jews. This argument should be assessed as completely false, since most of the companies run by Jews were family companies. Mostly family members found employment

---

20　Ibid., 148.
21　Ibid., 150.

there, therefore they were usually Jews (mixed marriages in Galicia were rare). Of course, it was primarily about making work difficult for Jewish merchants and reducing their income. The fight for Sunday rest was present practically all over Europe and everywhere the Jews came out of it unscathed (of course, until the war). Similarly, Jewish entrepreneurs from Kazimierz circumvented the regulations, illegally opening wholesale outlets for Jewish retailers who ran shops in Christian districts closed on that day. According to various sources, in some localities in Poland peasants also bought on Sundays. We know that this is what the Goldmans did—despite the notice with the inscription "Closed," they entered wholesale outlets through the back door. Only after early shopping did the family have time to spend Sunday afternoons together.

Despite the distance to religious matters, the Goldmans led kosher kitchen, mainly because of pious maternal grandparents, so that they could eat at their place. They also observed certain daily rituals, which is associated with an interesting observation. Jews and Christians lived side by side, so it is not surprising that they closely watched each other, often drawing quite simplified conclusions, sometimes turning into stereotypes. Thus, for example, Christians, seeing the general well-being of some Jewish families, became convinced that it must be related to the *mezuzot* placed above their doors.[22] There were Christians who hung *mezuzot* on the doors of their apartments, hoping that it would bring them happiness. In turn, Jews, looking at Christians, believed that their strength and vitality must result from the consumption of pork. Also in Marcel's memory, the childhood conviction he shared with his mother that Christian children are strong because they eat ham is preserved.

> Opposite our shop at Zwierzyniecka Street there was a grocery shop, which was called Racja. It was a chain of shops that also offered pork ham. Due to the fact that my parents ran a kosher kitchen, it was impossible to bring ham into the house or eat it on a plate, so that it would not become *trefa*. Therefore, for the money received from my mother I would buy a ham roll. The sellers wrapped it in paper for me. I returned to the other side of the street and ate the roll from a piece of paper at my parents' shop.[23]

---

22 *Mezuzah*—a wad containing texts of prayers taken from the Torah secured in a small container, usually placed above the door of the house. Jews, when crossing the threshold, used to touch them, and often kissed the hand or fingers that came into contact with the *mezuzah*.
23 Interview with Marcel Goldman carried out on February 8, 2017.

The good financial situation of the Goldman family allowed them to hire a maid: "The 'gentile' maid cooked, in prewar Poland there were maids who knew kosher cuisine better than their 'mistress.'"[24] They also occasionally employed other people to help with housework. Therefore, under their roof, Polish and Jewish customs were mixed up, both sides helped in cultivating them, partly adapting them to their needs. An example is the Christmas tree. Marcel recounts that:

> Of course, my parents did not celebrate Christmas, but its atmosphere infected them. The proof of this is that they put a Christmas tree at home during Christmas. They officially explained its presence by wanting to please the servants. The thing is that the Christmas tree stood in the living room, and not in the rooms occupied by the servants.[25]

It was evidently intended for household members, and especially for children.

Self-identification does not have to be consistent with the way one is perceived by outsiders. Marcel is fully aware of this. In his book *A w nocy przychodzą myśli* he notes: "As part of the activities of the Polish Institute in Tel-Aviv, a meeting was held in which professors from Polish universities took part. One of them, of Jewish origin, said that he was 100% Jewish and 100% Polish. I allowed myself to ask him how his Polish community sees him? The answer was evasive."[26] The Goldmans were distinguished from the Polish community even by their surname, which was derived from the German language (a cluster of two words: "gold" and "man"). The history of Polish Jewish surnames is tied to the partitions of Poland. It is worth recalling that in Old Polish times Jews did not have surnames, until the partitioners introduced the obligation to have them. The Austrians probably made that decision for order purposes, but at the same time they used it for Germanization—Habsburg officials gave Jews German names. Recognised historians, Stanisław Grodziski and Eligiusz Kozłowski, write even about "the German baptism":

> Thus, at the end of the eighteenth century in Galicia, there was a mass "German baptism" of Jews who received German, often very strange, names in circuses. They were also ordered to use German in trade.

---

24 M. Goldman, *A w nocy przychodzą myśli*, Krakow 2012, 20.
25 Interview with Marcel Goldman carried out on February 8, 2017.
26 Goldman, *A w nocy przychodzą myśli*, 13.

Their loyalty to authorities, their German names, especially legal regulations—all this separated Jews even more from the community in which they had been tolerated for centuries and became one of the reasons for the intensifying antisemitism.[27]

Certainly German and, to a large extent, distinctive surnames became a sign additionally stigmatizing Jews as strangers among Poles. The attempt to fully assimilate with Polish society required a change of surname. This type of practices was known but never took on a mass character. The Goldmans decided to take such a step only during the war, in the face of life danger. In their case it was not a change of name in the generally accepted sense, it was more about a complete change of identity. False birth certificates were obtained for them—certified by a priest who did not even have to know (though he could have thought) that they were intended for a Jewish family. Marcel's father chose the surname "Galas," which he knew from Silesia. He did not want his surname to end with "ski" or "cki," because most Jews who bought Aryan papers demanded such surnames.[28]

One more detail still needs to be added. The officials representing the invader used the procedure of forcibly naming Jews as a source of additional income. To avoid an offensive or funny name, one had to give the official an appropriate amount of money. Only the wealthy could afford to "acquire" the right to a surname that could be considered ennobling, impressive, or at least pretty, such as Rosenberg, Gross (Gros), Grossman (Grosman), or Goldman. On this basis, it can be concluded that Marcel's ancestors, at least the males in his father's line, were not poor people. It can also be assumed that the female ancestors in his father's line were equally well off. It is known that Jews paid close attention to their names and the marriage of someone named Gross with a person named Klein would be treated as a misalliance (the names of Polish nobility stood out in a similar way). The chosen fiancée had to come from an equally good home, which could mean a no less important name, and if she did not have one, a generous dowry could be a kind of compensation. Please note that Marcel's mother's maiden name was Goldberger (from German, "gold mountain"), as prestigious as Goldman.

Their typical Jewish family surname did not cause a lack of acceptance on the part of Polish neighbours, friends, and contractors. Theoretically, it could

---

27 S. Grodziski, E. Kozłowski, *Polska zniewolona 1795–1806*, Warsaw 1987, 23.
28 Interview with Marcel Goldman carried out on February 8, 2019.

be a manifestation of the cordiality of Poles encountered in their lives, but in practice the situation was more complicated. There are a few important things to keep in mind. The external appearance and way of being did not reveal that they were Jews; their clients and contractors, entering into relationships with them, could get the impression that they were dealing with Poles. Marcel Goldman himself emphasizes:

> My mother came from the country and her vocabulary was typical of people from the country. The shop run by my parents was located near Kleparz, which was visited by peasants from the villages around Krakow. My mother spoke to them using "their language." As a result, they not only accepted her, but also willingly visited the shop run by her. They felt good there. Nobody looked down on them and restrained them with the metropolitan refinement, because my mother simply did not have it.[29]

Therefore, it is difficult to determine to what extent the behaviour of peasants constituting the core of the Goldmans' clientele testified to their attitude towards Jews. When buying from them, they probably did not know that they were dealing with Jews, or they knew (guessed) it, but that Jewishness was so vague and unobtrusive that it was within the tolerance threshold they could have managed to deal with:

> My parents ran their shop under their own name. The name was written on the shop window, but in small letters so that Polish customers would not pay attention to the fact that it was a Jewish shop. It is interesting that when Piłsudski died, my parents bought a plaster portrait of Piłsudski, hung it over the door of the storage, and lit a lamp in front of it. Catholic clients who came to us did not see what it was from afar, they thought it was the Mother of God. So they were convinced that they were buying in a Catholic shop! Of course, no one proved them wrong....[30]

The Goldmans were therefore tolerated, but with some distance. Let us not forget that it was typical for Christian-Jewish relations of prewar Europe that a Jew remained a Jew, no matter how far assimilation took place. The late nineteenth and early twentieth century brought a series of anti-Jewish pogroms in the western part of the former Russian empire, from Odessa in the south to

---

29 Interview with Marcel Goldman carried out on February 8, 2017.
30 Pordes, Grin, *Wywiad*, 153.

Petersburg in the north. Thousands of Jews were murdered and robbed, many were injured. In 1894, the so-called Dreyfus affair took place, when Alfred Dreyfus (1859–1935), an officer in the French army, was wrongly accused of espionage simply because he was a Jew. Soon after that, antisemitic protests took place in Paris and other French cities. A direct observer of these events was Theodor Herzl (1860–1904), a Jewish journalist from Austria-Hungary, later the creator and leader of the Zionist movement, who saw the solution to the Jewish problem in the creation of a separate Jewish state. In his flagship work titled *The State of the Jews*, he wrote:

> Everywhere, we tried to honestly blend in with the societies around us, and only keep the faith of our fathers. We were not allowed to. We vainly become loyal, sometimes even exaggerated, patriots, we vainly make the same sacrifices in goods and blood as our fellow citizens, we labour in vain to increase the fame of our native countries in both art and science, in order to increase their wealth through the development of trade and economic relations. In the countries where we have lived for centuries, we are still described as strangers, often by those whose ancestors were not yet in a given country, when our fathers struggled there.[31]

Marcel also suffered because of his nationality, although not to such an extent as in many cases (after all, anti-Jewish riots took place also in Krakow). He began his school education at the Public School of Saint Adalbert,[32] which at that time had a very high level of education. However, an antisemitic prank took place there. He remembered that once, when he was eating a *challah* sandwich during the break between classes, one of the students ran up to him and started shouting: "Look, a Jew is eating *challah*!," which was picked up by other children. He felt lonely against general hostility, the whole class stood up against him. At home, he told his mother about the incident, trying to understand what happened. What does the word "Jew" mean? Who is that "Jew"? After the incident, his parents decided to change the boy's school, when the headmaster

---

31 T. Herzl, *Państwo żydowskie. Próba nowoczesnego rozwiązania kwestii żydowskiej*, trans. J. Surzyn, Krakow 2006, 50–51.

32 This institution was located in a wooden, no longer existing building at 14 Krowoderska Street. It continues to operate (although at a different address) to this day and is considered the oldest in Krakow and one of the oldest elementary schools in Poland. It was established on November 18, 1797, two years after the third partition of the Polish-Lithuanian Commonwealth.

> **i** The word "Zionism" comes from "Zion," the name of one of the hills of Jerusalem, which was later used to designate the Temple, Jerusalem, and the whole Land of Israel. Zionism is an ideological, political, and social movement seeking to rebuild the national seat of Jews in the Land of Israel (Hebrew: Eretz Yisrael). It can also be called the movement of national revival of Jews. The concept of "Zionism" was created in 1890 by Natan Birnbaum, a Jewish activist in Vienna, who also introduced the expression "political Zionism" in 1892. Therefore, for earlier efforts to build Jewish statehood in the areas of former ancient Israel expressed by rabbis, mystics, and politicians, the term "proto-Zionism" is appropriate. The proto-Zionist trend includes, for example, Lovers of Zion, an important figure in this movement was Leon Pinsker (1821–1891), who in 1882 published the program manifesto entitled *Auto-Emancipation. Warning to His Fellow People, from a Russian Jew* and organized the first congress dedicated to the issue of rebuilding Jewish statehood, which took place on November 6–11, 1884 in Katowice (currently in Poland, then the territory of the Prussian partition). A breakthrough in the development of the Zionist movement came with the activities of Theodor Herzl (1860–1904), who published a famous program work entitled *The State of the Jews* with the subtitle *Proposal of a Modern Solution for the Jewish Question* (*Der Judenstaat. Versuch einer modernen Lösung der Judenfrage*, 1st edition, Vienna and Berlin 1896) and organised the First Zionist Congress in Basel in 1897. Initially, some proto-Zionist and Zionist activists also considered locations other than the Land of Israel for the Jewish state. Pinsker, for example, suggested the United States, while Herzl and his colleagues explored the possibility of developing Jewish settlement in South America, Africa, and Cyprus. However, these options were relatively quickly rejected, and at the beginning of the twentieth century the activities of Zionist organizations were directed exclusively to the Land of Israel. When making that decision, practical and political considerations were also taken into account, but the primary role was played by the historical and religious relationship of the Jewish people with Zion and the strength of its influence on the imagination of Jews.

was still trying to dissuade them from this decision, Marcel remembered his words: "Please think about it. Separating yourself from Polish society is not a good solution." However, they did not change their mind.[33]

---

33 Interview with Marcel Goldman carried out on February 8, 2017

Childhood (1926–1939) | 53

Fig. 10. Boys' Public School of Saint Adalbert No. 1, at 14 Krowoderska Street, public domain

Fig. 11. Marcel Goldman at the age of seven, first-grade student at the Primary School of Saint Adalbert in Krakow, 1933, family collections of Marcel and Bianka Goldman (Tel Aviv)

In this way, our protagonist went to the elementary school that operated at the renowned Hebrew Gymnasium in Krakow.[34] Aleksander B. Skotnicki draws attention to the quite symptomatic problems of the school in the first period of its existence: "The Orthodox community saw an open path to assimilation in the newly created school. On the other hand, the community of a certain fraction of progressive Jews showed reluctance to the school, seeing too many conservative elements in its programs."[35] However, the following years brought the Hebrew Gymnasium reputation and recognition far beyond Krakow. The influence of the Zionist idea was evident at school, visible not so much in political initiatives as in the curriculum, which emphasised the learning of the Hebrew language and the history of Eretz Yisrael. At the same time, Polish patriotism was promoted in the institution, treating Polish history, literature, culture, and art with care. Many teachers of the school were outstanding personalities. The best example is Juliusz Feldhorn,[36] who was remembered as an extraordinary, but at the same time very demanding teacher arousing young people's passion for literature, history, art and beauty.[37] Natan Gross (1919–2005), who settled in Israel after World War II, many years later recalled lessons with him in the following way:

---

[34] The initiative to establish this institution came from the members of the Żydowskie Towarzystwo Szkoły Ludowej i Średniej (English: Jewish Society of Folk and High School) established in 1904 in Krakow (some sources and historical materials point to 1902 as the date of the establishment of the Society and its name as the Towarzystwo Hebrajskiej Szkoły Ludowej, in English: Society of the Hebrew Folk School). Thanks to it, in the 1908/09 school year, the first grade of elementary school was launched. In 1918, a Private Co-Educational Gymnasium of the Jewish Society of Folk and High School in Krakow named after Dr. Chaim Hilfstein was created on the foundations of this institution. The school had a set of buildings at the corner of 5 Brzozowa Street and 8/10 Podbrzezie Street, which were built in 1918, 1924, and 1930. See M. Bosak, "Z dziejów żydowskiego szkolnictwa w Krakowie," in *To była hebrajska szkoła w Krakowie. Historia i wspomnienia*, ed. N. Gross, Tel Aviv 1989, 14–24.

[35] A. B. Skotnicki, *Juliusz Feldhorn. Poeta, pisarz, tłumacz, wybitny polonista Gimnazjum Hebrajskiego w Krakowie*, Krakow 2011, 52.

[36] Juliusz Feldhorn (1901–1943) was a Polish poet, prose writer, and translator. In 1923 he graduated from the Jagiellonian University in Polish Studies, and in 1927 obtained a doctoral degree. In the years 1926–1927 he held an important place in the editorial office of *Gazeta Literacka*. He translated Italian, French, German, Russian, and Serbian literature into Polish. He was fascinated by Slavic, especially Polish, literature, and planned to create a chair of Slavic languages at the Hebrew University in Jerusalem, see N. Styrna, "Juliusz Feldhorn (Jan Las)," in *Krakowianie. Wybitni Żydzi krakowscy XIV–XX w.*, ed. A. Kutylak, Kraków 2006, 168–170.

[37] Skotnicki, *Juliusz Feldhorn*.

... they had nothing to do with the teacher's routine and were far from the official school curriculum. He did not stop at Polish literature, which was his main subject. Teaching analysis, composition, interpretation of the literary work, he ventured deep into the fields of other arts. He taught to look and listen. He organised classical and modern music concerts from discs, introduced students to masterpieces of fine arts through projection. While giving lectures on Kochanowski, he developed a beautiful vision of the Italian Renaissance, full of palaces, sculptures, paintings, beautiful poems and bloody scores, humanists and condoliers, people and works.[38]

The end of the Hebrew Gymnasium came only after the outbreak of World War II—at the beginning of the 1939/40 school year, the German occupiers decided to close it. The same happened to all Jewish schools in Nazi-occupied Poland. In the last year of its existence, about 1,500 students attended the Gymnasium.[39] According to inaccurate estimates, about 1.5–2 thousand of all pupils of the school from 1908–1939 survived the war, about 800 of whom settled in Israel (in 1950 they established the Association of Former Students of the Hebrew Gymnasium in Krakow).[40] The rest died during the war. Juliusz Feldhorn, mentioned above, was hiding with Aryan papers, but his wife's looks raised suspicion and the Germans came to arrest her on August 11, 1943. They also detained her husband, who confessed that he was a Jew, and both of them were shot.[41]

The high level of the Hebrew Gymnasium is evidenced by the fact that its graduates were admitted without exams to the University of Warsaw and the Hebrew University in Jerusalem. Among its famous pupils was, for instance, the previously mentioned Natan Gross, writer, screenwriter, director, and film producer, one of the creators of Israeli cinema. The teaching staff of this school was made up of eminent intellectuals, including the already mentioned Juliusz Feldhorn, Szewach Walkowski,[42] Dr. Chaim Loew (1901–1976) and Nachman

---

38   N. Gross, "Rękopis znaleziony w piwnicy," in Gross, *To była hebrajska szkoła w Krakowie*, 53–54.
39   Bosak, "Z dziejów żydowskiego szkolnictwa w Krakowie," 14–24.
40   N. Gross, "Semper Fidelis," in Gross, *To była hebrajska szkoła w Krakowie*, 76.
41   Skotnicki, *Juliusz Feldhorn*.
42   Szewach Walkowski (1872–1943) wrote stories that were published in the Hebrew magazines *Machzikei HaDat*, *HaMagid*, and *HaMitzpe*. He also wrote a textbook for learning Hebrew, *Safa*. Gross, *To była hebrajska szkoła w Krakowie*, 40.

Mifelew (1886–1937), who jointly prepared a textbook for learning Hebrew *Yaldei Israel*, Dr. Menachem Stein,[43] or Samuel Stendig.[44] Many teachers of the Hebrew Gymnasium at different times of their lives lived in Eretz Yisrael or later in Israel, such as Bencjon (Bentzion) Katz, researcher and author of translations from classical Greek and Latin literature into Hebrew.[45] In 1946, Dr. Chaim Hilfstein, a physician, Zionist activist, and school president came to Israel. It was his name that the school bore. In 1949, Meir Bosak (born in 1912) emigrated to Israel, and continued his work there as a popular teacher and an award-winning writer.[46] The elementary school to which Marcel's parents enrolled him also had excellent staff.[47]

Visits of distinguished personalities from the world of science and culture were quite a distinction for the Hebrew Gymnasium. Among others, Chaim Nahman Bialik (1873–1934), a world-famous poet, prose writer, translator, and publisher, called the restorer of Hebrew poetry, visited the school in 1933.

Zionists influenced the ideological profile of the school greatly. The Jewish scout organization HaTzofeh was active there, Marcel Goldman also joined it. His instructor was Poldek Wasserman,[48] who talks about that organization in

---

43 Dr. Menachem Stein (1894–1943), lecturer at the Institute of Jewish Studies in Warsaw, was a researcher of *Midrash* and classical Greek culture, who translated Flavius from Greek and Latin. See ibid., 41–42.

44 Samuel Stendig (1900–1943) conducted ambitious research in philosophy, psychology, pedagogy, and history, he was also interested in palestinographic literature and cooperated with the Warsaw journal *Cyjonistiszer Leksykon*. Ibid., 42.

45 Katz also published critical texts on Hebrew literature and was a lector of Hebrew at the Jagiellonian University. He belonged to the founders of the University of Tel Aviv and became its second rector. Ibid., 43.

46 Bosak received literary prize of the Interior Minister H. M. Shipira and the Ramat Gan Award. Ibid., 40–44, 76.

47 Gross's book names several members of the staff. A teacher called Blindman, Benjamin Jeruzalimski, organizer of school events and celebrations, Joachim Izaak Kohn, head of the educational counseling center, and Naftali Jaakow Kwitner, or Celter, administrator of the Hebrew library, taught Hebrew language. A teacher called Hochman taught Hebrew subjects. Mosze Dobrowski taught handwork. Adela Fallman-Morgenbesser and Ilza Schinaglowa were teachers of gymnastics. Efraim Fiddler and Eliasz Haber, secretary of the Pedagogical Council, taught all subjects. Regina Haberowa, Albert Hochman, Zofia Leinkramowa, manager of the Polish library, Malwina Kleinberger, and Ignacy Müller taught subjects in Polish. Helena Mendelbaum Frandowa taught accounting, and Baruch Sperber taught singing. Ibid., 37–38.

48 Leopold Wasserman (later his name was Yehuda Maimon) was during World War II a member of underground formations operating in the ghetto: Akiba and the Jewish Combat Or-

Fig. 12. Chaim Nahman Bialik at the Hebrew Gymnasium in Krakow, October 21, 1931, collections of the Association of Cracowians in Israel

the afterword to this book. In the Hebrew Gymnasium, there were also other organizations typical of Polish schools at the time: Koło Ligi Obrony Powietrznej i Przeciwgazowej (LOPP, English: Group of the Air and Gas Defense League), Liga Morska (English: Marine League), Red Cross, school troop (military preparation), Commune School (school council), Student Self-Help, school orchestra, and various student clubs: literary, historical, philosophical, sports, sightseeing, and drama groups.[49]

The Hebrew Gymnasium became legendary. Its phenomenon has not yet been described in detail. Many interesting facts remain to be discovered, for example, the extraordinary popularity of the school terrace. Jewish youth eagerly organized parties, dances, or meetings there, as well as certain activities, such as assembling aviation models. Why did young Jews choose that place? Was the terrace such a significant place in the history of any other Polish school? Doubtful. The Jewish students could use a small square located just in front of the school, although Planty Dietlowskie stretched a little further, clean and tidy at that time.

---

ganization. He participated in the famous attack on German officers in the café Cyganeria at 38 Szpitalna Street in Krakow. See "Yehuda Maimon," http://www.centropa.org/photo/yehuda-maimon, accessed May 18, 2017, and the biographical note in the afterword.

49 N. Gross, "Uczyłem się gładko," in Gross, *To była hebrajska szkoła w Krakowie*, 66.

Why did they use the terrace then? The answer is simple—it was located almost at roof level, fenced off on one side by the last floor of the building, and on the other, with brickwork. It was a real enclave, inaccessible to antisemitic troopers who increasingly terrorized Jews, especially merchants, students, and pupils of other schools.

That excellent Jewish school can become a starting point for a broader view of the intricacies of Jewish existence in Krakow in the early twentieth century, including the Goldman family. The school is an example of evident educational success of Jews. Its pupils had all the qualifications to co-create the intellectual elite of Poland in the future, the teachers working there constituted the flower of the Polish intelligentsia. Unfortunately, they had to live in times of growing antisemitism, and their future was uncertain. Nationalists tirelessly tried to limit (by introducing *numerus clausus* laws, from Latin: closed number) or even eliminate (*numerus nullus*—Latin: no number) Jews from university benches. At that time, an economic propaganda campaign aimed at Jews took place, with the slogan: "Do not buy from a Jew!" There was also a political battle, increasingly accompanied by street clashes. Under those conditions, Jews at least partially assimilated to Polish culture had a better chance of functioning normally. Of course, assimilation did not mean full acceptance by Christians. It allowed, however, to temporarily move away from the direct line of antisemitic propaganda and physical assaults. Yet, it increased the feeling of separateness among Jews, which was further exploited by antisemitic propaganda that used the slogan of "Jewish separatism." Jews felt that they could only count on each other, which intensified their friendships and created an atmosphere of solidarity and shared responsibility. This is clearly seen in the example of the Hebrew Gymnasium: friendships made there lasted a lifetime. Already after World War II, school graduates organized conventions in Israel, where students and teachers of that legendary institution met. In 1989, in Tel Aviv, a book about the school entitled *To była hebrajska szkoła w Krakowie* (English: It was a Hebrew school in Krakow), edited by Natan Gross, was published.

Marcel, despite several unpleasant antisemitic accidents, remembers his childhood as a good time. Thanks to the resourcefulness and diligence of his parents, the family had decent living conditions. At that time, Krakow offered its youngest residents various opportunities for rest, recreation, and spending free time. Near the second shop run by the Goldmans at 22 Zwierzyniecka Street (closer to the Vistula), an ice rink was organised in the winter. "We didn't have skates at the time. They were prepared in such a way that with the right tools

Childhood (1926–1939) | 59

Fig. 13. Science lesson with Rachel Goldwasser on the terrace of the Hebrew Gymnasium, 1930s, collections of the Association of Cracowians in Israel

Fig. 14. Purim at the Hebrew Gymnasium in Krakow, with the Hebrew teacher Bentzion Katz, 1934, collections of the Association of Cracowians in Israel

and screws the skates were attached to sports shoes,"[50] recalls Marcel, who often went on the rink with a friend living nearby. Riding a tram was also a big attraction for our young protagonist, and since he started going to elementary school in Krakow's Kazimierz, he used this means of communication almost every day. At that time there was no direct line connecting his home with the school, so he changed to another tram next to the Main Post Office and got off at the corner of Miodowa Street. He also remembers his carriage trips to his grandmother's house on Sunday. Marcel quickly learned to read, and, on his way, he entertained himself by studying advertising signs. When visiting his grandmother, who lived at Rękawka Street, he often played with non-Jewish children. They organised trips to Krzemionki, from where a beautiful panorama of Krakow could be seen. So, while at school he was surrounded by Jewish children, he spent most of his free time among Poles. This had to affect his choice of language, accent, and attitude towards Poles. He says about himself:

> I became a staunch Polish patriot. I studied Polish literature passionately. First of all, I fell in love with the books of Henryk Sienkiewicz. I was very impressed with his *Teutonic Knights* and the *Trilogy*. In the *Trilogy* there is a touching text about the battle of Zhovti Vody fought by the Polish and Cossack troops [the first battle of the Khmelnytsky Uprising]. That fight was a defeat for the Polish forces. Ending the story about it, Sienkiewicz wrote the following sentence: "The Commonwealth lay in dust and blood at the Cossacks' feet." Reading this passage, I just cried...[51]

In his youth, Marcel's literary taste was influenced by his home and school environments. Teachers in Jewish schools greatly appreciated Polish writers. Jews eagerly read the novels of Henryk Sienkiewicz, which resonated with readers rooted in Polish culture as well as those who (often maintaining their love for Poland) tied their future with Eretz Yisrael. In this situation, it is not surprising that Sienkiewicz's works were translated into Hebrew, and then together with Polish Jews they went to Eretz Yisrael (of course Marcel read them in the Polish original). In the years 1919–1921, the Warsaw publishing house Sztybel issued a Hebrew version of *With Fire and Sword*. It was Sienkiewicz's first novel translated into Hebrew. Włodzimierz Żabotyński was not indifferent to that publishing initiative, as Ryszard Löw points out:

---

50   Interview with Marcel Goldman carried out on February 8, 2017.
51   Ibid.

He praised . . . Sztybel's publishing house for publishing the novel and called it for a quick edition of *The Deluge*, which is the continuation of this "great book": "It's a good choice, we need definitely more such works . . . that can influence the national spirit. For us, a reviving nation, literature calling for action is indispensable. For we need a generation of young people able to lay foundations and then build, young people ready for adventures and an invigorating movement, able to discern the right path in the most overgrown woods, able to gallop on a horse and climb a tree, swim in cold water, use the fist and the rifle; a generation of people with vivid imagination and strong will, striving to lead the fight for life."[52]

It should be noted that in Poland of the interwar period, the propagation of patriotism was firmly inscribed in the educational curriculum, and in this respect Jewish schools were in no way inferior to Polish ones. This is documented by a considerable number of historical sources, including the preserved "School Chronicle of Jewish Female Students from 1933–1939" of the Municipal General School No. 15 named after Klementyna Tańska-Hoffmanowa and located at Miodowa Street in Krakow. The Jewish girls from this school wrote with great respect about the heroes of Polish history and the leaders of the Polish state. They celebrated the name day of Polish President Ignacy Mościcki and Marshal Józef Piłsudski. For example, on February 1, 1934, it was noted: "We marked the name day of the President, Professor Ignacy Mościcki, with a solemn morning celebration. Little sisters performed beautiful declamations, songs, and dances. We wished the President health in many years and strength to work for the whole of Poland."[53] Jewish children celebrated the Constitution Day on May 3, as well as other important national holidays and the anniversaries of births and deaths of leading Polish literature writers and artists. In the already mentioned "School Chronicle" we can also find confirmation of multiple payments of money collected by Jewish girls for charitable purposes serving Poles and Jews, the Society for the Support of the Construction of Public General Schools, the National Defense Fund, the League of Air and Gas Defense, Jews displaced from Germany, and Poles abroad.[54]

---

52   Löw, *Literackie podsumowania*, 43.
53   *Kronika szkolna uczennic żydowskich z lat 1933–1939 Miejskiej Szkoły Powszechnej nr 15 im. Klementyny Tańskiej-Hoffmanowej przy ul. Miodowej w Krakowie*, intro A. B. Skotnicki, Krakow 2006, 37 (22 in the original document).
54   Ibid., passim.

In the Goldman family, the maternal grandmother occupied an important position. In comparison with her, the grandfather was a secondary character, as Marcel says, a non-person.[55]

Fig. 15. The twelve-year-old student Marcel Goldman with his mother Sara and five-year-old sister Nela during a walk in Planty, Krakow, 1938, family collections of Marcel and Bianka Goldman (Tel Aviv)

Fig. 16. Marcel Goldman with his father on vacation in Iwonicz-Zdrój, summer 1939, family collections of Marcel and Bianka Goldman (Tel Aviv)

While his grandmother was a hard-working person focusing the attention of the whole family, his grandfather preferred to step back and sleep well.[56] It was in his grandparents' apartment at 14 Rękawka Street that Marcel was born under the care of a midwife. There is a family story associated with renting this property in Podgórze. His grandparents, when they were still living in Zbydniowice, were not doing well. Sara's mother, however, was attached to the farm, she could not imagine living without her own cow, she served only homemade butter and cheese at home. She prepared them in sterile conditions, as she trusted such

---

55   Interview with Marcel Goldman carried out on December 22, 2016.
56   Ibid.

Fig. 17. Marcel Goldman's maternal grandparents: Chana and Jakub, interwar period, family collections of Marcel and Bianka Goldman (Tel Aviv)

food only. Sara, following the spirit of the times, bought dairy products from the so-called *baba*, that is, a woman from the village, who delivered agricultural produce and self-made food to the recipients in the city on agreed days.[57]

After the wedding of Sara and Maks, her parents should have paid the previously promised dowry. Satisfying their own financial needs with difficulty, they could not afford such an expense. However, Maks insisted and with time suggested that his in-laws sell the farm. According to Marcel's testimony, he also took into account the improvement of the in-laws' conditions. The biggest trouble was the cow, which Marcel's grandmother necessarily wanted to take with her to the city. Maks solved the problem by finding the abovementioned apartment at Rękawka Street, located near Krzemionki Podgórskie hill. At that time, several farms operated in that area. The prewar Krakow was not yet a fully urbanized city and farm animals were part of the landscape of some of its districts. The family agreed with the owners of one of the farms, who, for an appropriate fee, were to keep Marcel's grandparents' cow in their cowshed. His grandmother often sent his grandfather to milk the cow, which says a lot

---

57 Ibid.

about his position in the family: after all, milking was a typical occupation for teenagers, girls and boys (less often for farm workers, as it would be too easy for them). Earlier, when they were still living in Zbydniowice, the grandfather also used to herd the cow. He did not refuse to do it, because it gave him the opportunity to doze in the meadows. It happened, however, that the unattended cow did damage by entering into neighbouring grain crops and the grandmother later had to pay the related charges.[58] For Chana, her own cow was so important because, as Marcel claims, "she did not use milk unless it flowed directly from the udder into her scrubbed vessel."[59]

The property swap turned out to be beneficial for the in-laws. Sara's three brothers of also benefited. Maks helped each of them set up their own haberdashery shops. Two shops in Podgórze, located at Salinarna Street, belonged to the youngest of them, Janek, and to the grandparents (Janek was actually looking after them). The middle brother, Moniek, opened a shop at Długa Street. The eldest, Izaak, became the owner of the shop at Starowiślna Street. Maks invested in the aforementioned shop at Słowiański Square.[60] Sara liked to spend Sunday afternoons in her parents' apartment at Rękawka Street. Hanging out there and talking to her mother were, for a long time, her favorite forms of relaxing after the week's work.

> My father rebelled a bit against this because he had higher aspirations. He loved the operetta, especially songs performed in German. He often took me to the operetta. Other times to the cinema. It was not uncommon for us to go together, just the two of us. Without my mother who spent her free time with her mother. Such trips were also a great opportunity to get to know those areas of Krakow that I didn't go to on a daily basis.[61]

Marcel remembers that his grandmother loved him and spoiled him. He was her first and favorite grandson, he received two zlotys a week from her, at that time relatively a lot, especially for a child. He spent it on sweets; often, returning from school, he would buy portions of halva, 200 grams each. Because of that, he was often unable to eat dinner at home, and even went to the doc-

---

58 Interview with Marcel Goldman carried out on December 22, 2016.
59 Interview with Marcel Goldman carried out on February 8, 2019.
60 Interview with Marcel Goldman carried out on December 27, 2016.
61 Interview with Marcel Goldman carried out on February 8, 2017.

tor once because his mother was worried about his lack of appetite. The matter cleared up quickly...[62]

The shop at Słowiański Square brought the Goldmans enough income to think about another child, better apartment, and moving the shop to a more attractive place. In 1933, Maks's aspirations to open a haberdashery shop in a better district came true; they rented a place at 22 Zwierzyniecka Street. At the same time, they moved to a more comfortable and larger apartment (with their own bathroom) on the second floor of the house at 5 Tatarska Street. The first floor was inhabited by the owner, Mr. Grünberg, who also owned two other houses and a woodwork factory located at the back of the lot at Tatarska Street.[63] In the new place, Marcel quickly found companions to play with, among others, from the caretaker's and building administrator's family. In late afternoons, when the factory was closed, they sneaked there and played on the trolleys used to transport goods or jumping on sawdust.[64]

Just before the family moved to Zwierzyniec (a district of Krakow), Marcel's sister Nela was born. It can be assumed that the change of flat was related to expanding the family. The improvement in the material status of the Goldmans is also evidenced by the fact that Nela was not born at home, like Marcel, but in a private Polish clinic at Garncarska Street. In the new apartment, they could afford to employ, in addition to the maid, a babysitter to help with the children, first German (which was typical of well-off houses), and then Polish (Catholic).[65] The same year when the Goldman family grew bigger, Adolf Hitler came to power in Germany, Nela was six when the war broke out, and she had not started school education yet.

Before that happened, however, the Goldmans' life was as successful as before. In Zwierzyniec, they also lived in rather Polish surroundings, even though another Jewish family, the Silbergs, lived nearby. Marcel remembers their daughter Halinka as a beautiful girl and his first love. At the parents' request, for safety, they commuted to the Hebrew Gymnasium together.[66] Polish neighbours were usually not hostile, and although Marcel sometimes heard critical remarks about Jews, they were more general in nature and he did not take them

---

62　Interview with Marcel Goldman carried out on December 22, 2016.
63　Interview with Marcel Goldman carried out on May 20, 2017.
64　Ibid.
65　Ibid; Pordes, Grin, *Wywiad*, 149.
66　Pordes, Grin, *Wywiad*, 149.

personally. He admits: "I basically did not come across active antisemitism before 1939."[67]

The Goldmans' experience is not representative of the majority of Krakow Jews. In particular, it is different from the fate of their fellow believers living in the Jewish quarter of Kazimierz. The reactions of Marcel, who used to go there with his parents for commercial purposes, are meaningful, as he treated "Jews dressed in black coats" as people from a different world.[68] However, that world was not completely unknown to him, as he was accustomed to Jewish religious practices thanks to men from the family: "Very clearly, I have in front of my eyes the silhouette of my father wrapped in a *tallis*, next to him the figures of my uncles, my mother's brothers, and of course my grandfather, my mother's father, the last Mohican in the family, with a gray patriarchal beard."[69]

Meanwhile, political tension was increasing in Europe. Thanks to the daily reading of the German press, Marcel's father had an excellent account of what was happening in Germany after Hitler came to power. He knew very well about Hitler's threats against Jews and took them seriously. He had no doubt that the fate of Jews would be tragic if Hitler's army entered Poland, although he could not have predicted how much. In fact, as early as in 1938 it was widely predicted that a war would break out. During that period Maks became closer to Zionist activists in terms of political views, but did not declare accession to a specific organization. However, he talked with his wife about a possible departure to Eretz Yisrael or the United States, which she strongly opposed, not wanting to leave her mother to whom she was very attached. Marcel thinks that his family left the ghetto only because his grandmother was already displaced at that time (most likely she was already dead). Otherwise, they would probably stay there until the very end . . .

Marcel's father did not really insist on leaving Poland. One could risk saying that both he and his wife underestimated the scale of the threat, and, like millions of other Polish and European Jews in general, they were lulled into a false sense of security. Why? It is hard to get a definite answer because we are forced to move in the sphere of (at least partly) guesses. First of all, further questions should be asked. Was the vigilance of Jews really dormant or did they find themselves trapped with no (good) way out? What could Jews who were not

---

67 Ibid., 153.
68 Interview with Marcel Goldman carried out on August 2, 2017.
69 Goldman, *A w nocy przychodzą myśli*, 20.

politically empowered do? In many European countries they were an influential but nonetheless minority. Let's look specifically at Polish Jews. Feeling threat, they could run away. But where to? Western countries began to close their doors to Jews more and more firmly, moreover, some of those countries could not become a place of potential refuge because they were ruled by nationalists or even fascists. This greatly restricted Jews' options. It is hard to deny that many disregarded the Zionists calling for a departure to Eretz Yisrael at that time. The problem, however, is that even if they decided to leave, it was not certain that they could succeed. In the interwar period, Great Britain exercised power over that territory in the form of a Mandate, and its government, trying to unite the Arabs, severely limited the migration of Jews there. A large part of them, wishing to get there legally, received refusals. Not everyone could afford illegal migration. This remark applies to both financial and mental reasons. Reluctance to break the rules and expose oneself to detention or expulsion could have influenced the decision of some Jews to stay in Poland. The Goldmans were in a completely different situation. They could emigrate to Eretz Yisrael because, despite the impediments imposed by the British, people who could afford to deposit several thousand pounds had a chance to go there. They also had the so-called affidavit, that is, the permission to enter the United States. They did not use any of these possibilities. According to Marcel Goldman, it was because of, as mentioned above, "my mother's strong bond with her mother, which is an absolute, unbreakable psychological addiction."[70]

Let us also note that Europeans still remembered World War I very well. Although sometimes that war's events had a dramatic course, they were accompanied by specific rules protecting the lives of civilians. Even if these rules were violated, the scale of such offenses did not resemble anything that happened after 1939. Antisemitic riots and pogroms took place mainly in the last days of World War I or even after it. They were caused not by specific governments, but by anarchised, emaciated crowds and groups of demobilized soldiers who were demoralized by the war and the antisemitic propaganda. In this regard, some Jews remembered not without regret strong countries (such as Prussia and Austria-Hungary) in which they were guaranteed physical security. Many Jews fought in the armies of the Central Powers. At the time, only under the command of the Habsburgs, there were between 275 and 400 thousand Jewish soldiers.[71] There

---

70   Interview with Marcel Goldman carried out on May 20, 2017.
71   E. A. Schmidl, *Habsburgs jüdische Soldaten 1788–1918*, Wien–Köln–Weimar 2014, 115.

were cases when Jews recognized former companions from the trenches of the Great War among the Nazi soldiers, but it did not help them . . . Before World War II broke out, it was quite widely believed that Germany, as a "cultured nation," would not behave in a way that would bring it a disgrace. There was also a widespread belief in the value of security guarantees that Poland received from France and Great Britain.

Today, we do not know what motivated the behaviour of Maksymilian Goldman, but there are clear indications that, given the outbreak of war, he absolutely did not know how to prepare for it. There were also sober-minded Jews, such as Goldman's wife. This can be seen in one of family stories from December 1938. Marcel's mother was celebrating her birthday then. Maks knew that his wife valued particularly financial gifts, because she came from a poor family and had a clear need to feel stable and secure the material existence of the family. Therefore, he acquired the so-called dollar bonds, that is, securities that are a form of state internal loans. They were issued in zlotys, combined with the dollar exchange rate and subject to favourable interest rates. The purpose of that action was to collect a considerable amount of money that the Polish government wanted to spend on buying weapons for the army. On her birthday, Maks proudly handed the gift to his wife, but it did not end nicely for him, he did not meet with appreciation, but with harsh criticism.

> An incredible quarrel broke out at home, because my mother was not gentle in this respect, so that my father's feelings would not be offended, but she simply told him: you are an idiot, the war is on your doorstep, and when it breaks out these papers will lose their value. I remember this row to this day. My mother was undoubtedly right, but she expressed it without any gentleness. My father finally gave in and asked her what to do in that situation. My mother told him: resell these papers immediately, even at a loss. Buy gold coins for this money. Later, my mother sewed those gold coins into the corset, which was then a popular part of women's clothing. During the war, if necessary, she took out the coins and sold them. They undoubtedly helped us survive that difficult time.[72]

A similar situation took place in the family of Bianka Ebersohn, Marcel Goldman's future wife. Just before the war, her father bought his wife a half of a beautiful house in Bielsko. He did not foresee that they would have to leave the house very soon. They never returned there; after the war they did not even

---

72 Interview with Marcel Goldman carried out on February 8, 2017.

try to enter it, because it was already occupied by new residents and an attempt to regain it could end badly for them. Bianka came back there only for a moment during one of her visits to Poland in the 1990s. The residents of the tenement were scared by that visit, as they were afraid that it meant the beginning of property claims. Bianka never decided to pursue them. Henryk Grynberg's words perfectly describe people like the Goldmans and the Ebersohns: "They left more here than they had."[73] In this way Grynberg commented on the fate of the March '68 emigrants who left Poland with a one-way travel document. It should be emphasized that the Goldmans and the Ebersohns, just like the March emigrants, left not only their larger or smaller property in Poland, but also, or perhaps above all, hearts, years of youth, first loves, fascinations, friends, and colleagues.

The studies carried out on Marcel Goldman's childhood years allow me to state that they had a constitutive significance for his cultural identity. He writes about himself in the following way:

> I admit that Polish, despite being fluent in Hebrew, good at English and quite good at German, is my cultural language. I will not write a poem in a language other than Polish, even though I tried doing it in Hebrew with various results. I can quote Mickiewicz's poems, but not Bialik's. I can quote prose from the Trilogy by Sienkiewicz, I love Skrzetuski, I am entertained by Zagłoba, not to mention Podbipięta from Psie- or Mysiekiszki. Very early in my childhood I started reading books. I swallowed whatever I could, without selection. I was a great Polish patriot until the Germans came and did everything to convince me, not always gently, that I was only a Jew.[74]

Let's look at these words carefully, as we find in them notes common to many other Polish Jews living in Israel after World War II. Marcel Goldman was brought up in a family of Jews assimilated to Polish culture. For them, the language of everyday life was Polish. In this language they said their first words and wrote down their earliest experiences, formulated thoughts and expressed emotions. To understand how important this is, one must reach for the famous

---

73 These words were placed on the memorial plaque embedded in the building of the Gdańska Railway Station at 4 Słomińskiego Street in Warsaw. It was made in 1998 thanks to the efforts of the Shalom Foundation, http://www.sztetl.org.pl/pl/article/warszawa/39,zabytki-kultury-materialnej/3528,tablica-pamiatkowa-na-dworcu-gdanskim-ul-slominskiego-4-/, accessed May 10, 2017.

74 Goldman, *A w nocy przychodzą myśli*, 5.

maxim of Ludwig Wittgenstein: "The limits of my language mean the limits of my world." Each language has a unique sound, dynamics, grammar, style, and emotions, and cultural contexts hidden in it. The list of books we read, the circle of our friends and acquaintances depend on the language we use. It all has formative properties and impresses on us a mark that nothing can blur. Trying to explain the phenomenon and meaning of the term "Polish Jews," we must refer to borders and to language. It is therefore about the Jews who were born in the lands of the former Polish Republic before World War II, or within the contemporary borders of Poland, if they were born after 1945. These people are strongly connected primarily to Polish culture. Even if they come from the territory of today's Lithuania, Belarus, or Ukraine, we can speak of them as Polish Jews, because their cultural identification is with the Jewish or Polish heritage, and only sporadically with Lithuanian, Belarusian, or Ukrainian and with culture produced in these languages.

Another important observation regarding Marcel Goldman's childhood is related to his bourgeois upbringing, similar to thousands of other young Jews who lived in Krakow, Lviv, Łódź, Warsaw or Vilnius. Marcel's mother showed admirable resourcefulness in business activities and in this respect she remained highly independent of her husband as for the prewar conditions. Basically, however, they formed a typical patriarchal family in which, as Marcel Goldman recalls, "my father was the highest instance."[75] In the event of any misbehaviour, the children heard that "my father will get to know about everything and that he will draw consequences for them."[76] There was a rule: "children are to be seen but not heard." Marcel was convinced that his father's attention should not be taken by unimportant matters, his father was a mentor, but not a partner.

Bianka was brought up in similar cultural conditions. She was born in a wealthy intellectual family of Ludwik Ebersohn and Pola née Rechtman. Ludwik Ebersohn was born and spent the first years of his life in Jarosław. His father Samuel was a merchant. Family ambitions decided that Ludwik settled in Krakow and graduated from one of the renowned secondary schools. On October 6, 1910, he passed his final exams. Perhaps, wanting to be closer to his family, he moved to Lviv to study at the local University in the 1910/11 academic year[77]. After two years, he interrupted his studies in Lviv to study law at

---

75 Interview with Marcel Goldman carried out on December 27, 2016.
76 Ibid.
77 The University of Lviv in the interwar years took the name Jan Kazimierz University and grew into a leading Polish institution of higher education. Today it is the Ivan Franko Na-

Fig. 18. Ludwik and Pola Ebersohn with their daughters
(Bianka, Marcel's future wife, is up in the middle), Bielsko, 1935,
family collections of Marcel and Bianka Goldman (Tel Aviv)

the Jagiellonian University from the 1913/14 academic year. Due to the outbreak of World War I, he was mobilised to the Austrian army. Because both the army command and the university authorities were generally favourable to students appointed to the army, Ludwik did not have to interrupt his education. He continued it in absentia. On September 30, 1918 he completed his studies, and on December 20, 1919 he became a doctor of legal sciences.[78] Bianka's mother was brought up in Krakow in a very religious family. The rhythm of her parents' life was determined by the rules of Judaism, which her father, Bianka's grandfather, was especially eager to follow. He also wore a beard and sideboards, and a traditional coat. At the same time, he had a liberal approach to life, thanks to which his daughters could freely develop their passions and talents. They both showed musical interests. Bianka's mother's sister played the piano, she married a violinist, and they both played for the Polish Radio. Bianka's mother learned to sing. According to Bianka, her grandmother was more conservative than her grandfather. It happened that "the grandfather hid

---

tional University of Lviv, one of the main Ukrainian universities.

78 *Corpus studiosorum Universitatis Iagellonicae in saeculis*, vol. 3: *1850/51–1917/18, E–D*, ed. K. Stopka; *From the Works of the Archives of the Jagiellonian University*, ed. K. Stopka, M. Barcik, A. Cieślak, D. Grodowska-Kulińska, U. Perkowska, Krakow 2006, 10.

his daughter's score under the coat and took it with him so that she could go and take singing lessons."[79] During World War I, Bianka's mother worked as a nurse in a hospital in Vienna. After the war, she found employment as a clerk in one of Krakow's banks.

Fig. 19. Pola Ebersohn, née Rechtman, Bianka Goldman's mother, 1920s, family collections of Marcel and Bianka Goldman (Tel Aviv)

Fig. 20. Bianka Goldman's aunt (with unidentified persons), early thentieth century, family collections of Marcel and Bianka Goldman (Tel Aviv)

Pola and Ludwik got married in 1925, but they did not continue their lives in Krakow. Ludwik did not have a lawyer practice there, because in the interwar period the legal market in the largest Polish cities was already saturated. Anyway, it is worth adding that other Jewish lawyers already worked in this market, and even dominated it over time, so that they were competing mainly with each other. Hence, many graduates of subsequent years of law studies at universities in Krakow, Lviv, or

---

79 Interview with Bianka Goldman carried out on December 20, 2016.

Fig. 21. The Town Hall in Biała, 1937, public domain

Warsaw sought opportunities in the provinces, usually near their hometowns or academic centers where they graduated. The Ebersohns decided to live in Bielsko, and Ludwik opened his own law office in nearby Biała (in 1951 Bielsko and Biała merged, and the city of Bielsko-Biała was created). The choice proved to be right. Bianka's father found excellent conditions for professional development in Bielsko and Biała. The cities, located on the border between the Polish provinces of Silesia and Lesser Poland, and the border Poland and Czechia, next to Roman Catholics, were also inhabited by large Protestant and Jewish communities. Bielsko and Biała experienced economic prosperity at the time. At the end of the nineteenth and the beginning of the twentieth centuries, the Bielsko-Biała region was one of the largest industrial centers of Austria-Hungary. Many industrial plants were established there, new tenements, villas, and public buildings were erected.

The Ebersohns belonged to the elite in every respect. They nurtured bourgeois traditions. At home, they spoke only Polish, although they both knew German very well. They used elegant vocabulary. They brought up their children in a friendly atmosphere, but required obedience and good manners. They had a richly stocked library and read works of Polish and world literature. They collected beautiful furniture, porcelain service, and exquisitely made cutlery. They wore elegant clothes. Bianka was born in Bielsko (most likely at home at Piastowska Street). Over time, Ludwik bought a half of the tenement house at 15 Miarki Street. The Ebersohn family lived there in a beautiful five-room apartment furnished by an interior architect (after World War II it was divided into apartments for three families). After leaving Krakow, Pola did not work professionally. She devoted herself to raising children and running a house. After

Fig. 22. Bielsko, the synagogue at the former Franciszka Józefa Street (today 3 Maja Street), around 1914, public domain

Bianka's birth, a German nurse was hired to look after her. That is why Bianka, like her parents, learned to speak German quite well. In 1936, she began studying at an elite private Jewish school. The institution was secular, the language of instruction was Polish, but additional subjects such as the Jewish religion and Hebrew were added to the curriculum. By the outbreak of war, Bianka had completed three grades.

Fig. 23. Bielsko, Sułkowskiego Avenue (today Bohaterów Warszawy Street), 1930s, public domain

Both Marcel and Bianka transferred the models of upbringing and family patterns received in Poland to Israel. We will talk about this later... Before they entered their adolescence and left for Israel, they had to survive World War II. This is important because it had an undoubted impact on both the process of their maturation (the war accelerated it and gave it a specific touch), as well as on their decision to emigrate. 1939 brought the end to the world described in this chapter.

2

The Hell of Extermination— Youth, Part One (1939–1945)

The outbreak of World War II was not an unexpected disaster, but everyone was surprised by the scale of this genocide. Well, maybe not everyone… Now, eighty years after its beginning, we appreciate the texts of intellectuals living before the war: writers, social activists, politicians, who warned that the apocalypse was approaching, that a certain era was coming to an end, the order familiar to people was coming to an end. Today, this kind of warning can be found in the essays by Heshel Klepfish, philosophy doctor and rabbi in the Polish Army, who in 1932 wrote:

> There is a dreary mood in Europe today. Almost everyone feels that the twilight of Europe is coming, that our civilisation and culture are shaking, collapsing and falling. The feeling of fall can be read from every poem, and even more so when you look between the lines. Scientific work, novel, press—everything is saturated with this mood.[1]

He also recalled the alarmist thoughts of the great personalities of that time:

> The famous Jewish-Austrian writer Stefan Zweig has recently published an article in a French literary journal *Les Nouvelles Litteraires*, in which he shares pessimistic thoughts about the state of our civilization. We are facing the fall, the outstanding writer says bluntly. . . . On the literary market in Europe, the book of the well-known Viennese journalist Ludwig Bauer *Morgen wieder Krieg* [Tomorrow's war again] has gained great publicity. This is a somewhat prophetic work. The author reaches bold conclusions, he clearly shows in black and white that the danger of war comes from the development of Europe. Increasing confusion in the world leads to war.[2]

---

1 H. Klepfish, *Przedwojenny świat przez pryzmat młodego Żyda polskiego. Eseje 1931–1937*, Tel Aviv 1999, 13.
2 Ibid., 13–14.

In 1932, the then-twenty-five-year-old Ksawery Pruszyński (1907–1950) debuted with *Sarajevo 1914, Shanghai 1932, Gdańsk?*[3] The author predicted that another world conflict could begin in Gdańsk. As a side note, let me point out that Pruszyński had a deep friendship with Moses Pomeranz, a Zionist activist who emigrated to Eretz Yisrael. In the interwar period, Pruszyński visited Eretz Yisrael, which is documented in a series of reports published in the pages of *Słowo* (English: Word), a periodical published in Vilnius.[4] After World War II, he had a great impact on the emergence of independent Israel, devotedly working as chairman of the UN Subcommittee for the Partition of Palestine.

Like others, Ze'ev Jabotinsky warned Jews long before World War II that they should emigrate from Europe because they would face terrible danger there. Due to his Zionist charisma, he enjoyed great popularity among modernist Jews. Through his fiery speeches he was able to interest crowds. He often visited Krakow. This is how Rafael F. Scharf remembered him:

> Jabotinsky visited Krakow from time to time in and gave four-hour speeches in the Old Theater Hall. As an orator, he was second to none, he was inspired and at the same time calculating, a visionary and a demagogue modelled on authentic tribunes of the people. He was leaving Krakow for a detour of other cities, in this way Zionist agitation took place—the speakers visited their organisations in towns, spoke at rallies (I was at one of them myself). But Jabotinsky's visit was an event that was talked about long before and long after. It often happened that when he boarded the cab at the train station, his supporters unhooked the horse and pulled the vehicle to the hotel themselves, to the delight of the crowds. Jabotinsky was surrounded by a cult that no other Jewish speaker could experience.[5]

Jabotinsky was the leader of the Zionist revisionist faction. Many Jews read his warnings as part of the propaganda typical of that trend. The moment when Jabotinsky, frightened by the spectre of the impending cataclysm, called European Jews to emigrate, best to Eretz Yisrael, but if they could not, wherever they could to save their lives, was missed.

Many were deceived, as already noted, by the still vivid memory of the course of World War I, and they hoped that the next world conflict would take

---

3   K. Pruszyński, *Sarajewo 1914, Szanghaj 1932, Gdańsk?*, Warsaw 1932.
4   See K. Pruszyński, *Palestyna po raz trzeci*, Warsaw 1996.
5   R. F. Scharf, *Co mnie i tobie Polsko . . . Eseje bez uprzedzeń*, 2nd ed., Krakow 1999, 224.

Fig. 24. Ze'ev Jabotinsky speaking at the Seventeenth Zionist Congress in Basel in 1931, photo: Ze'ev (Wilhelm) Aleksandrowicz, public domain.

a similar form. During World War I, despite the determination of all warring parties, attempts were made to follow certain rules, such as the civilized treatment of prisoners of war or the burial of the dead. Indeed, the first signs that the latest scientific and technical achievements, such as airplanes and chemical weapons, would be used to eliminate opponents were already there. However, at the time, especially at the beginning of the war, aircraft were mainly used to recognize and detect enemy artillery. It was not until later that the idea arose to use them for carpet raids, during which cities and villages were bombed. Experiments with chemical weapons were also carried out at that time, but they were not always successful. For example, of a cloud of gas was unleashed, sudden changes in the direction of the wind could turn it back, which caused the greatest losses to those who decided to use it. The technique of using gas was improved later, but it was still only used on the battlefields. The possibility of using gas for mass killing of innocent people crammed into specially created chambers went beyond human understanding. The presence of soldiers in urban space was not associated with a lethal threat, but rather with the nuisance and spread of pathologies typical of the time of war (prostitution and sale of alcohol flourished around military garrisons, and numerous fights took place). Soldiers were also responsible for robberies, but that concerned mainly the final stage of the war due to demoralization in the ranks of the army and widespread hunger, because the military supply was often bad. It is true that, with the end of World War I, a series of pogroms against Jews took place in various places in Europe. However, they always happened in specific, complex circumstances, and their causes, in addition to antisemitism, should be seen, among others, in emotions accompanying the creation of nation states and provocations of the failing powers. They brought thousands of deaths, and even more Jews were wounded and robbed. However, each of these pogroms had its own local context. They had the same antisemitic motivation, but on a European scale no one coordinated them. In addition, they occurred in specific places, so in case of a pogrom in one town it was possible to save oneself by escaping to another, even if located nearby.

The scale of aggression directed against Jews, unheard of in earlier history of the world, must have surprised them. Entire mechanisms at the disposal of the civil administration and the war machine were launched against them. The Nazis started to exterminate Jews in all the territories they occupied. In implementing that murderous plan, three attitudes among the non-Jewish population favoured them: fear that paralyzed decent people, indifference of broad social groups to the fate of the Jews, and antisemitism, which pushed many to denounce Jews, blackmail them, or even participate actively in acts of aggression directed against the Jewish population, such as pogroms or spontaneous murders). The Nazi idea, especially after the Wannsee conference (January 20, 1942), was obvious: they planned to bring about the total annihilation of the Jewish nation.

In Germany and in the countries occupied by the Third Reich, Jews could not feel safe anywhere, but not everyone could escape to the territory of the Soviet Union, where they also experienced persecution. Besides, while in the Nazi-occupied lands Jews began to die en masse only because they were Jews, in the Soviet Union they were in mortal danger as potential class enemies—buyers, lawyers, doctors, and so forth. The Soviet government sent them into exile, where they were threatened with death from hunger and overwork. Therefore, there are known cases of the return of Jews, who had previously fled to the Soviet zone, to the lands subordinate to Germany. Realizing what was happening around on the Soviet side, they chose, in their opinion, the lesser evil. Certainly, the desire to connect with the loved ones left there was not without significance. Ryszard Friedman (a Jew from Krakow) described such a situation in his memories. After World War II he served in the ranks of the American army. He came from a highly assimilated family, who only celebrated the most important Jewish holidays at home. After the attack of the Third Reich on Poland, he escaped with his mother and brother Zygmunt to the East. They reached Lviv. At that time, his father fought in the ranks of the Polish army, but his unit was quickly broken up, yet he managed to return home to Krakow. It was turbulent in Lviv, as Friedman recalls:

> Soon, peculiar arrests carried out on the streets by the NKVD began—the suspects were identified by their clothes and whether their hands were smooth or rough. The officers ordered people to show their hands

and if there were no visible bulges on their inner side, they took such a man for questioning.⁶

We talked with Zygmunt a lot about the Soviet oppression. "Maybe we'll get back to the other side, to the German occupation zone?," he wondered. After a short discussion, we decided that although Germans are our enemies, perhaps thanks to their education and culture they will be a bit milder and less dangerous.⁷

Ultimately, Ryszard and his mother crossed the border, Zygmunt decided to stay.⁸

The choice between the German and Soviet occupation zones or between life in the ghetto and escape from it was deeply tragic (in the original sense of the word, defining a situation from which there is no good way out, it can only be bad or worse). It also happened that Jews fled from the relatively small ghettoes in Lviv or Krakow to the great ghetto in Warsaw, hoping that in Warsaw their chances of survival would increase. And it turned out quite quickly that the fate of the inhabitants of the Warsaw Ghetto was just as dramatic as those who were imprisoned in the Lviv, Krakow, Łódź, Białystok, or any other ghetto. Moreover, many Jews died during the escape without reaching their destination.

There was also a possibility of escaping from the ghetto and living on the "Aryan side," as the Goldmans did. Such a decision was also connected with constant threats. Seeing that Germans were heading for the total extermination of Jews, Marcel's father began preparations to escape from the ghetto. In his opinion, it was the best solution, despite being connected with high risk. Marcel's mother's brothers assessed his behavior as too risky and irresponsible.⁹ Let's not forget that it was punishable by death. To start thinking about it at all, "right" contacts and a large supply of cash or valuables were needed. In addition, those who did not have a Semitic appearance had the best chance of survival "behind the walls." The Goldmans were lucky to meet both conditions. Marcel in his autobiography recalls those dramatic preparations in the following way: "By a friend, a Christian, we got records as Roman Catholics and on this basis also gray *Kennkarten* (the Jewish were yellow),¹⁰ which my mother hid at the

---

6   R. Friedman, *Jeden spośród wielu*, trans. J. Hunia, Krakow 2017, 35.
7   Ibid., 37.
8   Ibid., 38.
9   Correspondence with Marcel Goldman, November 18, 2018.
10 *Kennkarten* were identity documents obligatorily issued by the German occupation authorities.

Chapter 2. The Hell of Extermination

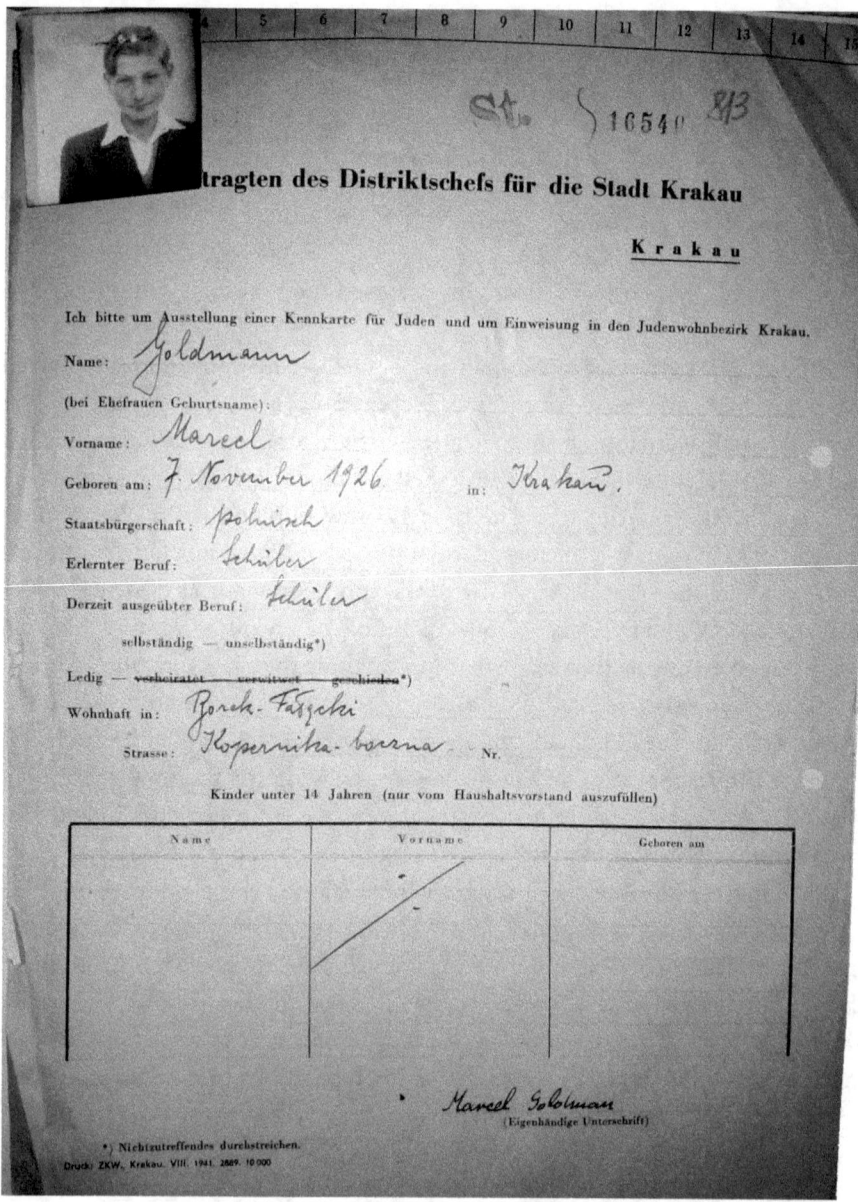

Fig. 25.
Maks Goldman's application for *Kennkarte*, NAK, department of applications of Jews from areas connected to Krakow, Files of the city of Krakow, reference number 29/33/SMKr 582 (folder "c");

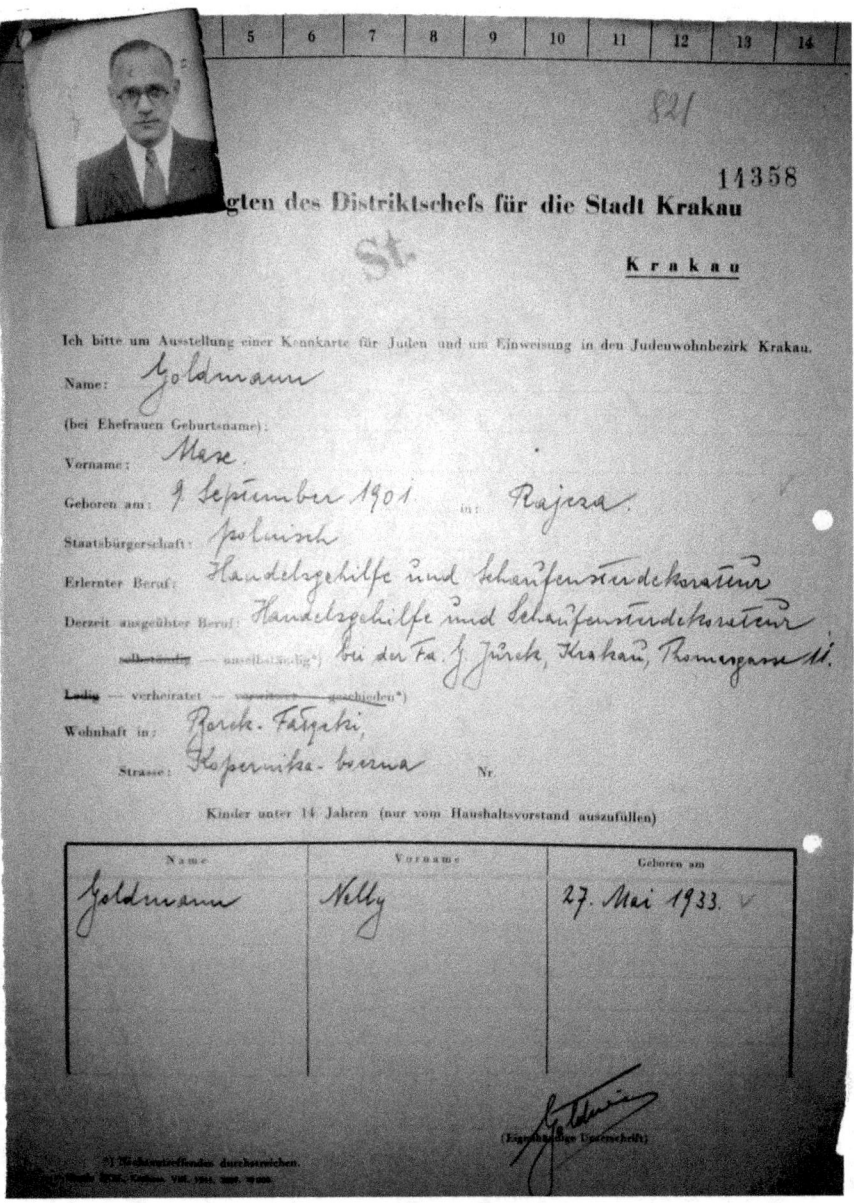

Fig. 26.
Marcel Goldman's application for *Kennkarte*, NAK, department of applications of Jews from areas connected to Krakow, Files of the city of Krakow, reference number 29/33/SMKr 582 (folder "c")

bottom of the trunk under underwear. 'We will use them as a last resort,' decided my father."[11] Their appearance also did not reveal their origin; moreover, Marcel's mother came from the village and exhibited certain types of behaviour and language specific to peasants, which was extremely rare among Polish Jews, so it additionally "masked" the Jewishness of her family.

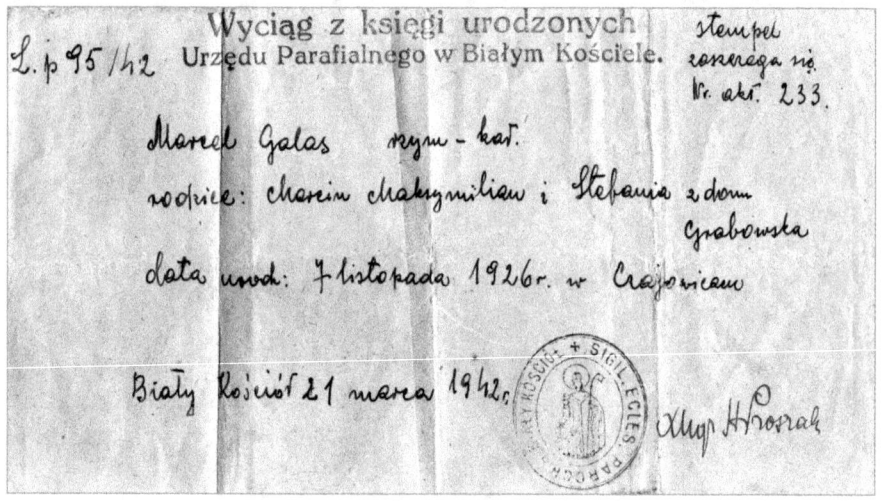

Fig. 27. Roman Catholic birth certificate
issued for Marcel Goldman with the name "Galas,"
family collections of Marcel and Bianka Goldman (Tel Aviv)

Undeniably, the documents they obtained—the Catholic birth certificate and the Aryan *Kennkarte*—saved the lives of the Goldmans. Marcel believes that the moment they received the documents with the name Galas became for them "the moment of being born again."[12] They got used to the new identity so much that, as Marcel emphasises, "from the moment we started using these documents, if someone on the street called 'Mr. Goldman,' I would not even look back."[13] The Goldmans decided to flee to the "Aryan side" in late autumn 1942, mobilized by two bloody expulsions from the Krakow Ghetto.[14] Before it happened, they experienced several odd and dramatic events.

---

11   Goldman, *Iskierki życia*, 3rd ed., 21.
12   Interview with Marcel Goldman carried out on December 18, 2016.
13   Ibid.
14   Goldman, *Iskierki życia*, 21.

The war broke out when a lot of people were returning from vacation. At bus and train stations, crowds of people hastily returning home and those who fled mixed up. Panic and confusion accompanied them. Many began to flee eastwards, but on September 17, 1939, Soviet troops entered from that direction. Poles, like Jews, consciously fled to the Soviet occupation zone at first, but having learned the realities there, they returned. The beginning of the war also meant the mobilization of men. Marcel's father discussed that topic with Mr. Frischer, a neighbour and at the same time a relative of the owner of the tenement house where the Goldmans lived. They did not believe the rumour that Jews were excluded from mobilization. They went to the assembly point at Zwierzyniecka Street, near their place of residence.

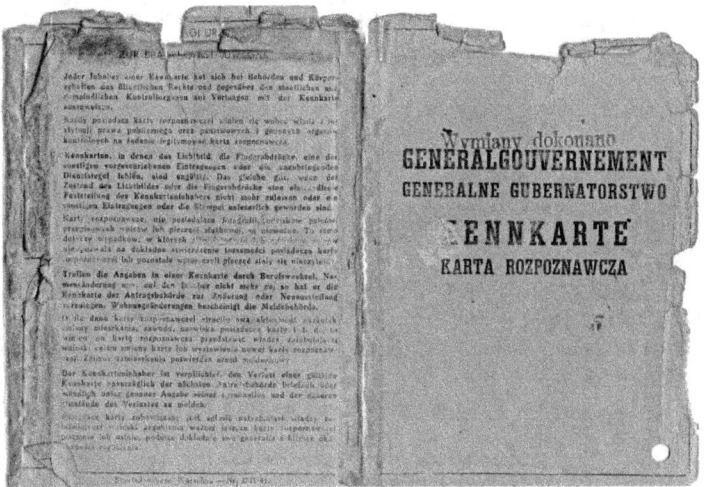

Fig. 28. The cover of the Aryan *Kennkarte* issued for Marcel Goldman (now Galas), family collections of Marcel and Bianka Goldman (Tel Aviv)

They stood in line with other reservists confident that they would be allocated when suddenly the officer conducting the appeal issued the command: "Jews, come out! As an uncertain element in the Polish Army, you can go home!" It's hard to believe, but in the first days of the war with Hitler, the most persecuted nation turned out to be an uncertain element.[15]

---

15 Ibid., 8. The Polish Army did not lack antisemitic incidents, but it does not convey the whole truth about it. Jews served in the Polish army and constituted valuable support for it, as many of them had professions useful in the armed forces, such as technicians and doctors.

Fig. 29. The Aryan *Kennkarte* issued for Marcel Goldman (now Galas), family collections of Marcel and Bianka Goldman (Tel Aviv)

Mr. Frischer convinced Maksymilian that such behaviour of the officer would not be repeated elsewhere, and they decided to reach the army themselves. Just outside Krakow, they could observe the Polish units withdrawing inertly.

> My father reached Nisk. There, the Germans caught up with him. Further attempts to reach the Polish army no longer made sense or had any chance of success. My father, after many adventures and a temporary stay in Lviv, occupied by the Russians, returned to Krakow, thus ending his private September campaign.[16]

German troops occupied Krakow in the morning of September 6, 1939. They entered the city from the south through the Piłsudski Bridge (they were

---

Military careers of Jews were often related with their assimilation. An example of this is Bernard Mond (1887–1957), who was born into a Jewish family. He reached the rank of general and commanded the Sixth Infantry Division in Krakow. In fact, it is difficult to consider him a representative of the Jewish population. Despite this, Polish Jews expressed pride in the fact that a man coming from their community had come so far within the structures of the army. Shortly before the outbreak of World War II, about one million citizens were mobilized, including about 150,000. Jews. During the war, Jews serving in the Polish Army were distinguished by their ferocity and discipline, which is confirmed by not only Jewish but also Christian testimonies. See T. Gąsowski, *Pod sztandarami Orła Białego. Kwestia żydowska w Polskich Siłach Zbrojnych w czasie II wojny światowej*, Krakow 2002; Shmuel Krakovsky, "Yehudim be-tzava ha-polani be-maarekhet september 1939," in *Studies on Polish Jewry. Paul Glikson Memorial Volume*, ed. E. Mendelsohn and Ch. Shmeruk, Jerusalem 1987, 149–171.

16 Goldman, *Iskierki życia*, 9.

met by Vice President Klimecki). In practice, they did not encounter resistance. In this region, the Polish army was already defeated. The Germans additionally secured themselves, taking twenty-five hostages for several hours. The German occupation of Krakow lasted exactly 1961 days. For various reasons, the Germans decided to establish the capital of the General Government (hereinafter: GG) there. The literature on the subject often emphasizes the aversion that Germans were to have towards Warsaw. Krakow was definitely culturally closer to them, for example, through its architecture or the earlier affiliation with the Habsburg monarchy. The presence of the Germans in the history of the city was widely known: it is sufficient to mention the outstanding sculptor, the author of the altar in St. Mary's Church, Veit Stoss, who lived around the years 1448– 1533. Historical premises suggested that Krakow would be easier to Germanize than Warsaw. Undoubtedly, Germany also took into account more practical factors, namely the fact that Krakow had 259 thousand residents, and Warsaw over a million, it was also definitely larger in terms of territory. In addition, Krakow was much closer to the former borders of the German Reich. The German element already present at Wawel (approximately a thousand people) was supported by the influx of people to the city, apart from soldiers: army support staff, policemen, officials, and a group of entrepreneurs who came there to do "the business of life." In total, according to various estimates, about 50,000 Germans arrived there. Hans Frank made his residence in Wawel, in 1939–1945 he was the general governor of the occupied Polish lands (GG). The general governor was installed in the building of the AGH University of Science and Technology. The seat of the Krakow district office was organized in the Palace under the Rams. In the very center of the city, German became the dominant language. The German character of the place was emphasized by the ubiquitous flags of the country, emblems, and uniforms, which were worn not only by soldiers and policemen, but also officials and German civilians. The first days of their presence in the city were remembered as full of uncertainty.[17]

In a short time, the Germans strengthened their position in Krakow and became convinced that they would stay there longer. They increased the city's territory more than three times, joining to it in 1941, among others, Przegorzały, Wola Justowska, Chełm, Bronowice Małe, Górka Narodowa, Łagiewniki, and Borek Fałęcki. At Królewska Street, they erected a functional housing estate,

---

17 For more information on this subject see A. Chwalba, *Dzieje Krakowa*, vol. 5: *Kraków w latach 1939–1945*, Krakow 2002; idem, *Okupacyjny Kraków w latach 1939–1945*, 2 ed., Krakow 2011.

marked out today's Konopnickiej Street and extended the Rakowice-Czyżyny airport. They continued work on regulating the Vistula, initiated before the war. The Nazis occupied the hill in Przegorzały (today a district of Krakow) and located an artillery battery there. Next to the existing residential stone tower (built in the interwar period by the well-known architect Adolf Szyszko-Bohusz), they began building a house for the head of the Krakow district, Otto Wächter. After a change of plans, the building was eventually used as a luxury holiday resort for Luftwaffe pilots.

In 1940, Nazi planners began to create concepts for the reconstruction of the cities they occupied, including Strasbourg and Luxembourg. According to their assumptions, Krakow was to become the "Nuremberg of the East." The outstanding researcher of cultural heritage Prof. Jacek Purchla found the plans of the German architect Hubert Ritter in the Archives of the Munich University of Technology. In 1941, Ritter designed a new government district to be located near Wawel in Dębniki. It was intended to build new and representative squares, streets, and public buildings there that could accommodate 10,000 government, military, postal, railway, and other officials.[18] Germans wanted Krakow without Jews, but also without Poles. At the beginning they started eliminating Jews, who constituted about a quarter of its prewar population (about 65,000), from the city space.[19] The Jews were the first victims of war in Krakow, and next to them was the Polish intelligentsia. On November 6, 1939, the Nazis carried out Sonderaktion Krakau. That day, at the Collegium Novum of the Jagiellonian University, Krakow scholars, mainly professors of the Jagiellonian University, convened to hear a lecture on the German point of view on science and higher education, as ordered by SS-Sturmbannführer Bruno Müller. Instead of the lecture, the audience heard only a brief announcement by Müller, who, starting with the statement that "as it is well known, . . . teachers have always been hostile to German science," announced the immediate arrest of all those present except women and threatened to shoot anyone who dared to resist. In total, 183 people were arrested, most of them eventually sent to the Sachsenhausen concentration camp. After international interventions on February 8, 1940, 101 prisoners were released. The others were sent to the Dachau concentration camp, from where

---

18   J. Purchla, *Kraków miał być Norymbergią Wschodu*, interview by S. Mancewicz, http://krakow.wyborcza.pl/krakow/1,44425,3021101.html, accessed December 31, 2017.

19   According to reliable estimates, in 1938, 64,958 Jews and 186,493 Christians lived in Krakow. L. Mroczka, *Krakowianie. Szkic do portretu zbiorowego w dobie industrialnej transformacji 1890–1939*, Krakow 1999, 45, 48.

Fig. 30. Celebrations related to the first anniversary of the outbreak of war, the renaming of the Main Square in Krakow to Adolf Hitler Platz, and the unveiling of a commemorative plaque placed at the Town Hall, Krakow, September 1, 1940, NAC, reference number 2-3267

most of them were released after several months. Some were murdered, others died of diseases and exhaustion caused by poor camp conditions.[20]

Germanization was carried out consistently, as planned. Squares and streets were given German names; some of them were translations of the previous ones, others had a completely new character. For example, the Main Square was renamed Adolf Hitler Platz, and the Juliusz Słowacki Theater became Staatstheater des Generalgouvernements (State Theater of the GG).

At the beginning of war, all schools and universities were closed. By decision of Governor Hans Frank of June 18, 1940, some primary and vocational schools resumed their activity with a very limited curriculum. The Nazis thought that it would be enough if people subjected to them were able to write and read (at elementary level), and were also able to practice professions useful for the economy of the Third Reich. In that situation, Marcel Goldman could not continue his education. It was only in the ghetto, with secret teaching, that he completed the first grade of secondary school and began the second one.[21]

Hunger prevailed quickly in the territories occupied by the Germans. It was a result of the occupier's plundering policy. Peasants lost their cattle, which were sent to the Third Reich, and then were charged with the obligation to provide food (milk, butter, eggs, grain, and other products). On the black market, food reached dizzying prices, people quickly began selling out valuables in order to survive.

The first restrictions imposed on Jews were unpleasant, but they did not foretell the Holocaust, which also prolonged the period of dormant vigilance.

---

20 See W. Konopczyński, *Pod trupią główką. Sonderaktion Krakau*, afterword E. Rostworowski, Warsaw 1982. See also A. Czocher, *W okupowanym Krakowie. Codzienność polskich mieszkańców miasta 1939–1945*, Gdańsk 2011.
21 Interview with Marcel Goldman carried out on January 25, 2019.

Already in September 1939, Jews were ordered to mark their shops and cafés with the Star of David. There were excesses, the victims of which were most often Orthodox Jews: some of them had their beards or sidelocks were cut off in public. Jews were forbidden to enter parks, special tram and train cars were allocated to them, and later they were forbidden to travel by these means of transport altogether. Synagogues were closed, and the use of Hebrew was banned. In November, confiscation of Jewish workshops and enterprises was ordered. Ruthless looting began. One of thousands of such scenes is represented in the memories of Ryszard Friedman from Krakow:

> One rather warm February day [1940—author's note] three German limousines, from which a group of uniformed Germans and three civilians got off, stopped by our house at 11 Karmelicka Street. They came up immediately and, making a wild noise, invaded our apartment. They kicked the door open and immediately pulled out their guns. . . . The "visit" lasted six hours. . . . Soon, five large trucks drove up to our house, and took almost everything we had, including gilded furniture, crystals, expensive ceramics, porcelain, silk bedding, with Persian rugs and paintings and all other movable property. My father had a collector's bent and passionately bought expensive works of art. They were all taken away from him then.[22]

The circumstances of appropriating property belonging to Jews are revealed by Marcel Goldman:

> In the capital [of the General Government—author's note], Germans needed many flats for the new, pure-blooded, fascist-Nazi administration. Hans Frank, the almighty Governor General, ironically called in Berlin the King of Poland, first wanted Krakow—*Judenfrei*, that is, free of Jews. Later he decided to organize a ghetto in Podgórze, a district of Krakow, in which quite a lot of Jews lived. For now, he began to take the appropriate housing from Jews living in non-Jewish quarters and allocate them to the Germans. Of course, we are talking about large, relatively new and comfortable apartments. That's what our two families had [M. Goldman means here a Jewish family of his friends from Krakow—author's note]. That is why we became neighbours in rented apartments outside Krakow. I would like to add that Jewish families who lost their flats were not allowed to stay in Krakow, even if they miraculously found another flat in the city.[23]

---

22 Friedman, *Jeden spośród*, 40–41.
23 Goldman, "W małym pokoju w Ramat Ha-Szaron."

As a result of a special regulation, from December 1, 1939, all Jews over ten years old were required to wear white armbands with the star of David (minimum ten centimeters wide) on the right sleeve of their clothes, including coats. From 1940, non-compliance with that provision was punishable by death. Jews aged between twelve and sixty were forced to work. They were used, for example, to backfill anti-aircraft ditches and remove snow from the city.[24] Marcel and his father also did this type of work, as he recounts in *Iskierki życia*. Early in the first days of November 1939, together with his father, they were directed by the Krakow Magistrate to Trzech Wieszczów Avenue:

> We started clearing the snow, chopping ice, softening the effects of winter. Everything was happening in a calm, muted rhythm. . . . Suddenly, groups of people, ordinary onlookers began to gather around us. Initially, they watched our work appreciatively, nodded their heads, but with time demons began to wake up in them. They became aggressive. They accosted us brazenly. The rout from the suburbs, typical Krakow urchins called the tune. For them, throwing snowballs at working Jews was great fun. While doing that, they directed at us remarks like: "Well, Jews finally got to work," "How does he hold a shovel, like a Jewess by the boobs," "You know only how to trade and cheat, so it's high time to do a decent job." They became sharper and more offensive. They started throwing at us, instead of snowballs, pieces of ice and stones. . . . Suddenly, an elderly gentleman came out from the tenement's gate, and at that time professors of the Jagiellonian University and the intellectual cream of the city lived in that avenue, the district belonged to elegant and refined people. He was dressed in a warm fur coat with a white handkerchief in his upper pocket, in woolen trousers, and his head was already sprinkled with gray hair and fresh snow. In his hands he held a tray with vodka in glasses and appetizers. "Gentlemen, allow me" he said to us in a warm, friendly voice. "Don't worry, gentlemen. The war will end soon and everyone will return to their place. This is just the temporary nature of the moment. Please help yourselves . . ."[25]

Before the mass extermination of Jews started, they were harassed in various ways, and forced labour was often used as a way to bully and mock the Jews. They had to work in circumstances that offended their dignity, also during the

---

24 K. Zimmerer writes extensively about the situation of Jews in occupied Krakow in *Zamordowany świat. Losy Żydów w Krakowie 1939–1945*, Krakow 2004. See also idem, *Kronika zamordowanego świata. Żydzie w Krakowie w czasie niemieckiej okupacji*, Krakow 2017.

25 Goldman, *Iskierki życia*, 12–13.

most important Judaism holidays. On October 3, 1940, on the first day of Jewish New Year, the *kahal* issued a notice saying:

> By the order of the authorities, all Jewish men and all Jewish women must attend work as usual on October 4 (the second day of Rosh Hashone [Jewish New Year]) and October 12 (Yom Kippur). All Jewish shops must be open and must sell.[26]

Work became a widely used tool to humiliate and destroy Jews. The most emblematic example of this is the inscription above the entrance gate to the Auschwitz-Birkenau camp: *Arbeit macht frei* (German: work sets you free), evidently deceitful, because in the camps, as commonly known, work, next to gas chambers and other deadly tools, was a means of the annihilation of Jews.

On May 18, 1940, the head of the Krakow district, Otto Wächter, announced that there could remain 15,000 Jews with families in Krakow—they were people temporarily needed in the economic plans of the occupier and special residence permits were issued for them. Others had to leave the city, the Goldmans among them. Uncle Wichner, the brother of Marcel's grandmother from his mother's side, managed a farm in Zbydniowice. Now, he came for Marcel's in a cart, and they lived with him for a year.[27] Marcel remembers that time well, because it was then that his family got documents, which later allowed them to survive the war:

> At that time, my father worked for one of the well-known Krakow shoemakers, for whom he kept books, money, and the entire administration. At that time, the Germans liquidated or took over many Jewish shops in the city. My father persuaded his employer to open a shoe shop and sell his products directly to the consumer. In that way he would earn much more. My father organized and ran the shop. It was a great success. Mr. Jurek (it was his surname, not first name) was so pleased that he offered my father to arrange Catholic certificates for the family and on that basis also ID cards for the assumed Polish-Catholic surname. Those so-called Aryan papers later saved our lives.[28]

Jurek rightly warned them to be ready to flee at any moment, because the fate of Jews was already bad, and was soon to become tragic. According to Mar-

---

26 Sz. Mendelsohn, *Polscy Żydzi za murami nazistowskich gett*, intro. and commentary M. Skwara, trans. M. Skwara, Szczecin 2017, 55.
27 Goldman, *Iskierki życia*, 15–16.
28 Goldman, "W małym pokoju w Ramat Ha-Szaron"...

cel, Jurek had extensive knowledge of German intentions thanks to contacts in the Polish Underground State (secret structures of the Polish state operating during World War II). He could give them the aforementioned help because he cooperated with a cell producing false documents for Poles who, due to their underground activity, had to change their identity or were forced to flee and hide due to denunciations.[29] The friendship with Jurek had one more advantage, namely that he allowed Marcel's father to use his address, which the Goldman family could enter in the application for a *Kennkarte* for Poles, issued for the name Galas. Later, Marcel's father used it as a contact address, placing a job advert in the newspaper (about which I shall write in a moment).

The war turned the Goldmans' lives upside down. Among the daily hardships unusual, sometimes even bizarre, events come back in memories:

> My father went to work in Krakow by bicycle every day. In fact, Jews were forbidden to use public transport. According to the ordinance, my father wore a white armband with a large blue star of David. The Jew had to be marked! One Saturday my father came home on foot. An SS man stopped him on the road and told him that he was requiring the bike because he had to get there and there as soon as possible. He gave him a receipt and promised that he would return the bike on the next day. He wrote our address exactly for that purpose. My father came home breathless, sweaty and tired, convinced that he had lost the bicycle for good. An SS man will make the effort to return a bicycle to a Jew? On Sunday morning, we sleep longer. We eat breakfast, we drink coffee, suddenly someone knocks on the door. My mom opens, and on the threshold there is our neighbour, the SS man, and ... the bicycle. He was looking for you, says the neighbour. And he points at the the SS man's black uniform with skulls. My mother invited the whole company for coffee, but the German refused. We were left with our mouths open! ...[30]

Soon began the deportations to the Krakow ghetto, created by the Nazis' order of March 3, 1941, in a part of Podgórze district. It only took up an area of about twenty hectares, and covered fifteen streets with 320 houses. The ghetto was surrounded with barbed wire. Later, a high wall was built with semicircular finials, which could be associated with the Decalogue plaques or *matzevot*—

---

29 Interview with Marcel Goldman carried out on January 25, 2019.
30 Ibid.

Jewish gravestones. Four closely guarded gates led to the ghetto. Poles who had lived there before were displaced, and Jews were ordered to move to March 20, 1941, the next day the ghetto was closed.³¹ The Goldmans moved into a ground floor (if it can be described in this way) apartment at 4 Zgody Square, the largest square in the ghetto, which was called after the war the Bohaterów Getta Square (English: Ghetto Heroes Square).

Fig. 31.
Construction of the ghetto walls on Lasota Hill, May 1941,
Bundesarchiv, Bild 183-L25516/CC-BY-SA 3.0

Leaving the ghetto without special permission was severely punished. From October 15, 1941, the punishment was death. At first, about three thousand people lived in the ghetto, then seventeen thousand were crowded together.³² Among them, there were the Goldmans ... Time spent in the Krakow ghetto left an indelible mark on Marcel. We can find traces of this in his poem entitled *Rok 1942*, which he wrote in Tel Aviv on February 25, 2011,³³ nearly seventy years later:

---

31   Zimmerer, *Zamordowany świat*.
32   Ibid.
33   Goldman, *A w nocy przychodzą myśli*, 60.

Ja tu mieszkałem na Placu Zgody 4:	I lived here at 4 Zgody Square:
Mała izdebka, dwa okna od ulicy,	A small room, two windows overlooking the street,
Sześcioro ludzi tam się gnieździło,	Six people were crowded together there,
A jeszcze dwoje „nielegalnych" w piwnicy.	And two more "illegal" ones in the basement.
Ten plac podgórski, spokojny,	This quiet square of Podgórze
Zaawansował w czasie wojny,	Advanced during the war,
Stał się przedsionkiem piekła ten plac	This square became the vestibule of hell;
I robił za „Umschlagplatz."	It worked as *Umschlagplatz*.
Pisał polski poeta:	A Polish poet wrote:
„Z kurzem krwi bratniej do Ciebie Panie bije ten głos"	"With the dust of your brother's blood to you Lord strikes this voice"
Do Ciebie? Panie?	To you? Lord?
Tyś z Twoimi aniołami cały ten okres przespali,	You and your angels slept through this whole period,
Kiedy Twój „naród wybrany"	When your "chosen people"
Dla siebie groby kopali.	Dug graves for themselves.
Dziś, gdy łgarze, podli i bezczelni	Today, when liars, mean and insolent,
Twierdzą, że się nic takiego nie działo,	Claim that nothing like this happened,
Jest nadal osób niewiele,	There are still few people
Które to jeszcze widziało.	Who saw it.
Ja to zeznaję! Jak długo?	I testify it! How long?
Nikt przecież nie wie, kiedy oddychać przestanie,	Nobody knows when he will stop breathing,
Ale te sceny... i obraz...	But these scenes... and the picture...
W stygnących oczach zostanie.	It will stay in the cold eyes.

In June 1942, displacements from the ghetto to the death camp in Bełżec began. Over 7,000 Krakow Jews were killed then. Among those deported there were Marcel's grandmother and grandfather.[34] On October 28, 1942, another 5,000 were transported to Bełżec. On March 13–14, 1943, the Nazis finally

---

34 Goldman describes the details in his book *Iskierki życia*, 26.

94 | Chapter 2. The Hell of Extermination

Fig. 32. Deportation of Jews from the ghetto, Lwowska Street, March 1943, public domain

Fig. 33. Property abandoned by deportees, Lwowska Street, with the third gate to the ghetto in the background, March 1943, public domain

liquidated the ghetto. The remaining residents were displaced to the Płaszów camp or to Auschwitz, some were murdered on the spot.[35]

The Goldmans escaped from the ghetto in September 1942, knowing they were risking their lives. If they had been targeted by blackmailers, the Polish Blue Police, soldiers, or the Gestapo, their fate would have been sealed—they would die on the spot or in one of extermination camps. The drama was that staying in the ghetto meant a certain, though perhaps more remote in time, death sentence. Marcel's mother's brother, Uncle Moniek, experienced that. Soon after the Goldmans escaped, the Germans began to divide the ghetto, and some of its inhabitants were placed in the labour camp in Płaszów, where there was no place for children, so their fate was sealed. Moniek decided to save his little daughter Gieniusia and smuggle her out of the ghetto (she was not yet a year old when the war broke out). Going to work outside the ghetto walls, he carried her in her backpack. He had previously given her sleeping pills. One of the SS men saw him. He went with Mońek and Gieniusia in his arms to their apartment. There was no one there because his wife and older daughter were at work. Moniek begged the SS man for mercy, but he was adamant:

> The German took Gieniusia in his arms and sat her on an empty barrel that stood in the yard. Gieniusia was crying, waving her hands, holding them out to her father. She almost fell off the barrel, but the SS man held her and put a candy in cellophane in her small hand. That calmed Gieniusia down. Intrigued by the rustling of cellophane, she began to open it, and finally she brought her small fingers to her mouth, looking at the man in black uniform standing in front of her. Moniek froze. He looked at the big blue eyes of his daughter, then again at the German, who was playing with the gun taken out of the holster. They probably want to intimidate me, he thought hopefully. And suddenly . . . God merciful! A shot was fired. One and only. And a terrible, inhuman howl pierced the air. Then there was silence, and only a whine of a man holding a dead child in his arms.
>
> Moniek and the rest of his family did not survive the war. They had no desperation, strength, and will to fight for their lives at all costs. And this was equivalent to agreeing to the judgement of fate. It was like suicide.[36]

---

35 Zimmerer, *Zamordowany świat*.
36 Goldman, *Iskierki życia*, 18–19.

The vast majority of the Goldmans' relatives, acquaintances, and friends did not survive World War II. Some deaths are known, each time they are a record of a nightmare that is hard to imagine. Others vanished without trace; they left the house and never returned there—most likely caught during one of the round-ups, shot, battered to death . . . In the case of the Goldmans it was right to stake everything on one card, but leaving the ghetto did not decide anything, and the fate of Marcel and his loved ones was uncertain again and again. The escape was complicated by the family situation. Before the displacement, the Germans began to regulate the number of people entitled to remain in the ghetto, issuing special documents for those who were employed. Aunt Frania, Marcel's mother's sister whom he loved very much, did not have such documents. After the outbreak of war, her husband was mobilized to the army and, as it turned out, he died as a Polish soldier. Maks and Sara hid Frania and her less-than-five-year-old daughter Rózia in the basement. They had to use the most sophisticated conspiracy, because the Nazis threatened that if they found persons unauthorized to stay in the ghetto in any tenement house, they would murder not only the illegal residents, but all the other tenants as well. However, the basement did not guarantee proper living conditions for a small child, even if she was taken to the apartment at night. That's why Rózia got seriously ill. One day, delirious, she began to ask for milk. Aunt Frania decided that she would try to make her way through the yard to the part of Podgórze where there were still several farms with cows. Sara strongly advised her not to go, but she did not listen. She did not survive . . . The Goldmans later learned that the Germans stopped her in one of the courtyards, and because she did not have the necessary documents, she was immediately murdered. Marcel's parents took care of Rózia, but they did not let a small child in on the horror of the situation. As Marcel believed, Rózia knew that something terrible had happened, because from that moment on she held on to Sara, following her even to the toilet. Sara then put a condition on Maks that she would not leave the ghetto without Rózia. If the girl was to stay, she would stay with her. In that case, Sara suggested that her husband should run away without her, taking Marcel and Nela. Maks worried that Rózia's appearance would allow strangers to identify them as Jews; moreover, he did not have the Aryan papers for her. In the end, he decided that they would take Rózia with them, but only after he was able to procure the Aryan papers for her. For Marcel, it remains a mystery to this day how his father, cut off from the world, was able to connect with people who could give him the documents for Rózia.[37]

---

37 Interview with Marcel Goldman carried out on January 25, 2019.

The carefully planned escape from the ghetto began on an autumn evening in 1942. Maks and Marcel left it first. A Blue Police commander named Grabowski led them through one of the ghetto gates. He received a diamond ring for that, which Maks gave to Sara just after Marcel's birth. As promised, the next morning, commandant Grabowski led Sara out of the ghetto with her two daughters, the older Nela and the younger foster child Rózia. That was the plan of action adopted earlier. Before the escape, Maksymilian placed an advertisement in *Krakauer Zeitung*: "A merchant, a Pole, a specialist in leather industry, fluent in spoken and written German, will accept a job, also outside Krakow."[38] It should be noted that using the phrase "also outside Krakow" was a tactical operation. Marcel's father assumed in advance that they had to leave Krakow, where everyone knew them. In response, they received many offers, from which they selected the footwear factory Bata in Radom. Straight from the ghetto, around 19:00, Maks and Marcel went to the train station, from which they departed at 20:00. They arrived in Radom around midnight, and because the area around the station was not safe at night, they took a coach to the hotel. On the spot, however, it turned out that the porter required a special residence permit, which they had to obtain across the street at ... the Gestapo headquarters:

> My father later told me that the duty officer was waken up and he was not happy about it. He asked my father why he came there, from where and how. My father explained with his perfect German what was going on and presented a telegram from the Bata company that he was to start work there. The Gestapo officer softened and he only wanted to know for how long we need permission.[39]

Having received the necessary document, they could take a hotel room. The next morning Maks had to go to the factory, Marcel was to stay alone in the hotel room. His father warned him not to go anywhere and not to engage in conversations with anyone. He explained that, after a long time living in the ghetto, the boy was not accustomed to living on the "Aryan side," and without knowing the new rules, he could expose himself and his father to death. Just looking through the window, which Marcel remembers to this day, made a great impression on him:

---

38 Goldman, *Iskierki życia*, 21–22.
39 Ibid., 22–28.

> Mothers walked with their children in prams, German soldiers paraded with their giggling girls, shops were open, people came in and out. Laughter and cheerful voices sounded in the air. And trees. Trees, from which ripe chestnuts were already falling on the pavement, were standing in all their autumn glory. I was stunned. No babies or toddlers were seen in the ghetto. There were no trees. There was no laughter.[40]

Marcel's father was right to warn his son, and the boy was to find out about it almost immediately. He could see a delicatessen shop of the Austrian company Julius Meinl from afar:

> There were sweets displayed. Cookies, candies, chocolate. Chocolate! I went down the stairs as if in a trance and straight to Meinl. A young lady attended to customers. "For you, Sir?" "Well, mainly chocolate, a hundred gram of sweets, pralines, that's all." She packed. "Coupons, please." I was petrified. I didn't have any coupons and I didn't know I had to have them. I came to my senses quickly and pretended to search my pockets. "Unfortunately I forgot, and what can you get without coupons?" "I think only cookies." "So I'll have them." I left the shop. It was written on the door in capital letters: "Nur für Deutsche"—"Only for Germans." Later I told my father everything. He looked at me sadly and anxiously. "You empty-headed, stupid boy, you could have brought death to our whole family." I will never forget those words of my father.[41]

At the Bata factory, Maks Goldman, now known as Marcin Galas, was given the job of a purchase manager. Later he was appointed director responsible for purchasing and storing all materials needed for production. Together with Marcel, he was assigned a studio apartment in the Bata building for unmarried employees. They ate meals in the canteen for clerks.

After three days in Radom, Maksymilian began an intensive search for an apartment so that his wife and daughters could join him. After leaving the ghetto, Grabowski helped them reach the agreed place, that is, Mr. Gierad's apartment on the Aryan side at Grodzka Street. The choice of this hideout is connected with another family story. Marcel's father had two sisters who lived in the Czech Republic. One of them was killed during the liquidation of the Czech ghetto, the other—Mania Donat—lived with her husband and son in Zaolzie, taken by Poland in 1938. After the outbreak of World War II, the Germans took

---

40   Ibid., 30.
41   Ibid., 30–31.

her husband to the camp, where he died. Mania and her son came to the Goldman family in Krakow. She was a beautiful woman, and she quickly organized her life in a new place. A young boy named Janek Gierad fell in love with her; he was a driver, and during the war he smuggled Jews to Hungary, which brought him a lot of money. He also took Mania and her son there. Equipped with false documents, they ended up in a Hungarian internment camp for Poles,[42] thanks to which they survived and settled in Israel after the war. In 1942, the Germans detained Janek while trying to smuggle Jews across the border with Hungary. Jews were shot on the spot, and Janek was sent to the Auschwitz camp. He managed to survive the war, and in spring 1945 he came to Radom. The Goldmans took him in and helped him recover. Maks was the director of Bata at the time, as the entire German management of the company escaped in fear of the advancing Russian army. He hired him as a driver. Janek soon got married and Marcel even managed to become his best man. During the war, it was thanks to him[43] that Sara and her two daughters, after escaping from the ghetto, and before leaving for Radom, found a safe haven in his father's apartment, which was located in Krakow at Grodzka Street.[44] Mr. Gierad, however, began to fear terribly that "dangerous" tenants would bring him trouble and urged Maks to take them. As Marcel recalls:

> The race against time begun to organize housing for the family. It was impossible in Radom. They did not register Poles because the Germans who had moved the district administration from Kielce to Radom needed flats for their officials with families who came from the Reich. Although the Radom ghetto was liquidated at that time, the locals took all the vacant apartments. We found a shop for the apartment in Glinice, a suburb that did not belong to the city at the time.[45]

On the fourth day after escaping from the ghetto, the "apartment" in the form of a shop in Glinice was already waiting for Sara and the girls. Marcel was asked by his father to prepare the place for living, he had to get a heating stove

---

42　After Germany, followed by the Soviet Union, invaded Poland, over 100,000 Polish civilian and military refugees ended up in Hungary to seek refuge there. The Hungarians placed them in internment camps that Poles could leave freely.
43　After 1989, Marcel unsuccessfully tried to find Janek, as he wanted to start the procedure of honouring Janek with the Righteous Among the Nations Medal.
44　Interview with Marcel Goldman carried out on December 28, 2018.
45　Correspondence with Marcel Goldman, February 6, 2019.

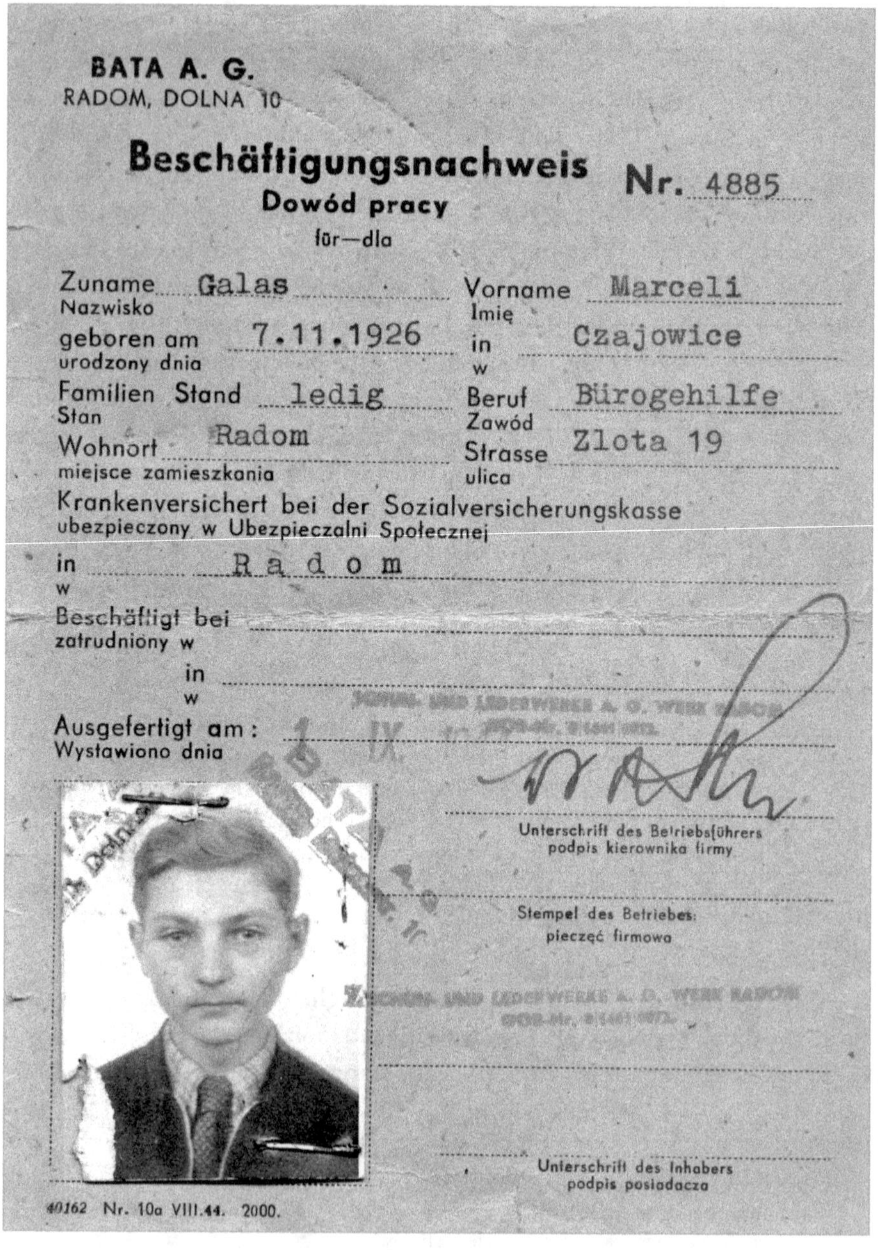

BATA A. G.
RADOM, DOLNA 10

Beschäftigungsnachweis Nr. 4885
Dowód pracy
für—dla

Zuname / Nazwisko	Galas	Vorname / Imię	Marceli
geboren am / urodzony dnia	7.11.1926	in / w	Czajowice
Familien Stand / Stan	ledig	Beruf / Zawód	Bürogehilfe
Wohnort / miejsce zamieszkania	Radom	Strasse / ulica	Zlota 19

Krankenversichert bei der Sozialversicherungskasse
ubezpieczony w Ubezpieczalni Społecznej

in / w   Radom

Beschäftigt bei
zatrudniony w

in
w

Ausgefertigt am:
Wystawiono dnia

Unterschrift des Betriebsführers
podpis kierownika firmy

Stempel des Betriebes:
pieczęć firmowa

Unterschrift des Inhabers
podpis posiadacza

40162 Nr. 10a VIII.44. 2000.

Fig. 34. The document confirming the employment of Marceli Galas
(Marcel Goldman) in the "Bata" factory,
family collections of Marcel and Bianka Goldman (Tel Aviv)

and curtains that would cover the old shop window so that no one would look inside. Maks took a truck with a chauffeur from Bata, which he drove to Krakow the next day to collect Sara, Nela, and Rózia. He had to fake a family relocation with furniture and luggage, because it was widely known that Jews escaped from the ghetto without any major objects, so if their family reached Radom as they had left the ghetto, it would raise suspicions. That is why Maks bought old furniture, a trunk with bedding and suitcases with clothes on a flea market in Krakow. On the fifth day they "celebrated" the arrival of the mother and girls to Radom. They lived for half a year in the temporary place in Glinice. Then they got a new, luxury apartment from Bata, which was still under construction when they arrived in Radom. There were four apartments in the building. A Pole named Momentowicz, who was a personnel manager, lived above the Goldmans, now known as Galas, and the remaining two apartments were occupied by German families of the Bata directors.[46]

Fig. 35. Marceli Galas (Marcel Goldman), at the typewriter, while working in the Bata factory, the period of World War II, family collections of Marcel and Bianka Goldman (Tel Aviv)

---

46   Ibid.

Bata produced footwear for the army and civilians. Shoes supplied to Germany had to be of the highest quality, leather was used for their production. Footwear made of linen and recyclable materials (for example, soles were made from used car tires) was intended for Poles. For the Germans, the factory was important, and, fearing sabotage, they only employed Germans and *Volksdeutche* in senior positions. For physical work, they used Poles and (for some time) a group of Jews isolated from everyone. Marcel's father in the position of purchasing director was the only non-German in Bata authorities.[47] Marcel also found employment in the factory soon: he got a job directly in production. In Marcel's opinion, it was the idea of his father who, attached to certain principles close to the German mentality, decided that his son should start from the lowest position to get to know the factory, its crew, and the principles of operation. So he started working on a machine sewing shoes. Later, the production manager named Blachut, a German from Silesia, appreciating his competence, promoted him to the position of "department manipulator"—it was basically the work of a department warehouseman. It became Marcel's responsibility to collect the goods needed for footwear production.[48] As a result of another promotion, Marcel took the position of "master manipulator," that is, the warehouse manager to whom the department warehousemen were subject (the entire division was managed by his father, who as the director was responsible not only for purchases, but also for the warehouses).[49]

The Galas family, although free, was in permanent danger, which can be illustrated by another story Marcel remembers. One day, the German police and the Blue Police surrounded their district. The police searched apartments for black-market dealers and goods. The Germans suspected, among others, that part of the footwear production was taken out and sold illegally, which was treated on the one hand as a classic violation of the law, but also as sabotage, because the army—due to problems with the supply of leather and reduced production capacity—increasingly suffered due to the lack of footwear. The Galas family could hide food products from the "black market," but in the apartment, there

---

47 Goldman, *Iskierki życia*, 34–36.
48 Cut-to-size parts of shoes were delivered to the departments and had to be sewn together. At the last stage, they were lubricated with a special paste for protection and polish. Each department produced an average of one thousand pairs of shoes a day. The factory consisted of about fifteen branches; each branch employed from thirty to fifty people. There was also staff outside of production, such as office workers, sales department support, and so forth. Interview with Marcel Goldman carried out on January 25, 2019.
49 Interview with Marcel Goldman carried out on December 28, 2018.

Fig. 36. Marceli Galas (Marcel Goldman) with Bata crew members (standing in the cap, the second from the right), World War II, family collections of Marcel and Bianka Goldman (Tel Aviv). First from the left in the second row is Gorczyk, commandant of the Werkschutz. At the barrier is Blachut, production master from Germany

was a *tallit*[50] in a basket in a visible place in the kitchen. Pulling it out and hiding it was out of the question, because Mrs. Katarzyna, who used to come to do the laundry once a month, was with them. There was no time to think about it, the German police (Schupo) knocked on their door. Marcel's father tried to gain time by asking about the reasons for the arrival, but the conversation could not last forever. Fortunately,

> the door of the opposite apartment opened. A German stood at the door, also one of the directors of Bata. He was not in his uniform . . . , but he had a visible sign of a NSDAP member in his buttonhole. "What's going on here?" he asked. My father explained what was going on. "Don't you know, gentlemen, that only the directors of Bata live in this house? You don't suspect that there could be a black market trader here?" our neigh-

---

50 The Hebrew term *tallit* (in Yiddish, *tallis*) means a rectangular shawl that Jews put on their shoulders or heads during prayer. Religious Jews also wear smaller *tallitot* under their clothes. Most often they are white with black or dark blue stripes along the sides. An important part of them are fringes, which are called *tsitsiyot*. Boys receive the first *tallit* at the Bar Mitzvah.

Fig. 37. During World War II with friends (the second from the left), family collections of Marcel and Bianka Goldman (Tel Aviv)

bour asked the policemen. They were confused and perplexed. They did not know who they were talking to and whether they stepped into something that could have unpleasant consequences for them. "Excuse us!" they said. They saluted and went away! My father died in Israel in 1956. After his death, my mother gave me a small package. "This is your father's *tallit*. Now it's yours." I am not a religious man, for many years I did not have the opportunity to wear the *tallit*. Up to my grandson's Bar Mitzvah in 2004.[51]

It seems interesting how the Goldmans remembered Polish-Jewish relations during World War II. What image of the Pole was engraved in their memory? It is difficult to indicate precise proportions here, but in general it is an image

---

51   Goldman, *A w nocy przychodzą myśli*, 22–23.

Youth, Part One (1939–1945) 105

Figs. 38–39. Marceli Galas (Marcel Goldman, the first from the left) while digging anti-tank ditches, the period of World War II, family collections of Marcel and Bianka Goldman (Tel Aviv)

oscillating between neutral and negative, it is certainly not positive. Why? In the general discourse regarding the attitude of Poles towards the Holocaust, the emphasis is usually placed on two issues. The first is Poles saving Jews. We hear words of appreciation for the Polish Righteous who, risking their own lives and the lives of their relatives, selflessly helped Jews by sheltering them in their homes or by providing false documents, the so-called Aryan papers. Under the ordinances of German authorities, in particular pursuant to the ordinance of the Governor General Hans Frank of October 15, 1941, every Pole who gave shelter or other help to a Jew was subject to the death penalty. As a classic example of collective responsibility, the penalty also applied to relatives, neighbours, and even entire local communities. In Western Europe, Germany did not go so far in terms of sanctions. Therefore, the fact that so far more than 6,000 Poles have been awarded the Righteous Among the Nations medal (awarded by the Israeli Yad Vashem Institute), which is today about a quarter of all Righteous, becomes even more meaningful. Enumerating these facts obviously raises further questions, including the most important, whether Poles could have saved many more Jews....

The second fundamental matter relates to the activity of blackmailers who handed Jews over to the Germans. The occupying authorities encouraged Poles to do so in various ways. In Warsaw, denunciators received a prize of 500 zlotys. In the province, depending on the place, 0.5–5 kilograms of sugar could be obtained for turning in a Jew. In some regions, a liter of spirit, or a small portion of grain or food served as a prize. That practice on the part of the Nazis contributed to the dehumanization and expulsion of Jews. Virtually anyone could kill a Jew without any punishment, and the Jewish life was valued at a few kilograms of sugar, sometimes only 500 grams... In that situation, unfortunately, thousands of people joined the activities directed against Jews, and blackmailers tracked down Jews in order to rob them and hand them over to the Germans. Most often the blackmailes came from the social margins, they were common offenders and criminals. However, some of them were motivated primarily by their antisemitism.

Today, Marcel does not wonder whether Poles could have saved more Jews, of course he assesses the blackmailers' attitude critically, like all civilized people, but most of all, he remembers the unjust hostility of the Poles towards the Jews. It is by no means a result of fear or of desire to achieve measurable benefits; we are talking about hatred that is unreasonable and completely incomprehensible. For example, a scene from the liquidation of the Radom ghetto is stuck in Marcel's memory. He was with his mother in the spice shop, which they often visited. The Germans ordered to move away from windows and doors. So they stood by the counter, but the glass doors and shop windows were just a few meters away from them, and they could see well what was going on outside. At one point, a group of Jewish children was being led by. As Marcel recalls: "My mother finally couldn't stand it and said aloud: 'What did those children do to anyone?' The shop owner said: 'Mrs. Galas, what are you saying, Jews will grow out of them! I would burn their eyes with hot metal!'"[52]

Marcel also remembers the constant fear and the fact that they were more afraid of Poles than Germans! That was simply justified: the Poles knew very well their Jewish neighbours, their customs, and other special features of Polish Jews. The Germans were not able to check every house, apartment, basement, attic, barn, and other places. They usually took action after receiving a denunciation. Hence, however tragic and unfair it may seem today, Jews feared Poles the most. A pattern emerges from Jewish memories: a German murder was often preceded by a Polish denunciation. It should be assumed that Poles never discovered the Jewish origin of the Galas family, if it had happened, they would have probably shared the sad fate of other hiding Jews who were turned in by organized blackmailers or spontaneous denunciators.

There are some indications that it could have been different. Marcel's younger (adopted) sister Rózia was the only one with dark hair in the family living in Radom. One day Mrs. Ruzik, their house owner's wife, "leaning confidently towards my mother, . . . said: 'Mrs. Galas, I'm telling you, don't put this dark pinafore on Różyczka, because she looks like a Jewish girl in it . . .' My mother got scared, but she responded to Mrs. Ruzik's remark with a smile, a wave of the hand. However, she did not put that pinafore on Rózia any more."[53]

After the war, when the Russians entered Radom, Mr. Ruzik said to Marcel's father: "Mr. Galas, don't think that we did not know that Rózia was Jewish."[54] In Marcel's opinion: "They apparently thought that we were a Christian family saving a Jewish child. I think, however, that the idea that the whole Galas family was Jewish did not even cross their mind. Mr. Galas, a director of Bata—a Jew? No, it was beyond their imagination!"[55]

---

52   Interview with Marcel Goldman carried out on March 3, 2018.
53   Ibid., 50.
54   Interview with Marcel Goldman carried out on January 25, 2019.
55   Ibid.

In Marcel's memory, there are also various reactions of Poles and Jews to the entry of the Red Army: "For most Poles known to us, the appearance of the Red Army meant a change of the occupier. For Jews, it was a signal that they were no longer in danger of death. Our family looked at all this, of course, through the eyes of Jews, but we also shared the emotions of our Polish friends, and we shared their point of view that a new type of threat appeared."[56]

Simultaneously, in different, but not less dramatic circumstances, the life of the Ebersohn family, including Bianka, Marcel's future wife, went on. They decided to escape from the war to the East. They went to Lviv, to Bianka's father's brother, Edward, who was also an attorney.[57] In the last days of August, they left Bielsko and went to Krakow, where they took the last train for civilians on August 31, 1939. They arrived in Lviv on September 1, 1939. Their luggage arrived just as the Germans bombed the local train station, it all burned in a fire that broke out. Bianka remembers that in her uncle's apartment they received one room and at first they lived there very modestly, but relatively peacefully. Her mother even managed to enroll her in school so that she could continue her education.[58]

The Ebersohns did the same as thousands of other Jews who, in fear of the impending Nazi army, chose the eastern direction. It was difficult to predict the further developments at that time. There was a widespread belief that France and Great Britain would hurry to help Poland, so when on September 3, 1939 the radio reported that the two countries had declared war on Germany, many people were crazy with joy. That enthusiasm quickly subsided, as it turned out, that move was on paper only. The threat of an attack from the Soviet side was real, but even if it were to happen, Stalin seemed to Jews to be less of a threat than Hitler. The Soviet program did not announce the physical destruction of the Jews, and from this perspective the occupation of the eastern territories of the Polish

---

56 Interview with Marcel Goldman carried out on December 28, 2018.
57 In the biographical note of Edward Ebersohn, published in 1937, we read: "Doctor, born in Krakow in 1877, attorney. After graduating from high school and the Jagiellonian University in Krakow, he devoted himself to the legal profession. Thanks to his outstanding legal abilities, high conscientiousness, great sense of honor, innate gentleness of feelings, righteousness, and kindness, he has gained universal respect among clients, in court, and with colleagues, and belongs to the elite among the Lviv Bar. He has held numerous offices in the Bar Association many times, and is currently the co-head of the practical law course for the last year of the attorney practice of trainee lawyers. Member of the disciplinary court." *Almanach żydowski*, ed. H. Stachel, Lviv–Warsaw–Poznań 1937, 380.
58 Interview with Bianka Goldman carried out on December 20, 2016.

Second Republic by the Red Army could even be read as a kind of protection against Nazi totalitarianism. If anyone had such illusions, they quickly had to part with them. Although communism was by definition a cosmopolitan ideology, hate campaigns with national or religious basis were also carried out in the Soviet Union. Enough to mention the "Polish operation" of 1937–1938, during the course of which, direct death sentences were executed at over 100,000 Poles, another 100,000 were sent to Kazakhstan, Siberia, and to the regions of Kharkiv and Dnipropetrovsk (many of them died). A similar fate awaited Jews, but their situation was marked by a certain paradox. Indeed, those who had been sent deep into the USSR by Stalin's order had the greatest chance of survival. When a part of Poland's territory was annexed by the USSR, Jews staying there were not treated as ethnic enemies, but they could have fallen into disfavor due to their improper social origin (in the communist jargon the concept of "class origin and affiliation" was used) or a refusal to accept a Soviet passport. Forced passporting of the population permanently resident in the occupied territories began in March 1940. As both Jews and Poles most often refused to accept the Soviet passport, the authorities had a convenient excuse to send them to Siberia or to other areas deep within the USSR. In the opinion of Tomasz Gąsowski who researches this issue: "There were not many willing to become Soviet citizens voluntarily, even former communists did not want this honour."[59]

The Jews who stayed free when the Third Reich attacked the Soviet Union found themselves in mortal danger. On June 22, 1941, Hitler and his allies threw more than four million soldiers against the Soviet Union, and the Soviets could use three million people. These numbers, however, do not reflect the essence of the matter. Stalin very quickly managed to mobilise another two million, but the problem was primarily in the disproportion of arms, of which the Germans had more and of better quality. In addition, the Soviet army was still in the phase of reorganization after the purge carried out by Stalin among the commanding staff. Ultimately, Hitler lost that duel, but the first days of war brought a stunning success of the Nazi army. The Germans entered Lviv in a flash, because under the Ribbentrop-Molotov pact of August 23, 1939, after the occupation of Poland, the division of its territory ran along the San–Bug–Narew–Pisa rivers.

---

59   T. Gąsowski, "Polscy Żydzi w sowieckiej Rosji," in *Historyk i historia. Studia dedykowane pamięci Prof. Mirosława Frančicia*, ed. A. Walaszek, K. Zamorski, Krakow 2005, 231. See D. Levin, *The Lesser of Two Evils. Eastern European Jewry under Soviet Rule, 1939–1941*, Philadelphia–Jerusalem 1995; M. Wierzbicki, *Polacy i Żydzi w zaborze sowieckim. Stosunki polsko-żydowskie na ziemiach północno-wschodnich II RP pod okupacją sowiecką*, Warsaw 2001.

That is why the Germans occupied the left-bank part of Przemyśl, where their armed formations were preparing to attack. In a straight line, Przemyśl is only ninety kilometers away from Lviv. Wehrmacht took Lviv on June 29, 1941 (the German occupation lasted until July 23, 1944). At that time the Ebersohns were no longer in Lviv.

In the summer of 1940, they were transported deep into the Soviet Union to Krasnouralsk in the Sverdlovsk Oblast of the Urals. Bianka remembers that moment very well:

> They came for us in the middle of the night. One of the soldiers had a list in his hand, which included our surname. We were told that we had twenty minutes to pack and go downstairs, where a truck would be waiting to take us. They left with us one soldier who was watching over us. My mother asked him if he knew where they would take us. He replied that he did not know where exactly, but certainly far into Russia. My mother asked him again what she should take with her, having two little children, two girls. He was smart and honest enough to say, "Wherever you go, you won't be able to buy anything, so take whatever you may need. No one will count these things on the truck." My mother kept asking if she should take a mattress, quilts, or pillows? He replied briefly: "Take everything." So my mother packed two mattresses, two quilts, two pillows, a pot for cooking soup and a few other necessary things. She took a deep plate, spoon, fork, and knife for everyone. This inquisitiveness and self-control of my mother later influenced our situation in a way that is difficult to overestimate. My dad at that time turned out to be quite helpless. He didn't know what to do at all. We went downstairs with the luggage prepared by my mother, where there were already a lot of people. Everyone was ushered into trucks, which took us to the railway station. There, a very long freight train waited for us. It had carriages, which we entered through a sliding door. Our carriage was equipped with two tiny windows at the top. Inside, there was a hole with a tube that served for physiological needs. Adults slept on the floor, and children and teenagers climbed on plank beds that hung above. Together with us, about forty people were pushed into this carriage. The vast majority of them were Jews. Although I remember one Christian woman who was a nurse by profession. She stuck in my memory because she once fainted, and I saw such a thing for the first time in my life. Our trip lasted about three weeks.[60]

---

60 Interview with Bianka Goldman carried out on December 20, 2016.

That journey was occasionally interrupted by stops, during which the door was opened and a pot of warm liquid, which was called soup, was placed next to the carriage. Some adults who had problems with defecation received permission to move away into some nooks or bushes. After a longer time difficult to determine precisely, individual carriages began to be detached. During one of the stops, the Ebersohns were instructed to get off and take their bundle with them. They went further by truck. Some of the people in their group ended up in a camp made of barracks, in which men were separated from women with children, regardless of whether they formed couples or not. The Ebersohns were lucky, the camp ran out of space and the soldiers did not manage to put them there. So they were taken to the newly built houses near the forest, in each of them there were two apartments consisting of a room and a kitchen with a stove. The Ebersohns were accommodated in one of them together with friends— a married couple with a son. In total, there lived seven people in that apartment. Apart from the abovementioned stove, there was no equipment in the kitchen. In this situation, the fathers of both families decided to look around the area to arrange, or, to write directly, even steal boards and nails from which they could make bunks to sleep. Bianka claims that she gave her parents the idea, reminding them of the bunk from the train. She also remembered that her father, while preparing a place to sleep for her, severely injured his hands, doing this type of work himself probably for the first time in his life. However, he had to get used to physical effort, because he was assigned to work in the woods. When heavy snowfall and forty-degree frost came, Ludwik Ebersohn managed to get a job as a carpenter. According to Bianka's memories, her father managed to get it only because a Russian foreman took pity on him, explained to him exactly what to do and helped if necessary. Pola Ebersohn also tried to work (Bianka does not remember in what capacity), but in the local climatic conditions she was severely bothered by rheumatism and had a big problem with her hands. From their stay in Krasnouralsk, Bianka also remembers bathing in a shared bathhouse, where she and her mother used to go together. The women first soaped themselves and then helped each other to pour water to wash themselves down.[61]

On June 22, 1941, the Third Reich attacked the Soviet Union. The Germans gave that operation the code name Barbarossa. Under the pressure of a massive attack, the Soviet authorities began to correct the state's internal and foreign policy. The British forced them to normalize relations with the legally active emigré

---

61 Ibid.

authorities of the Republic of Poland. On July 30, 1941, the Sikorski-Mayski agreement was concluded, which was signed in London by the Prime Minister of the Polish Government-in-Exile, General Władysław Sikorski, and the USSR ambassador to Great Britain, Ivan Mayski. It provided, inter alia, for the resumption of diplomatic relations with the Polish government by the USSR, unilaterally terminated after the attack on Poland on September 17, 1939, the release of Polish citizens arrested and deported by the NKVD, and the creation of the Polish Armed Forces in the USSR, which were to be subject to the legal Polish Government-in-Exile. General Władysław Anders, previously imprisoned in Lubyanka (colloquial name of the seat and prison of the KGB in Moscow) headed that formation, which became known colloquially as the General Anders's Army. Those great political events had a direct impact on the situation of Poles and Polish Jews in the USSR. The Ebersohns were informed that they were free and could move anywhere they wanted . . .

In that situation, Bianka's parents, after a conference with two friendly families with whom they shared the Soviet misery, decided that they would go south, because there was already a great hunger in Krasnouralsk. Bianka remembers that her dad and the other fathers from the abovementioned families were called the "holy trinity" made up of an engineer, a doctor, and a lawyer, her father. The basis of the Ebersohns' meals at the time were frugal soups, which Bianka's mother cooked using one potato and one onion. Everyone was also afraid of the next cold winter. The three families agreed that in the south it would be at least warmer and it would be possible to get rice and fruit sooner, which gave a better chance of survival. They left for Kyrgyzstan, a several weeks' journey, which was prolonged because Bianka's sister got sick with diphtheria on the road and had a very high fever. They had to stay in Tashkent (now the capital of Uzbekistan). Finally they reached Jalalabad, a city located in the western part of Kyrgyzstan (near the border with Uzbekistan). They intended to go on, but the train line they were travelling ended there. Therefore, they decided to stay in Jalalabad, where they remained until 1946. They lived in a room rented from a Kyrgyz woman. Bianka's father found employment in a footwear factory, where he worked as a guard, which was typical of Soviet conditions. Every now and then, transports with manufactured shoes left the factory, however, there was a risk that they would be stolen along the way. Ludwik Ebersohn was supposed to protect them, and on the way back he took the leather needed to make another batch of footwear to the factory. That work was lighter than in Krasnouralsk. The family members often did not eat well; they did not suffer hunger anymore, yet a slice of bread was still a luxury . . . Bianka's mother worked three shifts in a sugar beet processing plant, which made syrups and preserves. The work was associated with the privilege of receiving a jar of sweet beet jam or syrup once in a while. Bianka remembers that one day, when her dad was on a business trip, and her mother brought a jar of jam, the mother and the two girls decided to eat it immediately. It was already dark, there was no electric lighting in the house, and an oil lamp was lit if needed. Oil had to be saved, so they ate the jam with a spoon in the dark, savouring its taste, Bianka remembers to this day how wonderful and sweet it was, with crispy pieces of fruit . . . which in the morning turned out to be bees drowned in marmalade. Pola comforted the children that they consumed an additional portion of protein in this way.[62] Just like in Krasnouralsk, Bianka and her sister attended a Russian school in Jalalabad. Bianka graduated from the eighth form of primary school there. In the USSR, a ten-year school system was in force, thanks to which, after returning to Poland, she could enroll in the first form of high school. Children over the age of twelve often did various smaller jobs, which is why the girl helped, for example, to collect cabbage in the fields. And that is how the family survived until the end of World War II. They dreamed of returning to Poland, so they were glad to hear that a special train would soon be provided for repatriates. They got on it on April 15, 1946, on Bianka's birthday, and began a long journey to Poland.[63]

The tragic fate of Polish Jews in the Soviet Union was well documented by the Historical Department, appointed by the order of General Władysław Anders at the end of 1941, later transformed into the Historical Office. That institution collected documents and accounts of the deportees. It was installed in places where General Anders's Army was stationed: in Iraq, Eretz Yisrael, Egypt, and Italy. Its last headquarters was in Foxley, UK.[64] Thanks to the research of the Historical Office, we find out that friendly treatment of Jews in this country (often perceived by Poles as favouring them) lasted very shortly, they were quickly removed from positions related to administration, and were mainly directed to poorly paid manual labour. Merchants, craftsmen, and freelancers were deprived of their jobs, and often of houses or flats. Synagogues were closed and religious practices were forbidden. Russians made sure that Jews would work on Jewish holidays; lists of attendance, which had not been previously used, were

---

62 Ibid.
63 Ibid.
64 Gąsowski, *Polscy Żydzi w sowieckiej Rosji*, 224–225.

introduced at the time.⁶⁵ Cadet Corporal Dr. Menachem Buchweitz, who was employed in the Historical Office since June 1943, collected and compiled numerous examples of persecution of Jews:

> "I remember when one of the chiefs, seeing a Jew praying on the upper bunk [the thing happened in the camp—T.G.], pulled his *tefillin*, got him on the ground, and shouted brutally, 'We do not need God here!'" or "After my father's funeral I returned for a meal and right after finishing work I gathered ten Jews [to make the so-called *minyan* required for solemn prayer—T.G.] and I wanted to say a prayer, for which I was beaten so much that my nose was bleeding. I resisted. They punished me with two days of solitary confinement and fasting."⁶⁶

Birobidzhan, praised in various places around the world, the capital of the Jewish Autonomous Region created by the decision of Joseph Stalin, was assessed unambiguously by those who visited it personally: "As for Biro-Bidzhan, this would be perfectly explained by young boys from Zamość who volunteered to go there in 1935, and whose signatures from 1936 I saw in 1941 on the ceiling of a gulag barrack: 'Biro-Bidzhan is a concentration camp of Russian Jewry.'"⁶⁷

On May 7, 1945, just before three in the morning, the Nazis signed the act of surrender in the headquarters of General Dwight Eisenhower's Allied Expeditionary Force in Reims, France. Stalin categorically demanded the signing of the act of unconditional surrender of the Third Reich armed forces should be repeated the following day, that time at the headquarters of Marshal Georgy Zhukov, located in the building of the sapper school in Berlin. The final acts accompanying the war also prove that the wartime fate of the Goldmans and the Ebersohns was specific and differed from the experiences of most Poles and Jews. When the war was over, reactions to current events were most often twofold. In principle, nothing worse could happen to the Jews than the Nazi occupation, hence the coming Soviet army was welcomed with hope and sometimes even enthusiasm. That attitude was not understood by Poles, who commonly expressed fears that one occupation would be replaced by another. Neither the Goldmans nor the

---

65 Ibid., 227–233.
66 M. Buchweitz, *Żydzi polscy pod władzą sowiecką (przyczynki do zobrazowania sowieckiej rzeczywistości)*, quoted in Gąsowski, *Polscy Żydzi w sowieckiej Rosji*, 233.
67 Ibid., 235. Cf. A. Patek, *Birobidżan. Sowiecka ziemia obiecana? Żydowski Obwód Autonomiczny w ZSRR*, Krakow 1997; R. Weinberg, *Stalin's Forgotten Zion. Birobidzhan and the Making of a Soviet Jewish Homeland. An Illustrated History. 1928–1996*, Berkeley 1998.

Ebersohns had any illusions about installing the new political system in Poland. As a rule, Maks Goldman was reluctant to intrusive state interference in the economy and private lives of citizens. He preferred self-employment, responsibility and independence. He anxiously watched the Red Army robbing the "Bata" factory, taking absolutely everything that could be taken: outer and sole leather, threads, linen and auxiliary materials. Due to the approaching front, the Germans fled Radom, and the employees turned to Maks Goldman as the person in the top position to help save the factory employing 2.5 thousand people in the city. Maks was understood by the city commander, but they were not even admitted to the commander of the unit that took and plundered Bata. Their intervention proved to be in vain[68]. Marcel's father also directly experienced what Soviet "brotherhood" meant—seeing a soldier who had a broken lighter and could not light a cigarette, he offered him his own. After a while, he lost the elegant little thing, because the soldier not only took advantage of his favour, but also forced an exchange of lighters. Moreover, after a visit of Russian officers to the house, it turned out that Marcel's mother's watch and a silver "onion," that is, a silver watch with an opening dial, which was in a glass cabinet in the living room, were lost. Although broken, it had a sentimental value as a family memento. Then, Marcel's parents were attacked in the meadow when they were returning from work (Sara often met her husband on his way back). A group of soldiers attacked them, knocked them over, and robbed them—his father lost his watch, and his mother a gold chain, they also stole his purse and money.[69] As Marcel concluded with humour: "This is how we became a watchless family."[70] The Ebersohns knew what the "new order" coming from the East meant, even without this kind of incidents, since they had just returned from there. Probably, the thought of leaving Poland started to sprout in both families, to turn into confidence in the first postwar years.

The subject of war and the Holocaust inevitably raises questions about the situation in Eretz Yisrael at the time. It is not true that Zionist activists living there remained passive in the face of those tragic events. They did not really improve the position of Jews in Europe, but not because they did not want to, they simply could not. Before the war, they called on Jews to emigrate, those who listened to them had a much better chance of survival. During the war, they tried

---

68 Goldman, *Iskierki życia*, 78–79.
69 Ibid., 80.
70 Ibid., 81.

to reach European Jews with humanitarian aid, of course they could do little, because in the areas occupied by Nazi Germany, the field of activity for Jewish organisations was to a far extent limited. In Eretz Yisrael, the behaviour of Zionist activists (as well as the behaviour of politically uninvolved Jews born there) towards the Jews who had survived the Holocaust and arrived from Europe differed and was not always pleasant, which is confirmed by many preserved testimonies. The survivors remembered the hurtful words of contempt and misunderstanding. It was experienced by Celina Ortner (Shatil after marriage), who arrived in Eretz Yisrael on November 4, 1944 aboard the ship *Salah al-Din*.[71] During the first two weeks of their stay, together with other travel companions, they talked about their experiences in Europe. Initially, they had the impression that they were listened attentively, but:

> When they were allowed to leave Atlit, they were amazed that none of these stories appeared in the press. The entire Jewish community completely ignored them. Ignorance, self-exaltation, disbelief, and rejection were experienced by all those who tried to share their stories.... "We all shut ourselves away," says Celina. It was only after the Eichmann trial in 1961 that the atmosphere changed.[72]

Zionist leaders tried to get a clear picture of the situation in Europe:

> The leaders of the Jewish community, Ben-Gurion and Shertok (he later changed his name to Sharett) and Asher Ben Natan from Mosad, which was not Mosad at the time, came to listen to them. Celina had unique memory, almost phenomenal. For three days she sat with Asher Ben Natan, who wrote her accounts down, and told him her story.[73]

Celina Ortner's testimony also reveals several issues that should not escape our attention. The first, of course small, groups of Holocaust survivors began to reach Eretz Yisrael before the end of World War II. The British directed them to the internment camp for illegal immigrants fleeing Nazi rule they had created in Atlit on August 16, 1939. The camp was located in the territory of a military base, which was founded there by the British in 1938. Atlit was a small fishing village on the outskirts of Haifa with a large natural bay, which for obvious

---

71 E. Pillersdorf, *Celina*, trans. M. Sobelman, J. Stöcker-Sobelman, Krakow–Budapest 2012, 125.
72 Ibid., 128.
73 Ibid., 127.

reasons began to be used as a port. Both Jews and Arabs lived there. Under the UN General Assembly Resolution no. 181 of November 29, 1947, the place belonged to the Jewish state.

Fig. 40. A group of Jewish orphans who survived the Holocaust, after being registered in the Atlit camp, July 14, 1944, photo: Zoltan Kluger, public domain

Celina Ortner was not one of the first refugees from Europe to be accommodated in Atlit. Already in 1940, a group of over 1,000 people rescued from the ship *Patria* arrived there.[74] In 1941, about 800 Jews who fled from Bulgaria and Romania found themselves in the camp. In 1942, the British changed the purpose of the camp: first of all, they began to locate captured Italian and German soldiers there. However, Atlit was still a sort of gathering point for newly arriving

---

74 Before that, they were on the list of about 5,000 Jews whom the British administration considered illegal immigrants and decided to send back to Mauritius. It was intended to send them there on *Patria*. In response to that, the Jewish self-defense group Hagana detonated a bomb on that ship on November 25, 1940. The Hagana fighters only planned to do some damage to the ship, but as a result of a poorly calculated explosive, the ship, on which there were about 1,800 people, sank, together with over 200 people. Those who survived were transported to the camp in Atlit, and with time they were released.

Fig. 41. A nurse with an immigrant child, July 14, 1944,
photo: Zoltan Kluger, public domain

Fig. 42. Nurses playing with children in the Atlit camp, July 14, 1944,
photo: Zoltan Kluger, public domain

Fig. 43. Newly arrived Jewish orphans who survived the Holocaust in the Atlit camp, July 14, 1944, photo: Zoltan Kluger, public domain

Jews. Among them, there were, for example, orphans, for whom care had to be organised. The internment camp was active again in 1945–1948, when survivors of the Holocaust began to flow to Eretz Yisrael on a large scale.

After the creation of the State of Israel, the internment camp was officially closed. There was, however, a transit camp for newly arrived. In 1956 and 1967, Egyptian prisoners of war were detained there. In 1987, the Israeli authorities declared the camp area a historical site and decided to create a museum dedicated to illegal immigration and to the fight for the right to immigrate to Eretz Yisrael. A special wing of the museum was dedicated to the history of the Israeli Navy. In this way, the institution named the Clandestine Immigration and Naval Museum, Haifa was created. It allows us to understand the living conditions and problems of those who, trying to save themselves from the Holocaust, wanted to live in Eretz Yisrael. Combining two issues in one place: immigration to Eretz Yisrael and the history of Israeli naval forces is not accidental. The museum was opened in a historical space, through which it was given the value of authenticity. However, natural conditions predisposed this place to establish a maritime museum. Historical connections of immigration to Eretz Yisrael with Haifa (next to which Atlit is located) as well as with the birth of the Israeli navy are of paramount importance. When the port of Haifa opened in the 1930s, it became the destination point for the vast majority of Jewish immigrants arriving in Eretz

Yisrael, or later to Israel, by sea. Mount Carmel was usually the first sight of Israel appearing to newcomers before they could go ashore. Finally, a fundamental matter—the Israeli navy had two main goals: to defend the maritime borders of the state and to ensure the safety of the ships on which Jews migrated to Israel. Secret Israeli army missions were often associated with that. In addition, some of the ships on which immigrants arrived were converted into warships. Let us add that many of the Israeli navy creators were recruited from among those who arrived.[75]

The first groups of Jews who survived the Shoah, although they met with misunderstanding and a certain dose of arrogance in Eretz Yisrael, first and foremost experienced care and attention from the locals. It required considerable effort, because the local Jewish community was struggling with many problems related to matters of security and material existence. Zionist activists and members of local Jewish communities did a lot to make new immigrants feel as comfortable as possible, despite the objectively difficult conditions in which everyone was. They achieved measurable success in this respect, which can also be confirmed by the accounts of those who previously expressed their regret because of misunderstandings and various unpleasant situations. Let us give the voice to Celina Ortner again, who recalls the first moments spent in Eretz Yisrael: "We were in Eretz Yisrael, we were not afraid. We were not afraid that something bad would happen to us. We sang, talked about the kibbutz, there was a sense of community."[76]

The thesis that Zionist activists tried to cut themselves off from the problem of the Holocaust seems to be wrong. After all, the Warsaw Ghetto Uprising became one of the founding myths of the State of Israel. The heroism of the insurgents was compared to the heroic battle of the Maccabees. The Land of Israel became the first place where the Holocaust of Jews began to be commemorated. In 1943, the Yad Mordechai kibbutz was established, named after Mordechai Anielewicz. Moreover, this kibbutz played a strategic role during the War of Independence, because it stopped large forces of Arab troops that were pushing towards Tel Aviv. Thanks to that, Jewish self-defense forces (Hagana) were able to prepare the defense of Tel Aviv and saved the city from destruction. In 1948, the construction of the Lochamei HaGeta'ot kibbutz (Hebrew:

---

75 The Clandestine Immigration and Naval Museum, http://www.visit-haifa.org/eng/The_Clandestine_Immigration_and_Naval_Museum, accessed March 24, 2018.
76 E. Pillersdorf, *Celina . . .*, 127.

Fighters of the Ghetto) began. Among its founders there were Jews who survived the Holocaust, including insurgents from the Warsaw Ghetto, such as Yitzhak Zuckerman and his wife Zivia Lubetkin. In 1950, the Ghetto Fighters' House was created in the kibbutz. It was one of the first museums and educational institutions in the world to commemorate the Holocaust and the heroes of the Warsaw Ghetto Uprising. In 1953, Yad Vashem—the Institute of Remembrance of Martyrs and Heroes of the Holocaust—was created, about which I will write in more detail in the next chapter.

Fig. 45. Jankiel (Jaakow) Wiernik (1889–1972), building a model of the Treblinka extermination camp for the Museum in Lochamei HaGeta'ot, photo taken before 1959, public domain

It is true that the fate of Jews in Europe during World War II was difficult to comprehend. Questions that survivors could perceive as humiliating multiplied. For a more complete understanding of the essence of that drama, which was experienced by millions of Jews, a lesson related to the trial of Adolf Eichmann, which began on April 11, 1961 in Jerusalem, was needed. Eichmann was the coordinator and one of the main executors of the terrifying "plan of the final solution to the Jewish question." The testimonies of witnesses widely reported in the Israeli media (including, for example, Yitzhak Zuckerman, also known as Antek) were perhaps even more important than the words he spoke before the court. They allowed the Israelis to understand how tragic and hopeless the situation of European Jews during World War II was. Earlier it was suggested

Fig. 45. The Ghetto Fighters House in the Lochamei HaGeta'ot kibbutz, 2011, public domain

Fig. 46. Monument in the Lochamei HaGeta'ot kibbutz, February 2017, photo: Bukvoed, public domain

that Jews had given consent to be slaughtered without resistance. The process revealed the backstage of the war, including the fact that Jews were in absolute isolation. They had nowhere to escape, lacked the means to resist more. Few gave them a helping hand. Representatives of other nations mostly showed indifference towards their drama. There were also those who were ready to cooperate with the Nazi occupier, for instance the already-mentioned blackmailers. Not to mention the states openly collaborating with Hitler, which engaged their administrative apparatus in the process of exterminating Jews. Finally, the heroic act of the heroes of the Warsaw Ghetto Uprising, which lasted from April 19 to mid-May 1943, was recalled. A testimony of the Jewish underground and self-help during the war was given. At the same time, it turned out that, despite the tragic situation of Jews, their resistance against the Nazis was still one of the largest in Europe.

3

The Aliyah Time— Youth, Part Two (1945–1954)

The postwar period brought many new aspects to the history of Poland as well as the history of Jews. It was then that the Jewish life in Poland collapsed for good. First of all, only about 10% of approximately 3.5 million Jews living within the borders of the prewar Poland survived the Holocaust. It seems reasonable to ask whether in such conditions it was still possible to continue the heritage that we know from before the outbreak of World War II. Certainly not in the same shape, yet several hundred thousand Jews who survived could initiate something new. The largest group survived in the Soviet Union. Some Jews saved themselves, staying hidden in Poland occupied by Germany. Only a handful managed to see the release from German extermination and concentration camps.[1] Repatriates from the territories occupied by the Soviet Union were directed primarily to the so-called Recovered Territories, mainly to the territory of Lower Silesia[2]. It was there that Jewish labour cooperatives, cultural centers, schools, kindergartens, and after-school clubs were founded.[3]

Poland became part of the Soviet sphere of influence, which brought significant consequences for Polish-Jewish relations. For Jews, the end of the war simply meant liberation. On the other hand, many Poles, as I have already pointed out, thought that they fell from one captivity into another one, therefore, some of the underground and guerrilla formations members decided to stay hidden

---

1   Detailed calculations are presented by L. Dobroszycki in the book *Survivors of the Holocaust in Poland. A Portrait Based on Jewish Community Records, 1944–47*, Armonk–London 1994.

2   See B. Szaynok, "Ludność żydowska na Dolnym Śląsku 1945–1950," *Acta Universitatis Wratislaviensis. Historia* 146 (2000): 1–210; idem, "Początki osadnictwa żydowskiego na Dolnym Śląsku po II wojnie światowej: maj 1945–styczeń 1946," *Biuletyn Żydowskiego Istytutu Historycznego* 4, no. 2 (1994/95): 45–63; idem, "Żydzi we Wrocławiu po II wojnie światowej," *Rocznik Wrocławski* 4 (1997): 173–190.

3   See M. Grynberg, *Żydowska spółdzielczość pracy w Polsce w latach 1945–1949*, Warsaw 1986; A. Sommer Schneider, *Sze'erit hapleta. Ocaleni z Zagłady. Działalność American Jewish Joint Distribution Committee w Polsce w latach 1945–1989*, Krakow 2014.

and continue the fight, this time with the communists. Once again, there was a clear distinction in the situation of Polish citizens: Poles and Jews. Communist authorities contributed to this fact, purposely antagonising social relations and following the principle "divide and rule." The presence of Jews in the security organs became problematic for Polish-Jewish relations. Contrary to anti-Jewish propaganda, there was no over-representation of Jews in the secret police, although they held a number of exposed positions there and because of that were often associated with that body. The newly formed state was headed by the prewar Polish communist Bolesław Bierut (1892–1956), while the face of the secret police was Jakub Berman (1901–1984), also a communist but coming from a Jewish family. From 1944, he belonged to the Political Bureau of the Polish Workers' Party (PPR), and later to the Political Bureau of the Polish United Workers' Party (PZPR). In the years 1949–1954 he was a member of the Committee on Public Security of the PZPR Political Bureau, the body directly supervising the Stalinist security apparatus in Poland. In addition, Hilary Minc (1905–1974), minister for industry and trade and deputy prime minister for economic affairs, also a Polish Jew, became a symbol of the abolition of economic freedom. So, Bierut, Berman, and Minc formed the top leadership of the party and the state. Two of those three powerful people were Jews. These proportions gained symbolic significance, but in the reality of the Jewish population in Poland and its involvement in the communist apparatus, they meant nothing. Just like Bierut did not pursue Polish interests, Berman and Minc did not represent Jews or act in their favour. This is evidenced by the fact that the wave of persecution they had started also affected Jews. The owners of various Jewish institutions of business were also victims of Minc's "battle for trade." The percentage of Jews in the apparatus of repression (in relation to the total number of this group's members) was not relatively higher than the percentage of Poles present in it. However, symbols often speak to human imagination louder than facts. To make matters worse, after years of war-induced demoralisation, violence spread, and it often took the form of antisemitic aggression. The culmination was the anti-Jewish pogrom in Kielce on July 4, 1946, when several dozen people (including pregnant women and children) were brutally murdered, and many others suffered serious injuries.[4]

---

4   See B. Szaynok, *Pogrom Żydów w Kielcach 4 lipca 1946*, intro. K. Kersten, Warsaw 1992; J. Tokarska-Bakir, *Pod klątwą. Społeczny portret pogromu kieleckiego*, vol. 1, Warsaw 2018; idem, ed., *Pod klątwą. Społeczny portret pogromu kieleckiego*, vol. 2: *Dokumenty*, Warsaw, 2018.

After the Kielce pogrom, the mass emigration of Jews from Poland to Eretz Yisrael intensified; it was an important impulse to act, but in addition there were other factors pushing Jews out of Poland. There were many reasons for emigration, above all, the political circumstances mentioned above, the atmosphere of postwar lawlessness and violence (not only physical, but also verbal), and a sense of hopelessness. Many people did not see their future in the place where all their loved ones died. There was also a strong belief in the need to build an independent Jewish state.

At first, the Goldmans tried to shape their lives in Poland, which was due to practical issues to a certain extent. First, they extended their stay in Radom so that Marcel could graduate from the gymnasium, here he received the so-called small high school diploma (Polish: *mała matura*). Then, however, they left the city because they did not consider it safe:

> Radom was not a big city, we can say that everyone knew everyone. Meanwhile, the atmosphere around us began to thicken, because in addition to Janek Gierad, who had Slavic looks, our mother's brother, who managed to survive the war, appeared in our house. His looks, in turn, indicated that he was a Jew. Our neighbours were, so to speak, confused with this situation and began to make various guesses. Because there were various acts of aggression against Jews around, my parents decided to leave for Krakow.[5]

In his hometown, Marcel began to attend the State High School of Administration and Commerce. After graduating, he started studies at the Krakow Academy of Commerce (today's Krakow University of Economics).[6] He managed to finish the first year of studies with success and started the second one. Theoretically, that was not much, but allowed Marcel to gain valuable competences:

---

5   Interview with Marcel Goldman carried out on January 25, 2019. In the years 1946–1947, Poland was visited by Mordechai Tsanin, an Israeli journalist who was born in Poland. He reached the former centers of the Jewish population and described them in a series of reportages, which was published in book fom in 1952 in Tel Aviv in Yiddish, under the title *Iber sztejn un sztok. A rajze iber hundert chorewgeworene kehiles in Pojln*. In 2018, a Polish translation of the book was published *Przez ruiny i zgliszcza. Podróż po stu zgładzonych gminach żydowskich w Polsce*, trans. M. Adamczyk-Garbowska, Warsaw 2018. In this book, the reader will find as interesting as depressing descriptions of what was left of the former Jewish life in Poland immediately after World War II, including texts directly related to Radom (339–345) and Krakow (399–413).

6   Interview with Marcel Goldman carried out on January 7, 2018.

> I assess the level of education at the Krakow University of Economics very highly. Great emphasis was put on practical skills. To pass the first year of studies, each of us had to demonstrate the ability to create a company's balance sheet and close annual accounts. Thanks to that, I was able to look for a job as an accountant in Israel. In addition, we had extremely valuable classes in the preparation of trade documents. The professor who taught that course put a lot of passion into it and was very knowledgeable in this respect. I remember the first class with him. He told us to prepare a document, and then we were given the task to delete all unnecessary words from it. Thanks to that, I acquired the ability to write in a matter-of-fact way, without taking the reader's time to read unnecessary words and phrases—it is also important now, after all, we live in the times when people do not have time to read long elaborates.[7]

In Krakow, the Goldmans lived in the flat they were allocated on Wrocławska Street. Marcel remembers that it was quite neat, giving the impression of being built in the 1930s. The caretaker's son already lived in the apartment they had occupied before the war. The Goldmans did not even attempt to recover it. Marcel says that they did not want to kick anyone out. This, of course, can be understood, the thing is that they did not even ask for the furniture and paintings that had remained there. This leads to the conclusion that Maksymilian and Sara knew that attempts to recover prewar property, which was already managed by Poles, often ended tragically for Jews.

In 1947, Marcel's parents returned to their real surname. On that basis, they obtained passports and ID cards. Marcel enrolled in high school, still using documents issued during the war. Therefore, he acted as Marceli Galas, a Roman Catholic. He began to use the name Goldman again in 1949, on his way to Israel. Looking for a source of income for the family, Sara and Maksymilian, together with friends, opened a haberdashery and clothes warehouse at Starowiślna Street.

In 1948, Marcel's parents decided to emigrate from Poland. In Marcel's opinion, they decided to take that step mainly under the influence of tragic news about the postwar fate of Jews. One depressing event was the pogrom which took place in Krakow on the Sabbath day of August 11, 1945, which was directly caused by the rumour of an alleged ritual murder committed by Jews on Polish children (at least one person died then, Róża Berger, who survived the stay in the Auschwitz-Birkenau camp, many others were injured, including several

---

7   Interview with Marcel Goldman carried out on January 26, 2019.

Youth, Part Two (1945–1954) | 127

Fig. 47. Marcel Goldman at Krakow's Market Square, 1947, family collections of Marcel and Bianka Goldman (Tel Aviv)

Fig. 48. State High School of Administration and Commerce in Krakow yearbook, 1946/47 school year, class Rc, the first student from the left is Marcel Goldman, here under the name Galas, family collections of Marcel and Bianka Goldman (Tel Aviv)

serious cases).⁸ However, what shocked them most and scared them was the already mentioned Kielce pogrom of July 1946 with dozens of victims of that brutal murder. The communist system built in Poland, to which Marcel's parents had a strongly critical attitude, had to play a role too. The government seriously hampered the lives of everyone who wanted to run an independent business. At that time, his father's arguments that it was not worth spending the rest of their lives in a communist country did not yet get to Marcel, although he remembered his words forever that "he does not want to live in a country where they 'give,' but in one where you can buy for money."⁹ His father's values and experience gathered in Poland had an influence on Marcel. Leaving Poland, he was deeply convinced that the state should not interfere too much in the economy and social relations. He also decided that he would avoid state jobs.

Fig. 49. Marcel Goldman with his sister Nela on a walk in Krakow, around 1947–1948, family collections of Marcel and Bianka Goldman (Tel Aviv)

Initially, Marcel did not want to leave Poland, there were many reasons for staying: his started studies, a little sense of stability, new friendships, passionate feelings for a girl he met, and fear of new challenges in the emerging Jewish State. It became clear, however, that his parents would leave without him. During that

---

8   Anna Cichopek estimates that there were five fatal victims in that pogrom. See A. Cichopek, *Pogrom Żydów w Krakowie 11 sierpnia 1945*, Warsaw 2000, 87.
9   Interview with Marcel Goldman carried out on December 18, 2016.

time, they could no longer legally get out of the Iron Curtain. With the Polish passport they could, however, cross the border with Czechoslovakia, which also belonged to the Eastern Bloc after the war. And from Czechoslovakia it was still possible to legally emigrate to Israel.

When Maksymilian and Sara Goldman started their journey from Czechoslovakia to the new homeland, they were provided with passports and all other necessary documents, and even managed to send a package containing their small belongings. They covered part of the route to Israel by land, then they took a ship to Haifa, but it is not known exactly which or from which port.[10]

It is possible that their departure to Czechoslovakia resulted from something more than the circumstances outlined above. It cannot be ruled out that Marcel's parents still had some doubts related to the emigration to Israel. It seems unlikely, but it can be assumed that Czechoslovakia was to be a test. The communist system was also imposed on this country, but it was considered more friendly towards Jews. The Czechoslovak authorities supported Israel not only diplomatically, but also with arms deliveries. Well, this dilemma cannot be unequivocally resolved, because Sara and Maksymilian are dead, and the materials they left behind do not give any clues in this matter. The fact that Marcel's father's sister lived in Prague certainly helped: the Goldmans had a starting point. For the time it took them to prepare appropriate living conditions in Prague, both their daughters were placed in a Jewish children's home in Krakow. Marcel, who was already studying and working at the time, took care of them there. In his free time, he looked after the girls and took them for walks. In a short time, almost the whole family (without Marcel) found themselves in Prague. They also submitted papers to leave for Israel relatively quickly. So even if we assume (quite riskily) that the stay in Czechoslovakia was to be a kind of experiment, apparently their experiences were negative.

The Ebersohns also decided to leave Poland. It sounds a bit paradoxical: they paid for their ties with Poland with exile (they did not accept the Soviet passport). They waited a long time for a chance to return to the country. They remembered Bielsko with nostalgia... The journey from Kyrgyzstan was not easy, they spent several weeks on the train. At that time, no one provided them with food, they had to take care of it themselves amd buy food when the train stopped on its way. Nobody knew for how long the train stopped—it could be half an hour, an hour or even longer, they had to ask the train staff about the duration.

---

10 Ibid.

In those difficult conditions, women proved to be the most resourceful. In the Ebersohn family, Pola looked for women who earned extra money by selling food and supplied the family with necessary products, such as bread, cheese, and milk. Sometimes tradeswomen would come to the train station, so they could save some time and not only buy something, but also calmly prepare a meal. Bianka's mother took some vegetables with her, and during the train stops she cooked soup on a hastily lit fire—she set up two bricks on which she put the pot. It happened that the engine driver started without looking at anything. In such situations, Bianka's mother had to run with a pot of soup behind the train to quickly get on it. In Poland, they intended to get to Katowice, persuaded by the Potok family, one of the three families with whom they made a heartfelt friendship during their stay in the Soviet Union. The Potoks were sure that some of their loved ones survived in Katowice and would definitely help the Ebersohns. Indeed, their aunt lived in the city, and invited everyone for a warm meal, allowed them to rest and take a bath. Bianka remembered the long table waiting for them, covered with refreshments, she recalls that she had trouble finding herself in civilized conditions:

> During several years of my life in the Soviet Union, I ate meals, mainly using a plate and a spoon. Here I saw a table set for a meal, various types of plates and cutlery. I asked my mother what to do with all that. My mom said: "See how adults eat and imitate them." Now I know how wild I had become in the exile. I was fifteen or sixteen years old at the time, and I could't handle cutlery properly. I would add that I had another problem. I disaccustomed myself from using the toilet. During my exile I got used to the fact that when I wanted to settle my physiological needs, I simply went to a secluded place and crouched. Now I had to learn to sit on the toilet bowl again.[11]

The Ebersohns probably used that hospitality for two days, then they went to Bielsko. Their house was occupied and the parents were afraid to try to regain it, so after arriving, they left Bianka with her sister at the train station, and went to the local Jewish religious community, which offered them a one-room apartment in a tenement on the fourth floor without a lift. The Ebersohns returned to the station to collect the children with the keys to that place. Bianka was delighted with it: "It seemed to me the most beautiful in the world. It had electricity

---

11   Interview with Bianka Goldman carried out on March 3, 2018.

and its own toilet—these were 'luxuries' long unknown to me."[12] Soon they moved to another, three-room apartment. Bianka does not remember in what circumstances they came into its possession. Bianka's father adapted one of the rooms and opened a law office there. The other two were occupied by the family. Bianka returned to school. Her mother paid for the teacher who gave her extra lessons on history and the Polish language, as she had fallen behind in these two subjects, but soon managed to catch up. Normality returned to their lives slowly. It was, however, a normality that left much to be desired... It is difficult to consider normal a situation in which a family's home cannot be recovered. Ludwik Ebersohn soon realised that running a law office in People's Poland would not be the same as before the war. Bianka applied for medical studies twice without success. The family believed that she was well prepared, but her social background was improper. Every day they could observe how, in Poland, the communist system was being assembled, with which they had already had previous experience from the Soviet Union.

During family meetings they agreed to emigrate from Poland. They managed to do it legally, but they had to renounce Polish citizenship. Why did they choose Israel? According to Bianka, they finally wanted to live where they could feel at home. They did not want to roam the world and risk that something bad would happen to them again in another country because they were Jews. Perhaps the decision was influenced by Bianka's sister, who joined a Zionist organization. In any case, in March 1950, the Ebersohns emigrated to Israel.[13] They came aboard the *Galil* ship, which, like *HaAtzmaut*, had previously been a cargo ship, barely adapted to the needs of human transport. Bianka remembered that there were only two shower cabins on the ship, one for the captain, and the other used by the head of the technical team. The latter told the girl that, if she wanted, she could use his cabin and take a shower. Bianka quickly ran down to the lower deck to tell her parents about that possibility. Today she recalls that the man, when he saw her with her parents, was put clean out of countenance... He probably had a different development of the situation in mind.[14]

What was happening to Marcel at the time? News about thousands of Jews migrating to Eretz Yisrael and then to independent Israel did not motivate him to leave. The example of his parents and sisters and his separation from them did

---

12 Ibid.
13 Interview with Bianka Goldman carried out on December 20, 2016; Correspondence with Bianka and Marcel Goldman, January 2, 2017.
14 Interview with Bianka Goldman carried out on June 13, 2018.

not seem to impress him at first. He remembered that the period from late 1946 to spring 1949 was full of strong and happy experiences for him. Economically, those years were not easy, indeed, they were part of the context of the postwar poverty. He had to earn a living. He was alone in the apartment abandoned by his parents. Regardless of everything, it was a period of peace, so he could try to enjoy life again. The wartime became inscribed in the biographies of his friends from high school, and then from university. At the time, young people wanted to live carefree, they organized numerous parties, often with a lot of alcohol. They had constant habits—on almost every Saturday evening they would meet to play bridge, and on Sunday mornings or afternoons boys went to the church to pick up girls leaving the mass. That group also included a female friend named Kazia, whose parents had a large house near Krakow, hence the parties often took place there. Marcel remembered that, after the parties, everyone went to sleep in the hay barn, and couples were made up there...[15]

In high school, Marcel met his first love—Marysia Dobrzyńska, who was a student in one of the parallel classes. She came from a family of petty nobles, her father died during the war, she lived with her mother in Krakow (the family also had a house in Swoszowice, currently a part of Krakow). Marcel was deeply involved emotionally, and associated serious plans for the future with Marysia, hence the subsequent separation resulting from his departure was an extremely painful experience. Marysia was such an important part of his memories that when he returned to Poland after forty years in 1989, he went to her address:

> I remembered where she lived. I was sure she would be there. A young man opened the door. I asked him if Mrs. Dobrzyńska lived there? He replied that Mrs. Dobrzyńska was already dead. I thought he was talking about Marysia's mother, who was an elderly person. I clarified that I meant her daughter, that I was asking about Marysia Dobrzyńska. The man replied that she was also dead. I still asked if her children were alive. It turned out that she died childless. The man told me her husband was alive. I didn't want to talk to her husband. If there were children, they would be a part of her and I would love to meet them. I didn't have anything to talk about with her husband. My heart ached. I was deeply affected by that situation, I felt great sadness.[16]

---

15   Correspondence with Marcel Goldman, March 23, 2018.
16   Interview with Marcel Goldman carried out on January 7, 2018.

In the spring of 1947, they both finished high school and enrolled at the Academy of Commerce. Marcel wanted to marry Marysia, however, he claims that his mother, who visited him every few weeks coming from Prague, dissuaded him from doing it. She did not forbid him to marry Marysia, but she said that the decision in that matter should be postponed, because they (she meant the rest of the family) were about to emigrate to Israel, and it was possible that Marcel would decide to do the same one day. She argued that, if their feelings survived, he would bring her to Israel after his possible emigration.

After starting his studies, Marcel had to find a job to cover the costs of living and studying. He found employment in the Trawers construction company owned by engineer Gutter—a Jew who survived the Holocaust in Slovakia with his whole family. After returning to Krakow, he managed to regain his company specializing in trade in construction timber, which he had ran before the war. It was based at Grzegórzecka Street, where a large warehouse was located. Anatol Sylwin[17] joined him, and they formed a company that received contracts, among others, for the construction of houses in Silesia.

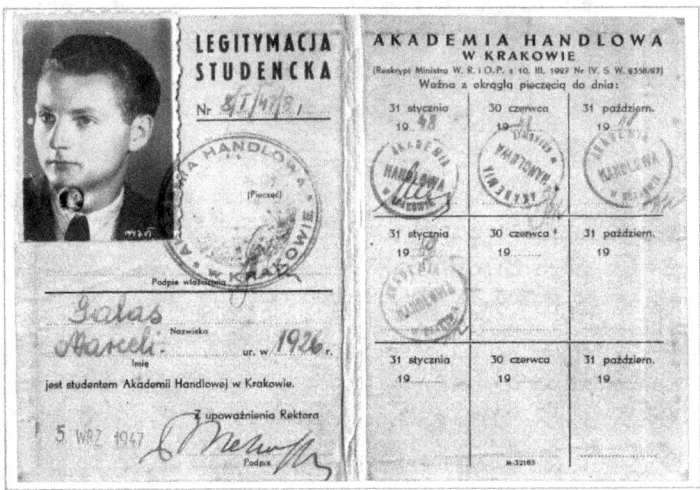

Fig. 50. Marcel Goldman's student card, still with his "war" surname Galas, family collections of Marcel and Bianka Goldman (Tel Aviv)

---

17 Anatol Sylwin, born in 1915 in Krakow, died in 2002 in Warsaw. He was a civil engineer, a graduate of the Lviv Polytechnic, an architect, and urban planner. He and his wife returned from exile in the Soviet Union after the war. Before World War II, he designed residential buildings in Krakow. After the war, he ran a construction company with Gutter. After retiring, he became involved in writing, and in 1986, the Iskry Publishing House published his debut book mixing memoirs and fiction entitled Śnieżyca.

Although the communist Polish government fought against private entrepreneurship, when it was beneficial or necessary for it, it deviated from that policy. In Silesia, the prospects for the development of mining and other industries were large, but there was a shortage of flats, so there was a risk that not only new employees would not come there, but the existing residents would leave. Therefore, private companies began to be admitted to the local construction market, the urgency of that task was even greater because coal became the basic energy source of postwar Poland. Houses were to be built quickly, their standard was not given much importance. The Trawers company, building wooden houses, was one of the companies selected to carry out that order.

Fig. 51. Marcel Goldman (third from the right) with friends in Krakow, around 1948 or 1949, family collections of Marcel and Bianka Goldman (Tel Aviv)

Fig. 52. Marcel Goldman (first from the left) with Maria Dobrzyńska and Tadeusz, a friend from Radom school, around 1948 or 1949, family collections of Marcel and Bianka Goldman (Tel Aviv)

Marcel remembers that the company employees often discussed the fact that the authorities require a rapid pace of construction, disregarding the living conditions of future tenants. For example, to save building time, toilets were placed outside—we are talking here about the so-called privies. Marcel recalls that one day engineer Sylwin, presenting the architectural plans of their housing estate in the office, jokingly stated: "The toilets will be scrumptious." Marcel first worked as a bookkeeper, but soon became a cashier and office manager. He also managed to get a job for his girlfriend Marysia. Absorbed in work and social life, he did not have time to regularly attend classes at university. As he recalls, he gave his student record book to his colleagues who collected the necessary signatures for him. When going to the exams, he often saw the lecturer for the first time. Marcel also worked for his parents as a typical sales representative. In the afternoons, he went to those shops, which were then considered elegant, within the district designated for him (it included, among others, Grodzka, Szewska and Sławkowska Streets). He put on his academic cap (green with a red rim) and walked with a suitcase that contained the designs of the goods offered by the parents' wholesaler. Supply shortages were so great that the sale of those goods did not pose any major difficulties. The commission he received on that account, as he remembers, was equivalent to his salary in a managerial position of the construction company.[18]

Except for engineer Gutter, no one at Trawers knew that Marcel was a Jew. Together, they decided that the disclosure of his origin could be badly received by the non-Jewish part of the crew, especially now that Marcel was promoted to the managerial position, earned twice the average salary in Poland, had a driver at his disposal to go to the offices, to the bank, or to Silesia, when it was necessary to pay salaries to workers, and managed the personnel. At that time, Polish-Jewish relations were very tense, so they were afraid that a young Jew in the managing role would be perceived badly.

A related story also tells about the issue of hiding one's Jewish identity after the war. The Sylwins, a Jewish family, pretended to be Christians. As Marcel recalls, the wife of engineer Sylwin was convinced that their religious affiliation was beyond doubt, while the truth was different. One day, she asked Marcel to collect her umbrella, which she had left in the Europejska café, near the Main Square. Marcel, after having taken care of business matters at the bank, went to the café in question and asked about the umbrella left by engineer Sylwin's wife:

> The waitress was comfused: "Engineer Sylwin's wife . . . ?" She didn't know who he meant. Other waiters working in the café echoed her. A discussion ensued between them. Finally one of them said: "Ah! I know . . . She is that fat Jewess who comes here for coffee! Yes, her umbrella is here, here you are." The fact that Mrs. Sylwin was a stout woman,

---

18 Interview with Marcel Goldman carried out on December 18, 2016.

so she could be called fat, is one thing. But I was very moved by the fact that she was known as a Jewish woman.[19]

This is obviously an isolated situation, but it is one of many proofs that Poles still identified Jews as a separate nation and did not take into account how the Jews wanted to present themselves.

Marcel was a keen observer of the reality surrounding him, so he drew conclusions from what was happening around him. The reality of Poland, poor and ruled by communists, was not optimistic. One must also take into account his longing for the family with whom he had so much in common. In addition, Marcel emphasises in strong words: "Having lived for about seven years on Aryan papers, I had the 'pleasure' to hear a lot of hateful, antisemitic statements. It made me feel inferior. A Jew is someone worse, and I didn't want to be worse."[20] However, the direct impulse for emigration was the news of his father's heart attack. Marcel's mother came to Krakow at that time and convinced her son that he should join the family, because due to the illness his father would not be able to provide for them. Marcel decided that he should be with his parents and take care of them.[21] So the moment of Marcel Goldman's departure from Poland came . . . Despite his young age, his life was to be thoroughly reoriented for the second time. The first time the reason was war, now emigration. Leaving Poland, he broke off with the life he had already formed. He had to part with friends and acquaintances, and above all with his beloved Marysia. Falling into the vortex of new events in Israel, facing the very difficult reality there, he did not have much chance of staying in touch with her. Due to the fact that Poland was behind the Iron Curtain, it was impossible to bring her to Israel. What is more, Marcel's own path to Israel was to be long and bumpy . . .

Before the Goldmans and the Ebersohns decided to go to Israel, several Jewish migration waves had already arrived there. The term *aliyah*, which has many meanings, is used to describe Jewish migration to Eretz Yisrael and Israel. It means "rising" and "ascending," which is why it was associated with emigration to Israel—it is a journey upwards. Given that Jerusalem is located on seven hills, these words can be taken literally, but above all they refer to higher values, because in the spiritual dimension Jerusalem is the highest place. In addition,

---

19 Ibid.
20 Correspondence with Marcel Goldman, July 8, 2019.
21 Ibid.

one must be mature in the spiritual sense for an *aliyah* (rise to the heights). Somewhat jokingly, but in accordance with the truth, we can say that anyone who decides to emigrate to Israel will have to climb a hill. On the other hand, the opposite term was used for the phenomenon of emigration or re-emigration from Israel—*yerida*, which means "descent." Jews who migrate to Israel rise to heights, those who leave it, descend. This symbolism is very meaningful and has roots in the Torah: when reference is made to Jews leaving Canaan, the term "descent" is used. For example, in the Book of Genesis we read: "Now there was a famine in the land, besides the former famine that was in the days of Abraham. And Isaac went to Gerar to Abimelech king of the Philistines. And the Lord appeared to him and said, 'Do not go down to Egypt; dwell in the land of which I shall tell you'" (Genesis 26:1–2). The rabbinical commentary explains: "Do not go down to Egypt—For you are an *ola temima* [perfect burnt offering] and it is inappropriate for you to be outside the Land" (Rashi).[22] Elsewhere, it was written: "When Jacob saw that there were provisions to be had in Egypt, he said to his sons: 'Why are you looking [like that]? I hear that there are provisions to be had in Egypt. Go down and provide for us from there, that we may live and not die'" (Genesis 42: 1–2). Jacob did not use the simple verb "go" (Hebrew: *lechu*), he said "go down" (Hebrew: *redu*), as Rabbi Sacha Pecaric notes, "thus alluding to the two hundred and ten years they will be exiled to Egypt. The gematria (numeric value) of the word *redu* is 210."[23]

At the end of the nineteenth century, Zionists reached for that phraseology, and adapted it to their own propaganda needs. The first *aliyah la-aretz* (Hebrew, "ascending to the land [of Israel]," 1880–1903) took the name BILU. It is an acronym of the biblical call: *Beit Ya'akov lechu ve nelcha*, or O house of Jacob, come ye and let us go (Isaiah 2:5). The second part of this sentence was omitted: *be darkei Adoni*, "in the light of the Lord." In the years 1904–1914 the second *aliyah* took place. It was a crucial stage in the process of building the independent Israel. This *aliyah* was largely made up of people motivated by a difficult financial situation, but there were also those inspired by Zionist or socialist ideas. Among the participants of the second *aliyah* there was, among others, David Ben-Gurion! As part of the third *aliyah* (1918–1923), many pioneers (Hebrew: *halutzim*) from Zionist youth organisations such as HeHalutz, HaShachar, and HaShomer HaTzair came to Israel. A significant percentage of the fourth *aliyah*

---

22 *Tora. Pardes Lauder*, book 1: *Bereshit*, ed. Rabbi S. Pecaric, Krakow 2001, 162.
23 Ibid., 264.

(1924–1926) were Jewish middle class representatives. They decided to emigrate from Poland because of the new, unfavourable to them, tax and monetary reforms made by Władysław Grabski,[24] which is why it is often referred to as the Grabski *aliyah*. The fifth *aliyah* (1929–1939) was made up primarily of European Jews fleeing from the growing antisemitism.

Marcel's emigration in this context was not unusual. It was part of the biography of millions of people living in Poland, both Jews and Christians (in the nineteenth and twentieth centuries, many Poles left Poland due to economic or political reasons). Besides, the migration concerned not only Polish territories, as Jews from other countries also moved frequently. The motif of the wandering Jew is universal, but also, unfortunately, antisemetic.[25] The problem has long troubled many artists, writers, scholars and ordinary people, some even tried to look for a quasi-religious explanation for it, others saw the causes of the phenomenon primarily in politics. Meanwhile, a single man was lost somewhere in it, with his dramas and experiences. Even when entire groups were leaving, they were co-created by people, each of whom experienced the departure in their own way. That is why it is so important to emphasize that Marcel's journey had a unique character. It was not accompanied by the enthusiasm of Zionist pioneers migrating to Eretz Yisrael before the outbreak of World War II. However, he did not feel this ambivalence or even contempt for Israel, which was often felt by communists forced to leave People's Poland for various reasons and in various circumstances. Unlike the emigrants from before World War II and the period immediately after it, he did not go to Eretz Yisrael, but to independent Israel. The proclamation of state independence took place on May 14, 1948, and Marcel Goldman was there in 1949.

---

24 Władysław Grabski (1874–1938), Polish minister of treasury and two-time prime minister.

25 The antisemitic genesis of this motif is highlighted by Władysław Panas, who writes: "The Jew Wanderer (Ahaswer) . . . is a legend spread since the Middle Ages about a Jew who allegedly insulted Christ led to Golgotha or did not let him be his guest. As a punishment, he was sentenced to eternal wandering, which was to end with the return of Christ. In this form, the topos became part of the folklore and many European literatures, as well as antisemitic literature. This is one semantic level of this topos. Another is the later universalisation that elevates it outside the Jewish context: as a universal archetype of a pilgrim, a wanderer. In this sense, Ahaswer's theme often appears in Romantic literature, and in the twentieth century in the period of Young Poland. . . . There is also another use of this motif: as a topos imposed on writers dealing with Jewish issues, as a "place" of confrontation." W. Panas, "Topika judajska," in *Słownik literatury polskiej XX wieku*, ed. A. Brodzka, M. Puchalska, M. Semczuk, A. Sobolewska, E. Szary-Matywiecka, Wrocław 1992, 1095–1104.

Most Polish Jews who came to Israel shortly after World War II experienced the death of their relatives—grandparents, parents, siblings, and others—during the Holocaust. Marcel was lucky that his parents and sisters were waiting for him in Israel. Shortly after the war, Jews in Eretz Yisrael, and later also in independent Israel, were looking for those who had a chance to survive. As a result, special radio programs were broadcast, press releases were issued, and even random people were asked. When the death of loved ones was confirmed, further family members were sought. Even if that failed, attempts were made to contact people who had once lived in the same Polish cities and towns. Various compartiots' organizations proved to be helpful in that situation. Members of such organizations supported each other in adapting to local conditions, in completing official formalities, and finding a job. Some associations of this type were established before World War II: for example, in 1925, the Association of Cracowians was established in Tel Aviv. Initially, it operated informally, and in 1983 it was officially registered as the "Association of Cracowians in Israel" (Hebrew: Irgun Yotzei Krakov be-Yisrael).[26] Jews from various countries founded their own associations. Polish Jews were distinguished by the fact that they organized themselves more often in communities gathering former inhabitants of specific cities, for example Krakow, Warsaw, Łódź, Kielce, and Białystok. This applies also to smaller towns, to mention only Wadowice. Other Jews were more willing to refer to the territory of the entire country they had previously lived in, such as Germany, France, or Italy. Why is there a difference? Based on the source database analysed so far (I mean mainly sources of the memorial and epistolographic types) I suggest that it resulted mainly from the fact that Poland was partitioned for 123 years. At the time when the Zionist movement began to form, Poland did not exist on the political map of Europe. At that time, many Jews and Christians living in the former Polish lands identified not with the partitioning powers, but first of all with their "little homelands," the cities and regions from which they came. In 1918 Poland regained independence, but certain habits had a long life span. In addition, contrary to popular belief, not everyone had reasons to fully identify with the Second Polish Republic. Lower social strata (including peasants and workers) as well as national and religious minorities could not count on equal treatment. After World War II, Poland found itself politically dependant on the Soviet Union. There were not many reasons

---

26   Organizacja Żydów z Krakowa w Izraelu, http://www.cracow.org.il/pl/cos-o-nas/, accessed November 26, 2018.

to identify with such a state. However, the heritage of the cities was proudly emphasized.

Community organizations also thrived during the first few decades of independent Israel. Among the more known and active ones, is the organization of the graduates of the Hebrew Gymnasium in Krakow. The bond connecting these people was manifested not only in the form of conventions held in Israel, but mainly in the help they provided to each other, even when they did not know each other directly. The already mentioned Celina Ortner describes, for example, her trip in a group of architects to South America. She was received there "like a queen" by the Israeli ambassador to Peru, Michael Michael[27] (he was born in Krakow as Michał Teodor Feldblum and emigrated from Poland in 1936),[28] and his wife Ester. The ambassador in Argentina, Ram Nir Gad, treated her similarly. Celina Ortner even joked about their unique and close relationship and commented that they were creating the "Krakow mafia."[29] Later, some regional and community organizations lost their impetus or even ceased operations, primarily because of the natural order of things—the oldest members gradually began to pass away. The members drifted apart, each on their various life and career paths, and differences in worldview issues also came to light.

After World War II, the Goldmans and the Ebersohns reached Israel, the territory of which was still in a civilizational syncope. It should be noted, however, that over the previous few decades, thousands of Jewish pioneers (*halutzim*) had created solid foundations for the construction of the state. In addition, the activity of the British was not without significance. They took control of strategic places in Eretz Yisrael as early as in 1917, and in 1923 Great Britain finally took the Mandate over Eretz Yisrael.[30] The British transferred many solutions already known in Europe to Eretz Yisrael. They also intended to shape this area according to methods known to them. Therefore, they soon applied there proven legal,

---

27 He had the same first and last name.
28 P. Figiela, *Losy i kariery uczniów Gimnazjum Hebrajskiego*, in Gross, *To była hebrajska szkoła w Krakowie*, 239.
29 E. Pillersdorf, *Celina*, trans. M. Sobelman, J. Stöcker-Sobelman, Krakow–Budapest 2012, 29.
30 On December 9, 1917, Marshal Edmund Henry Allenby entered Jerusalem, and on July 1, 1920, Britain introduced its own civil administration there. On that day British politician and diplomat Herbert Samuel officially became the first British Mandate commissioner in Eretz Yisrael. On July 24, 1922 the League of Nations adopted the draft of the British Mandate over Eretz Yisrael, colloquially referred to as the Palestine Mandate or the British Mandate. On September 29, 1923, the League of Nations officially and finally granted Great Britain a mandate over Eretz Yisrael.

administrative, and economic solutions. First, they focused on the development of roads and municipal infrastructure. They were facing a challenge because it was a neglected area for a long time, and also heavily affected by the destruction of World War I. That is why they started by repairing the existing infrastructure.

At the beginning of the 1920s, the most important motorways in the British Mandate were: Jerusalem–Bethlehem–Hebron–Beersheba (82.1 kilometers), Jerusalem–Ramla–Jaffa (61 kilometer), Jerusalem–Jericho (34.5 kilometers), Jerusalem–Nablus–Janin–Nazareth–Tiberias (173 kilometers), Jerusalem–Nablus–Tulkarm–Haifa (156 kilometers), Gaza–Beer Sheva (56.35 kilometers), Gaza–Chan Junus–Rafah (32.2 kilometers), Gaza–Lod–Tulkarm–Haifa (174 kilometers), Haifa–Nazareth (37.5 kilometers), Haifa–Tiberias–Safed (68 kilometers), Beit She'an–Jenin (43.5 kilometers), Beisan–Nazareth (38 kilometers), Beersheba–Rafah [El-Kantara] (61.2 kilometers).[31] The first bus connections appeared at that time. A bus ran almost every day between Jerusalem and Tiberias (via Nazareth). Twice a day there were bus connections between Haifa and Nazareth, Jerusalem and Bethlehem, Jerusalem and Jaffa, and Jerusalem and Hebron.[32] Regarding the railroad, before World War I, there were only two narrow gauge lines in Eretz Yisrael: Jaffa–Jerusalem (87 kilometers) and Haifa–Dara (161 kilometers). The second of those lines was a branch of the larger Turkish Mecca railway. The acceleration of rail investments was brought by World War I. For the needs of the British army, a 180-kilometer standard gauge railway was built, running from the Suez Canal (at Al-Kantara) up to the Turkish border (March 1917). As the front progressed (after November 1917), this line was extended to Lod, and then its branch from Tulkarm to Haifa and Jaffa was built. After the war, new steam engines and carriages were brought from England, with inscriptions in English, Hebrew, and Arabic. Sleeping and restaurant cars began to run between Egypt and Haifa, which was treated in business terms, hence the tickets were expensive. In October 1920, the railroad management passed from military to civilian administration.[33] During the British Mandate, Jerusalem transformed from a provincial city of the Ottoman Empire into a modern metropolis with important administrative, political, educational and cultural functions. At that time, the city underwent demographic, territorial and construction development. New houses, hotels and public buildings appeared,

---

31 W. Szczepański, *Palestyna po wojnie światowej. Światła i cienie*, Krakow 1923, 325.
32 Ibid.
33 Ibid., 326–330, 335.

the investors of which were private parties, Jewish organisations (such as Gymnasia Rechavia,[34] the second modern school in Eretz Yisrael after the Tel Aviv Herzliya Hebrew Gymnasium) and central government (Government House—residence of the High Commissioner, Central Post Office, Government Printing House). Many houses were built according to the assumptions of the modified Bauhaus style (with elements such as rounded balconies, decorative metal staircase railings, and iron external gates).[35]

Until the outbreak of World War I, postal agencies of Austria-Hungary, France, Germany, Russia, and Italy operated in Jaffa, Haifa, and Jerusalem. They handled the outgoing and incoming external mail to Eretz Yisrael relatively efficiently. The much less effective Turkish post was responsible for the postal service within Eretz Yisrael—letters were often lost or reached the addressee with a delay. The telegraph did not work well and there were no telephones at all.[36] After World War I, English postal services held a monopoly on all postal items in Eretz Yisrael (external and internal). The quality of postal and telegraph services improved, but it still lagged behind the European level. Except on Sundays, there was daily postal service between Jerusalem, Jaffa, and Haifa and train stations. On average, the post reached towns that were not connected to the railway network once a week. Daily mail traffic was maintained between Jerusalem and Haifa and Europe. Initially, mail was transported by train to Egypt, from where it was sent on ships departing from Port Said or from Alexandria. Due to British interests, Eretz Yisrael was included in the air mail system connecting Egypt with Iraq.[37] The direct telegraph connection of Jerusalem with the main cities of Eretz Yisrael, as well as with Cairo and Beirut, became a great convenience for the population. Messages from Eretz Yisrael to England or back were delivered within twenty-four hours, it took five hours on the Eretz Yisrael–Italy line. Thinking about merchants, in January 1922, telegraph night shifts were introduced between Eretz Yisrael and Egypt.[38] In July 1921, the length of telegraph lines in Eretz Yisrael was 12,244 km. There were twenty-eight post offices at the

---

34 The school was founded in 1909. In 1928, it received a new building in the Rechavia district at Keren Kayemet Street.

35 L. Eylon, *Jerusalem. The New City Comes of Age. Architecture in the British Mandate Period*, https://mfa.gov.il/mfa/mfa-archive/1999/pages/focus%20on%20israel-%20jerusalem%20-%20architecture%20in%20the%20b.aspx, accessed June 30, 2019.

36 Ibid., 330.

37 Ibid., 331.

38 Ibid.

time, which employed 719 officials (mostly Jews).[39] A major obstacle for the postal activity was the lack of street names and house numbers. In Jerusalem, although the streets had names, no correspondence was delivered home. People had to buy a private PO box or collect their mail from the post office. Shimon Peres recalls the situation from Tel Aviv:

> In Tel Aviv, you can still see, at the corner of Bograshov and HaYarkon Streets, a house on the front of which there is a plaque with the information: "Beit Rahel Friedmann"—the House of Rachel Friedmann—reminding that there were no street names a few decades ago. People, wishing to inform the world about their place of residence, placed their own names on the fronts of their houses.[40]

In comparison with other countries, the prices of postal services in Eretz Yisrael were considered high. The telephone network was slowly forming, the intercity connections functioned slightly better, the interurban ones left much to be desired. In large cities there was a shortage of public telephones, at the beginning of the 1920s there were only two telephone booths that were set up in Jerusalem.[41] To improve the travel conditions of pilgrims, the British authorities opened the Society for Travel to Holy Places in February 1922.[42]

The quality of inland navigation also left much to be desired. At the beginning of the British Mandate, primarily primitive fishing boats and several small motorboats worked in the Sea of Galilee. Only one larger motorboat was sailing there, which provided communication between Tiberias and the marina in the vicinity of today's kibbutz Degania Alef.[43] A license to operate in the Dead Sea was granted to a private entrepreneur, Hasbun, who maintained several sailing boats and three motorboats there. They ran between El-Dedeide and Mezraa once a week on average.[44]

---

39   Ibid.
40   S. Peres, *Podróż sentymentalna z Teodorem Herzlem*, trans. B. Drozdowski, Warsaw 2002, 31.
41   Szczepański, *Palestyna po wojnie*, 332.
42   Ibid., 333.
43   Ibid.
44   Ibid. Historical sources testify that sailing in the Dead Sea was already possible in ancient times. See P. Briks, "Ślady żeglugi po Morzu Martwym w starożytności (VII w. przed Chr.–II w. po Chr.): stan i perspektywy badań," part 1, *Klio. Czasopismo poświęcone dziejom Polski i powszechnym* 36, no. 1 (2016): 3–16.

The first attempts made by Zionist activists to launch their own maritime shipping took place in July 1921, when Zion National Steam Navigation Co. in London began efforts to launch a regular connection between England, Eretz Yisrael and Syria.[45] However, it was not until 1933 that the *Caramel*, registered in Jaffa, sailed into the Mediterranean as the first ship under the British and Jewish (white-blue) flag. The first voyage from Haifa to Egypt was made with 1000 boxes of oranges and 300 tons of other goods on board.[46] The British and British-Jewish fleets were complemented by ships under foreign flags. For example, in 1933 orange exporters had at their disposal ninety-six foreign ships (fifty from Jaffa and forty-six from Haifa).[47] From the point of view of the Jewish state's builders, passenger ships were of key importance, along with freight ones. Thanks to them the development of tourism in Eretz Yisrael was possible, as well as the influx of successive waves of *aliyot*. In this context, an important event was the launch of connections on the route from Constanta to Jaffa and Haifa by the Gdynia–Ameryka Linie Żeglugowe S.A. Society in September 1933. The *Polonia* ship, which previously operated on the Poland–USA route, was used.[48]

LOT Polish Airlines was the first air carrier connecting Europe with Eretz Yisrael. On June 9, 1936, a LOT aircraft made a reconnaissance flight on the Warsaw–Tel Aviv route, which took three days with stopovers in Lviv, Istanbul, Aleppo, and Haifa. Regular courses were launched in April 1937.[49]

Eretz Yisrael was intensively working on electrification. Engineer Pinkus Rutenberg from Odessa submitted a project to build a dam at the mouth of the Jordan from the Sea of Galilee. It was planned to create a large water reservoir, which, thanks to a significant decrease in area (forty meters), could be used to produce electricity (100 million kilowatts of power per year). Initially, there was a lack of funds on the road to efficient implementation of those plans, and then a dispute about whether the company managing the power plant should be in British or Jewish hands.[50]

In the interwar period, plans to build in Eretz Yisrael a channel that would connect the Mediterranean Sea with the Red Sea began to be considered. Ideas

---

45 Szczepański, *Palestyna po wojnie*, 319.
46 *Nowy Dziennik* 32 (1933).
47 *Nowy Dziennik* 33 (1933).
48 A. Klugman, "Pomoc Polski dla żydowskiego ruchu narodowego w Palestynie," *Więź* 5 (1997): 145–146.
49 Idem., *Polonica w Ziemi Świętej*, Krakow 1994, 60.
50 Szczepański, *Palestyna po wojnie*, 343.

of this kind had been reported before, including in the decade of the 1870s, and later in 1883 and 1884. The demand for such an investment was high, but the problem was that the originators failed to convince the British who, for practical reasons, showed greater interest in the Suez Canal built in 1859–1869 (thanks to it the sea route from London to Mumbai was shortened by approx. 7.5 thousand km). In December 1921, F. A. Maier announced in *Bremen European Press* a project to dig a channel between Haifa and Aqaba. It was planned that it would consist of two parts: the first (northern) was to connect Haifa with Afula (length 43 km, height 60 m), the second was to run from Ain Buweirde to Aqaba (length 117 km, height up to 350 m). They were to be connected by a 236 km long lake, stretching from Afula through Beit She'an to Ain Buweirde. However, it turned out that the parameters of the channel would not be so competitive with the Suez Canal that the British government or any private investor would want to finance it. The economic and environmental implications were also feared. In addition, the implementation of the plan would have blocked the previously adopted Eretz Yisrael electrification project by engineer Rutenberg.[51]

Because the interests of companies from many countries that operated in different currencies met in Eretz Yisrael, the demand for banking institutions grew naturally. There were relatively many of them, but most operated without sophisticated tools and products, usually content with servicing domestic and international remittances, currency exchange and generally providing small short-term loans (usually for buyers). Those circumstances hindered significantly the development of trade, agriculture and industry in Eretz Yisrael. The most significant banks at that time included: The Anglo-Egyptian Bank, Banco di Roma (Italian), Crédit Lyonnais (French), Imperial Ottoman Bank (international), and, of course, the Bank of England also operated here. On May 15, 1933, a branch of Bank Polska Kasa Opieki S.A. (Pekao), which handled mainly transactions concluded by entrepreneurs conducting trade between Poland and Eretz Yisrael, was opened in Tel Aviv.[52] It remained open even after 1967, when, following the Soviet Union, communist Poland broke off diplomatic relations with Israel. The branch existed until 2003.

Against the background of banks running an average, limited coverage activity, Anglo-Palestine Bank stood out. Teodor Herzl himself demanded that

---

51 Ibid., 345–349.
52 On the subject of economic exchange between the markets of Poland and the British Palestine Mandate, see J. Łazor, *Brama na Bliski Wschód. Polsko-palestyńskie stosunki gospodarcze w okresie międzywojennym*, Warsaw 2016.

a financial institution be created to handle investments related to the development of Jewish settlement in Eretz Yisrael. It was also to be an institution providing financial resources for the Zionist Organization established during the First Zionist Congress in Basel (from 1960 under the name of the World Zionist Organization). According to his thought, the Jewish Colonial Trust was founded, and then on February 27, 1902, the subsidiary The Anglo-Palestine Company (APC). Zalman David Levontin from the Zion Lovers movement made a great contribution to the success of that founding action. In addition, the function of the first chairman of the Bank's board was held by David Wolffsohn, who was the successor of Herzl as the chairman of the Zionist movement. The Anglo-Palestine Company started operations with a small capital of 50,000 pounds (according to some sources, 40,000 pounds). The first branch of Anglo-Palestine Bank was opened on August 2, 1903 in Jaffa. Before the outbreak of World War I, branches were also opened in Jerusalem, Beirut (then the region's main commercial center), Hebron, Safed, Haifa, Tiberias, and Gaza. The bank supported the activities of Zionist organisations. It credited the purchase of land, import of goods, concession fees, and others. It offered long-term loans to farmers. It also granted loans for the construction of the first sixty houses built in Tel Aviv. In terms of capital, those were not significant operations. Compared to credit operations of banks operating in Europe, it is difficult to call them even medium. However, they were of strategic importance for the development of Jewish settlement in Eretz Yisrael. Herzl's thought was confirmed that even the most beautiful, righteous and thrilling idea would not come true without accumulating the right capital. For this, a responsible and reliable bank was needed, which, while maintaining the right balance between revenues and expenses, was not, however, under pressure to increase profits. During World War I, the Turks treated the Anglo-Palestine Bank as a hostile institution because it was founded in Great Britain. The Turkish authorities ordered the liquidation of branches of the bank and the confiscation of the money at its disposal. However, the bank's management succeeded in securing financial resources and the liquidation of branches was carried out with an intentional delay. Thanks to that, the business was provided with small, secret, but still significant funds for continuing operations. The bank also survived World War II. It used the supply of cash to develop the local industry.[53]

---

53 "Company History," https://english.leumi.co.il/articles/38067/; "Zionism: Jewish Colonial Trust," https://www.jewishvirtuallibrary.org/jewish-colonial-trust, accessed March 1, 2019.

Shortly after Israel proclaimed its independence, its authorities signed a special agreement with the Anglo-Palestine Bank, making it their financial representative. Although Israel became a sovereign state, the currency of the British Mandate, the Palestinian pound, was still in use at first. The Anglo-Palestine Bank was entrusted with the creation of the state monetary system. First, the Israeli pound was introduced (the first banknotes were printed in the United States). Then Israel issued a completely separate currency called the Israeli lira. Since the task required independence from the British, in 1950 Leumi LeYisrael Bank (Hebrew: National Bank of Israel) was founded, which on May 1, 1951 took over all liabilities and assets of the Anglo-Palestine Bank. With the opening of the Bank of Israel (the central bank for this country) in 1954, Bank Leumi became the largest commercial (universal) bank of Israel, with numerous branches today in Europe, North America, South America, Africa, Asia, and Australia.[54]

Zionist activists rendered a service to the socio-economic development of Eretz Yisrael, not only by expanding the banking sector, but also by contributing to the development of education at all levels.[55] In 1912, a teacher's college was opened in Tel Aviv, named after Elhanan Leib Levinsky (1857–1910), a respected Zionist activist, writer and Hebrew journalist from Podbrodzie near Vilnius. It is symbolic and meaningful that the first Hebrew college in Eretz Yisrael was founded with teachers in mind. They were to decide about the future of Jewish education in this

Fig. 54. Work in kibbutz Degania Bet, 1945, photo: Zoltan Kluger, public domain

---

54 Ibid.

55 In the 1920/21 school year, there were 135 private schools with 12,830 children attending them in Eretz Yisrael. 523 teachers worked in those institutions. In the same year, Zionist organisations had, in Jerusalem alone, 11 elementary schools, 5 high schools, 3 handicrafts schools, and 12 children's gardens. Only one-fifth of Jewish children (about 3,000) attended non-Zionist schools, which belonged, among others, to Alliance Israélite, Anglo-Jewish Association, and Talmud Torah. Szczepański, *Palestyna po wojnie*, 356.

Fig. 55. Moshav Nahalal, 1937–1938, photograph taken from a plane by Zoltan Kluger, public domain

place. Currently, this university is called Levinsky College of Education. In January 1925 Technion was created in Haifa, currently it is the leading in Israel and one of the most important technical universities in the world, which operates under the name Technion—Israel Institute of Technology. On April 1, 1925, the Hebrew University in Jerusalem was ceremoniously opened, being the third Hebrew-language university in Eretz Yisrael, and the first university with Hebrew as the language of instruction.

The first kibbutzim were created by pioneers (Hebrew: *kibbutz*—community, seat). By this term we understand cooperative farms in which land, means of production and income were jointly used. On the one hand, they were the realization of the Zionist idea that Jews should learn teamwork, grow into the land of Israel, and develop it, on the other, it was a response to the real needs of settlers who had to guarantee their own food. Before Israel was established, kibbutzim also began to act as its armed vanguard and in fact marked the future borders of the state. Degania (from the Hebrew word meaning "grain") is referred to as the first kibbutz, formed in 1910 at Lake Tiberias. In 1920 kibbutz Degania Bet was founded nearby, so to distinguish the former, now considered the "mother of all kibbutzim," it began to be called Degania Alef. Apart from kibbutzim, there were moshavim—they accepted the existence of private property, but there were joint investments and joint distribution of manufactured goods. The first was founded in 1921, it is known as Nahalal and located in northern Israel in the Jezreel Valley.

Emigrants from Central and Eastern Europe dominated among the founders of kibbutzim, and a significant percentage were people from the lands of the former First Polish-Lithuanian Commonwealth, especially from Galicia. The first "Galician" kibbutzim include Kfar Stand (established about nineteen miles south of Lake Tiberias), created in 1921. About fifty former residents of Galicia, mainly from Lviv, lived there. Most of them had higher education, usually they were doctors and engineers.[56] In 1927, two kibbutzim were established with the participation of Krakow Jews: Kwutzat Shiller and Beit Zera. Already in 1891, Jews from the areas of former Poland and Lithuania created Hadera, a settlement halfway between Tel Aviv and Haifa.[57] It was a breakthrough event, because for the first time in the history of modern Jewish settlement in Eretz Yisrael, Zionist activists had bought such a large territory. Hadera was located in a swampy area, therefore the land had to be dried first (the first inhabitants were decimated by malaria). Then citrus groves were established there with great effort. In the 1930s, Hadera began to transform from a rural settlement into an industrial town. In 1952 it gained city rights.

The appearance of kibbutzim and moshavim brought significant progress in the field of agriculture in Eretz Yisrael. Before the outbreak of World War I, Eretz Yisrael was part of the Ottoman Empire. For the Turkish state, it was a peripheral territory, but important in military and prestige terms (supremacy over Jerusalem). From an economic perspective, it was important only because of the significant communication routes passing through, which connected Europe and Asia with Africa. The Turks had neither reason nor more resources to invest in modernizing agriculture in Eretz Yisrael. After World War I, the British ruled there, but for them urban centers counted primarily. Only Zionist activists showed sufficient determination and found the appropriate funds to finance large-scale projects related to the reclamation and irrigation of inhabited territories, which were often located in desert, semi-arid, marshy, and malarial areas. In fact, they paid a high price for it, because infectious diseases and harsh living conditions took a considerable toll on them. Pioneers generally came from families that had no farming traditions. That is why they made use of innovative (at that time) knowledge from agricultural textbooks. Some of them even went

---

56 CDIA, f. 701, desc. 3, Jewish Religious Community in Lviv, case 171, Correspondence of Keren Kayemet LeYisrael, Repository for Eastern Galicia with the Superiority of the Jewish Religious Community in Lviv regarding a subsidy.

57 S. Aleksandrowicz, *Polska i Palestyna—dwie ziemie i dwa nieba. Żydzi krakowscy w obiektywie Ze'eva Aleksandrowicza*, ed. E. Gawron, T. Strug, Krakow 2012, 40–41.

to agricultural schools and colleges thinking about their future emigration to Eretz Yisrael. In Galicia, the Agricultural University of Dubliany enjoyed great popularity among Jews.[58] It was founded for sons of landowners, but they overestimated their knowledge and skills and thought that they did not need such education. Jews, on the other hand, were aware of their shortcomings in that respect and were more and more willing to enroll in that university. That is why farmers in Eretz Yisrael were open to experiments and to using new technologies from the very beginning. In addition, a large part of their customers were townspeople from Europe, who were accustomed to a diverse supply, so the farmers had to offer a wide range of products.[59] In the nineteenth century, Jews reactivated viticulture. Despite ancient traditions, in the years preceding the development of Jewish settlement in Eretz Yisrael, vineyards were rare and the means of production used there were obsolete. The Rothschild family, among others, invested in this business. Later, a producer syndicate was established, which promoted the best vineyards located in Rishon LeZion and Zikhron Ya'akov.[60] The main export goods of the British Mandate in Eretz Yisrael were: oranges, soap, wine, barley, peas, melons, apricots, sunflower, and broad beans. On the other hand, larger quantities of the following products were imported: cotton, sugar, rice, flour, clothes, tobacco, kerosene, coal, iron, steel, and construction timber.[61]

In kibbutzim, also inventions were born, which today are applicable all over the world, such as the drip irrigation system constructed by an engineer from Warsaw, Simcha Blass. It consists in the fact that water is distributed underground or just above its surface using a network of microtubes that allow even hydration and high water savings (in Israeli climate conditions, irrigation by spraying would result in a large loss of water due to evaporation). In the 1930s, in kibbutz Hatzerim, he started experiments that gave rise to the rational use of water for irrigation of agricultural crops and green areas. That system was developed by his son who founded in 1965 together with the Hatzerim community the company Netafim specializing in the production of irrigation equipment.

---

58 The institution was established in 1856 as the School of Life Sciences, it was transformed into the Agricultural University in 1858, and raised to the rank of an academy in 1901.
59 The basic agricultural products produced in the interwar period in Eretz Yisrael included wheat, barley, olives, peas, vetch, broad beans, lentils, sesame, oranges, melons, lemons, grapes, figs, and almonds. Szczepański, *Palestyna po wojnie*, 306.
60 Before World War I, they produced around 3.5–4.5 million litres of various wines and around 30,000 litres of cognac per year. Ibid., 308.
61 Ibid., 316.

Currently, it is the world leader in irrigation technologies used mainly in agriculture, and especially for irrigation in urban areas. Irrigation and water saving are such important subjects in Israel that in 1988 they were presented on postage stamps.[62]

Kibbutzim have stood the test of time, they still exist, although they had to undergo profound transformations to adapt to new social, political, and economic realities. The pioneers who founded them were often motivated by ideological reasons. After World War II, groups of Jews who already showed a great distance, even if not in relation to the state itself, but to its ideological background, began to reach Israel. Many young people chose an individual career, hence they left kibbutzim (if they had lived in them before) or purposefully bypassed them. In addition, the community-raised generation grew up, which had contact with biological parents only a few hours a day. In the 1970s and 1980s that practice was abandoned, but some people who considered themselves hurt could no longer stay in a kibbutz. Israeli media widely commented on that problem. It was described, among others in the popular book *We Were the Future* by Jael Neeman.[63] In 1977, when Menachem Begin became the Prime Minister of Israel and began to form the first right-wing government in the history of Israel, kibbutzim were forced to adapt to the rules of the free market. Because terrorism was spreading in cities, kibbutzim—once perceived as a social avant-garde—began to be criticised as alienated enclaves enjoying convenience and security. Giving in to pressure, some kibbutzim changed their business formula and underwent at least partial privatisation. Over time, their commercialisation became common. In addition to agricultural production, they began to focus on services (mainly tourism), trade and industrial production. They also diversified greatly in terms of ideology. The first ones had a clearly socialist profile. The right-wing current of Zionism attached more importance to city life, to organizing self-defense, and to learning the Hebrew language. Currently, there is a synagogue in almost every kibbutz. In addition to left-wing kibbutzim, right-wing and even religious ones were also created.

Already at the time of leaving Poland, Marcel Goldman ruled out the possibility of living in a kibbutz. He came from a middle-class family and assumed that he would work and shape his life as independently as possible. He was not

---

62 T. Ulanowski, "Każda kropla święta," http://wyborcza.pl/1,75400,19813985,kazda-kropla-swieta.html, accessed May 16, 2019.
63 J. Neeman, *Byliśmy przyszłością*, trans. A. Jawor-Polak, Wołowiec 2012.

alone in that quest. In the memoirs regarding Polish Jews we can find many testimonies that they treated life in a kibbutz or in a moshav as their last resort resulting from the lack of financial resources to buy a flat in the city (preferably in Tel Aviv). An example of this are the memories of Nili Amit, who came to Israel in 1957 as a child, as part of the Gomulka Aliyah: "My parents cannot find a job, we have nothing to live on. We are leaving the transit camp and settling in the countryside, and the city, as in *Three Sisters*, becomes a distant, unattainable dream. We have become farmers."[64] Marcel's financial situation after reaching Israel was difficult, it did not guarantee him staying in the city, so he had to show incredible determination and diligence in this regard. Like almost all other emigrants from the Vistula, he left without any belongings. It is enough to look at the photo (Fig. 56) in which Marcel (first from the left) stands in a group of several people next to a suitcase and a few packages.

Fig. 56. Marcel Goldman (first from the left) on his way to Israel, Salzburg 1949, family collections of Marcel and Bianka Goldman (Tel Aviv)

---

64 N. Amit, *A miałam być księżniczką z bajki*, trans. K. Mazurczak, Krakow–Budapest 2009, 62–63.

In *Iskierki życia*, he accurately enumerates what he took with him: a suitcase with clothing, a leather coat, high shoes, documents with two different names, a business card of a professor from New York, whom he had met in Krakow recently (the professor was buying Judaic items in Poland, and Marcel was his guide for some time), a student index of the Academy of Commerce in Krakow, and a few dollars hidden just in case, which he had received from his father.[65] In the memories of the Gomulka Aliyah and March '68 emigrants, we most often read that they took only a few books and gramophone records, sometimes small household appliances, a few keepsakes, and clothes, most of which were to be useless in Israeli climatic conditions.

Marcel's emigration was undoubtedly a personal experience for him, but it is hard not to notice the similarities between his situation and the situation of tens of thousands of other Polish migrant Jews. Before he left, he had to face a number of dilemmas and quandaries. He considered for a long time whether it is worth taking that risk or whether he would manage in Israel. In Krakow, he had already started economic studies, he was on a straight path to his career, although he was aware that it would have to take place in a poor communist state. He did not hide the specific life and professional goals he had set for himself. He knew that he would be declassified in Israel, simply because of his lack of knowledge of the Hebrew language. Marcel already experienced that during his journey to Israel, about which I will write later. He ruled out working in a kibbutz or in a moshav.

Marcel's journey was illegal, it took place under the so-called *bricha*, which in Hebrew means "escape." It is particularly sad that the Jews who had managed to save their lives during the war could not just go to Eretz Yisrael or later to Israel. Those who left just after the war had to take into account being arrested by the British. It happened, for example, to a group of survivors from the German concentration camp in Buchenwald who arrived at the port in Haifa on June 15, 1945. In 1948, Jews already had an independent state, but the sovereignty of Poles, whose country was politically dependent on the Soviet Union, was lost. The communist authorities closed the borders for everyone. Later they were placated for some time. In April 1949, when Marcel decided to emigrate, Poland could be left almost exclusively illegally (legal travels were very limited

---

65 Goldman, *Iskierki życia*, 102, 115.

and required a number of time-consuming formalities).[66] Therefore, Marcel volunteered to a recruitment point of the Hagana (which initiated the Israeli army) and took the challenge of crossing the so-called green border on the Polish-Czechoslovakian section at night, next to Cieszyn (divided by the river into the Polish and the Czechoslovakian part). He was in a group of several people. The problems began with the absence of the guide who was supposed to pick them up on the other side of the border, luckily, they soon found her. Later Marcel fell into much more trouble, and it was at his own request. He came to the conviction that, since he knew Czech very well, he could do better alone. He also believed that in terms of clothing or behaviour he would not stand out from the surrounding people. So he informed the guide that he would travel separately from the group, and no one objected. He headed for the train station. Standing at the ticket office, he asked for a ticket to Bratislava, from where he intended to travel to Vienna. Suddenly, two undercover agents appeared and demanded documents that he obviously did not have. He was escorted to the interrogation room in the station building. He could not provide convincing explanations. Counterfeit documents, dollars, and a business card of the American professor all spoke against him. Next to the allegation of illegal crossing of the border, there could also be an accusation of espionage. He was sent to custody, where he spent two weeks. Then a trial took place, during which he was sentenced to two weeks in prison, and as he had already spent that time being arrested, the sentence meant immediate release.[67] It must be noticed that the Czechoslovakian justice system was very gentle with Marcel. Had he been sent to Poland, he would have been imprisoned for at least a few years, and the interrogations could have been far more brutal. After his release, he learned that several people from his group were looking for a guide and came across a man who later filed a notice with the police. The police officers surrounded the station and stopped Marcel easily, while the members of his group, undisturbed, went to the previously chosen place of accommodation, and then safely reached Vienna through Bratislava.

After leaving prison, Marcel also went to Bratislava (the city was an assembly point for Hungarian Jews who migrated to Israel). There he was taken under the care of representatives of Israel, who prepared the further journey,

---

66   B. Szaynok, "Nielegalna imigracja Żydów z Polski—1945–1947," *Przegląd Polonijny* 2 (1995): 31–46.

67   Interview with Marcel Goldman carried out on December 18, 2016.

arranged the necessary formalities, and, if necessary, conducted negotiations with Czechoslovak border guards and Soviet soldiers who were guarding the Czechoslovak-Austrian border. Marcel remembered that Hungarian Jews dominated in his group. Their first station outside the Iron Curtain was Vienna, where they were located in the Rothschild Hospital converted into a DP camp, that is, a camp for the so-called displaced persons.[68] In Vienna, the male part of the group Marcel came with was subjected to verification that they were certainly Jews, most likely, in fear of Soviet spies. It is also possible that the Israelis wanted to secure themselves against the possibility that people of other nationalities would benefit from the journey program for Jews. In any case, Marcel and his travelling companions were asked to read a fragment of the prayer book in Hebrew. The Hebrew alphabet was also brought, from which they had to read individual letters. Marcel admits that he could not read Hebrew, he did not recognize even one letter from the alphabet. Because a larger group of boys and men who did not speak Hebrew gathered, it was decided to check whether they were circumcized. The procedure was not very pleasant: they were arranged in a row, with their members exposed, and checked by a female doctor.[69] One might be wondering why Marcel did not know Hebrew at all, since he had been learning the language in elementary school for five years. He explains: "From the moment I started living on Aryan papers, until my departure in 1949, seven years passed. At that time, something happened in my memory that completely erased Hebrew from my brain."[70]

After two weeks in Vienna, Marcel continued his journey to Israel. Along the way, transit camps in Salzburg and Trani (southern Italy) were waiting for him. From there, he went to Haifa on the board of *HaAtzmaut* (Hebrew: independence).[71] All in all, it took him two months to get to Israel. The pleasant part of the cruise is presented in two photographs in the text (Figs. 57 and 58), and the word "pleasant" should be put in brackets, because the conditions on the ship were by no means luxurious. It was a former cargo ship, quickly adapted to transporting people. There were no toilets or showers. Rooms were very

---

68 At the end of World War II, such camps were established in various places in Europe (most in Germany, Austria and Italy). They accepted people who were out of their homeland as a result of the war. Most often, "DPs" were people deported to forced labour in the Third Reich and freed from concentration camps.
69 Correspondence with Marcel Goldman, February 6, 2019.
70 Correspondence with Marcel Goldman, August 1, 2018.
71 Ibid.

crowded and filled with amazing stench. Hence, not only the desire to observe the sea, but also, and perhaps above all, the need for fresh air was the reason for Marcel's frequent visits on the upper deck (documented in photographs).

Talking of Marcel's journey, one more important point should be noted. Most of the ship's passengers were Hungarian and Romanian Jews, because legal emigration was still possible from these countries. Polish Jews were definitely a minority. In Italy, Moroccan Jews boarded the ship. Marcel mentions that, watching them, he felt consternation because their behaviour and morals were completely alien to him. In his opinion, European Jews stuck together and did not show a desire to integrate with Moroccans. It seemed that the Moroccans felt the same way.[72]

The *aliyot* of the Moroccan Jews were a big challenge for Israel. Morocco, from 1912 under the protectorate of France, gained independence in 1956. A large Jewish community lived there, but representatives of its business, academic, and cultural elite were at least partially assimilated with French culture, which is why they most often emigrated to France. However, its worst educated (often illiterate) and poorest members, often poor shepherds from the foothills of the Atlas Mountains, travelled to Israel. They lived in similar conditions as their Arab neighbours and adopted many customs from them. For those reasons, their acclimatization in Israel lasted a long time, but brought great results. Representatives of the third generation of Moroccan Jews already occupied the highest positions in government, army, and economy. By the way, it is worth adding that the majority of Jews from Algeria, which until 1962 was a French colony, emigrated to France. In total, of approximately 130,000 Algerian Jews, about ninety percent went to France, and only about ten percent, to Israel.

Despite the harsh conditions on Marcel's ship, enthusiasm and hope reigned there. These feelings intensified when after four days of sailing the passengers finally saw Mount Carmel in Haifa[73]—the same view had been admired by generations of pioneers migrating to Eretz Yisrael before World War II.

The port of Haifa was built in the 1930s. Before that, Jaffa (today part of Tel Aviv) served as the main Mediterranean port. That port had a fresh water intake, and a magnificent panorama stretched from the waterfront, but deep-sea ships could not moor there because of the rocks located some distance from the shoreline. Larger ships could not reach the shore, and travellers and goods had

---

72 Interview with Marcel Goldman carried out on June 13, 2018.
73 Interview with Marcel Goldman carried out on December 18, 2016.

Figs. 57 and 58. Marcel Goldman aboard the HaAtzmaut ship on his way to Israel, 1949, family collections of Marcel and Bianka Goldman (Tel Aviv)

to be transported from the ships to the shore by boats. People often drowned and packages were lost. Therefore, activists of the Zionist movement considered it necessary to build a fully professional and safe deep-water port, and convinced the British to start the project. The importance of that investment is difficult to overestimate, as it is not easy to imagine the reception and unloading of further *aliyot* through the port of Jaffa. However, the port in Haifa could not handle all passenger and freight traffic alone. Tel Aviv had great needs in this respect, as in the 1920s and 1930s it experienced rapid demographic and economic development. The first plans to build a separate port in Tel Aviv appeared already in 1913, shortly after the foundation of the city. In 1925, the port design was prepared by a Scottish city architect Sir Patrick Geddes. However, the plan he created was abandoned for almost a decade. Among other reasons, the charismatic mayor of Tel Aviv, Meir Dizengoff, did not agree with Geddes's proposed location of the port near to the place where Allenby Street ended. Undoubtedly, the biggest obstacle to realising the idea of building a port in Tel Aviv was the lack of adequate funds. All funds that Zionist activists managed to collect were directed to the construction site in Haifa, because there were optimal topographic conditions for a fully professional port capable of servicing every vessel. The discussion of a separate port in Tel Aviv came back with full force after April 19, 1936, when Arab dockers announced a strike in Jaffa. At that time, the inhabitants of Tel Aviv decided to become independent of Arab-dominated Jaffa. In addition, they were

Fig. 59. Exodus 1947, photo: Frank Shershel, public domain

Fig. 60. Evacuation of a sick person from the Jewish State ship, which arrived at the port of Haifa, October 1947, public domain

Fig. 61. View of the harbour and bay in Haifa, 2014, photo: Łukasz Tomasz Sroka

mobilized by an Arab revolt, which broke out in the Palestine Mandate on April 21, 1936. After negotiations with the British, Tel Aviv authorities received appropriate permits and began building the port. It was decided that the new port would be located south of the mouth of the Yarkon River. First, a wooden pier was created, but it was damaged the following day, so the next one was made of steel.[74] On May 19, 1936, the first freighter under the Yugoslav flag with a load of cement on board arrived at the port of Tel Aviv. The port was built with due discretion, because nobody wanted to provoke the Arabs. At the time of its inauguration, however, the inhabitants of Tel Aviv felt the sublime atmosphere. It was immortalised in the reportage by a Polish writer, Maria Kuncewiczowa, who in 1936 came to Eretz Yisrael following the invitation of the Hebrew Pen Club.[75]

---

74 *About Tel Aviv Port,* http://www.yarid-hamizrach.co.il/English/?catid=%7B636083 F1–CD24–486E-BA3C-EADBB9C240C5%7D, accessed March 11, 2018.
75 A. Szałagan, "Maria Kuncewiczowa w podróży," *Pamiętnik Literacki: Czasopismo Kwartalne Poświęcone Historii i Krytyce Literatury Polskiej* 3 (2014): 227.

A bunch of men were hanging around the beach, beams were being carried, people were wading around in the water, some piles were driven into the bottom, a piece of pier pierced ready over the waves, two women were striking their hammers.
—What's happening?
—Please, go away, the public is not allowed here.
The policeman spoke with a smile. Porters—dropping their weight—stopped and also smiled mysteriously. My companion pulled me aside.
—You'll see in the evening.
Unfortunately, in the evening I stayed too late with new friends. I was coming back along Allenby road—a street as crowded as if there was still a demonstration there. Near the square, where most cafés stand, where the temporary Habima seat is in the cinema—a blockade and shouts of *Hatikvah*. In the very center of the crowd, a truck loaded with sacks moved under a white-blue flag. It wasn't driven by a chauffeur—people were pushing it. People were jumping out of the crowd, grabbing a sack from the platform and bumping it on their backs. On the sacks it was written in Serbian: cement. Those who could not get to the car got on each other's shoulders to look at this cement at least once, many people cried, kissed, and shouted. A small, thin man, bent under the load, hit me with his sack, a familiar eye flashed. Companion!
—Lord, what are you doing? What does all this mean?
He stopped, shining with sweat.
—I'm carrying the first load unloaded in Tel Aviv to the museum. What does that mean? Victory. Did you see in the morning? In two weeks they finished the iron bridge. The ship that brought cement from Yugoslavia did not have to be unloaded in Jaffa. We've been trying for it for six years! The High Commissioner always refused . . . Until the beloved Arabs helped. Is life going to end in Palestine because they are on strike? For now, it's called Custom Station. But in a few years everyone will say: it is the Jewish port in Tel-Aviv![76]

The official opening of the port in Tel Aviv took place in 1938. During World War II it was manned by British troops. During the War of Independence in 1948–1949, the port in Tel Aviv, as well as the port in Haifa, played a strategic role in shipping the soldiers of the Israel Defense Forces. In the following years it was planned to expand the port, but the adjacent area turned out to be too small, so in 1965 it was closed. Initially, craft warehouses and workshops were located in the former port space. In the 1990s, the area was developed as

---

76 M. Kuncewiczowa, *Miasto Heroda. Notatki palestyńskie (1938)*, Warsaw 1982, 17–18.

a shopping, entertainment, and restaurant center. On one side, it has a natural extension in the form of a wide beach, on the other, the Yarkon park extends. Haifa has maintained its unquestioned leader position among the Mediterranean ports of Israel.

The fate of the Jewish Holocaust survivors, who were left wandering around Europe, only changed after the declaration of Israel's independence. With all Israel's imperfections, it became a haven for Jews from all over the world from the very beginning. Even if the travel was not easy, and sometimes accompanied by various adventures like in the case of Marcel Goldman, each of the newcomers knew that in Israel no one would reject them and send to another place, that they would be accepted, although, let's add, not always so cordially as one could expect. This guarantee and a reference to the Jews scattered throughout the world and their longing for Eretz Yisrael is included in the Israeli Declaration of Independence:

> The Land of Israel was the birthplace of the Jewish people. Here their spiritual, religious, and political identity was shaped. Here they first attained to statehood, created cultural values of national and universal significance, and gave to the world the eternal Book of Books.
>
> After being forcibly exiled from their land, the people kept faith with it throughout their Dispersion and never ceased to pray and hope for their return to it and for the restoration in it of their political freedom.
>
> Impelled by this historic and traditional attachment, Jews strove in every successive generation to re-establish themselves in their ancient homeland. In recent decades they returned in their masses....
>
> The catastrophe which recently befell the Jewish people—the massacre of millions of Jews in Europe—was another argument in favor of the urgency of solving the problem of its homelessness by reestablishing in Eretz Yisrael the Jewish State, which would open the gates of the homeland wide to every Jew and confer upon the Jewish people the status of a fully privileged member of the comity of nations.
>
> Survivors of the Nazi holocaust in Europe, as well as Jews from other parts of the world, continued to migrate to Eretz Yisrael, undaunted by difficulties, restrictions, and dangers, and never ceased to assert their right to a life of dignity, freedom, and honest toil in their national homeland....
>
> THE STATE OF ISRAEL will be open for Jewish immigration and for the Ingathering of the Exiles; it will foster the development of the country for the benefit of all its inhabitants; it will be based on freedom, justice and peace as envisaged by the prophets of Israel; it will ensure complete equality of social and political rights to all its inhabitants irrespective of religion, race, or sex; it will guarantee freedom of religion,

conscience, language, education, and culture; it will safeguard the Holy Places of all religions; and it will be faithful to the principles of the Charter of the United Nations.

THE STATE OF ISRAEL is prepared to cooperate with the agencies and representatives of the United Nations in implementing the resolution of the General Assembly of November 29, 1947, and will take steps to bring about the economic union of the whole of Eretz-Israel.[77]

The Israeli Declaration of Independence was announced by David Ben-Gurion, born in Poland. Entrusting him with such an honourable and responsible role was a recognition of his own achievements, but also those of the entire community of Polish Jews. The solemn declaration of Israel's independence took place on May 14, 1948, during the assembly of the Provisional State Council in Tel Aviv. The text of the Israeli Declaration of Independence along with the signatures below it has become an iconic motif in Israeli culture. It is often seen on postage stamps, postcards, and posters decorating school and university rooms, libraries, community centers, and other public institutions. In remembrance of the establishment of the State of Israel, the state festival of Yom Ha-Atzmaut (Independence Day) is celebrated, the same day the Arabs celebrate Nakba, or Day of the Catastrophe.

Jerusalem was initially considered as the site for proclaiming Israel's independence, but because it was under siege by the Arab army, the idea was abandoned, and Tel Aviv, the first modern and fully Hebrew city in Eretz Yisrael, was chosen. The Tel Aviv Museum of Art, located in the house of the first mayor of Tel Aviv, Meir Dizengoff, at the Rothschild Boulevard, was chosen as the place suitable for the rank of the event.[78]

May 14, 1948 was Friday, which forced some haste to complete the ceremony before Sabbath. The next day, the British Mandate over Palestine was to expire. The meeting of the Provisional State Council began at 4 p.m. with singing *Hatikvah*, which became the official anthem of Israel. Then David Ben-Gurion stood at the centrally placed microphone. A portrait of Teodor Herzl and two Israeli flags hung on the wall behind him. He held in his hand the text

---

[77] Original recording of the text delivered in Hebrew by David Ben-Gurion in Tel Aviv on May 14, 1948, Israeli Ministry of Foreign Affairs website: http://www.mfa.gov.il/mfa/foreign-policy/peace/guide/pages/declaration%20of%20establishment%20of%20state% 20of%20 israel.aspx, accessed December 28, 2014.

[78] Meir Dizengoff (1861–1936), the first mayor of Tel Aviv, held this office in 1921–1925 and 1928–1936.

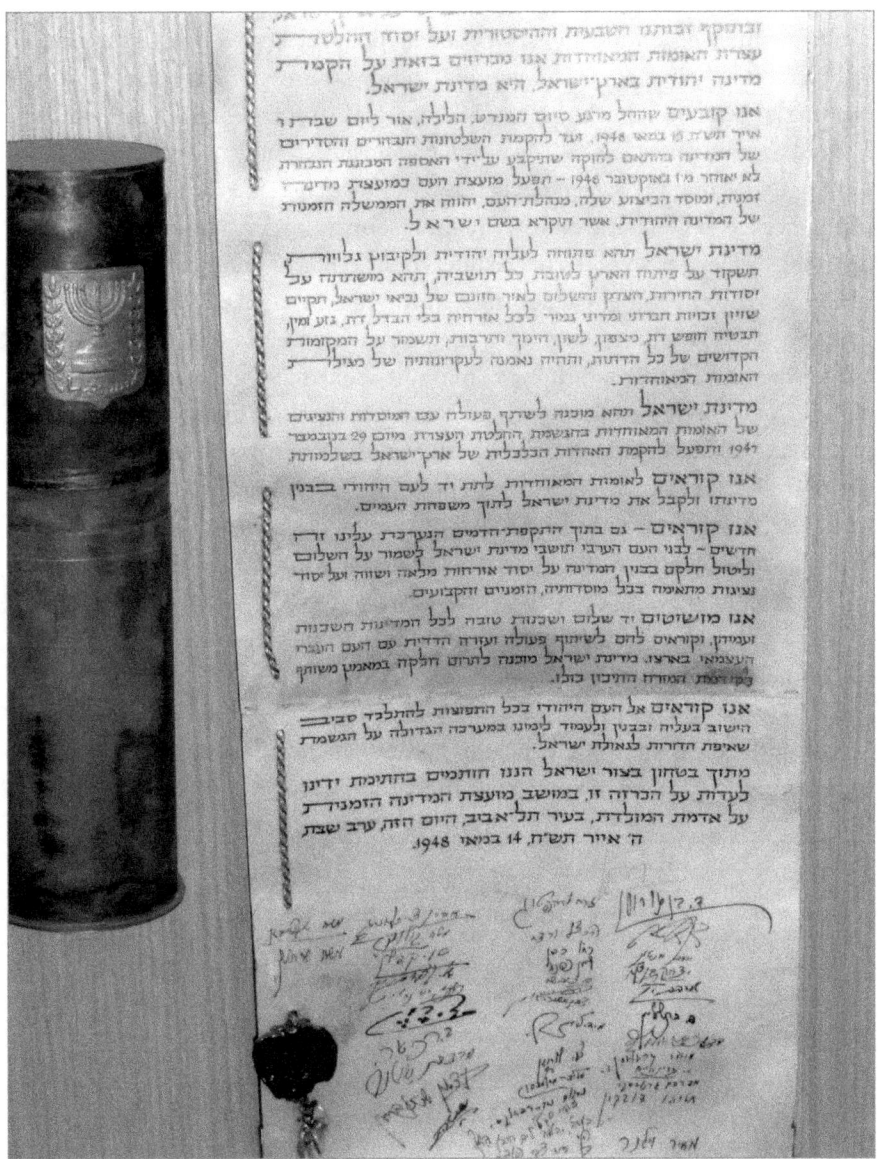

Fig. 62. A reprint of the Israeli Declaration of Independence hung in a display case at the Beit Berl College Library in Kefar Sava, Israel, 2008, photo: Łukasz Tomasz Sroka

of the declaration of independence, which he read in his characteristic firm and somewhat rough voice.

After the declaration of Israel's independence, David Ben-Gurion asked Rabbi Yehuda Leib HaCohen Maimon,[79] who was present in the hall, to say the blessing of Birkat Shehecheyanu, which is usually said when something new is learned or experienced. Rabbi Maimon had unsuccessfully tried to convince Zionist activists that the Israeli declaration of independence should contain a direct reference to God. The core of the Zionist organizations, however, was made up of secular Jews who preferred to refer to the ethos of their work and sacrifice. That is why in the initial part of the text the role of pioneers and defenders of Eretz Yisrael is emphasised, as they "revived the Hebrew language, built villages and towns, and created a thriving community controlling its own economy and culture, loving peace but knowing how to defend itself, bringing the blessings of progress to all the country's inhabitants, and aspiring towards independent nationhood." Although the second sentence of the declaration mentions the "spiritual, religious, and political identity" of the Jews, which was shaped in Eretz Yisrael, words that can be interpreted as a reference to God are only found in the last paragraph: "Placing our trust in the Rock of Israel,[80] we affix our signatures to this proclamation at this session of the Provisional Council of State, on the soil of the homeland, in the city of Tel-Aviv, on this Sabbath Eve, the 5th day of Ijar, 5708 (May 14, 1948)."

After the blessing of Rabbi Maimon, the signatories[81] signed the document establishing the independent Israel, then *Hatikvah* was sung again and Ben-

---

79   Rabbi Maimon headed the Jewish religious party Mizrachi, which aimed to connect the religious and the Zionist circles. Maimon came from Bessarabia, graduated from the yeshiva in Vilnius, decided to take part in the *aliyah* in 1913, and settled in Tel Aviv. He supported Ben-Gurion, and in the independent Israel he became the first minister of religion. He received the Israel Prize in the field of biblical literature.

80   Maimon originally wished to use the words *Elokei Israel*, "God of Israel." However, the final version of the text uses the phrase *tzur Yisrael*. The Hebrew word *tzur* is ambiguous: it means "stone," "strength," or "flint." It can also be understood as one of the attributes of God, signifying His strength and the support that He gives to His people. The wording "Rock of Israel" is a result of a free, non-literal translation. In this case, I refer to historical tradition—in English translations, the term "Rock of Israel" is the most common—but I am aware of the imperfections of such a solution. .

81   David Ben-Gurion, Daniel Auster, Yitzhak Ben-Zvi, Mordechai Bentov, Eliyahu Berligne, Fritz Bernstein, Rachel Cohen-Kagan, Eliyahu Dobkin, Yehuda Leib Fishman, Wolf Gold, Meir Grabovsky, Avraham Granovsky, Yitzhak Gruenbaum, Kalman Kahana, Eliezer Kaplan, Avraham Katznelson, Saadia Kobashi, Moshe Kolodny, Yitzhak-Meir Levin, Meir David Loewenstein, Zvi Luria, Golda Meyerson, Nahum Nir, David-Zvi Pinkas, Felix Rosenblueth,

Fig. 63. David Ben-Gurion publicly announces the Israeli Declaration of Independence, with the portrait of Teodor Herzl visible above the gathered people, exhibition hall of the Museum of Art in Tel Aviv, May 14, 1948, photo: Rudi Weissenstein, public domain

Gurion announced the end of the ceremony. Thanks to the broadcast by Israeli radio, that immortal event could be followed not only by people gathered in the Museum of Art, but also by crowds gathered in homes, squares, and streets of Israeli cities. Shortly after the declaration of independence, Arab aggression against Israel began. During Ben-Gurion's radio speech prepared especially for the United States, bombs exploding in Tel Aviv were already heard. Ben-Gurion had to explain the noise to the confused American audience.

Let's go back to the signatories. Even a person moderately familiar with Israel's history must wonder why Chaim Weizmann,[82] an eminent scholar and

---

David Remez, Berl Repetur, Zvi Segal, Mordechai Shatner, Ben-Zion Sternberg, Bechor-Shalom Sheetrit, Haim-Moshe Shapira, Moshe Shertok, Herzl Vardi, Meir Vilner, Zerach Warhaftig, and Aharon Zisling

82   Chaim Weizmann (1874–1952) came from Motol (now the territory of Belarus), where he received elementary religious education. His talent in chemistry came out in high school. He studied at the Polytechnic in Darmstad and Berlin. In 1899 he obtained a doctorate degree at the University of Fribourg. In 1901 he got a job at the University of Geneva. In 1904 he became a lecturer in chemistry at the University of Manchester. The fame of a talented scientist helped him in his political career. He conducted, among others, an effective campaign

the leader of the Zionist movement, cannot be found in that noble group. It is impossible to give a fully convincing and source-based answer. There have been hypotheses that are certainly interesting, but they should be treated with caution. The most likely seems explanation seems to be the difficult relationship between Weizmann and Ben-Gurion. Until the outbreak of World War II, the position of both politicians could be regarded as equal. In the interwar period, Ben-Gurion became the leader of the *yishuv*,[83] but Weizmann had excellent relations in British political circles, which had a colossal impact on his political position. We are talking about the period during which Great Britain exercized a mandate over Palestine. It is difficult to say whether Ben-Gurion had reasons to have a Weizmann's complex. It is certain that both politicians aspired to the leader's role in the reborn Israel. Only one of them could win that competition. Initially, Weizmann was in the leading position, but the geopolitical transformations brought by World War II also changed his situation profoundly. Weizmann believed in the power of Great Britain until the last moment and maintained close contacts with the politicians of that country. During that time, Ben-Gurion focused on strengthening ties with the American milieu, which already during the war, and even more after it ended, began to pay off. A bipolar system developed in the world, in which the United States and the USSR played major roles. Those transformations allowed Ben-Gurion to push Weizmann into the background. We can assume that the prospect of signing the declaration at the very end did not suit his ambitions, in that situation he preferred not to do it at all. However, these are only speculations . . . Still, the talents and international esteem enjoyed by Weizmann were large enough that Ben-Gurion did not want or could not afford his withdrawal from politics.

They found an honorable solution—Weizmann agreed to take up the function of the first president of Israel. In the Israeli political reality, it is a noticeable, but only honorary position. Weizmann wanted to give up his presidential salary, but he confused the officials with it. It was agreed that he would receive a salary, but as low as possible. Those were the gestures he made as a man of

---

to build the Hebrew University in Jerusalem. In 1918, he participated in the solemn laying of the foundation stone for the construction of this university. He also showed great involvement in Zionist activity, for instance, regarding the revival of the Hebrew language. He was the president of the World Zionist Organization twice (1921–1931 and 1935–1946).

83 In Hebrew, the word *yishuv* means a settlement. It is often used to refer to the Jewish settlement in Eretz Yisrael before the creation of Israeli statehood, in the full version: *ha-yishuv ha-yehudi be-Eretz Yisrael*.

Fig. 64. David Ben-Gurion (standing in the car) after returning from a visit to the United States, passing through Ramat Gan, June 7, 1951, photo: Teddy Brauner, public domain

an exceptional class, but he was already very wealthy at the time.[84] In 1934 he founded the Daniel Sieff Institute in Rehovot, which officially took his name on November 2, 1949. Today, the Weizmann Institute is one of the best scientific universities in the world.

He was undoubtedly a man of charisma, able to draw crowds with him. Against the background of his great achievements, the fact that he ruled with a "firm hand" becomes less important. For several decades, he imposed left-wing

---

84 Weizmann made a fortune, among others, on inventions and scientific patents applicable in economy.

narrative in Israeli internal policy, in fact discrediting and marginalising right-wing representatives. Although he expressed leftist beliefs, he quickly orientated Israeli diplomacy to building and strengthening a close alliance with Western countries, especially the United States. Even before World War II, he accurately predicted that soon the United States would become the main power and for a long time would exert a decisive influence on the history of the world. Squares and streets in many cities of Israel are named after Ben-Gurion. In 1973, his name was given to the University of Beersheba. In 1975, the airport in Tel Aviv, the largest in the country, was named in his honour (previously it was called Lod Airport, because it is located next to the city of Lod).

Marcel Goldman arrived in Israel in August 1949. We can treat this date symbolically. Just a month earlier, the young state celebrated the first anniversary

> David Ben-Gurion, the first prime minister and one of the main founding fathers of the Israeli state was born as David Grün in 1886 in Płońsk (then in the Russian partition). His father Avigdor Grün was a lawyer and a leader of the Zionist organisation Chovevei Zion (Lovers of Zion). In his hometown, young David attended the Jewish school founded by his father. His mother died when he was eleven years old. In 1904 he moved to Warsaw. He began studying at the local university, where he became involved with the Poalei Zion (Workers of Zion) organisation, which formed the left wing of the Zionist movement. In 1906 he emigrated to the Land of Israel, then belonging to the Ottoman Empire. There he continued to be active in Poalei Zion. After some time he moved away from politics. He worked as a farm worker in Galilee. In 1909 he joined the Hagana and supported the establishment of self-defense units in subsequent Jewish settlements. In 1912 he started to study law at Istanbul University. At the outbreak of World War I, he was in Eretz Yisrael. He was active in Jerusalem. In 1915, the Turkish authorities deported him to Egypt. In 1915 he settled in New York. There he met his future wife Paula Munweis, with whom he had three children. In 1918 he volunteered for the British Army. In the interwar period, he played a primary role in the creation of trade unions, including the General Organisation of Workers in the Land of Israel, founded in 1920 (Hebrew: HaHistadrut HaKlalit shel HaOvdim B'Eretz Yisrael, the organisation is most often referred to under the abbreviated name Histadrut). In the following years, he contributed to the unification of a significant part of the Zionist left, from which the Mapai party (Hebrew: Mifleget Poalei Eretz—Workers' Party of the Land of Israel) emerged

Fig. 65. David Ben-Gurion (in the middle) and Simon Peres (first from the left) in the Sde Boker Kibbutz, March 1, 1969, public domain

that he headed shortly after its creation. Ben-Gurion became the main political leader of *yishuv*. In 1948 he read the act of proclaiming Israel's independence and became its interim prime minister. As a result of the first parliamentary elections in 1949, his party won the leading position on the Israeli political scene, and Ben-Gurion received a democratic legitimacy for continuing to rule in Israel. At the beginning of 1954, he resigned as prime minister and withdrew from politics. He settled in kibbutz Sde Boker in the Negev Desert. In 1955 he returned to politics and became Israel's third prime minister. He resigned once again in 1963, but continued to have influence over the Israeli political scene. He eventually retired from public service in 1970. In 1973 he suffered a stroke and died. He is remembered as one of the "founding fathers" and "co-creators of Israel." He lived very modestly, which is confirmed by, among others, the decor of his houses in Tel Aviv and in Sde Boker, which now house museums dedicated to him. Even when he already held governmental functions, he would state that his occupation was "agricultural worker" (after he arrived in Eretz Yisrael, he worked for some time as a farmer in a kibbutz). He did not favour his relatives and did not solicit lucrative positions for them. His brother sold soda water and juice at a kiosk at the intersection of Nordau and Dizengoff streets in Tel Aviv (as Ryszard Löw recalls, he told various family stories for a small fee).*

---

* Interview with Ryszard Löw carried out on May 17, 2019.

Fig. 66. The house of David Ben-Gurion in Tel Aviv, which currently houses a museum dedicated to him, 2008, photo: Łukasz Tomasz Sroka

of the proclamation of independence. On May 11, 1949, Israel was admitted to the United Nations. Marcel began to take his first steps there almost at the same time as the emerging independent State of Israel. In the following years, he witnessed its intensive development, making his contribution to it.

Marcel spent the first years of his life in Israel in Haifa. Beginning in the interwar period, the city experienced an impressive boom, and the port became the driving force behind it. Until the construction of the port in Ashdod,[85] Haifa was the only deep-water port of Eretz Yisrael and later of Israel. Two more Mediterranean ports functioned, one in Tel Aviv and the other in Jaffa. The latter, however, began to be withdrawn from use. Another port was in Eilat on the Red Sea. In 1968, the Ashkelon Port, which is an oil terminal south of Tel Aviv, was opened.[86]

---

85 The Port of Ashdod, located about twenty-five kilometers south of Tel Aviv (closer to the Gaza Strip), was designed at the turn of 1957/58. It was officially opened in November 1963. Its construction was mainly related to the development of extraction and processing of mineral resources from the Dead Sea. There was also intensive development of agriculture in the southern part of the country. The construction of the port in Ashdod made it possible to shorten the inland transport of exported mineral resources as well as crates with oranges. In the following years, this port also began to handle passenger traffic (it remained mainly a freight port and now handles more than half of the cargo reaching Israel by sea). Ashdod has grown into one of Israel's major industrial centers. The largest workplaces include oil refinement. The city authorities also invest in the development of tourism and related water sports. An additional attraction of this place are ruins from past centuries, including remains of the former Ashdod fortress. In 2015, the city had over 220,000 residents. See Population. City, http://population.city/israel/ashdod/, accessed April 6, 2019.

86 Ashkelon is located on the shore of the Mediterranean, about thirty-one kilometers south of Tel Aviv, only ten kilometers north of the border with the Gaza Strip. Although the place has settlement traditions dating back to distant ancient times, the construction of the city basi-

Fig. 67. Port of Ashdod, aerial view, December 2012, photo: Amos Meron, public domain

Haifa, next to Jerusalem and Tel Aviv, is one of the three largest cities of Israel. It is associated with the work ethic, which is reflected in the saying popular in Israel: "Jerusalem prays, Tel Aviv plays, Haifa works." This saying has English

---

cally began from scratch after the proclamation of the independent State of Israel. At the end of 1949, only about 2.5 thousand people lived there. In 1961 there were 24,000 residents in Ashkelon. In 2015, there were already approx. 130 thousand. In terms of demographics, the city was largely inhabited by immigrants from the former Soviet Union and Ethiopia. The construction of the port contributed to the economic prosperity of the city. In addition to this, food, electrotechnical, chemical, automotive, and defense industries developed there. In 2005, one of the world's largest desalination stations was opened in Ashkelon (honoured with the Global Water Awards). Much effort was put into making Ashkelon an important tourist center, thanks to its wonderful, sandy beaches. A marina for yachts was built near the port. The Ashkelon National Park, which includes coastal dunes and ancient buildings, was created. Museums, sports and recreation centers and hotels were built. Great attention is paid to science, culture and public health. The Barzilai Medical Center, founded in 1961, has outstanding reputation. In 1971, it was named after the minister of health, Israel Barzilai, who died in June 1970 and who had laid the foundation stone for its construction. The Ashkelon Academic College (AAC), which was founded in 1965 as a branch of the University of Bar Ilan, is thriving. In 2007, the Council for Higher Education in Israel recognised this university as one of the largest and most important academic centers in Israel. Keren-Ashkelon, http://www.keren-ashkelon.org.il/8675/ (link not active now), accessed April 6, 2019; "With 32,000 New Housing Units Ashkelon to Become Israel's 6th Largest City," https://www.jewishpress.com/news/breaking-news/with-32000-new-housing-units-ashkelon-to-become-israels-6th-largest-city/2015/10/30/, accessed April 6, 2019; Population.City, http://population.city/israel/ashkelon/, accessed April 6, 2019; "Rząd Izraela zaaprobował plany budowy wielkiej stacji odsalania," https://inzynieria.com/wpis-branzy/projekty/2/20299,rzad-izraela-zaaprobowal-plany-budowy-wielkiej-stacji-odsalania, accessed April 7, 2019; "General Information," Ashkelon Academic College, https://www.aac.ac.il/en/about-us/general-information/, accessed April 6, 2019.

Fig. 68. Panorama of the city of Ashkelon, October 2007, public domain

roots, not Hebrew. Haifa enjoyed high status already when Marcel took his first steps there. Today it belongs to the richest cities in Israel. Its prestige is determined not only by the port, but also by the Technion Institute, oil refinery, and a number of industrial plants. Matam Industrial Center, the largest modern industrial park in Israel, operates here. It was created by Intel, Microsoft, Amdocs, Google, Yahoo, Elbit, IBM, and other companies. Convenient rail connections of Haifa with Netania, Yokneam, Karmiel and other areas are noteworthy. Haifa is less than 100 kilometers away from Tel Aviv and can be comfortably reached by train, by car, or bus, using a modern highway connecting both cities. In all variants, the journey takes about an hour.

Haifa's topography is also ideal for describing social inequalities occurring to this day in Israel (and perhaps even more visible now than ever before). The city consists of three parts arranged in a terrace system from the foot to the top of Mount Carmel. The first, the lowest one, surrounds the port. This is the poorest part of the city, life goes on there dynamically, as in every port. It is relatively easy to get a job there, especially not requiring high qualifications. In the first decades after the port was built, employment could be found there for port mechanics, merchants, cooks, porters, and cleaners. To this day it is easiest to

Fig. 69. Haifa around 1948, 1949, public domain

meet there newcomers who settled near Arab houses (at the turn of the 1980s and 1990s many emigrants from the former Soviet Union lived there). The next level of Haifa is the middle part called Hadar, which is inhabited by the Jewish middle class. In that district one can find elegant boutiques, delicatessen, and restaurants. The richest residents of the city settled in the highest-situated Carmel district. Banks and other prestigious institutions related to local government, finance, and services market opened their branches there.

Haifa belongs to cities with a relatively high percentage of the Arab population.[87] A large proportion of the Arabs in Haifa are Christians. Possibly thanks to their religious affiliation, during the Arab-Jewish war of 1948–1949 many Arabs

---

87 For example, in 2017 Haifa was inhabited by 217.6 thousand Jews (77.4% of the total population), 31.8 thousand Arabs (11.3%), and 31.7 thousand representatives of other ethnic groups (11.3%), in total 281.1 thousand people. In the same year in Tel Aviv there were 401.5 thousand Jews (90.4%), 19.7 thousand Arabs (4.4%), and 22.7 thousand representatives of other ethnic groups (5.1%), in total 443.9 thousand people; in Jerusalem, 546.1 thousand Jews (60.59%), 341.5 thousand Arabs (37.8%), and 13.7 thousand other (1.52%), in total 901.3 thousand people; and in Beersheba, 181.0 thousand Jews (87.2%), 5.1 thousand Arabs (2.5%), and 21.4 thousand other (10.3%), in total 207.5 thousand people. Central Bureau of

Fig. 70. Haifa, in the foreground the Baháʼí World Center buildings on Mount Carmel and the port, 2003, photo: Michael Paul Gollmer, public domain

in Haifa did not leave their homes, despite calls from Arab military commanders to leave those lands before the crushing blow that would "push Jews into the sea." The instigators of the war promised the Arabs that they would be able to return to their homes and even take what the Jews managed to build and gather. Those who trusted them were seriously disappointed, but the Arabs who remained in Haifa still live there today. In the public space one can see that there is a relative consensus between them and the Jews. An example is public transport—Haifa is the only city in Israel where buses run also on the Sabbath.

The location of Haifa on Mount Carmel and the magnificent view of Haifa Bay from the city makes many consider it the most beautiful city in Israel.

The name of the city harmonizes with this: according to the most common interpretation, it results from the combination of two Hebrew words: *Hof yafe*, or "Beautiful Coast." The city is called the "Israeli San Francisco." Both due to its topography and to the port, it has a special focus on the Mediterranean Sea.

Statistics, https://www.cbs.gov.il/he/Pages/default.aspx?fbclid=IwAR2PM0MxCXGBxeD qY3C-wTye9C0zEWkhxosdIiMi3hsiwBa0kunJtWHM_2rw, accessed January 7, 2019.

Fig. 71. The shop window of the Ata clothing shop, around 1940, public domain

Tourists are attracted by the unique Baháʼí temple and gardens (see Fig. 70), which together make the Baháʼí World Center, a UNESCO World Heritage Site.[88] Buildings of the former German colony and numerous museums are also very popular, the most interesting being the Atlit Detainee Camp—Museum of Illegal Immigration in Israel, National Maritime Museum, Madatech-Israel—National Museum of Science, Technology, and Space, Railway Museum, Hecht Museum of the University of Haifa (presenting contemporary art and archaeological excavations), Haifa City Museum, the Mané-Katz Museum, and the Tikotin Museum of Japanese Art. There is also the Dagon grain silo in Haifa, which houses a museum showing the history of crop production and use. The Haifa Theater and the Haifa Symphony Orchestra also enjoy great popularity.[89] The city has well-developed public transport, a network of elementary and high schools, thriving libraries, and community centers. Numerous hospitals and

---

88 Bahaism is a monotheistic, syncretic religion (it combines elements of Judaism, Christianity, Islam, Babism, and other religions), which was created in the nineteenth century in Persia.

89 Port of Haifa, http://www.haifaport.co.il/template/default_e.aspx?PageId=159, accessed April 6, 2019; Mané-Katz Museum, https://www.mkm.org.il/eng, accessed April 7, 2019.

medical facilities take care of residents' health, among which Rambam Medical Center, one of the leading hospitals in Israel, occupies an important place.[90]

When Marcel Goldman came ashore in Haifa, living conditions in Israel were hard. The state had just had its first bloody clash with the Arab army. Defense, construction of municipal infrastructure, and broadly understood structures of the state: government and parliament seats, local authorities, schools, kindergartens, hospitals, power plants, factories, farms, and others required significant expenses. Israel's economic foundations at the threshold of the birth of its statehood should be considered very weak. Due to shortages of supplies, ration coupons for basic foodstuffs were introduced, and the proposed range of products was also limited. Bianka Goldman recalls:

> At present, in Israeli grocery shops, for example, a cheese counter sometimes stretches several metres in length, and several dozen different types of cheese are lined on it. I remember that in the first years of my life in Israel, the same question was asked in shops: "Would you like red or yellow cheese?" The choice was therefore between two types of cheese. It was similar with wine. Two types of wine were sold in Israeli shops: sweet and sour, which was supposed to be dry.[91]

In the 1950s and 1960s, manufacturing was primarily based on small workshops. The basis of industry was a group of only six major enterprises. The Osem company was the leader in the production of pasta and cereal products. Olive oil production was the domain of the Shemen company. The Elite company stood out in the field of chocolate production. Nesher (Hebrew: eagle) made cement. An oil refinery operated in Haifa. In the clothing industry, the Ata company, which produced cotton clothing, was important.[92] Climatic and financial conditions resulted in the fact that Israelis dressed very practically, so most of their needs were met by the said company. It mainly offered shirts with long and

---

90 "Community Housing—Haifa," https://www.nbn.org.il/aliyahpedia/community-housing-aliyahpedia/community-profiles/haifa/ (link not active now), accessed April 07, 2019.

91 Interview with Bianka Goldman carried out on January 26, 2019.

92 The company was founded in 1935 in Kiryat Ata by the Müller family from Germany. Kiryat Ata is located near Haifa. Traces of settlement in this place date back to ancient times. A modern settlement in the form of a moshav was founded in 1925 by emigrants from Poland (at that time it was called Kefar Atta). The moshav suffered greatly as a result of an Arab attack in 1929, when the residents were evacuated. Normal life was not restored there until the following year. The Ata company contributed to the flourishing of the moshav, transformed in 1941 into a separate local government unit.

Fig. 72. Production of shirts at Ata, photo taken between 1950 and 1953, public domain

short sleeves in khaki. The poorer bought shirts with long sleeves, because after rolling them up or down they could serve respectively on hot and colder days. The wealthier, however, were supplied with two shirts, one with short sleeves and the other with long sleeves. Short pants—also khaki—were worn as part of the set. On Sabbaths and public holidays, white shirts and long gray semi-cotton trousers were worn.[93] In a short time, the company became the leading clothing manufacturer in Eretz Yisrael, and then in independent Israel, and was one of the largest companies at the time. At the end of the 1970s and in the 1980s, when the financial standard of Israelis increased significantly, the modest assortment of Ata ceased to be enough for them. Changes were initiated in the company, and not only due to practical considerations: world fashion trends were also taken into account. At that time, errors in its management by foreign owners were noted, and in 1985 it was closed down.

The biggest challenge for the young state was the absorption of incoming migration waves. The admission of a population several times larger than the one living in that territory in a relatively short time is a phenomenon that has

---

93 Interview with Marcel Goldman carried out on June 26, 2018.

no equivalent in earlier world history. The closest example is the United States, which after World War II also took in large migration waves, but the proportions recorded in that case were of a different nature. In addition, it was already a stable state, with well-formed and efficient administration, and it was also wealthy. The state of Israel was only in the shaping phase. With lean finances, it had to build administration, infrastructure, the army, education, healthcare, and other systems from scratch.

At the first stage of building the state, problems became visible in many areas, especially in the economy. The shortage of foreign currency, mentioned above in this book, and especially of the American dollar, which at that time was the main means of payment in international trade, was a serious problem for the state under construction, but it was later turned into a success. The Israeli authorities, forced to save foreign currency, had to carefully plan imports, limiting them to the necessary minimum in the first two decades of the state's existence. This stimulated internal production. Other countries in the region, rich in oil, adopted a different direction. With petrodollars, they chose shortcuts and began to meet the consumption needs of their citizens through imports. So they chose an unfavourable economic model, exported natural resources themselves, and imported highly processed goods, ranging from food to electronics. In consequence, they did not develop their own technical thought, and the related regress did not really start to be made up until the beginning of the twenty-first century, when the prospect of depletion of oil deposits and other raw materials appeared on the horizon. In addition, the trend of caring for ecology and promoting renewable energy sources, which is dangerous from the point of view of energy-exporting countries, has developed worldwide.

Israeli enterprises, having guaranteed a certain (local) market, could develop and improve the quality of their products. If they had had to face more modern competition, for example, from Western Europe and the United States, at the very beginning, they could not have coped with it—they would have fallen or would be subordinated (bought) to foreign capital. When in 1977 Begin's right-wing government began market reforms, Israeli entrepreneurs had already reached such a stage of development that they were capable of international competition. It was also important that in Israel the economy was treated in terms of general state security. This is how pioneers who built the foundations of statehood in the end of the nineteenth and the beginning of the twentieth centuries reasoned. The creation of kibbutzim and moshavim was associated not only with ideological but also with practical reasons. Zionist activists rightly assumed that in the foreseeable event of a conflict with the Arabs, the Arabs would stop supplying food to the Jewish population. That is why they focused on independence and self-sufficiency in food production. Because Israel is a country lacking great quantities of natural resources, it failed to implement a policy of self-sufficiency in all sectors of the economy. Instead, it was ensured that whenever possible, at least part of the production process took place in Israel. In order to do that, conditions favorable to the transfer of knowledge from academic centers directly to enterprises were provided. The foundations of the Israeli economy were thus built in the circumstances of the state's engagement and even protectionism. In this sense, one can notice elements specific to the economies of socialist countries, but at least one detail significantly distinguishes Israel from the countries of the Eastern Bloc, headed by the Soviet Union. In Israel, private initiative was never treated with hostility, the state apparatus was not used to combat entrepreneurs. On the contrary, from the very beginning entrepreneurs were respected, they were in the center of interest of subsequent Israeli governments. Until now, their voice has been taken very seriously, which is associated with the fact that economy is of great interest to most Israelis.

It should also be added that Israel's first prime minister and founding father, David Ben-Gurion, was democratically chosen to rule, but he was never tempted to resort to instruments used by dictators (though his political opponents had no reluctance to call him "a little dictator"). Instead, he put in a lot of effort to secure Israel's democratic system against potential threats. In fact, he concentrated great power in his hands, but thanks to that he gained great decision-making possibilities and agency for his far-reaching visions. By creating the project of the State of Israel, he allowed its content to be determined by specialists in particular fields. For example, he was able to impose an afforestation program for Israel, but he did not have the ambition to play the role of the forester choosing specific tree species. He entrusted that task to Joseph Weitz,[94] thanks to which that friend of his and expert on the subject lived to be called "the father of Israeli forests." As we know, Ben-Gurion also propagated the idea of developing the Negev Desert. However, he did not limit himself to the slogans: he took real actions towards the development of this area. First of all, he made sure that an expert base was created for each project. It is worth emphasizing that in his governing practice Ben-Gurion always planned for the long perspective and had the courage to impose his ideas on his countrymen. He knew his value, but he never

---

94 Joseph Weitz was born in 1890 in the town of Burmel in Volhynia on the territory of the former First Republic of Poland, now Ukraine, he died in 1972 in Israel.

despised others. He corresponded with many Israelis from various social strata, and kept in touch with some of them for years, even though he never met them personally. All that happened at a time when Israel was struggling to maintain independence and faced civilization challenges.

In the first few years after World War II, more Jews arrived in Israel than had lived there before the war. In the 1930s, around 200,000 Jews lived in Eretz Yisrael (about twenty percent of the total population). In 1945, there were already about 550 thousand of them (about thirty percent of the total). In the years 1948–1951, 687,000 immigrants arrived, mainly survivors of Nazi extermination camps in Europe, as well as members of Jewish communities from Arab countries in Asia and North Africa.[95] Israel helped in the evacuation of the latter because they were in mortal danger. Their relations with the Muslim population had not always been easy. After the proclamation of Israel's independence and the first Arab-Jewish war, they became, as could be expected, the target of retaliation. In November 1949, the Israeli army organized the "Magic Carpet" operation, during which about 49,000 Yemeni Jews exposed to persecution by the Arab population were evacuated by air. In May 1950, the action "Ezra and Nehemia" was carried out, thanks to which the lives of around 140,000 Iraqi Jews were saved. That year, about 33,000 Jews from Libya were evacuated as part of a secret action. In 1984, the Israeli government started to evacuate Ethiopian Jews, who are called Falash Mura (they call themselves Beta Israel, or the House/Community of Israel, and believe that they come from ancient Israel). The decision to bring them to Israel was accelerated by famine. In addition, in 1974–1991 there was a civil war in Ethiopia, which also posed a direct threat to the health and life of local Judaism followers. At the turn of 1984 and 1985, the Israel Defense Forces, with the support of American intelligence, conducted an air operation under the code name "Moses." In 1991, operation "Solomon" was carried out. In total, tens of thousands of Falash Mura reached Israel. Currently, their population in Israel is about 150 thousand people. The decade of the 1980s brought political changes in the Soviet Union that enabled the emigration of local Jews to Israel. The beginnings were rather modest. In the years 1980–1988 only 30,000 Jews from the USSR area emigrated to Israel.[96] The turn

---

95 "Population of Israel: General Trends and Indicators," https://mfa.gov.il/mfa/pressroom/1998/pages/ population%20of%20israel-%20general%20trends%20and%20indicator.aspx, accessed March 16, 2019.

96 K. Chaczko, "Społeczeństwo izraelskie," in K. Chaczko, A. Skorek, Ł.T. Sroka, *Demokracja izraelska*, preface S. Weiss, Warsaw 2018, 119.

of the 1980s and 1990s brought the political transformation and the collapse of the Soviet Union. As a result, the migration of Jews to Israel significantly accelerated. From 1989 to the early 1990s, over half a million Jews from the former Soviet Union came to Israel. The events cited here are reflected in the statistics presented in Tables 1 and 2.

Table 1. The population of Israel in 1949–1993 (*in millions*)

Year	Population	Year	Population	Year	Population
1949	1,174	1964	2,526	1979	3,836
1950	1,370	1965	2,598	1980	3,922
1951	1,578	1966	2,657	1981	3,978
1952	1,630	1967	2,776	1982	4,064
1953	1,669	1968	2,841	1983	4,119
1954	1,718	1969	2,930	1984	4,200
1955	1,789	1970	3,022	1985	4,266
1956	1,872	1971	3,121	1986	4,331
1957	1,976	1972	3,225	1987	4,407
1958	2,032	1973	3,338	1988	4,477
1959	2,089	1974	3,422	1989	4,560
1960	2,150	1975	3,493	1990	4,822
1961	2,234	1976	3,575	1991	5,059
1962	2,332	1977	3,653	1992	5,196
1963	2,430	1978	3,738	1993	5,328

Source: Israel's Ministry of Foreign Affairs, https://mfa.gov.il/mfa/pressroom/1998/pages/population%20of%20israel-%20general%20trends%20and%20indicator.aspx, accessed March 19, 2019

For the young State of Israel, the influx of so many migratory waves was as much a gift as it was a problem. People who could build and defend the country arrived. However, they had to be provided with decent living conditions: shelter, work, education, medical care, and so forth.

Full and exemplary fulfillment of these obligations proved impossible. Many activities were spontaneous, improvised, and incoherent. The immigrants, among whom there were people who barely escaped death during the Shoah and still had vivid memories of "the hell on earth" in their minds, were often frustrated by their new lives. Today, this is often not remembered. Some articles

Table 2. Immigration to Israel in 1948–1993 (*in thousands*)

Year	Number of immigrants	Year	Number of immigrants
1948	101,828	1971	41,930
1949	239,954	1972	55,888
1950	170,563	1973	54,886
1951	175,279	1974	31,981
1952	24,610	1975	20,028
1953	11,575	1976	19,754
1954	18,491	1977	21,429
1955	37,528	1978	26,394
1956	56,330	1979	37,222
1957	72,634	1980	20,428
1958	27,290	1981	12,599
1959	23,988	1982	13,723
1960	24,692	1983	16,906
1961	47,735	1984	19,981
1962	61,533	1985	10,642
1963	64,489	1986	9,505
1964	55,036	1987	12,965
1965	31,115	1988	13,034
1966	15,957	1989	24,050
1967	14,469	1990	199,516
1968	20,703	1991	176,100
1969	38,111	1992	77,057
1970	36,750	1993	76,805

Source: Israel's Ministry of Foreign Affairs, https://mfa.gov.il/mfa/pressroom/1998/pages/population%20of%20israel-%20general%20trends%20and%20indicator.aspx, accessed March 19, 2019

in the Israeli media even claim that new immigrants are treated worse than those who had lived in Israel in the first decades of its existence. For example, there is a certain tension between Ashkenazi and Sephardic Jews, who often believe that the Ashkenazi elites of Israel care more about Ashkenazi immigrants. One of their arguments is that the Ashkenazi Jews received housing from the state. In fact, Israel made the effort to build affordable municipal housing, but their supply could not keep up with the rapidly growing demand. Therefore, immigrants in the first years of Israel's existence had to show their determination to get their own housing. Most began with transition camps (Hebrew: *ma'abarot*). There, they occupied small rooms in barracks and tents. There were several families quartered in individual rooms, separated only by small curtains. Shared bathrooms and kitchens were normal. The road to the nearest bus stop often led through fields devoid of any infrastructure (such as sidewalks or lighting). For many immigrants, the first days and years of life in Israel meant the necessity of struggling with difficult living conditions and the trauma of World War II.

We can describe the situation of at least some of the newcomers as dramatic, since there were attempts to return to communist Poland.[97] The participants of the Gomulka Aliyah generally had their return path blocked. As a rule, the authorities of People's Poland denied the Israeli Jews the right to settle in Poland again. Exceptions were made very rarely. The Jews forced to leave Poland during the events of March '68 also knew that for them it was a one-way trip. After the Six-Day War, when the government of the Polish People's Republic decided (following Moscow's similar decision) to break diplomatic relations with Israel, not only return to Poland, but also visits to relatives, friends, and acquaintances, even those who were seriously ill, were forbidden. However, return was possible for Jews from Western countries.

In 1948–1982, emigration from Israel reached twenty percent of immigration, in 1983–1992 it was at thirty percent. Emigration from Israel was partly caused by failures in the acculturation of earlier immigrants.[98] The Israeli government tried to combine help for newcomers with the rational use of their potential. Immigrants from Poland usually had higher education. Many of them had engineer and doctor diplomas needed in Israel. That is why they were settled in large urban centers, such as Tel Aviv. It is hard to say that they were favoured in that matter; they were simply directed to where they were needed, where they could make the most of their skills. Jews from European countries were most often the "flower of society" of the countries they lived in. Polish or Russian Jews had previously held high positions at universities, in the media, in shipyards, factories, and architectural offices. In Israel, they often had to start from

---

97 See M. Silber, "'Immigrants from Poland Want to Go Back.' The Politics of Return Migration and Nation Building in 1950s Israel," *Journal of Israeli History* 27 (2008): 201–219.

98 "Population of Israel."

scratch, which gave them the right to feel outclassed. The government tried to prevent this so that their frustration would not increase and manifest, because it could have a deterrent effect on subsequent groups of Jews considering an *aliyah*. On the other hand, the living conditions of immigrants from African and Asian countries, often without education, still improved, even if they lived in small, remote locations, in kibbutzim and moshavim.

The Goldman family also took the path from the tent to their own apartment (we are talking here about Marcel, his parents, and sisters). At the beginning they received a tent with iron beds, mattresses, blankets, mess pots, spoons, and an oil lamp. Marcel remembers that just after disembarking someone gave him a few oranges . . . Marcel found himself in a comfortable and unique situation because he came to Israel healthy (after the Shoah many Jews had to undergo a long treatment to improve their physical or mental health). He could join his parents accommodated in the already mentioned Atlit transit camp. His sisters lived in kibbutzim at the time.[99] Marcel's first memories of Israel and his thoughts about it are interesting:

Fig. 73. Marcel's parents: Sara (first from right) and Maks accompanied by aunt Mania (father's sister), 1949, family collections of Marcel and Bianka Goldman (Tel Aviv)

---

99   Interview with Marcel Goldman carried out on December 18, 2016.

Like many other immigrants arriving in Israel by ship, I also saw Mount Carmel rising above Haifa. This view made an indelible impression on me as well, but it did not lead me to any special exaltation. I remember that some, coming ashore, kissed the ground . . . I didn't feel such a need. I remember better that an Israeli official could not communicate with me either in Hebrew, the knowledge of which I had denied during the war, or in Yiddish (Jewish), which I never knew, because we spoke Polish at home. I was surprised to see my father . . . It's possible that I wouldn't have recognized him on the street. He did not resemble that elegant man from Krakow he had used to be. I get the impression that he played the role of an Israeli just as he had imagined him. He was wearing khaki pants. He also bought this type of shirt. He probably believed that by wearing a costume promoted by Zionists, he would somehow seal his Israeliness in a symbolic way. I must point out that I have never worn this type of clothes, although of course I adapted my wardrobe to the local climate.[100]

The key to explaining the actually successful absorption of immigration waves that reached Israel in the first decades of its existence is not only the government's policy, but also the attitude of the inhabitants of the new state, who took nothing for granted and were always oriented towards the result. They wanted not only to take, but also, and above all, to give something from themselves. Marcel's impressions of life in kibbutz Kabri,[101] where he visited his sister Nela, who lived there for some time, is informative in this respect. From Marcel's statement it can be concluded that his sister was in the kibbutz only for practical reasons, certainly not ideological, which does not deny the fact that after World War II kibbutzim were often created by people who treated their work as a mission. During that visit, Marcel's mother noticed a man milking a cow, which interested her, as she came from the village. She came up to him and asked: "How much do you get for it? He replied: 'I do not get, I give.'"[102]

The Goldmans lived in the transit camp, which was treated as a kind of quarantine, for a short period of time. Later they were transferred to a camp located almost on the top of Mount Carmel, which was taken over from British soldiers.

---

100 Interview with Marcel Goldman carried out on March 16, 2019.
101 Kibbutz Kabri is located in northern Israel near the border with Lebanon on the slopes of the hills of Western Galilee.
102 Interview with Marcel Goldman carried out on June 13, 2018.

There was Beit Olim or House of Newcomers.[103] Next to it, there were tents referred to as Hindu, because they consisted of double canvases to reduce the heat inside. One of them was assigned to the Goldmans. The area of the camp corresponded roughly to today's campus of the University of Haifa. At that time, getting there required a long (about two kilometers) climb, because the buses reached only the Achuza Central stop.

The Mount Carmel camp was not temporary. Emigrants stayed there longer: some stayed half a year, others a year or even two years, depending on when they were allocated housing by the state. Those who had funds could leave the camp earlier. The Goldman family stayed there no more than two months.

Participants of the following *aliyot* also went through transit camps. The life there was described by Nili Amit, who came to Israel as part of the Gomulka Aliyah:

> I feel at home in the transit camp of asbestos barracks built on the sands near the town of Bat Yam. Everyone around speaks Polish . . . . Many old friends of my parents are here, and with most children I went to the same school or even the same form in Wrocław. . . . In summer . . . an *ulpan* is organised for children and adults. We are all diligent in learning Hebrew. . . . Following their [teachers'—Ł.T.S.] advice I changed my Polish name Nela to Hebrew Nili, thanks to which I have the impression that I am becoming an almost indigenous *sabra*! We also learn Israeli songs: *Opposite Mount Sinai*, composed on the occasion of the 1956 Suez campaign, and *Who will Eulogize the Deeds of Israel*, and we are full of patriotic pride.[104]

Marcel's father found a flat at a bargain price, previously owned by Arabs. It was abandoned in 1948, when the flats and houses of the Arabs who escaped during the First Israeli-Arab War were taken over as "abandoned property" by the state commissioner. That particular apartment which Maksymilian Goldman became interested in was taken over by the family of a doctor from Germany, so Marcel's father did not really buy it, he only paid them 2,000 dollars for leaving it. Those were their last savings from the sale of the house in Podgórze, which Marcel's mother inherited from her brother. The new apartment was located in the lower district of Haifa, on the first floor of a small two-storey house, which had another apartment on the ground floor. Apart from the tap in the

---

103 In Hebrew the word *aliyah* means "climbing upward," and the phrase *olim chadashim*, as already explained, means "newcomers."

104 Amit, *A miałam być księżniczką z bajki*, 62–63.

kitchen, there was no plumbing at home. The Goldmans decided to renovate the apartment. As the only residents of the first floor they adapted a part of the staircase to their needs to arrange a toilet and a shower. Marcel also remembers the peculiar surroundings of the house: "On the one side there was a cemetery, and on the other there were railway tracks through which a train running between Haifa and Tel Aviv passed."[105]

Today, housing troubles are still present in memories of many Polish Jews. Shevah Weiss's family immigrated to Israel after World War II. First, he and his brother arrived there, then (with considerable delay, mainly due to the illness of his father) his parents and sister joined:

> Uncle Shaye, my mother's brother, lived in Israel and took my parents home. I had some savings because I was earning already in the tenth grade. I was a guide of a younger group in Hadassim, an agricultural school near Netanya. I had about eight hundred liras. My brother also worked and collected three hundred liras. For this thousand, we bought a small one-room flat with a shared kitchen and a toilet in the corridor. In 1955, my parents received compensation from Germany. Rather modest. But it was enough to buy a two-room apartment in Haifa.[106]

The high price of real estate in Israel was not only determined by geopolitical conditions (which I will describe in more detail in the next chapter). The difficult situation of tens of thousands of emigrants created a unique earning opportunity for property owners and builders. Of course, demand shapes supply under all latitudes and vice versa. The problem is that the situation on the Israeli real estate market was difficult to reconcile with publicly proclaimed slogans about the solidarity of Jews building their state. Deep indignation in this respect can be seen in the diary of Apolinary Hartglas,[107] who after escaping from Poland to Israel was not able to find a flat at a decent price: "The apartments were not rented, only the right to rent them was sold for amounts I could not have dreamed of in my wildest dreams."[108] To his satisfaction, the then labor minister

---

105 Interview with Marcel Goldman carried out on December 18, 2016.
106 Weiss, *Pamiętam*, 57.
107 Apolinary Hartglas (1883–1953), an influential Zionist politician and parliamentarian in prewar Poland, escaped from Poland to Eretz Yisrael (via Trieste) during World War II. He and his wife first lived in Jerusalem and then moved to Tel Aviv in July 1948. He later became a high official in Israel's Ministry of the Interior.
108 A. Hartglas, *Na pograniczu dwóch światów*, intro and ed. J. Żyndul, Warsaw 1996, 406.

Golda Meir (later the minister of foreign affairs and the fourth prime minister of Israel) intervened in the real estate sector:

> [She] finally decided to say a few harsh words to construction workers, accusing them of the fact that most of them collect usury in the black construction market and that this could force her to bring construction workers from Italy, otherwise the government would not be able to build houses necessary for the admission of new immigrants. There was unrest, protests, and the central secretary of the Construction Workers' Union twice called Mrs Meyerson's statement "extortion."[109]

Marcel Goldman's parents lived in a modest Haifa house until 1956. Those years were not easy. Maks had a problem with finding a job, because the local labor market, needed people either young and strong (for work in the field, in industry, and road construction), or older, but with appropriate professional qualifications (doctors or lawyers with fluent knowledge of the Hebrew language). For obvious reasons, Maks did not belong to either group. He endured

> **i** Golda Meir (Meyerson) was born on May 3, 1898 in Kiev as Golda Mabovitch, she had seven siblings. At the age of eight she went to the United States with her family. After turning fourteen, her parents wanted her to get married, but she did not comply and moved to her sister living in Denver. There she met her future husband, Morris Meyerson. In 1921, she emigrated with him and her sister to Eretz Yisrael. She settled in kibbutz Merhavia. She proved to be a talented leader and a committed socialist who fought for women's equality. In 1924 she moved to Jerusalem. She co-founded the Social-Democratic Workers Party of Israel (Mapai) and the General Organisation of Workers in Israel (Histadrut). In the years 1969–1974 she was the prime minister of Israel. She became famous for her decisive rule, because of which she was dubbed the "Iron Lady" long before the British Prime Minister Margaret Thatcher. After the massacre of Israeli athletes by Palestinian terrorists during the Munich Olympics in 1972, she gave Mosad the order to eliminate the members of the Black September organization and the Popular Front for the Liberation of

---

109 Ibid., 407–408.

Fig. 74. Golda Meir with children in kibbutz Shefayim during the opening ceremony of the Tel Aviv–Netaniya road, 1950, photo: Teddy Brauner, public domain

Palestine, who were responsible for that act. Those events became the basis for Steven Spielberg's 2005 film *Munich*. At the same time, she was caring and protective, which was reflected in her nicknames, "mother" and "grandmother" of the Jewish nation. The government's propaganda service used that, and purposefully showed Golda Meir as a mother gathering all of Israel's children around her. An example of this is a popular photo (Fig. 74) of Golda Meir with children in kibbutz Shefayim. These character traits resulted from her own experience, but were also in line with her political profile (she was a member of socialist formations) and union career (during which she helped those in need). The government meetings, which she often conducted at her home, are shrouded in legend. They were conducted in a warm atmosphere, Meir prepared meals, and the ministers helped to lay the table. On April 11, 1974, she resigned from the office of prime minister, mainly because of the defeats suffered by Israel in the first phase of the Yom Kippur war. After retiring from public life, she devoted herself to writing books. She died on December 8, 1978 in Jerusalem.

that situation very badly. He was the type of prewar gentleman; for him, to guarantee dignified living conditions for his family was the matter of honour, which proved impossible in his new life. In an intimate story titled "Spowiedź starego człowieka" (English: An old man's confession), published in 2014 in the Israeli daily *Haaretz*, Marcel writes:

> My father was looking for a job. He would go from one office to another, to employment services, to Histadrut, he talked with people, he went outside of Haifa. And all for nothing. For a forty-eight-year-old man after a heart attack and with very limited sight there was no work. After running out of energy that was still in him, he fell into apathy and almost depression. He was hanging around the apartment, trying to do something. He disturbed my mother. He wasn't used to sitting at home. During almost four years of German occupation he was the director. In communist Poland he was the general director of a shoe factory. Even after leaving for the Czech Republic, he earned well to support his family. Now he has become unnecessary!
>
> I can still see my father. He is sitting at the table and reading. He always read *Readers Digest* in German, which could be bought at kiosks at the time. Hunched, because he could read only with a magnifying glass. He held the magnifying glass near his better eye, very close to the text. A tragic figure of a man who rolled down from the top to the very bottom in a very short period of time.[110]

Maksymilian also endured badly the fact that Marcel had to take on the burden of supporting his family, finding employment as an accountant in the construction company Palroad[111] run by a Polish Jew named Perec. To this day, Marcel is bothered by the words spoken by his father during one of the conversations. Hearing what serious responsibilities were entrusted to his son in his new workplace, he said: "I will not be the one to take you out of jail!"[112] Why was his attitude so unfavorable? According to Marcel, in those words "there was a critical assessment of my professional competences, but there was certainly some regret and bitterness related to the fact that I was developing while he was stuck."[113] With his new work, Marcel showed great determination to acquire new competences, and above all to learn the Hebrew language: "I decided to learn

---

110 Goldman, "Spowiedź starego człowieka."
111 The company Palroad (short for Palestine Road) was founded during the British Mandate. On behalf of the British, it built roads and airports.
112 Interview with Marcel Goldman carried out on January 26, 2019.
113 Ibid.

Hebrew so that I could at least communicate. So I bought the book *1000 Words in Hebrew* and started swotting up, and as after two weeks I started to work, the time to learn was only at night. By the candle."[114]

Restoration of the Hebrew language for everyday use became a part of the Zionist project. Zionist activists assumed that the Hebrew language would become an important bond connecting the Jewish people in their own state. The rejection of the Yiddish language and the national languages of the countries in which the Jews had previously resided was part of the break with the diaspora heritage. Resurrecting the language that had for centuries been used mainly for liturgical purposes was not a simple task. In fact, poets and writers also used Hebrew, but in Jewish homes people did not speak that language on a daily basis. Yiddish dominated among European Jews, and the Sephardi Jews mostly used Judeo-Spanish, or Ladino. Jews assimilated and accultured to the main cultural trends of specific countries used the languages of their former homelands: Polish, Russian, German, English, Hungarian, Romanian, and so forth. The task of reactivating and modernizing Hebrew, along with inventing new words for things and concepts that appeared since ancient times, was taken by Eliezer Ben-Yehuda,[115] a linguist, writer, and Zionist activist. When he began his work, he was affronted both by those who did not believe in the chance of success and the seriousness of his work, and by the Orthodox Jews who maintained that the use of Hebrew in everyday activities desecrated the religious nature of that language. Still, he did not give up. Thanks to his support and perseverance, the Zionist activists managed to complete their plan and succeeded in reviving the Hebrew language. Today one can find streets named after him in all of Israel. Ben-Yehuda died in 1922, the same year when Hebrew gained the status of one of the three official languages of the British Mandate in Palestine (alongside English and Arabic). Before that happened, Zionist politicians themselves were doubtful about the success of Hebrew as everyday language. Even Teodor Herzl wrote the following in his diary: "We cannot communicate with each other in Hebrew. Who of us knows Hebrew enough to buy, for example, a train ticket in this language? It's impossible."[116]

---

114 Goldman, *A w nocy przychodzą myśli*, 7.

115 Eliezer Ben-Yehuda (1858–1922) came from the village of Łużki (now Belarus, formerly the territory of the First Republic of Poland). In 1881 he emigrated to Eretz Yisrael.

116 T. Herzl, *Państwo żydowskie. Próba nowoczesnego rozwiązania kwestii żydowskiej*, trans. J. Surzyn, Krakow 2006, 132.

In 1948, Hebrew naturally became the official language of Israel (next to Arabic). Later, Maria Lewińska coined an accurate statement: without knowledge of the Hebrew language in Israel, one could feel like "an illiterate with higher education."[117] In a short time, Hebrew penetrated all areas of people's life: the most important newspapers and magazines were published in this language, radio programs were broadcast, printed forms, notices, and official letters were issued, signs, advertisements, packaging, in a word, it was everywhere. Knowledge of Hebrew was necessary for middle and senior positions in companies and public institutions. It was promoted by the Israeli authorities, who assumed that Hebrew was a convenient tool for uniting Israeli society, made up largely of immigrants from different countries who used separate languages. Going one step further, the government began to impose on citizens the Hebraization of their names and surnames. To give an example, the politicians did so themselves, including David Ben-Gurion (formerly Dawid Grün), Golda Meir (Golda Meyerson), Menachem Begin (Mieczysław Biegun), Shimon Peres (Szymon Perski). The Goldmans avoided that compulsion. Apolinary Hartglas, who was mentioned earlier, retained his name, and commented on that situation in an interesting way:

> Names are Hebraized, which is quite right, but forcing the officials of the Ministry of Foreign Affairs and the army officers to Hebraize is already an exaggeration. If the Prime Minister Ben-Gurion himself had long ago Hebraized his name, it was his private affair, in which he lost nothing, because he began his career, distinguished himself, and became famous under that name, and before that no one in Poland knew or was interested in the young Grün from Płońsk.... Once at a Knesset commission meeting, ... before the meeting was opened, a well-known workers activist, Ben-Tzvi, jokingly mentioned that my name had such a German sound that it would be appropriate to change it. I told him that, first of all, I have no reason to be ashamed of my father, and, secondly, my name is the only property I took from the diaspora along with two small suitcases.[118]

The sad paradox is that the "Jewish" names of newcomers first disturbed the Europeans, then the Israeli government. They contributed to the rejection of the diaspora heritage and the Yiddish culture.

---

117 See M. Lewińska, *Analfabeci z wyższym wykształceniem*, Krakow–Budapest 2016.
118 Hartglas, *Na pograniczu*, 371–372.

People with state posts, especially diplomats in the broad sense, felt the strongest pressure to Hebraize their names and surnames. The Israeli authorities decided that the state could only be represented by people with Hebrew names. Others could avoid it more easily. Such a change was often made by the officials responsible for registering newcomers, especially children, for whom officials or teachers took decisions. In memoir literature, it is often recounted that children were presented with a fait accompli. They heard from their teachers: "I sign you up in school documents as . . ." Admittedly, efforts were made to match the old name (or at least its sounds) as close as possible. In this way, Lidka could receive the name Lili, and Marysia returned home as Miriam . . . Also during registration in the army, Hebraization of names or surnames often happened. For these reasons, some Israelis had several names. For example, Alona Frankel, a book illustrator and writer, explains: "In Krakow I was Ilona, during the war I was named Irena in my Aryan papers, in the school in Tel Aviv I became Ilana, and when I went to the army, . . . someone made a mistake and I became Alona."[119] At the end of the twentieth century, citizens gained more freedom of choice in this respect, and nowadays various, sometimes original and foreign-sounding (from the Hebrew perspective) names are used.

As a side note, it is worth mentioning that the liberalization of the Israeli government's policy towards foreign names is a sign not of weakness, but of the strength of the state. It does not contradict the affirmation of the Hebrew language in Israel's public space, but it interacts with the change of course in the attitude of the country's authorities. While in the first decades of the state's existence, the diaspora's heritage was rejected, now Israel is trying to be its depository. An emblematic example of this is the frescoes of Bruno Schulz, which he painted in 1942 in the villa occupied by Felix Landau, the head of the Gestapo in Drohobych.[120] In an attempt to preserve them, the Israelis removed the surviving fragments of the frescoes to Yad Vashem in 2001. Moreover, on August 7, 2016, the Supreme Court of Israel issued a verdict ordering Eva Hoff, daughter

---

119 Alona Frankel, "Rozdwojona," interview with Katarzyna Bielas, *Wysokie Obcasy* 25 (2007): 14.
120 Drohobych—a city within the borders of the First Polish-Lithuanian Commonwealth before 1772. In 1772, after the partitions, it became a part of the Habsburg monarchy, and in the years 1918–1939, it returned to the revived Second Polish Republic. During World War II, it was alternately occupied by Soviet and German soldiers. After World War II, Drohobych was part of the Soviet Union, and from 1991 it is within the borders of independent Ukraine. Bruno Schulz, the outstanding Jewish writer, artist, painter, illustrator, and literary critic, lived in Drohobych. On November 19, 1942, he was murdered by a German officer.

of Esther (Ilse), a friend and secretary of the writer Max Brod (1884–1968), to hand over the manuscripts and documents of Franz Kafka (1883–1924) to the National Library of Israel.[121] Benjamin Balint, an Israeli-American journalist (born in 1976 in the United States, his great-grandparents came from Bytom) aptly comments on this situation:

> Today, official state policy aims to make Jerusalem the place where the history of the Jewish diaspora ends. The port that all Jews scattered around the world are supposed to reach and where they are supposed to bring their stories, experiences, and memories. And this is where the cultural heritage of all the people of Israel spread around the world, including manuscripts and books, will come.... To understand all this, one needs to know that after 1945—after the war ended and a moment later, after the creation of the state of Israel—its attitude towards the diaspora and its achievements was largely based on denying what had been created beyond its current borders. Zionist leaders dreamed of a revolution, a new beginning, cutting off from the trauma of the past and the accretion of cultures that had let the Jews down. Everything that had happened before was denied, so opposition to the diaspora culture was also very strong. Especially diasporas from Central and Eastern Europe, using not the revived Hebrew, but German or Yiddish. Later events, growing pride, further conflicts and solidification of the state changed, however, Israeli optics. It was recognized that everything related to Jewish tradition and culture must return home. That is, to the present Israel.[122]

This is a clever action, because it constitutes Jerusalem as the treasury of the greatest achievements of Jews from around the world. This policy does not interfere with the course of the state aimed at supporting *aliyah*, but facilitates it, because it seems to suggest to Jews living in different places in the world: come as you are, with what you have.

At the time of the proclamation of Israel's independence, the main tool of social communication in the world was the press. That is why the government conducted a thoughtful policy in this respect, adapting it to the changing realities. Despite the pressure on Hebraization, it was obvious that an immigrant who did not speak the language at all would not start reading Hebrew-language newspapers overnight or even from week to week. That is why Hebrew titles

---

121 Brod mentioned this legacy in his last will after his friend Franz Kafka had entrusted it to him with a request to burn it. See B. Balint, *Ostatni proces Kafki*, trans. K. Kurek, Warsaw 2019.

122 Benjamin Balint, "Czyje gołębie powinien karmić Kafka," interview by Michał Nogaś, *Gazeta Wyborcza*, March 23–24, 2019.

were preferred, but the existence of press published in diaspora languages, such as Polish, German, Yiddish, Bulgarian, Romanian, and Hungarian, was also allowed. The abolition of foreign-language press would have forced many immigrants resident in Israel to live outside the circulation of information and away from the cultural mainstream. This would have brought the opposite effect from what was intended. Elżbieta Kossewska comments on the policy of the Israeli authorities:

> Shortly after the creation of the state, the increase in foreign-language publications made them a sector dominating over the Hebrew-language press. The waves of Jews coming to Israel did not increase the Hebrew population, on the contrary—they diluted it, reducing the distance between it and the foreign-language community. The Israeli authorities, in a situation of a significant influx of new citizens, had to face a serious problem of protecting the Hebrew language. An important step in that direction was the establishment of Hebrew language courses—*ulpanim*, conducted under the auspices of the Hebrew Language Department and the Education Department. The first *ulpan* was created in mid-September 1949 at Etzion Immigrant Home in Jerusalem, the second was opened in Machane Israel, and Jews from Poland benefited greatly from this offer.[123]

Bianka Goldman and her father benefited from the Hebrew language learning program. Marcel decided to master Hebrew himself, because he had to learn the language and at the same time work to support his family. He was motivated to learn Hebrew quickly by his immediate supervisor, the head of the office, a Yemeni Jew, Avram Garti. Every day Garti gave Marcel Hebrew press to read and asked him to answer the phone. Telephone conversations were particularly stressful for Marcel, because most of them had to be conducted in the language he was learning. He also remembers that it was thanks to Garti that he first tasted hummus, a traditional Israeli dish.[124]

Through the prism of Marcel Goldman's biography, interesting patterns accompanying the evolution of the Hebrew language in Israel's private and public space can be seen. In conversations and memories, many Polish Jews in Israel admit that, while they tried to "switch to Hebrew" at work or in public places,

---

123 E. Kossewska, *"Ona jeszcze mówi po polsku, ale śmieje się po hebrajsku." Partyjna prasa polskojęzyczna i integracja kulturowa polskich Żydów w Izraelu (1948–1970)*, Warsaw 2015, 39.

124 Interview with Marcel Goldman carried out on June 11, 2018.

they still communicated in Polish at home. An exception were mixed marriages, if the husband or wife did not speak Polish, the Hebrew language became a natural tool for their daily communication. Marcel and Bianka Goldman remember precisely when they decided to change their everyday language from Polish to Hebrew. It was 1956, when their daughter Orit was born:

> With Bianka, we decided to talk to the child only in Hebrew to facilitate her perception of the language. We knew that soon she would have to communicate with her peers in this language, first in kindergarten, then at school. So we wanted to make learning the Hebrew language easier for her. However, in a situation where we were sure that the children could not hear us, we communicated in various languages, we often switched from Hebrew to Polish.[125]

Marcel bravely admits that, although he quickly learned the Hebrew language and speaks it fluently, his language is a street language—simple, and certainly not literary. That is why, as I have already mentioned, the medium for his work is the Polish language acquired at home, writing in which he can be sure of a high literary level. It is worth adding that, in Israel, adolescence usually coincides with the period of military service. At the time when European youth take up studies and fill university campuses, young Israelis, after graduating from high school, begin military service and settle in barracks. This development cycle is reflected in the specific shape of Hebrew commonly used in Israel. It is characterized by functionality, simplicity, and frequent use of abbreviations—this applies, for example, to names. Many people, even those who hold the highest positions in the state, often appear under nicknames, such as "Bibi" instead of "Benjamin" or "Rafi" instead of "Rafael." It is interesting that the Hebrew language lacks more sophisticated curses, so that cursewords are borrowed from other languages, most often from Yiddish and Arabic. It is worth adding that Israeli writers and scientists are aware that their language, despite the great and ancient traditions, is rarely known outside Israel and outside the Jewish communities in the world. That is why Israelis attach great importance to translating their work into foreign languages (first of all, English, then French, Spanish, German, Russian, and Italian). All in all, Marcel quickly mastered the Hebrew language, the knowledge of which, along with professional skills and competences as well as appropriate character traits, lay at the heart of his pro-

---

125 Interview with Marcel Goldman carried out on March 16, 2019.

fessional successes. Many older immigrants who were unable to learn to speak Hebrew fluently could not work in positions equivalent to those previously occupied in Poland or corresponding to their aspirations.

Marcel's sisters also quickly became independent and formed their lives. At the age of eighteen, Nela married a Czech Jew, but she quickly divorced him without having children. In 1957, she got involved with Henryk Grycendler (I will talk about him in the next chapter), a machine construction engineer, who had arrived from Poland as part of the Gomulka Aliyah. She had a happy life with him; they had two daughters. Marcel remembers her as a person who combined artistic talent with the ability to act precisely. She started as a kitchen help in a restaurant, but photography was her passion. She completed a special course and worked as a retouching photographer in the largest studio in Haifa. She also learned how to make beautiful flower sculptures. She was a very cultured person and ran a wonderful home. She died of cancer at the age of forty-eight. The younger, adoptive sister Róża married a Romanian Jew, they had two sons. Their financial situation was difficult—neither she nor her husband Sando found lucrative jobs. She became widowed fairly quickly: Sando was just over fifty when he died suddenly. However, she received consolation from her sons, who surrounded her with affectionate care. The elder worked in the banking sector, and Marcel helped him find a job. Being a deputy director in a Tel Aviv bank, Marcel proposed hiring his nephew in a rank-and-file position. Later, as Marcel declares, he was no longer interested in his nephew's career, and the young man managed without his help. He took a number of courses to gain managerial qualifications and competences, and worked his way up to the position of a branch manager. He enjoyed a good reputation among clients as a polite and obliging person. The younger son worked in a social security institution in the investigation department. Marcel describes him as an energetic man who loved his family deeply. He showed great interest in his mother's history, and together with Marcel he even travelled to Poland—they followed in the footsteps of Róża, visiting, for instance, the orphanage, where she had stayed for some time between 1947 and 1948. At the end of 2017, Róża celebrated her eightieth birthday. In addition to two sons, she had, at that time, five grandchildren and one great-grandson.[126]

In Israel, Marcel consistently adhered to the principle that he would not work in a state position and would not join any political party. His father had done the

---

126 Interview with Marcel Goldman carried out on January 7, 2018.

same before the war. Postwar experiences from communist Poland only assured both of them that such a decision was correct. In Israeli conditions, apoliticality brought considerable costs, because initially the left-wing party Mapai and its associated trade union Histadrut were almost omnipotent. In addition, in a state built practically from scratch, ambitious and well-educated people had a chance for a rapid promotion in the state administration, diplomacy, army, and special services. Marcel did not take advantage of that option and never regretted it later. It was not, however, a kind of dogma, but rather a consequence of experiences derived from Poland. He did not mind that his grandchildren worked for the state. Still, Marcel's daughter also never took a job in a state institution. She was the head of the kindergarten at the Hadassa Hospital in Jerusalem[127] run by the international Jewish women organization WIZO (Women's International Zionist Organization), which was established in 1920 in London.

As the sole breadwinner, Marcel's military service was postponed for more than two years. In 1951, the recruitment committee informed him that further delay was no longer possible and that he would soon be assigned to the appropriate military unit.[128] This is not particularly surprising, because in Israeli society the army occupies a very important place, it is simply the guarantee of the country's survival. Both men and women must complete compulsory military service. After military service, they do not lose contact with the army for a long time. Until the age of forty-five, they are called to monthly reservist exercises. This is an extremely problematic burden on the economy, especially for small businesses. For individual entrepreneurs, this often requires suspension of business during exercise, and the related losses are difficult to make up for. Moreover, the history of Israel is woven with wars, so one also has to take into account going to the front, which happened to Marcel. Major armed conflicts have a destabilizing effect on the economy. Also, in case of military conflicts, the mobilization may be extended by several months or more.

Before joining the army, he managed to agree with the owner of the company that his father would replace him in his position. Initially, his father was not formally employed, Marcel officially held the position and the salary was paid in his name: "I convinced the owner that I would introduce my father to my duties and explain everything to him in Polish, because he still could not speak Hebrew

---

127 Interview with Marcel Goldman carried out on December 20, 2016; Correspondence with Marcel Goldman, February 6, 2019.
128 Interview with Marcel Goldman carried out on December 18, 2016.

well at the time. I argued that my father was a merchant for many years and later worked in a factory as general manager."[129] After apprenticeship of about two months, the office manager gave a positive opinion about Marcel's father taking over his duties to the owner of the company, thanks to which an official employment contract was concluded. Thanks to finding a job for his father, Marcel could go to the army without further concern.

Marcel's father maintained his job until 1954 or 1955, when the company went bankrupt. Its collapse had no relation to the work of Maksymilian, who dealt with simple matters. During that time, many companies that had been opened under the British, were liquidated because they were unable to adapt to new social, political, and economic realities. After losing his job, Maks and Sara tried to run an independent business—they opened a haberdashery shop as they had done in Krakow. It gave a certain illusion of occupation, but certainly did not bring income. Years later, Marcel claims that the location of the shop in the lower part of the city was primarily at fault. People living there at the time limited their expenses to the minimum because of poverty. The purchase of new buttons, bags, belts, or decorative ribbons was not among their priorities. In addition, the loose style of clothes adopted by many Israelis did not place such details too high in the hierarchy of needs.[130]

Initially, Marcel's military service was to last for two years, but it was half-a-year longer.[131] He was assigned to the Golani unit, which today has an elite character. At the time when Marcel served in it, it consisted of people randomly chosen, poorly armed, and not necessarily trained at the highest level. It seems that the Israeli army was still experimenting then, testing different models of training its soldiers, and certainly suffered from underfunding. According to Marcel's memories:

> The basis of our arms supply were the weapons dating back to World War II. We had Czechoslovak rifles. Some of them still had engraved swastikas, because the Protectorate of Bohemia and Moravia produced them for the needs of the Third Reich. Our unit was made up of people from very different countries, from different cultures, often with habits absolutely incompatible with the requirements of the army. I remember that some colleagues were afraid of night service. One time, night exercises were announced. Not everyone understood the commands in

---

129 Ibid.
130 Interview with Marcel Goldman carried out on December 18, 2016.
131 Ibid; Correspondence with Marcel Goldman, March 23, 2018.

Fig. 75. Marcel Goldman in the Israeli army parade, first in the second row, circa 1951–1953, family collections of Marcel and Bianka Goldman (Tel Aviv). This photograph and the preceding one perfectly document the condition of the Israeli army at its dawn: Israeli soldiers, British uniforms, Czechoslovak rifles

Hebrew. Some thought that a war broke out. One of my colleagues threw his rifle on the ground and said that he would not fight, and certainly not at night. Of course, there was also a certain dose, as I judge it today, of stupidity on the part of our officers. I will give an example: at some point we were obliged to fill the bottle with water when entering the training ground, but we were prohibited from drinking it. Returning to the unit, we were to give back full bottles. Apparently, the commanders thought that in that way they would accustom us, or more precisely our organisms, to function longer without water. Complete nonsense. You can't do that. Therefore, some soldiers, especially our colleagues from the Orient, approached Arab villages and looked for the remnants of watermelons thrown away by the Arabs, the inedible but juicy shells, to suck water out of them.[132]

Marcel believes that it took a long time before the army became an institution integrating Israeli citizens. He remembers that even during his service, the separatism of individual groups was clear: European, Moroccan, or Middle East-

---

132 Interview with Marcel Goldman carried out on June 13, 2018.

Fig. 76. Marcel Goldman in the uniform of the Israeli army, circa 1951–1953, family collection of Marcel and Bianka Goldman (Tel Aviv)

ern Arab Jews preferred to stay in their group and shun the others as much as possible. The integration and educational programs adopted by the army finally had a clear effect and today this situation looks much better.[133]

In 1953, in the last year of his military service, Marcel decided to resume economic studies he began in Krakow. In the years 1953–1956 he studied economics at the Haifa branch of the Tel Aviv School of Law and Economics (Beit Sefer Gavoha LeMishpat VeKalkala), which was based in the Hadar district (the school was made up of two faculties: Economics and Law). Marcel was admitted to the second year because he graduated from the first year at the Krakow University (he did not manage to pass the second year, as mentioned). In addition, he was required to pass an exam in Hebrew and to confirm his knowledge of the Tanakh (the Hebrew Bible). The studies were paid, but as *ole chadash* he could count on a discount. He faced a real challenge—he had to find time for his military service as well as studies.

His schedule was quite tight: after receiving the pass, he had to hurry, often run, to get on the bus leaving around 17:00 to Haifa, to make it to classes that started around 18:00. He finished between 21:00 and 22:00, then he went to the family home. There, a supper prepared by his mother was always waiting for him by the bed. He had a few hours to sleep, but at five in the morning he had to get up to return to the military unit located near Afula in northern Israel before eight o'clock.[134]

---

133 Ibid.
134 Interview with Marcel Goldman carried out on December 18, 2016.

Fig. 77. Marcel Goldman and his wife Bianka on their wedding day,
August 12, 1954,
family collections of Marcel and Bianka Goldman (Tel Aviv)

In the third year the situation got complicated because the university authorities, despite earlier assurances, closed the branch in Haifa. From then on, students from that institution had to commute to Tel Aviv to attend classes.[135] There were twelve people from Haifa studying with Marcel in the same year. They decided to share their duties—every day one person from the group went to Tel Aviv, listened to the lectures, took notes, and borrowed the assigned reading material. Marcel's last two years of education took place after he had finished his military service. Certainly leaving the barracks made it easier to finish education, but at the same time he faced new challenges related to family and professional life. That time he combined studies with work and new responsibilities resulting from starting his own family. On August 12, 1954, he married Bianka née Ebersohn.

He met his future wife in 1952 thanks to his father's cousin's husband, Polajner.[136] One day, the Polajner family invited Bianka's parents as well as Mar-

---

135 Shortly after Marcel Goldman graduated, the university was absorbed by the newer Tel Aviv University.

136 Polajner came from Poland and was a civil engineer by profession. He emigrated before the proclamation of Israel's independence. He worked on the construction of roads and coopera-

cel for Saturday afternoon tea. Circumstances indicate that it was an attempt at matchmaking known in Jewish culture. The hosts knew that in 1950 the Ebersohns came to Israel with two marriageable daughters. They probably thought that Marcel, a bachelor who had recently settled in Israel and was just finishing his military service, would be a good candidate for one of them. However, Marcel remembers that during the first meeting his attention was drawn primarily to Bianka's father, with whom he made friends very quickly: "That day I fell in love not with Bianka, but with Bianka's father," he jokes.[137] He often met with the father for long conversations, during which they talked about various topics related to politics, economics, and other areas of life. As he states: "On such occasions I often 'had a look' at Bianka and I liked her a lot."[138] During one of the meetings he suggested going to the cinema together. Later, they went for long walks. They both lived very modestly at the time, so they could not afford sophisticated cultural entertainment. Most often they walked along the streets of Haifa, stopping at more elegant shops and dreaming that one day they would be able to buy there. There were some exceptions, for instance, they managed to attend Shoshana Damari's concert,[139] who was one of the most popular singers in Israel at that time. Only soldiers could buy a ticket to her performance in the Haifa cinema Armon (Hebrew: palace), and Marcel, then a senior sergeant, coincidentally took over the function of the quartermaster in the regiment. He had to replace a lieutenant who had just been released from the unit because he had failed his superiors. As the quartermaster, Marcel also had better conditions to study.[140]

Before the wedding, Bianka first lived with her parents and sister in a one-room apartment in the barracks of the transit camp (originally built for the British soldiers), located about half-an-hour away from Haifa by car. Then they moved to *ma'abara* (Hebrew: transit camp) Mahane Israel (Hebrew: Israel's Camp) near Tel Aviv. A few months after arriving in Israel, Bianka got her first

---

tive estates for newcomers, the so-called *shikuns*. He was employed in a construction company, the same in which Marcel, with his help, got his first job in Israel.

137 Interview with Marcel Goldman carried out on December 18, 2016.
138 Ibid.
139 Shoshana Damari (1923–2006) was born in Yemen. In 1924, after the outbreak of anti-Jewish persecution, her family emigrated to Eretz Yisrael. She showed musical talent early in her youth, she had a unique voice and charm. Many of the songs she sang became popular in Israel. N. Shahar, "Shoshana Damari," https://jwa.org/encyclopedia/article/damari-shoshana, accessed February 10, 2019.
140 Interview with Marcel Goldman carried out on December 18, 2016.

job at a jewellery shop in Tel Aviv. Family connections helped, because she had neither education nor experience in this field. Thanks to the kindness and trust of the owner, she was quickly trained to deal with new responsibilities. Every morning, she weighed out the right amount of gold for the jewellers coming to work, and afterwards she received gold from them, weighed it, and recorded the result in a special notebook. She also learned how to calculate the weight of jewellery waste. She worked there for almost two years.

During that time, her sister went to Netanya, where she lived with her cousin, who had come to Eretz Yisrael before the outbreak of World War II. She worked in a café. Bianka's parents also left the camp, her father obtained accommodation in Jerusalem, where he started a Hebrew course for academics, her mother followed him. So Bianka was left alone. Her father successfully completed the course, but he did not learn Hebrew well enough to work as a lawyer. He would also have to validate the diploma obtained in Poland, which was not easy, so he decided to find another job. He got a job at the tax office in Haifa and at the same time was allocated to a two-room apartment in a cooperative block in Kiryat Motzkin. Bianka, on the other hand, began working as a civilian in the army as one of two secretaries employed in the office. At first it was difficult for her, because, although she had learned to speak Hebrew fluently, she could not manage to learn spelling for a long time. To get a job, she could not admit it. Therefore, she had to deal with embarrassing situations later, such as receiving an urgent order to prepare a text on a typewriter:

> On the first day of work, a high-ranking officer called me to him and told me to type the letter he would dictate to me. I got heart palpitations because I didn't feel ready for it. I positioned myself so that he would not see that I noted it all in a phonetic way. Later, I asked my friend to help me put the right letters. The beginnings were certainly not easy...[141]

Bianka also worked in the social insurance office in the department of sickness benefits.[142] After starting a family, she no longer thought about making a career. She decided to dedicate herself to raising children and running a home. Like thousands of other European Jews, the Goldmans repeated the familiar patriarchal family model in Israel. It was based, among others, on the fact that the husband's career was prioritized, and the wife moved to the background. From

---

141 Interview with Bianka Goldman carried out on December 20, 2016.
142 Ibid.

the end of the 1960s, liberalization of social relations began to progress in Europe, which was seriously opposed by Orthodox Jews in Israel. That is why Israeli women were less likely than Europeans to succeed in politics and business. We are currently observing the intense clash of liberal and secular social groups with orthodoxy that is trying to preserve Israel's family and public relations.

Marcel and Bianka's wedding was religious, despite the fact that he is a declared atheist. They decided to do so because of the legal rules prevailing in Israel, according to which only people married in a ceremony sanctioned by a rabbi are considered a husband or a wife.[143] The wedding ceremony was performed by a rabbi from Kiryat Motzkin, where Bianka's parents lived at the time. The wedding was very modest, because both families had no money to organise an expensive party. Bianka's mother belonged to the already mentioned WIZO organisation, which made a room in Motzkin available to the family for free. The ceremony and the reception for the members of the immediate family and a selected group of friends took place there. Bianka prepared food, while Marcel provided drinks: thanks to one of his friends he could buy alcohol with a big discount.[144] For a week's honeymoon, they went to Nahariya, a popular seaside resort in northern Israel, very close to the border with Lebanon. Later they went there again when Bianka was pregnant with Orit. A leisure trip abroad was at that time beyond the financial possibilities of the Goldmans, as well as of the vast majority of Israeli families. Marcel and Bianka's daughter was born in 1956 on the Jewish holiday of Hanukkah (Hebrew: rededication [of the Jerusalem Temple]), commemorating the Maccabees' victory over the Seleucids

Figs. 78 and 79. In Nahariya during honeymoon, 1954, family collections of Marcel and Bianka Goldman (Tel Aviv)

---

143 Interview with Marcel Goldman carried out on December 18, 2016.
144 Ibid.

in 165 BCE. Because it is a festival of lights (Hebrew: *orim*), she was given the name Orit: in Hebrew, *or* means light.

After getting married, the Goldmans' financial situation was complicated by the fact that Marcel was still studying. He had a chance to take a well-paid bookkeeper's job in construction, where he already had experience, or in other industry. However, he would have to work until four or five in the afternoon. Meanwhile, he needed the afternoons free to be able to study and make it for his classes in Tel Aviv at the latest at 17:00 or 18:00. Therefore, he took a bank job, where he was already free at 15:00. He began, as he recalls: "from the lowest level. I went to the Central Bank with my briefcase of checks every day, I was like a little smarter messenger."[145] At the beginning (1953–1956) he worked at Union Bank (Hebrew: Bank Igud). The director of the Haifa branch of the institution was Ernest Jaffet from a famous family of Jewish bankers from Germany.[146] His family also had a bank in Israel, however, Ernest was making his own career at Union Bank. He was an influential figure and had extensive contacts in international banking circles, especially in Germany. It is confirmed in a story from the early 1950s (1953 or 1954). At that time, the grain needed to meet Israel's food needs was entirely imported, so no one was surprised to see two cargo ships filled with grain entering the port of Haifa. A big commotion began when it turned out that the state treasury lacked a large sum in dollars to pay for the grain. Government representatives turned to Jaffet for help. He went to Germany and there, after meeting with the head of Deutsche Bank, arranged a loan for the amount needed to buy the cargo.[147] Marcel draws attention to two related matters:

> The story cited here proves how efficient Jaffet was as a banker, above all, however, it makes us understand that Israel, which currently [in 2019—Ł.T.S.] has a foreign currency reserve in the amount of 120 billion dollars, in the first years of its existence had a problem with paying the basic bills. If I remember correctly, the grain in question cost about

---

145 Goldman, *A w nocy przychodzą myśli*, 7.

146 By the way, it is worth mentioning that at the dawn of Israeli banking, mainly German Jews were in the lead, followed by Iraqi Jews. The Jaffet family founded the Jaffet Bank. Apart from it, other banks founded by German Jews also operated: Bank Ellern, Bank Feuchtwanger, and the Export Bank belonging to the Mayer family, Correspondence with Marcel Goldman, January 19, 2019.

147 Interview with Marcel Goldman carried out on September 21, 2018

two million dollars. From the perspective of the current state finances it is a small amount.[148]

It was not until 1954 that the Bank of Israel was established. Until then, the Israeli government and Bank Leumi LeYisrael performed the functions of the central bank. David Horowitz became the first director of the Bank of Israel. In the years 2013–2018, the director was Dr. Karnit Flug,[149] born in 1955 in Poland, the first woman in the history of Israel in this position.

Israel began the decade of the 1950s without a foreign currency hedge that would allow the government to meet the consumption needs of a country experiencing large immigration flows. An urgent task was to curb inflation, which was rising because the government was printing money that was not covered by commodities. It was only the newly created Bank of Israel, modelled on other central banks in the world, that received the appropriate instruments to maintain the value of money and curb the inflation. However, the task turned out to be very difficult, because all the circumstances favoured the depreciation of the Israeli currency. That is why the Bank of Israel used drastic methods—in an attempt to stop the money supply, banks were required to secure 100% deposit liquidity. In practice, it meant that if, for example, a client brought 1000 Israeli pounds to the bank to deposit, the bank had to transfer the entire amount to the Bank of Israel. In such a situation, the bank could not pay interest to the person depositing the money, and it did not have the capital to grant loans. Various solutions were invented that used or bent the laws to bypass the draconian system introduced by the Bank of Israel. According to Marcel Goldman, trading in bills of exchange was the most popular one. When someone applied for a loan, they could hear from the banker:

> "We do not have sufficient capital to grant you a loan, but we can be an intermediary between you and our client who has a surplus capital and is ready to lend the expected amount in the form of a bill of exchange. However, it will be a loan at a higher interest rate than the standard one."
> In fact, black market interest rates appeared in the banking world.[150]

---

148 Ibid.
149 In 1980, she graduated from the Hebrew University of Jerusalem with a degree in economics, and in 1985 obtained a PhD in economics from Columbia University in New York.
150 Interview with Marcel Goldman carried out on April 18, 2017.

The bank acted as an intermediary between lenders and borrowers who remained anonymous to each other. Formally, the bank was not responsible, the bank guarantee was not included in its books. In fact, however, the bank that brokered such a transaction was responsible for it. That system of informal loans quickly took the form of a speculation bubble, which at the turn of 1956 and 1957 was clearly swollen. Bills of exchange were not repaid, they were exchanged for further bills of exchange. A large part of the capital borrowed in that way went to people who could not settle their liabilities. That situation led to the threat of a complete collapse of Israeli banking, which would have catastrophic consequences for the economy of the entire state. Therefore, the government urged the Bank of Israel to intervene. Restrictive regulations requiring 100% collateral for deposits were withdrawn. Bills of exchange were gradually converted into classic loans and recorded in the banking books, where bills of exchange could not be recorded. The whole operation took a few years. However, it was not without a crisis, which was keenly felt in the 1960s. It resulted mainly from a large number of unpaid loans in form of bills of exchange. There was a stagnation on the real estate market. It was not until the Six-Day War in 1967 that the crisis was completely averted. The impressive actions and success of the Israeli army brought euphoria that enveloped the entire country and became an impulse for the economic development of the state. The multiplied inflow of foreign investments also helped.[151]

Similarly to the economic situation of the state, Marcel and Bianka, after getting married in 1954, also started very modestly. First of all, they did not have enough funds to buy an apartment for cash. At the same time, they did not meet the requirements to obtain a loan. They could hardly afford to rent. They accepted an offer to install themselves as subtenants in an apartment that Bianka's friend hired from one of the army officers. In fact, they lived illegally. The officer did not know that there were two couples in his apartment, each occupying one room. The Goldmans paid half of the rent to the mentioned friend, which was beneficial for both young couples. The total cost of rent was fifty Israeli pounds at the time, so the Goldmans had to pay twenty-five pounds. At the time, Marcel earned around 200 pounds and Bianka's salary was slightly lower.[152] They bought their first flat in the summer of 1955, a year after their marriage. They had to take a loan that in the beginning seriously affected their household budget.

---

151 Ibid.
152 Interview with Marcel Goldman carried out on December 18, 2016.

According to Marcel: "In the second year after our wedding, we lived on one salary and the other went to pay installments for the flat. Our neighbors who knew about it (nothing is a secret in Israel!) checked every morning whether we were still alive, because they thought that one salary was not enough to live off."[153] In those hard moments, Marcel's former instructor from the school scout organisation in Krakow, Poldek Wasserman, offered his help. In Israel, Poldek became a lieutenant colonel (in Hebrew: *sgan aluf*) in the navy. This position is only two ranks lower than a general.[154] It turned out that he lived in Haifa in a cooperative block intended for officers of the Israeli army, which was located on the same street at the corner of which Marcel lived with Bianka and their newborn daughter Orit. After an accidental meeting on the street or in one of the shops nearby, their acquaintance revived. Marcel recalls:

> Bianka and I will never forget it. It was one of the first days of December. In our modest apartment we didn't have heating. Although it is not freezing in Israel at the time of the year, it is getting colder. It also rains often. That's why it gets cold and humid in unheated apartments. This is very bad for babies, especially when changing diapers, but we didn't have enough money to deal with it. Meanwhile, Poldek knocked on our door accompanied by his wife. They brought us an electric stove to heat the apartment so that Orit would not freeze. This gesture moved us greatly. Bianka and I are still grateful for that help.[155]

The Goldmans chose an apartment in Haifa located on the Carmel in the highest and most elite part of the city. They could choose a larger and nice two-room apartment located lower, in the suburbs of Haifa in Bat Galim. However, it was a rather poor district, inhabited by people from lower social strata. Marcel convinced Bianka that it was better to buy a smaller one-room apartment (with a kitchen, bathroom, and a large porch), but located in a better district. They preferred an address that gave the prospect of a good neighbourhood, greater security, and in the future the possibility of sending their child to a better kindergarten or school. After two, maybe three years, they moved into a two-room flat with a kitchen (in an even better location).

---

153 Correspondence with Marcel Goldman, March 23, 2018.
154 The Israeli army has the same ranks in all types of armed forces.
155 Interview with Marcel Goldman carried out on November 16, 2018.

In 1956, Marcel's father died. He was fifty-five years old. His death at such a young age could be related to the traumatic experiences of World War II, heart disease, and a sense of personal disappointment he suffered in Israel. Organizing his father's affairs and closing his parents' shop, Marcel had to pay off their debts.[156] At the time of her husband's death, Sara Goldman was only fifty-three years old. She decided to remarry, and married a distant cousin who bought a new apartment for them.[157] Maksymilian did not live to see the birth of any of his grandchildren, neither Orit born in 1956, nor Michael, who was born in 1959.

Shortly after the birth of their son, Marcel and Bianka decided to move to a larger, three-room apartment. At that time, Bianka's father died, and Marcel decided to look after her mother. Therefore, when buying a new apartment, he paid the developer the cost of an additional one-room flat for her in the same property.[158]

All the family members called the young Michael Miki. He began to demonstrate mathematical talent very early, and his parents contributed to his development in this direction. Marcel recalls: "When he was five he got to know the concept of negative numbers. I managed to teach him, for example, that 4 can be subtracted from 3."[159] Miki, an extremely developed boy, quickly understood new content in maths lessons, he was looking for his own solutions for the tasks presented by the teacher, which was not necessarily well received by her. Marcel remembers one of the parents' evenings when his son attended the Hebrew Reali School in Haifa:

> The maths teacher told me that Miki did not solve the tasks according to the key she presented to the classroom, but used his own ideas. She admitted that he did it successfully. I asked if she had many such students who did not repeat what she did, but solved tasks in their own way. She replied that only Miki did that. I told her that she should be happy that he did it that way, because it proved that he did not repeat everything passively after her, but, by understanding her lesson, he could allow himself to face mathematical problems in an independent and alternative way.[160]

---

156 Interview with Marcel Goldman carried out on December 18, 2016.
157 Ibid.
158 Ibid.
159 Interview with Marcel Goldman carried out on November 5, 2018.
160 Ibid.

He wanted to know everything that interested him in detail. Marcel heard from him more than once: "Dad, you are not accurate enough." Considering the fact that Marcel was a banker known in his community for accuracy and precision, his child's remark must intrigue and surprise. Marcel explains it:

> Miki had a strictly mathematical brain and mindset. On the other hand, I worked as a banker who faces other types of challenges and tasks. They were very well defined by the professor of The London Institute of Banking and Finance (unfortunately I don't remember his name today), who wrote in the introduction to one of his books—here I am quoting from memory: "It could seem that every educated person—a lawyer, economist, accountant—can be a good banker. And there are many such people. But in practice it is not like that. A good banker doesn't have to study any subject in depth. It is enough if he knows the essentials in many areas and has a large dose of common sense. He faces clients day after day: petitioners: buyers, industrialists, businessmen, people providing various services in various industries, pensioners, people from the insurance industry, and so forth. There are also fraudsters, thieves, and counterfeiters. The banker has to deal with all this." I think this diagnosis is a clue to why my son thought I wasn't deep enough in specific matters.[161]

Miki became a cybernetic engineer. He was a graduate of the renowned Technion Institute in Haifa. He also planned to study mathematics. However, he failed to achieve those goals. He started working for an Israeli ICT company that performed orders in South Africa. Then he decided to open his own business. Unfortunately, in 1992 he died in tragic circumstances. He was thirty-three years old at the time. That was definitely a premature death, which caused unsoothable pain in Marcel and Bianka. Miki's death is remembered by everyone who managed to meet him with undisguised sadness and regret. He is remembered as a remarkably talented young man who, as it seemed, had a great business or scientific career ahead of him ...

The Goldmans changed their apartments several times, which reflects the social and economic advancement they became involved in. They were building their financial well-being, and Israel's prosperity was being shaped at the same time. Of course, not everyone made a fortune at the same pace as Marcel Goldman. However, the Jewish state created decent income opportunities for its citizens. Although it took the country a long time to be out of the woods, its

---

161 Correspondence with Marcel Goldman, November 4, 2018.

inhabitants coming from Poland quickly realized that in terms of living conditions, and especially personal freedom, they found themselves in a much better position than in communist Poland. However, the high quality of life was often accompanied by some kind of snobbery, frowned on by the founding fathers of Israel and misunderstood by fellow citizens from the Orient, and treated as a pejorative indicator. In the interwar period, German Jews were referred to in Eretz Yisrael as *yekes*, from the German word for jacket (*Jacke*), because they wore jackets with pleasure, which in those climatic and political conditions was perceived as a manifestation of eccentricity and exaltation. The community of Polish Jews is referred to as *polanim*.[162] They are commonly associated with bourgeois culture and intellectual professions. In many other countries of the world, their manners would receive the highest praise, but Israel was built on the principles of egalitarianism, where the ethos of the manual labor and kibbutz work was spread. In addition, many habits derived by Polish Jews from their family homes did not fit in, such as the desire to have a set of elegant clothes and cutlery, or serving coffee and tea in appropriate porcelain cups with saucers, lined on beautifully embroidered napkins. For casual observers they were whims. Polish Jews, who had already reached a certain position in Israel, probably remembering their old lives, considered their new situation the minimum they could live with. In consequence, a stereotype developed regarding the Polish Jewish women (*polaniyot*), according to which they were considered to be overly exaggerated, old-fashioned, and haughty. We find traces of such thinking in Israeli mass culture, for example, in films.[163] There were also a lot of jokes about them. I will cite a few:

> A *polaniyah*'s husband is on his deathbed. He calls his wife: "I can smell a wonderful strudel, give me a piece." "No. It is not yet fully baked and, besides, it is intended for the funeral reception!"
>
> Two *polaniyot* meet on the street. "Where are you going from?" "I was in a Beauty Institute!" "Was it closed?"
>
> A *polaniyah*'s husband died. Shortly after the funeral, a friend meets her and asks: "Where did you get a ring with such a magnificent diamond?" "I bought it myself with the money that I found in my late hus-

---

162 Their story was told in an interesting way by Karolina Przewrocka-Aderet in the book *Polanim. Z Polski do Izraela*, Wołowiec 2019.

163 See G. Padva, "Mocking the 'Polaniyah': Marginalization and Demonization of Israeli Women of Jewish-Polish Origins in Israeli Cinema and Popular Culture," in *Polish–Israeli Cooperation Experience, from Zionism to Israel*, ed. Ł. T. Sroka and B. Brutin, Krakow 2017, 206–222.

band's things. There was a fairly large sum of money with a note attached to it that said: for the stone."

The *polaniyot* were criticized because they did not adapt to the living conditions in Israel. For example, they were often ignorant of oriental cuisine and spices. Bianka Goldman admits that in Israel she continued her cooking habits from Poland for a long time. To this day she serves, for example, cabbage soup, completely unknown to Oriental Jews. She copied many recipes from her mother, who had instructed her before the wedding that she should take care of her husband who would come home hungry after work.[164] Polish parents, and above all mothers (Hebrew: *imma polaniyah*), were accused of overprotection, moralizing, cultivating old (conservative) customs, and being oversensitive about their children.

The Goldmans also became a *polanim* family. Their daughter Orit was deeply affected by the fact that Marcel was definitely different from many other fathers—raised and formed in Eretz Yisrael or already in independent Israel.[165] He was not relaxed, lacked the distance to life and the reality that surrounded him, he took everything and everyone very seriously. He could not smooth away the barrier separating him from his growing children—who expected fun, spontaneity, and far-reaching understanding. Years later, Marcel recalls that over time in his life there was a reflection that due to his harsh (at least for Israeli conditions) personality he lost a lot and something began to escape him in relations with his children: "I had this type of thought for the first time during one of our holiday trips when I tried to be their companion, fool around with them and make jokes. However, I realized that it is too late for that. 'These horses have already run their way.'"[166] Earlier, he had not paid attention to Bianka's requests in various situations that he should not dress their children down and treat the pranks typical of their age with greater indulgence. As a side note, I would like to add that at their children's presence they conducted conversations of that kind in German, because they did not want them to know that in a particular case there was a disagreement between them.[167] However, it can be assumed that the children... figured it out quite well. Let's give the voice to Orit:

---

164 Interview with Bianka Goldman carried out on December 20, 2016.
165 O. Goldman, "Congratulations to My Father on his Ninetieth Birthday," November 2016, family collections of Marcel and Bianka Goldman (Tel Aviv).
166 Ibid.
167 Ibid.

> As a little girl I looked at you with various feelings. I wanted a soft and warm father. Whom I could access and who would be a partner to play with. Just like a *sabra* [born in Israel] father. Father-friend.
>
> At that time, I did not know and could not assess the culture in which you grew up, your very high requirements from the society, and above all from yourself, and the strength that was in you.
>
> I began to approach you at a relatively adult age, when suddenly a shy girl was transformed into a young lady, who also had something from you.[168]

These are not easy words, but they are certainly not a kind of reproach. Orit is aware that her father, with his strong personality, has become a pillar of the family. While children and parents playing together is an educating experience, Marcel raised his children by his own example. He required a lot from them, but even more from himself. He was strict but fair. After years, his children appreciated it, which Orit's speech confirms. However, it is a fact that Orit and Michael, like tens of thousands of children from the *polanim* families, were brought up in a certain dissonance. The surroundings in which they lived were Hebrew, but their homes were Polish. Ilona Dworak-Cousin's words express it perfectly:

> From the age of seven I was brought up and grew up in Israel. A real Israeli outside: school, youth organisation, army. A real Israeli in love with the Hebrew poetry of Alterman, Lea Goldberg, Rachel, Amichai. But our home was Polish. There was Polish cuisine and we behaved in the Polish way. The culture and atmosphere were also Polish.[169]

Regardless of how we respond to different opinions on the *polanim*, whether we accept them or reject them, it must be admitted that the model of upbringing in Polish families was apparently not bad, since the children from those families grew up to become exemplary citizens, a part of the Israeli society, and achieved successes in private and professional lives. The same applies to the attachment of Polish Jews to bourgeois culture. It was this culture that finally prevailed—the inhabitants of kibbutzim and moshavim never constituted more than about ten percent of the total population—and today dominates in Israel. Therefore, it is worth asking about sources of criticism and ironic comments about Polish Jews. Jews from other countries and continents also had (or even still have) their spe-

---

168 Ibid.
169 I. Dworak-Cousin, *Dybuk wspomnień*, Krakow–Budapest 2008, 104.

cific features, but they did not become such frequent targets of colourful criticism and jokes appearing in private and public space. There are several reasons for that. The quantitative and qualitative significance of Polish Jews seems to be decisive. They became one of the most numerous cultural groups who co-created Israel, and they had a lot of influence in various spheres of life (politics, army, culture, science, economy). Representatives of Polish Jews joined two characteristic communities, which in certain periods of time fought in various circles—on the one hand, the secularized Jews who were attached to the bourgeois culture, and on the other, Hasidim, who strictly observed tradition and who today have created compact and influential centers of religious life in Israel. It is a fact that Polish Jews associated with the establishment cannot count on preferential treatment on the part of media people, who often mitigate the tone of their statements due to political correctness when it comes to Jews originating from regions such as Africa, because, according to many Israelis, they were often mistreated by the administrative apparatus and the elite of the state.

From the proclamation of independent Israel, David Ben-Gurion made sure that the country developed evenly. Of course, Zionist politicians attached special importance to Tel Aviv, but all Israelis could not live there. For political, economic, and military reasons, attempts were made to settle the entire territory of Israel. Ben-Gurion was fascinated by the Negev (Hebrew: dry) Desert. He believed that Jews should develop it and partially settle it. In his memories he noted:

> The desert gives us the best opportunity to begin again. This is a vital element of out renewal in Israel. For it is through mastering nature that people learn to control themselves. . . . When I looked out my window today and saw a tree standing before me, the sight awoke in me a greater sense of beauty and personal satisfaction than all the forests that I have crossed in Switzerland and Scandinavia. For we planted each tree in this place and watered them with the water we provided through much effort. Why does a mother love her children so? Because they are her creation. Why does the Jew feel an affinity with Israel? Because everything here must still be accomplished. It depends only on the individual Jew to participate in this privileged act of creation.[170]

---

170 Cited after Peres, *Podróż sentymentalna*, 91.

Fig. 80. New houses in Beersheba, December 1, 1950,
photo: Teddy Brauner, http://www.gpo.gov.il/, public domain.
At the time these houses were built, there was a desert area around

i The Negev desert area is dominated by barren rocky peaks and massive plateaus crossed by riverbeds of periodic rivers (*wadi*). In summer the temperature here is very high, while in winter there are hurricanes, sandstorms, rainfall does not exceed twenty-five milimeters on an annual basis. Although the desert is typically an unfriendly environment for people, Negev has been teeming with life for centuries. This is confirmed by biblical sources: Abraham, looking for pasture (Genesis 12:9), Ishmael, father of the Edomites (Genesis 21:20), and Isaac stayed in the Negev. The Israelites who left Egypt lived there before occupying Canaan. Along the way, they had to face the Amalekites. After occupying Canaan, the Negev Desert fell to Simeon and Judah. In the tenth century BCE, in the time of David, the Israelites ruled the entire Negev. Later, this territory fell to Idumeans, descendants of the Edomites, who in the first century BCE were supplanted by the Nabataeans.* At the beginning of the second century, the Romans had a victorious war with the Nabataeans. The end of the Nabataeans, whose kingdom in the peak period (from the second century BCE to the second century CE) extended from Sinai to Damascus, occurred in the fourth–fifth centuries CE. The Negev Desert experienced another glory period in Byzantine times, when hermitages and monastic life developed there. In 636, the area was conquered by Muslims. For the third time, the

---

* People coming from the depths of the Arabian Peninsula.

Fig. 81. A new housing estate in Beersheba, August 1, 1955, photo: Dawid Eldan, http://www.gpo.gov.il/, public domain

Negev was to flourish in connection with the implementation of Zionist policy. Beersheba, a city located 40 kilometers east of the Dead Sea and 120 kilometers southwest of Jerusalem, became "the capital" of the Negev. In ancient times, Beersheba was the southernmost center of religious worship of Israel. It is mentioned in the Old Testament. Abraham went nearby while looking for pastures. There, he dug a well for his flocks, at which he made a covenant with Abimelech (Genesis 21:22ff). According to Genesis: "So that place was called Beersheba, because the two men swore an oath there" (Genesis 21:31). Further we read: "And Abraham planted a tamarisk tree in Beersheba, and called there on the name of the Lord, the Everlasting God (Genesis 21:33–34). In Beersheba, God appeared to Isaac. In the following centuries it was a small settlement, which did not play a major political and economic role. However, it attracted the attention of various rulers, because it had a strategic location on the route from Africa to Asia Minor. In the interwar period, Arabs started riots here, as a result of which most Jews left Beersheba. In 1947, the United Nations decided that Beersheba would be part of the British Mandate granted to the Arabs. During the first Israeli-Arab war in 1948, Egyptian troops took over Beersheba. In the same year, Israelis recaptured it.

Fig. 82. Construction of a water supply system at a new housing estate in Beersheba, December 1, 1950, photo: Teddy Brauner, http://www.gpo.gov.il/, public domain

Thanks to Ben-Gurion's determination, Beersheba grew into an important economic and university center. In the 1950s, housing estates were erected here, which were inhabited by newly arrived Jews. The fact that the Israelis built Beersheba almost from scratch deserves to be highlighted. That is why, like Tel Aviv, it became an experimental space for architects. Here, for example, the concept of workers' homes, that is, the so-called *shikuns* (see Figs. 80, 81, and 82) was introduced on a large scale. Those houses were to express the idea of social equality and create a sense of community. In the following years, more testimonies to expressive and creative architectural ideas of architects appeared in Beersheba. The architecture of the local town hall, theater, and court is noteworthy (see Figs. 83, 84, and 85).

Currently, Beersheba is the largest city in the Negev Desert, it has about 200,000 residents, nearly of whom are Jews. Many of them are emigrants from the countries of the former Soviet Union and Africa. It is also the home to the Ben-Gurion University, founded in 1969, its researchers conduct advanced research on the climate and vegetation of the desert. An important part of their work are studies on the possibility of developing the desert, cultivating it, and using modern irrigation technologies. Soroka University Medical Center has an international reputation. Dimona, an important nuclear research center, the

Youth, Part Two (1945–1954) | 219

Fig. 83. Town hall with an observation tower in Beersheba, October 12, 2014, photo: בוכניק נתי, public domain

Fig. 84. The Goodman Theater and Acting School in Beersheba, May 2013, photo: Orrling, public domain

Fig. 85. Courthouse in Beersheba, December 2, 2010, photo: טייכר אבישי ר״ד, public domain

alleged storage site for Israeli nuclear weapons, is located about thirty kilometers west of Beersheba. Beersheba has well-developed road, rail, and air connections to Tel Aviv, Jerusalem, and Eilat. The chemical, machinery, and food industries are developing successfully there.

An important role in the spatial design of Israel was played by Arieh Sharon,[171] who was entrusted with that task by David Ben-Gurion. In the years 1949–1953 he worked as the director of the State Planning Department. Initially, the institution operated under the Ministry of Labour and Construction. In an effort to raise its importance and improve its work, it was incorporated into the structure of the Chancellery of the Prime Minister of Israel. Israel's national and spatial development plan was widely remembered as Sharon's "national plan."[172] That engineer developed the concept of dividing Israel into twenty-four settlement zones, which were to be settled as evenly as possible. In addition, he prepared projects of new cities, settlements, roads, highways, bridges, and viaducts. His achievements also include designs of houses and housing estates as well as many public buildings.[173] Sharon's plan provided a solution to the problem of having to absorb thousands of Jews who came to the State of Israel. We are talking about survivors of the Holocaust, the inhabitants of Iraq, Iran, and North Africa, as well as numerous groups of Ethiopian Falash and immigrants from the former Soviet Union who appeared in the new towns at the turn of the 1980s and 1990s,.

For obvious reasons, all immigrants could not be accommodated in the three largest cities, namely Tel Aviv, Haifa, and Jerusalem. Moreover, Israel only gained control over Jerusalem as a result of the Six-Day War in 1967. In addition, great importance was attached to increasing the Jewish population in the peripheral areas of Israel. The proverbial "apple in the eye" of Ben-Gurion was the settlement action in the Negev Desert. Kibbutzim and moshavim had their specifics and not everyone had the appropriate predisposition to live and work in them. In that situation, Sharon envisioned another characteristic form of

---

171 Arieh Sharon (1900–1984) came from Jarosław (today the Podkarpackie Region in Poland). He was a graduate of the Bauhaus School in Dessau. In 1920 he emigrated to Eretz Yisrael.

172 A. Jasiński, *Architektura i urbanistyka Izraela*, Krakow 2016, 104.

173 Including the three buildings of the Weizmann Institute in Rehovot (1955–1959), the Israeli pavilion at the Brussels World Expo (1958), the complex of buildings for the Technion in Haifa (1954–1960), the Memorial Hall of the Yad Vashem Institute, which he designed together with Arieh Elhanani (1959–1964), two buildings for the Hebrew University of Jerusalem (1961), cable car station to Masada (1965–1971), the building of the Bank of Israel in Jerusalem (1965), and the sanatorium on Lake Tiberias (1973).

Jewish settlement, the so-called development towns (Hebrew: *ayarat pituach*). They appeared in the 1950s and were often based on transition camps (Hebrew: *ma'abarot*) for *olim chadashim*. It is assumed that Beit Shemesh (Hebrew: House of the Sun) was established as the first development town, located sixteen kilometers west of Jerusalem. Its base was the camp for the newly arrived immigrants from Bulgaria, and then from Iraq, Iran, Romania, and North Africa, founded in 1950. Other development towns include: Arad, Kiryat Shmona, Migdal HaEmek, Mitzpe Ramon, Or Yehuda, and Sderot. They were planned as complete entities, that is, they were to house flats built from scratch, municipal infrastructure, educational and cultural institutions, and of course workplaces. In general, small factories associated with various industries and food processing plants were established there. Development towns were democratic and egalitarian. The basis of housing construction were cooperative (workers') houses, so-called *shikun ovdim*. The simple form and modest equipment of the apartment blocks partly resulted from ideological premises, but at the same time were a consequence of Israel's limited financial capabilities. Development towns undeniably played a large role in the history of this country. They gave shelter to hundreds of thousands of newcomers, enabled them to get their first job, housing, and so forth. Along with the army and kibbutzim and moshavim, they became a space where immigrants from different countries and cultures fused into one Israeli society.

The efforts of David Ben-Gurion and Arieh Sharon to evenly develop Israel can be summarized as follows: contrary to the expectations of the founding fathers of Israel, the inhabitants of this country mostly preferred life in urban centers and bourgeois culture. Therefore, development towns were more attractive than kibbutzim and moshavim, but Tel Aviv most of all, and Jerusalem and Haifa were next. According to a popular saying in Israel, quoted earlier: "Tel Aviv plays, Jerusalem prays, and Haifa works," but one can also hear that "in Jerusalem you study and function, work in Haifa, and earn in Tel Aviv."[174] The problem of development towns is not only that in the eyes of people focused on career and urban life they are definitely less attractive than Haifa and Jerusalem, not to mention Tel Aviv. Contrary to the intentions of the founding fathers of Israel, they ceased to be zones of egalitarianism. When Israel entered the path of capitalism (especially after 1977), many *shikun* residents left them and moved

---

174 Ritterman-Abir, *Nie od razu Kraków zapomniano*, 19.

to more comfortable housing. The wealthiest Israelis chose luxury apartment buildings and villas. In turn, areas of poverty and backwardness formed.

This does not mean, however, that the three large cities only provided living spaces for the rich. On the other hand, high-level schools, access to healthcare, and cultural centers also reached a high level in the development towns. In addition, successful start-ups have brought a new prosperity there, because they are based on information technology and often provide services over the internet so they do not need to be based in the largest cities, where the prices for buying or renting office and warehouse space are very high. For this reason, start-ups and companies from the high technology industry are increasingly willing to locate themselves in development towns, and even in kibbutzim and moshavim. It should also be expected that the growing number of inhabitants of this small, in terms of occupied territory, state will force some relocation of resources.

If currently anything is a barrier to living in Tel Aviv, these are certainly not ideological premises, but the purchase and rental prices of properties, which are much higher than in other cities. Tel Aviv is associated with cosmopolitanism, openness, business, science, culture, and entertainment. It has become the object of desire for young and creative people, as well as those wealthy and valuing the comfort of life at the highest level. There are many business centers here, as well as leading science and culture centers. The attractiveness of Tel Aviv is also determined by aspects such as the Mediterranean climate, seaside location, and sandy beaches, unique architecture, excellent land connections, and the international airport of David Ben-Gurion. Around Tel Aviv, the metropolitan area of Gush Dan has grown, which consists of the cities of Bat Yam, Bnei Brak, Givatayim, Herzliya, Holon, Kiryat Ono, Or Yehuda, Ramat Gan, and Ramat HaSharon. Starting from Herzliya located in the northern outskirts of Tel Aviv, through Netanya to Haifa, numerous luxury housing estates and office centers of major global companies and start-ups from the ICT, biotechnical, medical, and other industries were built along the charming coastal belt.

Haifa invariably enjoys the reputation of the city leading in the economic sphere. Here is Israel's largest seaport, one of its main "windows to the world." Haifa is also a city of one of the world's leading technical universities, Technion. Leaving Haifa for Tel Aviv is still considered a promotion, as was the case with the Goldmans. It does not work the other way round (Tel Aviv will be also discussed in the next chapter).

In a natural way, Jerusalem occupies the leading position among the most important cities in Israel, because it is the capital of the state according to local legislation. Due to its capital nature, Jerusalem attracts the political, clerical, and business establishment. It is also a leading academic center as well as the spiritual and religious center of the state.

To date, most countries in the world do not recognize Israel's unilateral decision. The vast majority of countries maintain embassies in Tel Aviv. The reason for this is the ongoing Arab-Jewish dispute over the overall relations in Israel, and in particular about the status of Jerusalem (the Arabs would also like to have the capital of their own state there, strictly speaking, in the eastern part of the city). In this situation, the transfer of the US embassy from Tel Aviv to Jerusalem and the recognition of the city as the capital of Israel, following the 2018 initiative of President Donald Trump, took on a revolutionary character. Trump called that decision the recognition "of the obvious, the plain reality." Let us remind that in 1947 the United Nations proposed making Jerusalem and its immediate surroundings a neutral zone under international control. That plan was rejected by both the Arab and Jewish sides. As a result of the First Arab-Jewish War, Arab troops occupied most of Jerusalem. Jews were pushed to the western districts. The 1949 ceasefire provided free access of Jews to important religious sites such as the Western Wall (also known as the Wailing Wall). However, the Arabs broke up that agreement and did not let Jews into the eastern part of the city. In 1967, during the Six-Day War, the Israeli army occupied East Jerusalem. On July 30, 1980, the Israeli Parliament adopted the *Basic Law: Jerusalem*, under which the unified Jerusalem was recognized as the capital of Israel.

Shortly after the Six-Day War, general enthusiasm prevailed in Israel, which was intensified by the joy of regaining Jerusalem. Many young Israelis came to the city at that time and wanted to build their lives in this historic place. The influx of Jewish people to Jerusalem (as well as to other areas occupied during the Six-Day War) was supported by the government. After years, the "fashion" for Jerusalem decreased, which was influenced by various factors. While there is great political tension throughout Israel, in Jerusalem it is intensified by constant inter-group and intra-group conflicts.

The gates of Jerusalem, which surround the Old City, belong to the oldest, because their roots reach ancient times, and the most popular symbols of the city. They became an iconic motif for world culture. For example, the Polish composer Krzysztof Penderecki dedicated to them his Symphony No. 7: *Seven Gates of Jerusalem*. The piece was commissioned by the Jerusalem authorities in

Fig. 86. The Wailing Wall in Jerusalem (the Dome of the Rock visible in the background), 2008, photo: Łukasz Tomasz Sroka

Fig. 87. The Damascus Gate in Jerusalem, 2008, photo: Łukasz Tomasz Sroka

i Jerusalem is the holy city of three religions: Judaism, Christianity, and Islam. Here, like at the interface of several different tectonic plates, the greatest friction occurs, the reverberations of which is felt in all of Israel, and even in international politics. The Temple Mount raises the greatest emotions. From the perspective of Jewish believers, this is a holy place, where Abraham was ready to offer his only son Isaac to God. According to the Jewish tradition, Abraham called this hill Moriah (Hebrew: chosen by Jehovah). It was also called Zion. The First and Second Jerusalem Temple were located there.

For Muslims, the Temple Mount is the third largest religious site after Mecca and Medina. According to Islam, Muhammad, in the company of the archangel Jibril, was taken to heaven from a rock. The Dome of the Rock was built in that place (Fig. 86), and today it is one of the city's most popular landmarks. There is also the Al-Aqsa mosque on the Temple Mount.

For Christians Jerusalem is very important as well. For centuries they have been following in the footsteps of Christ who carried the cross through the streets of the Old City of Jerusalem along the so-called Via Dolorosa (Latin: way of suffering) to the Golgotha hill, where the mystery of his passion was completed. Thousands of Christians make a pilgrimage to the Church of the Holy Sepulchre, which commemorates the passion, crucifixion, burial, and resurrection of Jesus Christ. Next to this, the Church Ecce Homo enjoys great interest. It is located on Via Dolorosa, in the place where Pilate, exposing Jesus at the sight of the crowd, said the words: "Ecce Homo" (Latin: behold the man).

connection with the jubilee of the three millennia of the city's existence. Its first performance took place in Jerusalem on January 9, 1997.[175]

The defensive walls around Jerusalem existed before King David conquered the city. The current walls and gates were built during the Turkish rule in the sixteenth century. There are eight gates: Damascus, Zion, Jaffa, Mercy, Lions'

---

[175] It was performed by: Marian Nicolesco (soprano), Sylvia Greenberg (soprano), Jadwiga Rappé (alt), Evgeni Shapovalov (tenor), Reinhard Hagen (bass), Boris Carmeli (reciter), Symphonieorchester des Bayerischen Rundfunks, Jerusalem Symphony Orchestra, Chor des Bayerischen Rundfunks, MDR-Chor Leipzig, Südfunk-Chor Stuttgart, Lorin Maazel (conductor). https://ninateka.pl/kolekcje/trzej-kompozytorzy/penderecki/audio/siedem-bram-jerozolimy-vii-symfonia-na-5-solistow-recytatora-3-chory-mieszane-i-orkiestre [access: 26/05/2019].

Chapter 3. The Aliyah Time

Fig. 88. Moshe Dayan in September 1973, photo: Kodkod Tzahov, public domain

i Moshe Dayan was born in 1915 in kibbutz Degania Alef and raised in moshav Nahalal. In 1933 he joined the Jewish self-defense group Hagana. In 1939, along with several dozen Hagana fighters, he was arrested by the British Mandate authorities for illegal possession of weapons. He was imprisoned in Acre until 1941, when he was released and joined the Hagana's combat unit, which, in cooperation with the British army, began to recapture Syria and Lebanon from Vichy's sphere of influence. During one of the battles fought in Lebanon, Dayan was wounded and lost his left eye. After that, he began to wear a characteristic black patch, which became his hallmark. In the years 1949–1952 he was the head of the Israeli Southern Command, in 1952 he managed the Northern Command, and in 1952–1953 he managed secret operations. In the years 1953–1958 he was the head of the General Staff of the Defense Forces of Israel. He reached the rank of lieutenant general (*rav aluf*). From 1959, he sat in the Knesset, and in the years 1959–1964 he managed the Ministry of Agriculture. In 1966 he went to Vietnam as a correspondent to observe the war closely. He gained valuable experience regarding the modern battlefield, especially surprise operations with commando units and guerrilla warfare. Just before the outbreak of the Six-Day War, Prime Minister Levi Eshkol entrusted him with the position of the minister of national defense, which he occupied until 1974. On June 5, 1967, Moshe Dayan ordered the preemptive attack on the neighbouring Arab states that were preparing for war with Israel. The war was swift (hence its name) and brought Israel a stunning victory. As a result, Israel grew into a local power, social enthusiasm increased, new waves of immigrants came, and foreign investment accelerated. Dayan

(Christians call it the Gate of St. Stephen), New, Flowers (also known as Herod's Gate), and Dung (the name comes from the assumption that it was the gate through which garbage was thrown from the Temple).

In 1967, the Israeli army's occupation of Jerusalem's Old Town together with the Temple Mount opened the prospect of building the Third Temple. The idea was born in narrow religious circles, but soon gained the support of the larger religious wing of Zionism. Although formally Temple Mount has become an integral part of Israel, Moshe Dayan did not give permission for the Jews to take control over it by force.

On June 27, 1967 the Israeli authorities entrusted the administrative function over the Temple Mount to the Muslim religious foundation Waqf. The

> thus became one of Israel's national heroes. Due to his unquestionable commanding talent, he was hated in the countries of the former Eastern Bloc, which during the Six-Day War supported the Arab armies (by supplying them with weapons, ammunition, and so-called military advisers, who often performed regular staff and combat tasks). During the infamous events of March '68 in Poland, Dayan became well known to the Polish public, because the communist authorities made him the face of the alleged "Israeli militarism." His caricatures were on posters and banners used during workers' assemblies organized by the communist authorities. The slogan "Zionists to Dayan" was also used. During the Yom Kippur war in 1973, Dayan helped save Israel from defeat, but he felt guilt over the fact that, even though Israel had information that an armed attack would take place, it was still surprised by the attack on that specific date. This first attack by Arab troops was very painful for Israel and caused serious losses of personnel and equipment. The chaos that accompanied the first phase of the war was overwhelming. That is why Dayan resigned, but the then Prime Minister Golda Meir did not accept his resignation. In the report of a special commission examining the circumstances surrounding the war, it was concluded that Dayan was not personally responsible for the situation. In 1977 he assumed the position of Israel's minister of foreign affairs, where he remained until 1979. He belonged to supporters of dialogue with Arab countries, and made a significant contribution, among others, to the normalization of relations between Israel and Egypt. He died in Tel Aviv in 1981. In 1988, the Israeli Post honored him with a special post stamp.

government of Prime Minister Levi Eshkol promised to protect all holy places in the area occupied by Israel. Representatives of all faiths were guaranteed free and unrestricted access to their holy places.[176] Undoubtedly, the Third Temple would integrate the Jewish people. However, there is no good solution that would make it possible to implement this plan without violating the existing *status quo*. Proposed agreements on this matter, formulated in various political or religious circles in Israel, are strongly rejected by the Muslim side. For example, the Muslims did not accept the idea of dismantling the Dome of the Rock and the Al-Aqsa Mosque and moving them to another place. Palestinians are very distrustful of any Jewish activity near the Temple Mount. Because of that, numerous riots break out, resulting in fatalities on both the Palestinian and Jewish sides. Even conservation works, which the Israelis carry out around the Western Wall, look suspicious to the Muslims. In the opinion of a large part of the Muslim public, the archaeologists aim to destroy the Temple Mount in order to prepare the ground for the construction of the Third Temple. In addition, violent reactions are caused by every attempt to interfere in this space by the Israeli authorities. Serious repercussions were even caused by General Ariel Sharon's visit to the Temple Mount on September 28, 2000. Sharon was then the leader of the opposition party Likud (Hebrew: Union), in the years 2001–2006 he was the prime minister of the Israeli government). Before coming to the Temple Mount, he declared that his purpose was only to look at the progress and scope of construction works carried out by Waqf. In fact, he wanted to verify information about the alleged destruction by Palestinians of excavations carried out by Israeli archaeologists. The Palestinians, however, considered this visit a provocation and an attempt to violate the existing order. The incident contributed to the outbreak of the Palestinian uprising named the Al-Aqsa Intifada, which took place in the years 2000–2005.

In addition to great conflicts, Jerusalem's daily life is also marked by neighbourhood disputes between representatives of various faiths, most often Judaism and Islam. The Arabs and the Jews occupy separate districts, but they share borders with each other, so it is not difficult to find reasons for misunderstandings and skirmishes. Palestinian terrorists are also a problem, as they can relatively easily penetrate the Jewish districts.

---

176 R. Bania, "Status Jerozolimy a konflikt bliskowschodni," in *Międzynarodowe studia polityczne i kulturowe wobec wyzwań współczesności*, ed. T. Domański, Łódź 2016, 315–316.

Christian-Jewish relations are also far from trust and agreement. In the Israeli and world media at various intervals there are references to disagreements between clergy of Christian denominations and the Jewish Ultra-Orthodox. Major conflicts are far less common. In February 2018, representatives of three Christian communities taking care of the Church of the Holy Sepulchre announced its permanent closure. The custos of the Holy Land, Franciscan Francesco Patton, the head of the Orthodox Patriarchate of Jerusalem, Theophilos III, and the Patriarch of the Armenian Apostolic Church, Nourhan Manougian, issued a statement in which they protested against the planned statutory changes providing for the collection of taxes on property occupied by Christian communities. Their indignation was also caused by the fact that the Jerusalem authorities demanded greater control over treasury receivables, which could make it possible to seize the churches' bank accounts and property. In response to that protest, the Israeli authorities declared their willingness to agree with Christian communities and postponed the dispute over the problematic law. After a few days, the Church of the Holy Sepulchre reopened.[177]

Disputes also break out within individual religious groups. Jewish feminists are opposed to the division into the male (larger, forty-eight meters long and adjacent to the entrance to the synagogue) and female (smaller, twelve meters long) sectors at the Wailing Wall. In addition, feminists want to pray here in *tallits* and with Torah scrolls, although according to Judaic tradition this practice is reserved only for men. This provokes violent reactions from Ultra-Orthodox Jews. For about twenty-five years, the Ultra-Orthodox continued to block the feminists, who were often subjected to acts of verbal and physical aggression: eggs were thrown at them, they were spat upon and pushed. In addition, they were arrested for violating public order. Their position gradually improved. In the 1980s, they founded an organisation called Women of the Wall, and won the right to wear the *tallit* provided that its colors will differ colours from the one worn by men (therefore it cannot combine white and black or white and navy blue/blue) and it will not be worn on the shoulders.[178]

---

177 "Bazylika Grobu Pańskiego ponownie otwarta," https://www.tvn24.pl/wiadomosci-ze-swiata,2/bazylika-grobu-panskiego-w-Jerozolimie-zostala-ponownie-otwarta,818569.html, accessed March 16, 2018.

178 "Kobiety (w końcu) pomodliły się pod Ścianą Płaczu. 300 policjantów pilnowało porządku," http://wiadomosci.gazeta.pl/wiadomosci/1,114871,14066438,Kobiety__w_koncu_pomodlily_sie_pod_Sciana_Placzu_.html, accessed March 16, 2018.

Fig. 89. The Elegante shop in the Mea Shearim district of Jerusalem with a wide selection of wigs, November 13, 2011, photo: Djampa, public domain

Feminists had to wait quite long for further changes. The ruling of the Supreme Court of Israel in 2003 basically confirmed the monopoly of the Orthodox at the Western Wall, which was justified by the inability to guarantee the security of liberal Jews. In the following years, feminists aroused the interest of politicians and received support from various equality organisations. However, the Orthodox interpretation of the law was still in force, and on April 11, 2013, five activists praying at the Western Wall were arrested "for wearing prayer shawls, which the Supreme Court forbade."[179] It was then that a precedent-setting verdict of the court in Jerusalem declared the arrest of feminists unlawful and the police appeal brought in that case was rejected. Therefore, the interpretation given by the court removed the Orthodox primacy from this place, and gave it a pluralistic and nationwide dimension. However, it did not change the position of the Ultra-Orthodox. Therefore, each time groups of praying feminists must be protected by police officers.

---

179 Ibid.

Fig. 90. The Shabbath Square and one of the streets of the Mea Shearim District in Jerusalem starting there. Young boys wearing sidelocks (side hair strands) characteristic for Orthodox Judaism are visible in the foreground. In the photo you can see the *tzitziyot*, or tassels from the *tallitot*, coming out from under their clothes, March 9, 2007, photo: W. Robrecht, public domain

The Israeli government is looking for a compromise in this matter. One of the proposals for solving this issue suggests designating a third zone—a co-educational one. It could be located south of the Wall near the Robinson's Arch, where liberal Jews now pray. Progress is therefore visible, but Ultra-Orthodox religious activists are threatening that the rights granted to feminists can be completely withdrawn.[180] Disagreements between secularized and Orthodox (and especially Ultra-Orthodox) Jews also occur in other places where both communities meet. There are many such places in Jerusalem, such as housing estates and shopping centers. Some reasons for conflict include pressure exerted by the Ultra-Orthodox on the community so that the Sabbath and other religious holidays are strictly observed.

---

180 Ibid.

Fig. 91. Grand opening of the new Knesset building in Jerusalem, August 30, 1966, Israel National Photo Collection, public domain

Fig. 92. The Supreme Court building in Jerusalem, with the Knesset building in the middle of the background, followed by a panorama of the city, April 15, 2009, photo: Israel-tourism, public domain

Other communities living in Jerusalem are also not free from divisions and antagonisms. A well-known example is the dispute over every square meter of the Church of the Holy Sepulchre between several communities who participate in its management. Due to the lack of trust between them, the keys to the Church are now in the hands of a Palestinian family.

In Jerusalem, more than in other cities, some influential families have lived in Israel continuously from the time before the proclamation of the state's independence. It is the crème de la crème of the Israeli political, business, and scientific elite. The iconic place in this city is the parliament building, that is, the Knesset. It was built in the years 1958–1966 according to the design of Józef Klarwein, born in Warsaw in 1893. A specific element of the Jerusalem architectural landscape is the ubiquitous stone veneer on the facades of buildings. It is worth adding that it was the British who introduced the appropriate municipal ordinance, which required all new buildings in Jerusalem to be faced with stone. This law remains valid today and is generally observed.[181]

The famous Holocaust Martyrs' and Heroes' Remembrance Authority—Yad Vashem, founded in 1953, is located in Jerusalem. It is a part of the Holocaust History Museum, together with the Hall of Names, synagogues, archives, library, galleries, the Valley of the Communities, the International School/Institute for Holocaust Studies, and the Garden of the Righteous Among the Nations. Trees in this garden commemoratie the people who saved Jews during World War II. Due to the lack of space, newly discovered names are now engraved on a special memorial wall. In addition, there are several different monuments, one of them is dedicated to Janusz Korczak (see Fig. 93).

Such a large accumulation of objects important from a religious, historical and political perspective in one place makes Jerusalem a unique city not only in Israel, but in the whole world. It also causes a kind of pressure that can result in mental disorders in newcomers. Such disorders especially affect people who come to this city full of hope for deep spiritual experiences. The combination of their ideas with the experience of a place inscribed in the context of biblical history often results in shock and delusions. For example, they might identify with biblical characters. About 200 people a year are affected by this problem, mainly middle-aged religious men of different denominations. After a short hospitalisation and leaving Jerusalem, they usually recover quickly. In the 1980s,

---

181 Eylon, *Jerusalem*.

Fig. 93. Janusz Korczak Memorial, by Boris Saktsier, photo: Berthold Werner, Yad_Vashem_BW_2.JPG, 3 November 2011, public domain

the Israeli psychiatrist Dr. Yair Bar-El diagnosed this condition as "the Jerusalem syndrome."

The summary of this chapter provides a convenient opportunity to highlight two important issues. Marcel Goldman, like thousands of other Jewish immigrants, came to Israel in the early stages of the development of the young state. Because of that, he and other people of his kind started a new life in difficult conditions. The country was in the phase of development and, to make matters worse, in the state of permanent threat, unable to guarantee the newcomers help adequate to their situation. At the same time, it was a country in which economic divisions had not yet emerged. The vast majority of Israelis lived modestly. People who were better off did not flaunt it. The Israeli authorities, including David Ben-Gurion, promoted modesty, solidarity, and egalitarianism. Even if the slogans associated with that often did not correspond to the real life, those features determined the system of values of the state. As Israel began to develop quickly, the state built from scratch needed staff in virtually every field, such as government and self-government administration, the army, healthcare, lower and higher education, followed by the agricultural, construction, banking, insur-

Fig. 94. The Hall of Names, Yad Washem, December 2007, photo: David Shankbone, public domain

ance sectors, and many others. Working conditions and wages did not spoil the new employees, but opened for them a perspective of unlimited personal and professional development, which would be unimaginable in already developed countries. In each field, of course, at certain intervals, there were vacancies at many positions—from the lowest to the highest. It is true that success was not destined for everyone. In Israel, money was not on the street. While the market offered a large number of jobs, a significant part of them (one could even say, the majority) reflected the early state of progress of the Israeli economy and its priority needs. Thus, they were usually the lowest posts related to construction, agriculture, and the army. Higher offices (also in the aforementioned areas) required knowledge of the Hebrew language, proper education, ambitions, and determination. Marcel Goldman had all these qualities. In his biography, we see how much potential could be activated when a young, well-educated person, who was open to challenges and determined to succeed, responded to the needs of the labour market. We can also see in this story the seeds of intergenerational misunderstandings currently occurring in Israel. Israelis who are close to Marcel Goldman in age have many reasons to be proud of their achievements and the state they built. In their opinion, young people today have immeasurably better living conditions than they had, and the younger generation's complaints are difficult to understand. Sharp comments were caused by the wave of emigration of Israeli youth to Germany, which gained momentum due to economic reasons in the first decade of the twenty-first century. Germany (mainly Berlin) became such a popular destination, since many Israelis have German origin, which facilitates the legalization of their stay in this country. In addition, it is a country that offers relatively comfortable living conditions. In Israel, the pace of economic growth is impressive, but the relationship between earnings and cost of living remains less favourable than in Germany.[182] Only in 2011, 16,000 people emigrated from Israel, 10,000 of which decided to stay abroad.[183] The same year, tens of thousands of Israelis protested throughout Israel demanding the government to introduce social justice policies. The largest demonstrations took place in Tel Aviv, where about 20–30 thousand people took to the streets. Israeli people are, above all, affected by high prices of housing and food (including basic products such as bread and dairy). These problems have still not been resolved systemically.

In this way, we move smoothly to the second conclusion: the diversity of Israel. Guidesbooks to this country emphasize that, despite its rather small territory, there is a lot of diversity in terms of landscape, nature, architecture, and culture. They pay attention to divisions related to the national and religious factors. There is also information on the reasons and manifestations of differences between Ultra-Orthodox, Orthodox, and secular Jews. However, this does not show the full range of divisions in Israel. Against the background of the rest of the country, the cosmopolitan Tel Aviv clearly stands out. The cities scattered in the Negev Desert, including Beersheba, have their own specific features. The small towns scattered around Tel Aviv and located at a safe distance from the Arab communities have an exclusive character. Kibbutzim and moshavim live in a different rhythm. Jerusalem is unique. Located on the Red Sea, Eilat is a kind of tourist enclave: safe, prosperous, but not resonant with the state in general

---

182 For example, as reported by the economic portal forsal.pl in March 2014, since 2007 the cost of renting apartments in Israel has increased by 51%, while average earnings have fallen by 1.6%. During that time, prices increased by 16%. "Ekonomiczna kalkulacja przełamała tabu: Izraelczycy emigrują do ... Niemiec," http://forsal.pl/artykuly/783030,ekonomiczna-kalkulacja-przelamala-tabu-izraelczycy-emigruja-do-niemiec.html, accessed March 17, 2018.

183 Ibid.

(in this sense Eilat resembles the nearby Jordanian Aqaba or Egyptian resorts such as Taba, Dahab, and Sharm el-Sheikh). Israel is a constellation of micro-worlds. It seems that the challenge for the next decades will be to ensure their peaceful coexistence and maintain the flow of people, ideas, services, and all goods between them. Maintaining the unity of the state and society of such diverse and often mismatched elements is a serious problem, but also a great opportunity.

4

In the Land of Success—
The Mature Age (1954–2019)

Emigration to Israel naturally brought profound changes to Marcel Goldman's life. His "hunger for life" and its high pace proved unchanged. During World War II he showed great determination to survive. Already in his childhood spent alongside parents who ran their own business, he acquired useful qualities that he developed later, such as diligence, courage combined with prudence, and iron consistency in action. During the Nazi occupation, these traits of character allowed him to survive, and in Israel they made him succeed in private and professional life. After the first ten years of his life in Israel (of which he spent two-and-a-half years in the army), he was already married, had two children: an older daughter Orit and a younger son Michael, and had received a university degree in economics. He had his own three-room flat on Mount Carmel, in the exclusive Haifa district where he had a telephone installed. He also had a car. From the perspective of Israel at the time, it was simply a luxury! Of course, the photographs and postcards presenting Tel Aviv or Haifa in the 1950s and 1960s often show cars, but let's note that they are usually taken in city centers. The vehicles appearing there were largely of business nature—they were owned by companies and public institutions. They were much less common in the ordinary housing estates. A fragment of the story told by Ilona Dworak-Cousin, a socio-cultural activist and writer, about the visit of her father's cousin, aunt Stefa from Antwerp, is interesting in this context. In 1960, her aunt married the owner of a diamond-cutting business, and soon (in 1961 at the latest) her husband died. After that unpleasant event, she decided to visit her family in Israel: "At one point, a black taxi drove to the square near our building. For local residents [of the Ramat Aviv district—Ł.T.S.] it was quite a sensation, because taxis rarely came to the housing estate. The only vehicles known here were carts with horses or donkeys."[1]

---

1 Dworak-Cousin, *Podróż do krainy cieni*, 230.

It is also worth adding that at that time Marcel also looked after his parents. After the death of his father-in-law, with whom he was very close, he also took care of Bianka's mother—a fact worth emphasizing, because we are talking about a man who in 1959 (ten years after arriving in Israel) was only thirty-three years old, and spent the first months in Israel in a kerosene-lit tent . . . An in-depth analysis of Marcel's attitude was done by his daughter Orit, who wrote the following words dedicated to her father in November 2016 on his ninetieth birthday:

> You drink from the goblet of life to the bottom. And you always stay twenty years behind your biological age.
> But none of the young people present here knows the path you have taken. From a young charismatic man, dominating in any social group and of course also in the family, and above all galloping forward fueled by crazy ambition—you have become a mature man, by no means old, devoted to the family, warm, tender, and sometimes even capable of considerable emotions.[2]

We will return to Orit's words later. Now I would like to talk about the time when Marcel Goldman's first decade in Israel was coming to an end. It is a symbolic moment in many respects, important for him and for the whole country. Marcel, as shown, had impressive successes in private and professional life, and was to face further challenges. The State of Israel was in a similar situation. First, it had to prove that it was able to survive. The founding fathers of Israeli statehood predicted that a tribute of blood would be paid for it. During one of the press conferences accompanying the UN vote on the division and future of the territory that had previously been part of the British Mandate in Palestine, Chaim Weizmann was asked whether he was afraid that the creation of independent Israel would trigger a conflict that would bring victims. He replied that "a nation does not receive a state on a silver platter" (according to the *Haaretz* newspaper, "The state will not be given to the Jewish people on a silver platter").[3] His thought was developed to mean that each generation of Israelis has to fight for their homeland and give their lives for it. This is the silver platter on which the state will be handed to subsequent generations.

---

2 Goldman, "Congratulations to My Father on His Ninetieth Birthday."
3 "Silver Platter," http://zionism-israel.com/hdoc/Silver_Platter.htm, accessed April 7, 2019.

The outstanding Israeli poet Natan Alterman (born in 1910 in Warsaw, died in 1970 in Tel Aviv) wrote a poem motivated by Weizmann's statement entitled *The Silver Platter* that musicians readily use—it has become an integral part of Israeli culture and national identity. Here, I quote it in full:

Natan Alterman, *The Silver Platter*

...And the land will grow still
Crimson skies dimming, misting
Slowly paling again
Over smoking frontiers
As the nation stands up
Torn at heart but existing
To receive its first wonder
In two thousand years.

As the moment draws near
It will rise, darkness facing,
Stand straight in the moonlight
In terror and joy.

...When across from it step out
Towards it slowly pacing,
In plain sight of all,
A young girl and a boy
Dressed in battle gear, dirty,
Shoes heavy with grime.
On the path they will climb up.
While their lips remain sealed.
To change garb, to wipe brow,
They have not yet found time,
Still bone weary from days
And from nights in the field,
Full of endless fatigue,
And all drained of emotion;
Yet the dew of their youth
Is still seen on their head.
Thus like statues they stand,
Stiff and still with no motion,
And no sign that will show
If they live or are dead.

Then a nation in tears
And amazed at this matter
Will ask: who are you?
And the two will then say
With soft voice: We—
Are the silver platter
On which the Jews' state
Was presented today.

Then they fall back in darkness
As the dazed nation looks.
And the rest can be found
In the history books.[4]

All citizens' effort to work and fight with weapons in hand brought surprisingly good results. Israel had a chance for further development, although of course the threats did not disappear. In 1948–1949 Israel fought the first victorious war with the Arab states: Egypt, Iraq, Syria, Transjordan, and Lebanon. The reason for its outbreak was that the Arabs did not accept the United Nations resolution of November 29, 1947, which ended the British Mandate in Palestine and divided it into two states: Arab and Jewish (the resolution was supported by thirty-thre member states, including Poland). Let us add that the division was very unfavourable for the Jews. In 1950, the Kingdom of Jordan annexed the West Bank territories (Judea and Samaria). Almost at the same time, Egypt annexed the Gaza Strip, and in 1950 it occupied two islands in the Strait of Tirana, practically taking control of shipping in the Red Sea. Simultaneously, the Egyptians banned Israeli ships from using the Suez Canal. Arab *fedayeen* also attacked on a large scale.[5]

On July 26, 1956, the Egyptian authorities announced the nationalisztion of the Suez Canal. This decision upset the governments of Great Britain and France, which decided to crack down on Egypt, and involved Israel in the conflict. For Israel, it was a chance to be in the good company of countries that played out geopolitical clashes. As a result of secret British-French-Israeli negotiations, it was agreed to conduct an armed action against Egypt, codenamed "Musketeer." The operation planned for the Israeli army was called "Kadesh."

---

4 Trans. Dawid P. Stern, https://hartman.org.il/SHINews_View.asp?Article_Id=117, accessed April 6, 2019.

5 In Arabic *fedayeen* means someone willing to sacrifice their lives.

Specific decisions were made in Sèvres on October 24, 1956. On that basis, on October 29 of the same year, at 17:00, Israeli troops stormed the Suez Canal, followed by Gaza, Rafah, and Al-Arish. A day later, the English and French troops joined the attack. Under such pressure, Egypt had to give in. However, the leaders of the USSR and the United States forced the end of the war, fearing that it threatened their interests and position in the Near East. For Israel, the primary benefit of that conflict was regaining the possibility of free navigation through the Tirana Strait. And yet, the defeated Arabs did not abandon their plan to destroy Israel. The powerful blow of the combined Arab forces was only a matter of time. However, the Israelis did not wait idly. They subjected their army to further thorough modernization and rearmament. The army's strength was to be determined by elite commando units cooperating with modern aviation and armored-mechanized regiments. Undoubtedly, the earlier joint military operation with the French and British helped. Although this alliance began to dissolve relatively quickly, for some time it helped to bring modern weapons from the West to Israel. In close cooperation with the French, the Israelis launched their own atomic research program in a special center in Dimona (in the Negev Desert), which, as is commonly assumed, resulted in the construction of an atomic bomb.

The armed clashes listed above and all other issues connected with the military can give the impression that Israel and its inhabitants focused exclusively on the army, neglecting everything we call a normal life. Nothing could be more misleading. Since its inception, the State of Israel has strived for normality at all costs and does everything to guarantee its citizens peace and then work, access to culture, education, and healthcare at the highest possible level, comparable with other developed countries. Naturally, subsequent wars brought pain and suffering to millions of people, but at the same time they strengthened Israel's geopolitical position. Every terrorist attack is received by the citizens very personally here, because Israel is a small state. Victims of terrorist attacks are never anonymous. Each Israeli, who learns about a serious injury or death as a result of an attack, identifies the victims as family members, direct or indirect acquaintances. Despite these difficult circumstances, Israel is teeming with life. Wars and assassinations may paralyze it for a moment, but the return to normality is quick, and cafés, restaurants, and discos fill up again . . . Maybe there is even a kind of compensation and attempts to prove to themselves and the world that, above all, Israelis want, can, and will live a normal life!

The life of Marcel Goldman, like the country where he lived, gained momentum and became prosperous. In 1956, after graduation, his request to the bank's management for promotion and a payrise was refused, so he accepted the job offer of the Halva'ah VeChisakhon (Hebrew: credit and savings) Bank, which had a branch in Haifa at Yafo Street in the lower part of the city. It sought people for managerial positions not because of its growth, but because the newly created Bank of Israel introduced requirements that the existing staff could not cope with due to weak competence. Marcel was supposed to be the director of the branch, but employees protested that they did not want to be "ruled by a snot."[6] They argued that the branch has employees working for no less than thirty years—in their opinion, the longest-serving staff deserved the highest positions. A compromise was reached and Marcel became deputy director of the branch. He was probably the first banker in the history of Israel who was entrusted with such a high position at such a young age. A person who was not a banker assumed the role of the main director. He was limited to approving loans, while Marcel was responsible for most of the bank's affairs.[7] In this position, he gained new competences and expanded his group of influential friends. He worked there until 1959. The circumstances of his resignation are interesting because they shed light on the evident political-related intricacies of the Israeli banking at that time.

The branch of the Halva'ah VeChisakhon Bank in Haifa was unique compared to other branches of that bank, because people associated with the general and right-wing current of Zionism had a relatively high position there. It did not suit people associated with the leftist wing that dominated in the country. To increase their influence on the board of directors and eliminate political adversaries, they used the paradoxical system on which the bank was based. The shareholders of the cooperative were not those who had capital invested in it, but borrowers. The compulsory purchase of shares was associated with taking out a loan and not creating a deposit. In addition, at general meetings, each shareholder was entitled to one vote, regardless of how large his shares were, in contrast to joint-stock companies in which the number of votes depends on the capital. In that situation, the director of the bank did not hesitate to encourage even people from transition camps for *olim chadashim* to take out loans. He granted them small loans, although it was known that they would not be able to

---

6   Interview with Marcel Goldman carried out on February 9, 2019.
7   Family collections of Marcel and Bianka Goldman (Tel Aviv): documents and correspondence; Correspondence with Marcel Goldman, February 8, 2019.

Fig. 95. Pinchas Sapir (second from the left), famous Israeli minister of finance, then also the minister of trade and industry, during a visit to a footwear factory in Jerusalem, January 1, 1964, photo: public domain

pay back. However, he made them members of the cooperative and invited them to general meetings, which allowed him to pursue his own policy.

Marcel, who did not agree with that situation, submitted a letter to the bank's president (who was a member of Histadrut) in which he informed him that he would not attend board meetings anymore, because he believed that the bank was being managed incorrectly. The president accepted the letter but did not react, so Marcel began to look for another job. Through Bianka's father, he found the right contact at a Swiss bank in Geneva, in which the Israeli government had partial shares. The bank was also headquartered in Tel Aviv and planned to open a branch in Haifa. Marcel was invited to the headquarters in Tel Aviv. On the spot, he was asked to write a letter asking for employment. The meeting took place at 10:00, followed by a break until 12:00. Marcel is convinced that the application he wrote was forwarded for examination by a graphologist. When he returned, a contract was awaiting him for the post of deputy bank director in Haifa. He was offered significantly better financial conditions: previously, as a branch director, he was receiving 500 pounds, now he was to receive 1000. In addition, he was offered a preferential loan for a car and its maintenance, and then for the purchase of an apartment and its renovation. Marcel signed the contract and, having such security, resigned from his previous job. At the same time, he stated that he should retain the right to compensation while terminating the contract, even though compensation was usually offered to people dismissed because of their employer. According to the law, the dismissed person was entitled to severance pay in the amount of a monthly salary for each year worked. Marcel justified the request by saying that although he left voluntarily, he did so because he did not have the right conditions to work. By decision of the bank's management board, Marcel received a severance pay, and in that way his connection to Halva'ah VeChisakhon was finally severed.[8]

In 1959 he started working as deputy director at LeSahar Hutz Bank,[9] which then used the English name, the Foreign Trade Bank. The position of the main director was taken by a man who was previously the main cashier of the Haifa magistrate. The bank's top management assumed that employing a person related to the local government, with large connections, would bring them clients. However, it did not happen, because this person did not show any talent in that respect. Therefore, it was Marcel's task to find the clients.[10] However, after many years, he assesses the cooperation with his superior positively: "He was a well-educated man, fluent in several languages—especially English, because he had an English wife. In fact, he had a soul of a scientist. He would certainly be a great lecturer."[11]

Marcel worked there for nearly forty years until his retirement in 1997. In 1972, his bank, with the consent of Israel's finance minister Pinchas Sapir, merged with several others: Export Bank, The Israeli Industrial Bank, Atzmaut Mortgage and Development Bank, as well as with a number of independent loan funds. The merger resulted in the creation of HaBank HaBeinleumi HaRishon LeYisrael. It also officially began to use the English name, the First International Bank of Israel (FIBI). It was the largest foreign operating and universal bank in any country. Its main shareholder was the State of Israel (through the FIBI Holdings Company) and the American First Pennsylvania Bank, then the only foreign entity that invested in Israeli banking (it sold all shares in 1978).[12] David Golan became the first CEO, and performed that function in the years

---

8   Interview with Marcel Goldman carried out on September 21, 2018.
9   It was the "daughter" of an Israeli bank in Geneva, wholly owned by the State of Israel and servicing its international transactions.
10 Family collections of Marcel and Bianka Goldman (Tel Aviv): documents and correspondence; Correspondence with Marcel Goldman, February 8, 2019.
11 Interview with Marcel Goldman carried out on December 18, 2016.
12 "Fibi History," https://online.Fibi.co.il/wps/portal/FibiMenu/MarketingEN/AnInformation/AnInvestorRelations/AnAboutFibi/AnFibiHistory, accessed January 4, 2019.

1972–1980.¹³ One interesting fact is that in 1977 the FIBI took over control of the PAGI Bank, which specialised in providing services to the Ultra-Orthodox Jews in Israel.¹⁴ Golan was a *sabra*. His family had previously been called Goldman, but they were by no means Marcel's relatives. They changed their name, most likely, on the popular wave of Hebraization of surnames. Golan belonged to the so-called Sapir's children: usually young graduates of economic studies at the Hebrew University in Jerusalem, the closest associates of Pinchas Sapir,¹⁵ who was known as the "father of the Israeli economy" and one of the best finance ministers in the history of Israel. He brought the country's economy out of regional isolation and, through extensive international activity, caused foreign investment inflow to Israel. He built a model where economic development did not prevent covering the necessary expenses for defense and the social sphere (related, for example, to the costs of absorbing new *aliyot*).

Marcel's employment in the new position brought the Goldman family prosperity and a feeling of financial stability. Now, they could afford attractive journeys. Today, Israelis travel around the world willingly and frequently, to the most distant regions of the worl. For years, young people traditionally go on a long (lasting from several months to half a year or even more) trip after military service and before starting university studies. Travelling has become fashionable not only among young people. But at the turn of the 1950s and 1960s, only the richest Israelis could travel abroad. The state was built by people who came there deprived of their property, so their first priorities were to find a job and secure a roof over their heads. Then, they focused on furnishing their homes. Great importance was also attached to children's education, which required considerable labor and financial resources, which the parents had to provide from their relatively low salaries. Travelling was certainly not favoured by the double dollar exchange rate initially used in Israel.¹⁶ The state had a monopoly on currency trading, those who were travelling abroad could only buy ten dollars at the

---

13 Ibid.

14 Ibid.

15 Pinchas Sapir, born on October 15, 1906 in Suwałki as Pinchas Kozłowski, died on August 12, 1975 in the town of Kfar Saba (near Tel Aviv). He headed the Ministry of Finance (1963–1968 and 1969–1974), as well as the Ministry of Trade and Industry (1955–1965 and 1970–1972).

16 It resulted mainly from the foreign currency shortage recorded in the first years of the state's existence, especially the shortage of American dollars needed in international trade. In addition, the government tried to support exports and limit imports. Therefore, the dollar was valued differently for the export of goods (cheaper) and for the import (more expensive).

official rate. Later, when the economy was well established and capitalist reforms began, those practices were abandoned.

The Goldmans left abroad for the first time in 1962. They went to Cyprus, which is interesting in itself because this country became then and still is a popular destination for Israelis. It is at a relatively small distance from Israel; one can travel not only by air, but also by sea. Fast, comfortable, and cheap hydrofoils depart from the port of Haifa. From the Israelis' point of view, it is a rather safe and inexpensive country. Its climate is warm, but due to the mountainous terrain it is also easy to find refreshment.

The Goldmans went to Cyprus for leisure, but at that time many Israelis went there mainly for shopping purposes. Today, this may seem unbelievable, but at the beginning of the 1960s, Cyprus shops were much better equipped with household appliances. In Israel, there was a problem with access to electrical products at the time: there was a shortage of irons and almost no electric refrigerators, which was extremely burdensome in Israeli climatic conditions. Most often, food was stored in refrigerators cooled with lumps of ice, which merchants brought on carts pulled by donkeys or horses. People had to buy a lump of ice at the right time, put it in the fridge, and then pour out the slowly melting water. Supervision was necessary so as not to flood the apartment. Marcel also remembers such a "troublesome" fridge. While still living in Haifa, one evening they went to the cinema with Bianka. They forgot about pouring out the water, which accumulated all day and evening, and on their return home, they had an unpleasant surprise . . .[17] Marcel mentions that "everything was considered luxurious at that time."[18] For the vast majority of Israelis, owning a car was unimaginable. It was only with time that cars began to be assembled in Israel. Before that, used cars were imported from Europe, while new ones, because of the high price, were basically not bought. Industrial products were lacking mainly because in Israel they were generally not yet produced and import was very expensive. The state, as already mentioned, was struggling with a deficit of foreign currencies, therefore foreign products were imported in limited amounts that could not satisfy all Israelis' needs. Household appliances were needed urgently, hence the frequent flights of Israelis to Cyprus, which even gained the name of "iron trips." In terms of professional and material status, the Goldmans belonged to the small, recently formed Israeli elite. They bought goods that were

---

17 Interview with Marcel Goldman carried out on December 18, 2016.
18 Interview with Marcel Goldman carried out on December 20, 2016.

considered luxurious faster than others. In 1959 they bought an electric fridge. They had already had an iron then, but they do not remember for how long.[19] They also had, as mentioned earlier, a telephone and a car. The telephone was installed in 1959, immediately after Marcel signed the employment contract with the new bank. An average Israeli family waited for a phone from four to six years, it was treated as an indicator of social and professional status.[20] The only thing they still lacked was air conditioning, but Marcel points out that, living in the upper part of Haifa, they did not feel the need to install it. Indeed, in June, July, and August there was a high temperature in the house, but on all other days of the year, after opening the windows, a pleasant air flow came, and the sea breeze brought relief.[21] David Horowitz's research shows that a real revolution in supplying Israeli households with electrical equipment took place between the 1960s and 1970s. Progress in buying cars did not look that good. Data on this subject are presented in Table 3.

Table 3. Percentage ratio of electrical equipment and private cars in Israeli families between 1960 and 1970

Device	Year	Percentage of families in possession	Year	Percentage of families in possession
Electric refrigerators	1960	51,0	1970	96,0
Washing machines	1960	17,0	1970	46,0
Electric cookers and freestanding kitchen appliances	1960	64,0	1969	88,0
Mixers	1962	9,2	1970	27,7
Televisions	1965	2,4	1970	53,0
Private cars	1962	4,1	1970	17,0

Source: D. Horowitz, *The Enigma of Economic Growth. A Case Study of Israel*, New York 1972, 40

---

19   Interview with Marcel Goldman carried out on December 18, 2016.
20   Interview with Marcel Goldman carried out on December 20, 2016.
21   Ibid.

The data in the table show how few Israelis had televisions in the 1960s. It is worth mentioning that in Israel television appeared and spread with some delay in relation to other countries, because David Ben-Gurion was its fervent opponent. The founding father of the Israeli statehood expressed the fear that television would detach Israelis from serious social, professional, and family matters. Radio also did not develop quickly, although it was accepted as an important means of social communication. After all, thanks to widespread radio sets, Jews in Eretz Yisrael could hear Ben-Gurion reading the text of the proclamation of Israel's independence. When first waves of the Shoah survivors arrived, announcements were broadcast on the radio to help find relatives, friends, or acquaintances. Radio was also used to broadcast messages about the mobilization of reservists or about various types of threats. Interesting remarks about the radio were made by Shevah Weiss, who, before becoming an eminent politician and diplomat, made an impressive career as an athlete (which was interrupted after a car accident), a writer, a scientist, and a journalist:

> ... during my studies I was already a very popular journalist on the radio, author of several books for children. In the sixties and seventies, two radio stations operated in Israel: one military, the other national. The whole country was listening to the radio. In our country it is the norm, because everyone must know what is going on. I became very popular thanks to the radio. I hosted *The Evening with Shevah Weiss*, which lasted two hours. There were questions, riddles, games for adults.[22]

Israel struggled with supply problems, but there was never hunger. For people who survived the hell of World War II, it was of great importance. They patiently endured the inconveniences of the first decades of the state's existence. At that time food ration coupons for meat, eggs, sugar, chocolate, and other products were in force (among the goods rationed there was, for example, cement). Food portions guaranteed in that system were more than modest, but sufficient. The inhabitants tried to deal with those shortages in various ways, also bypassing the law. While Cyprus was the place to go for irons, food could be bought much closer, on black market or in Arabian villages. Naturally, various abuse occurred in the centrally regulated and rationed market. In Tel Aviv, for example, "sugar streets" were talked about. In this case, we are talking about buildings erected by one of the food manufacturers, who, with large sugar allocations, was able

---

22 Weiss, *Pamiętam*, 65.

to derive huge profits from the sale of some of his resources. The purchase of food from the Arabs involved the necessity of reaching the villages in which they farmed and raised animals. Then one had to come back home with purchases. Meanwhile, due to the Arab-Jewish conflict, at the entrances to the cities there were outposts where cars were searched. Soldiers primarily sought for hidden weapons, ammunition, explosives, and terrorists. However, they also checked if someone was trying to transport illegally acquired food. Despite those restrictions, food was smuggled, but it took place on a scale difficult to define precisely today. The procedure could have been organized or random and individual.

Marcel also made such purchases for his own household. In his first job at a transport and construction company, his duties included trips to construction sites in various provincial centers. He set off on average every two weeks accompanied by his manager. Once arrived, they paid the workers' salaries and controlled the consumption of materials. On the way back, they stopped to buy, among others, meat and butter from the Arabs. In Marcel's opinion, they crossed the border posts so often that the soldiers already recognized them and relaxed their control. "However, there were troublesome situations. I remember, for example, that once we were transporting chickens in the back of the car, and they started clucking loudly during controls. However, the soldiers did not hear or pretended not to hear it."[23]

In later years, the agricultural and food industries in Israel developed quickly, and thus the shop supplies improved not only in terms of quantity but also quality: a wider range of dairy products and sweets appeared, and, in addition to oranges, grapefruits, lemons, and bananas, new types of fruit: apples, pears, plums, cherries, and strawberries were offered. Israeli agricultural exports grew dynamically.[24] Progress was also noted in other areas of the economy, such as the textile industry. As a result, clothing shops also diversified their offer.[25] The Israelis began to dress according to world fashion. A loose style, providing comfort in a hot (for most of the year) climate remained their distinctive feature. The more expensive shopping centers and the more prestigious streets of Tel Aviv and other Israeli cities are now full of luxury boutiques and clothing shops belonging to global brands. The diamond industry and mining of natural resources

---

23 Interview with Marcel Goldman carried out on June 13, 2018.

24 Exports of agricultural commodities in 1960 reached the level of USD 37.8 million, in 1961—52.6 million, and in 1970 as much as USD 140.2 million. D. Horowitz, *The Enigma of Economic Economy. A Case Study of Israel*, New York 1972, 28.

25 Interview with Marcel Goldman carried out on December 27, 2016.

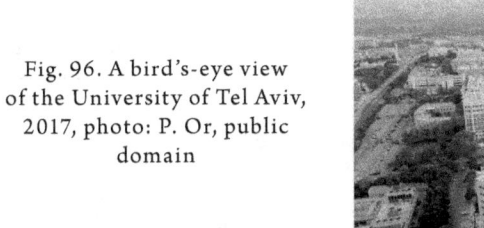

Fig. 96. A bird's-eye view of the University of Tel Aviv, 2017, photo: P. Or, public domain

Fig. 97. The building of the Porter School of Environmental Studies of the University of Tel Aviv, 2014, photo: Oren Rozen, public domain

also strengthened. These factors contributed to increase of exports in various areas,[26] and the provision of services also recorded impressive growth dynamics.[27]

The development of education, science, culture, and healthcare turned out to be of key importance for the future of Israel. Jews appreciate the importance of education, which is why the ambition of many parents, even those less affluent,

---

[26] There was an increase in citrus exports from USD 40.5 million in 1961 to 83 million in 1970; more products made of citrus fruits were also sold—the export increased from USD 7.9 million in 1961 to USD 35.1 million in 1970. In 1961, exports of other agricultural goods generated USD 22.5 million, while in 1970, they reached USD 43.4 million. In 1961, diamond export income was USD 64.9 million, and in 1970 it reached USD 202.9 million; in the same period, income from textile exports increased from USD 24.4 million to USD 96.3 million, the export of mining products increased from USD 13.4 million to USD 43.4 million, and the export of other industrial goods grew from USD 64.2 million to USD 210 million. Horowitz, *The Enigma of Economic Growth*, 124.

[27] In this area, among others, total amount of tourist services increased from USD 30.1 million in 1961 up to USD 103.5 million in 1970; transport services—from USD 84.5 million to USD 261.6 million, respectively; insurance costs increased from USD 25.3 to 116.3 million; and capital services grew from USD 13.1 million to USD 52.7 million. Ibid.

Fig. 98. View from the campus of the Tel Aviv University at Albert Einstein Street leading to it, 2018, photo: Łukasz Tomasz Sroka

Fig. 99. Campus of the Hebrew University in Jerusalem on Mount Skopus, 2010, photo: Grauesel, public domain

was to enable their children to get the best education possible. With the proclamation of independence, that attitude coincided with the policy of the state that began building an efficient education system. Kindergartens and schools accessible to all, with high-level education and innovative methods of teaching began to operate very early in all of Israel. They were the first step on the road to social and professional advancement of successive generations of Israelis, regardless of where they came from or who their parents were. Even in the smallest towns, and in kibbutzim, cultural centers, libraries, cinemas, and theaters appeared.

In Tel Aviv, Haifa, and Jerusalem, the colleges founded before World War II, were thriving: the Levinsky College of Education in Tel Aviv, Technion in Haifa, and the Hebrew University in Jerusalem.[28] The Weizmann Institute of Science grew into the world's leading scientific center. In 1955, the interdisciplinary Bar-Ilan University was founded in Ramat Gan.[29] The proclamation of Israel's independence created favourable conditions for the resumption of discussions on the establishment of the University of Tel Aviv.[30] The first step in that direction was made on August 16, 1953, when the City Council decided to transform the Biological and Pedagogical Institute into the Academic Institute of Natural Sciences. It had a campus in southern Tel Aviv and twenty-four students in the first year. In 1956, the city authorities officially opened the Tel Aviv University, in 1962 it acquired the status of an autonomous academic institution.[31] A modern campus for the needs of this university was built in the northern part of the city in the Ramat Aviv district. At the end of 2018, the University of Tel Aviv was the largest university in Israel.[32]

In 1969, the University of the Negev was created. It was inspired by Prime Minister David Ben-Gurion, who, as already mentioned, believed that the Negev Desert had great development potential. The first task assigned to this university was to conduct research on desert development. In 1973, the university was named after Ben-Gurion. It carries out research related to the natural

---

28   At the end of 2018, the Hebrew University of Jerusalem had 23.5 thousand students, 973 scientists, 7 faculties, 6 campuses, 14 schools. The pride of this university are 8 Nobel Prize winners and numerous winners of other prestigious awards: 14 winners of Wolf Prize, 46—Emet Prize, 100—Rothschild Awards, and 294—Israel Prize. The university has tens of millions of dollars in annual revenue from 9,826 patents, 2,753 inventions (150 per year), 600 commercial products, 880 licenses, and 120 spin-offs. "The University in Numbers," https://new.huji.ac.il/en/list-page/450, accessed December 29, 2018.

29   In 2018, it had eight faculties: Jewish Studies, Medicine, Engineering, Law, Life Sciences, Exact Sciences, Social Sciences, and Humanities. The university began with 70 students, and recruited 4.5 thousand of them during the academic year. In the 2018/19 academic year, it already had 17,000 students. "About the University," https://www1.biu.ac.il/en-about, accessed December 23, 2018; *Who's Who in Israel and in the Work for Israel Abroad 1969–1970*, Tel Aviv December 1969–January 1970, 352–353.

30   The discussion about the establishment of this university began in the 1930s, it was undertaken by the then mayor Meir Dizengoff. Chaim Levanon, deputy mayor of the early 1950s and mayor of Tel Aviv in the years 1953–1959, showed passion and commitment in this regard.

31   In the 1969/70 academic year, the university employed over 1,600 researchers and had 10,685 students, *Who's Who in Israel*, 349.

32   It had over 30,000 students, 9 faculties, 29 schools, and 98 institutes, see "About the University."

sciences, exact sciences, humanities, social sciences, medicine, business, and management.[33]

In the 1969/70 academic year, the Holon Institute of Technology was founded. In 1972, the University of Haifa opened. In October 1976, The Open University of Israel, specializing in distance education, began operating in Raanana. It was created for people on military service or engaged in work and family responsibilities.

The beginning of Ariel University dates back to 1982. The university was originally founded as a regional branch of Bar-Ilan University. Currently Ariel University offers education in the fields of engineering, natural sciences, health sciences, social sciences, and humanities. The mission of this university is to provide cutting-edge knowledge in all fields, but its main direction of work is associated with scientific and educational support for the development of high technologies in Israel.[34]

Israel has made very large investments in the area of science and education, overshadowed only by donations to the army and special services that condition the existence and security of the state. In fact, these categories were never treated separately, and even more so, they were not opposed to each other. There is a clear synergy between universities and research centers, the army, and the economy. From the beginning, the state spent a lot on science and education, because they were not treated in terms inconsistent with reality, abstract and illegible to the average citizen. These institutions have grown into the landscape of the main cities of Israel, but also of smaller towns. They are provide the population with "food" for the spirit, but also with many necessary and functional solutions and inventions used in virtually all areas of life. Scholars also work on modern technologies for the army, some of which have civil applications as well. Since the beginning of the state's existence, science, army, and business have been the best career paths. Moreover, there are visible connections between these environments that have a very positive impact on overall social and economic development. Scientists are welcome in the army. Former soldiers and

---

33   At the end of 2018, Ben-Gurion University had approximately 20,000 students and 4,000 lecturers, "About BGU," http://in.bgu.ac.il/en/Pages/about.aspx, accessed December 23, 2018.

34   In 2018, the university educated 15,000 students, it had the highest percentage of students born in Ethiopia in the country. Seventy percent of students came from central regions of the country, and fifteen percent came from the northern and southern peripheries, "About Ariel University," http://www.ariel.ac.il/en/about-the-center/students, accessed December 23, 2018.

experienced service officers are eagerly employed in the private sector. Sometimes soldiers themselves leave military service to try their hand in business.

Israel created autonomous universities taking into account global trends, which is why they rank high in the world rankings, but they do not necessarily occupy top positions. The highest places are dominated by American universities. In 2018, two Israeli universities ranked in the first hundred of Shanghai ranking: Technion in Haifa (77th place) and the Hebrew University in Jerusalem (95th place). The next two institutions are the Weizmann Institute of Science (places 101–150) and the University of Tel Aviv (151–200).[35] However, it should be borne in mind that the so-called Shanghai list rewards universities that attract foreign students and lecturers with an already recognized international position. Meanwhile, in Israel, universities are treated in terms of internal development. Inside Israel, these rankings are not treated as a kind of fetish, which unfortunately marks the debates around science in many other countries such as Poland.

In Israel, the focus is on innovation and inventiveness, in the humanities, the culture-forming role is also important. Universities, next to schools and the army, are the main institutions where or through which the integration of Israeli society takes place, and where newcomers and *sabras* are brought together. This path of integration was also followed by the protagonist of this book, Marcel Goldman. In addition, Israeli scientists are treated as a kind of state ambassadors. After all, knowledge, not energy resources or other goods, is the biggest driving force of Israeli exports. First, the government took care of creating decent working conditions for scientists in Israel, then made sure that they could do internships at leading foreign universities. Thus, contacts and friendships were established, which resulted in international cooperation. Donations from individuals and private institutions (largely from Jewish communities outside Israel) are a great support for Israeli universities. This is favoured by the combination of high recognition for the sciences that Jews have and the treatment of universities as one of the foundations of the state, which means that support for them is an act of patriotism. In the campuses of Israeli universities, there are numerous signs informing that acquisition of specific scientific equipment, library collections, or even building construction were financed by a specific person, family, or foundation.

---

35 "Academic Ranking of World Universities 2018," http://www.shanghairanking.com/World-University-Rankings-2018/Israel.html, accessed December 25, 2018.

In addition, Israel benefited a lot from the influx of well-educated immigrants, who often already had an academic degree. They enriched Israel's science with their unique knowledge and experience as well as their contacts with foreign scholars.

In order to increase the availability of studies for the average Israeli, the state has created appropriate scholarship systems. Those who came to Israel with little or no Hebrew language skills can use the free *ulpan* teaching system created specially for them. In a short time Israel's education policy brought visible effects.[36] In 1967, among civilian employees for every 10,000 people there were ten graduates in exact and technological sciences in Israel. This number placed Israel at the forefront in a group of countries such as the United States, Great Britain, and Japan, and higher than Canada, France, the Netherlands, and Belgium[37].

The government also attached great importance to publicly available medical care. Currently, Israeli doctors and hospitals are known for the most modern methods of treatment. Innovative hospitals and the pharmaceutical industry are becoming the next trademark of Israel.[38] According to the Bloomberg Index published at the beginning of 2019, Israel is the tenth healthiest country in the world.[39] In 2018, the average life expectancy in Israel was 82.4 years. According to forecasts, in 2040 this average will increase to 84.4 years. Three of the life duration leaders are in the Mediterranean: Spain, Italy, and Israel, and they share common eating habits. The diet of most inhabitants of these countries is based on whole grains and dairy products, vegetables, fruit, nuts, and fish, and they often use olive oil, which has health-promoting properties. In addition, religious Jews do not eat pork, which is critically assessed by dietitians (it can be purchased in some Israeli shops, but it is generally not popular). The health condition of the Israelis is also improved thanks to the state's care for the natural environment, universal access to clean water, and sanitation.

---

36 According to UNESCO data, in 1969, the number of students per 100,000 inhabitants was in the United States 3471, in Canada 2201, in Israel 1488 (data for 1966), in Japan 1398, in Sweden 1250, in France 1239, in Lebanon 1156, in Great Britain 716, in West Germany 695, in Egypt 565. Horowitz, *The Enigma of Economic Growth*, 66.

37 Ibid.

38 In 1967, there were 422 inhabitants per one doctor in Israel, for comparison, there were 650 in the United States, 710 in Denmark, 850 in Sweden, 860 in Great Britain, 1,230 in Lebanon, and 2,320 in Egypt. Ibid., 41.

39 In total, Bloomberg evaluated 169 countries. Israel is ahead of Spain, Italy, Iceland, Japan, Switzerland, Sweden, Australia, Singapore, and Norway.

Today, it is clear that the phenomenon of Israel cannot be explained with a popular, but essentially general, statement: "the state focused on sustainable development." It should be emphasized that the founding fathers of Israeli statehood programmed changes in Israel in such a way that universal access to schools, libraries, cultural centers, healthcare, and housing became the most important. Financial stability and priority development conditions were ensured for these areas. The whole country was covered with a dense public transport network, railway connections were built. At almost the same time as the state, on November 15, 1948, the Israeli airlines El-Al were established (the first employee of El-Al was Dr. Abraham Rywkind from Poland). The list of development priorities also included the transport of people and goods. Only in such conditions could innovation be discussed. On the other hand, all excess, everything that is the packaging, was in the background. The community center could be housed in a very modest building and it did not bother anyone as long as it had an ambitious program of activities. This is a different scenario from that used in many other countries of the world that take up the challenge of modernization. For example, in Poland at the end of the 1990s and in the first two decades of the twenty-first century, modern sports or cultural infrastructure facilities were erected in large numbers, but often only after their opening did the discussion on their tasks begin. At that time, modern trains appeared also in Poland, but the network of their connections was relatively sparse and they ran only between major cities. This is the opposite of what lay at the root of Israel's development. And finally, the question of consumption . . . The founding fathers of Israel tamed the consumption appetites of Israelis for some time, as they promoted a modest lifestyle and strengthened this message with their own example. It was only after the state and its citizens began to step confidently on the path of economic development that they slowly started to think about the pleasures of shopping and travelling.

The successful combination of various events allowed Marcel and Bianka to go on a journey around the world as early as in 1964. Two things are closely related to it—Marcel's family connections and his promotion. Marcel's brother-in-law Henryk Grycendler[40] (we will refer to him later), a shipbuilding engineer, was delegated by the Israeli shipyard in which he worked to Japan where he

---

40 Before emigrating from Poland, he worked as the production director at Gdańsk Shipyard. In 1957 (as part of the Gomulka Aliyah) he came to Israel and married Marcel's sister.

would supervize the construction of a freight fleet for Ghana.[41] He left with his wife. After a year, Marcel's sister, on her own and her husband's behalf, invited him and Bianka to Japan. That situation coincided with Marcel's new professional successes.

Marcel was no longer satisfied with the situation in which his position was described as deputy director, but he performed the duties of the branch director. He brought this issue to the general manager of his bank's head office in Tel Aviv and met with a positive response. The management of the bank had to fill the position of the director of the Hadar branch in Haifa, as its current director resigned and moved to the newly created Rothschild Bank. Marcel describes the change as follows:

> I received a branch based on retail trade and small craft. This was in harmony with the social and economic profile of Hadar. The companies responsible for international trade conducted in the port used the branch in the lower part of the city. My branch was growing all the time, but it was at the expense of that branch. I was called by the management of the bank and accused of picking up clients from the branch where I had previously worked. These were mainly importers and exporters operating in the port, as well as customs agents. I made extensive explanations that not only did I not pick up clients, but I even did everything I could to keep them where they were because that branch was the closest one for them. However, for various reasons, these clients did not want to stay there and started coming to the facility I managed. This even caused some complications for me, because my branch was small and had fewer employees.[42]

---

41 Israel had very good political and economic relations with Ghana at that time. In 1870–1957 Ghana was a British colony. In 1957, it regained its independence, and was now headed by the popular leader of the Pan-African movement Kwame Nkrumah (1909–1972). Nkrumah sought close cooperation with Israel, seeing in it clear benefits for his country. In turn, Israel diligently sought to expand the list of countries with which it could cooperate, so as not to fall into international isolation. Africa and the Middle East took a strategic place in Israel's foreign policy. After establishing diplomatic relations with Ghana, Israel sent there, for instance, agrarian instructors who were to help in establishing modern farms in Ghana. In addition, Ghana adopted an ambitious program to build its own maritime merchant fleet. Its government commissioned the construction of ships in the Japanese shipyard in Kobe. According to arrangements with the Japanese side, the engineer representing Ghana was to supervise the construction on site. The problem was that Ghana did not have a shipbuilding engineer. That is why its authorities asked the Israeli government, if possible, to delegate to Japan a qualified engineer who would live there for several years and oversee the construction of ships in Kobe. This order went to Marcel's brother-in-law.

42 Interview with Marcel Goldman carried out on January 4, 2017.

Fig. 100. In Kobe during the launching ceremony of a ship,
third from the left Bianka Goldman, 1964,
family collections of Marcel and Bianka Goldman (Tel Aviv)

Members of the works council related to the leftist trade union Histadrut, who worked in the lower branch, expressed their concern about the situation. They addressed a letter to the Bank's management board in Tel Aviv stating that they were afraid to lose all their customers to the branch managed by Marcel Goldman. So they asked that he be transferred to their branch again, preferably as main director. The management tried to persuade Marcel to return to the lower branch to his previous position, but he agreed to return only as the main director.

The board agreed to his conditions, although it meant they had to find a new job for the current director. Marcel worked as the director of the main branch in Haifa, and at the same time was the head of the northern region of the Bank. As he recalls, the usual work day started early in the morning. He went around all departments to get to know the current situation and react to possible staff shortages resulting, for example, from someone's illness or mobilization for military service.

He spent most of his time in the office, receiving clients, and tried not to deal with other matters, so that no one would have to wait too long for him. He also supervised work in the customer service room to keep the traffic flowing.

Fig. 101. A banquet accompanying the launching ceremony of a ship in Kobe, 1964, family collections of Marcel and Bianka Goldman (Tel Aviv)

For example, he intervened if he noticed queues in front of the cashier's window. Every day he had a break for a light dinner and a game of tennis[43] (there were tennis courts near the bank). In the afternoon there was time to review correspondence and write letters as well as for meetings and talks with the bank employees, branch managers subordinate to Marcel, and external shareholders. As region manager, Marcel did not control specific facilities directly, but he supported their managers and advised them on specific matters which they brought to him. On average, once every three to four weeks he visited the northern region (he began by going Haifa to Kiryat Shmona, or, at other times, from Haifa to Netanya). On average, every three or every six months, Marcel invited all branch managers to a meeting in a hotel in Haifa, where they also casual conversations at dinner or relaxing by the pool. Several times, the branch he managed received an award for best results, which was awarded during a solemn meeting attended by other regional managers and directors from Tel Aviv. The routine of those meetings was once broken in a rather unusual way:

---

43 Marcel usually played with his assistant, they finished a tennis course together.

> I was tricked. My assistant and one of the managers of branches subordinate to me proposed that the next meeting should take place in one of the theaters popular in Haifa at the time, which was to prepare a performance for us. I did not read that the program also included striptease! On the following day Tel Aviv boiled: "Goldman made a meeting of bankers with a striptease." I did not want to admit that I did not have time to check what that meeting would look like, so I could only make the best of a bad job. I could only say: well, people like it... After many years, I remember it with laughter, but then I had nothing to laugh at.[44]

Marcel's branch was successful, and the CEO of the Bank in Tel Aviv decided to reward his work:

> The director asked me a short question: "How can we reward you for your success?" I answered equally briefly: "My sister has been living in Japan for a year and a half, I would like to visit her." I heard it was not a problem. The director stated that the bank had offices representing its interests in Bangkok and Hong Kong. Therefore, I would be sent there at the expense of the bank to pay an official visit. From there I was supposed to go to Japan. So I went to a travel agency. It was the office of the famous British company Thomas Cook in Haifa. During the conversation, the director of the office pointed out to me that I should come back through the second part of the globe, because Japan's distance from Israel is half the world. That meant that the road to or from it is about the same number of kilometers, regardless of whether you travel to the east or the west of the globe. I liked that idea very much and I came home with him to discuss it with Bianka. She said that she would agree to the trip only if I took her with me.[45]

The cost of the trip was about two or three thousand dollars. It was a large amount then, although the largest expenses (accommodation, tickets for sea, land, and air transport) were covered by the bank. The children stayed with Bianka's mother. Bianka and Marcel went on a journey of a lifetime, which took them ten weeks. They wanted to visit India along the way, but it required extra effort, because Israel and India did not have official diplomatic relations then. The interests of India in Israel were represented by the Dutch embassy in Tel Aviv. Interestingly, the required visa was to be collected in... Tehran. At that time, Iran

---

44   Interview with Marcel Goldman carried out on January 4, 2017.
45   Ibid.

was ruled by Mohammad Reza Pahlawi (1919–1980), the last shah of Iran from the Pahlawi dynasty. He pursued a pro-Western policy and maintained friendly relations with the Israeli government.[46] Therefore, the Goldmans went from Tel Aviv to Tehran, and then to Mumbai and Delhi (they visited the city and the surrounding province), followed by Cambodia, Burma, Thailand, and Japan (first Tokyo and then Kobe).[47] The return trip led through Hawaii (Honolulu), then San Francisco, Los Angeles, New York, and Vienna, from where they flew to Tel Aviv.[48]

As a side note, it is worth mentioning that the young state of Israel from the beginning of its existence willingly shared its knowledge and experience with other countries. In the first place, help was directed to other young countries, often in a situation as complicated as Israel's. In addition to the previously mentioned Ghana, there was also Singapore,[49] a city-state located at the southern tip of the Malay Peninsula, not far from Indonesia. Both Israel and Singapore have freed themselves from the British domination and were now threatened by the nearest countries, with more population and better weapons. In the case of Singapore, we are talking about Malaysia and Indonesia. In those circumstances, the Singaporean authorities quickly recognized that the optimal solution for them would be to use the defense solutions known in Israel. As Dan Senor and Saul Singer write in response to the request of the first Minister of Defense of Singapore Goh Keng Swee: "IDF [Israeli Defense Forces] commissioned Lieutenant Colonel Jehuda Golan to write two textbooks for the emerging Singapore army: one on the theory of combat and the structure of the Ministry of Defense and the other on the subject of intelligence institutions. Later, six IDF officers moved to Singapore with their families to train soldiers and form a conscription-based army."[50] In the following years, providing various types of support to other countries became an effective tool in the hands of Israeli diplomacy.

---

46 In 1979, he was removed from power as a result of the Islamic revolution, its direct consequence was the immediate and strong deterioration of Iran's relations with democratic states, and above all with the United States and Israel.

47 Interview with Marcel Goldman carried out on January 4, 2017.

48 Ibid.

49 Singapore was founded by the British in 1819. The people of Singapore achieved independence in two stages: in 1963, as part of Malaysia, they freed themselves from the British rule, and on August 9, 1965, they declared independence, separating themselves from Malaysia. Already in this we can see the similarity between Israel and Singapore—both countries are small, the inhabitants of which had to contend for their independence with the British.

50 Senor, Singer, *Naród start-upów*, 125.

In assessing the phenomenon of the Israeli economy, it is difficult not to take into account the fact that it is a country almost devoid of mineral resources. It forced the nation and government to seek new, more technologically advanced ways to earn money. Unlike countries collecting foreign currencies from the export of natural resources, such as oil or gas, Israel had to aim at highly processed products. Those conditions were included in the group of factors stimulating the development of the local high technology industry, followed by start-ups, which was convincingly described by Dan Senor and Saul Singer in the above-cited book. It also significantly influenced the specific style of Israeli diplomacy. Because Israel has no way of influencing international politics by properly dosing the export of natural resources, it decided to share what was best and what it had in abundance: knowledge and experience. In 1964, in Kobe, during a banquet accompanying the launching ceremony of a ship built in Japan for Ghana, a Japanese man sitting next to Bianka Goldman asked her: "Do you know what Israel's largest export commodity is?" Bianka tried to give the right answer: citruses, chemicals, medicines... "No!" The interlocutor interrupted her, after which he answered the question himself: "Your brains!"[51]

Currently, in contacts with superpowers such as the United States, India, China, or Russia, Israel often uses knowledge in the fields of military, intelligence, high technology industry, agriculture, and environmental protection. They also help shape positive relations with other countries, including quite many with countries located in Africa, Central, and South America. Many of them have raw materials, but they lack access to high technologies that Israel can guarantee. In addition, as long as the Israeli army and intelligence are highly esteemed, the knowledge they acquire will be priceless.

Israel is one of the countries that, if needed, are the first to send rescue and humanitarian aid into the world. Undoubtedly, this has a positive effect on the international image and position of the state. Although Israel is located close to seismically active areas, it does not experience earthquake problems itself. However, it has rescue teams that are perfectly trained to act in the event of terrorist attacks. Operations carried out in blown-up buildings in many respects resemble those that are implemented in the event of building collapse due to an earthquake. On April 25, 2015, a 7.8-magnitude earthquake occurred in Nepal. Around nine thousand people were killed then, over twenty thousand injured. The Israeli authorities sent the most numerous team of rescuers to Kathmandu,

---

51 Interview with Marcel Goldman carried out on December 18, 2016.

the capital of Nepal.⁵² In 2017, Israelis helped Mexicans affected by an earthquake and Puerto Rican people who suffered a hurricane. In September 2017, in Mexico, Israelis used ultra-modern cameras with RF Ultra Wide Band (UWB) signal, thanks to which it is possible to generate 3D images even from objects covered with solid barriers, such as walls made of various popular materials, including cement, plaster, brick, concrete, and wood.⁵³ In 2018, the Jerusalem government supported Zambians who had to deal with the cholera epidemic.⁵⁴ There are many more examples of this type. They shape the identity of Israelis, who proudly emphasize that as a nation who has experienced so many troubles, they can show empathy for the weak and those in need of support.

An important part of the history of Israel is the so-called Gomulka Aliyah, the emigration of Polish Jews to Israel in the years 1956–1960. The context of the accompanying events is complex. In 1953, the Soviet dictator Joseph Stalin died. During the Twentieth Congress of the Communist Party of the Soviet Union (CPSU) on the night of February 24–25, 1956, the leader of the Soviet Union Nikita Khrushchev gave a speech entitled "On the Cult of Personality and Its Consequences." It was a signal for profound political changes throughout the Eastern Bloc. In Poland, political life became relatively more liberal, and the rigors of censorship were reduced. At that time, de-Stalinisation began, which, as part of internal party games, was an opportunity to get rid of some of the political competitors of the Jewish nationality. What is more, Władysław Gomułka, who was at that time the first secretary of the Central Committee of the Polish United Workers' Party, finally allowed people of Jewish origin to go to Israel.⁵⁵

---

52 The team consisted of over 250 doctors and rescuers, who conducted search and rescue operations on site. Within a dozen or so hours after arrival, they set up a field hospital that had two operating rooms, four intensive care rooms, and eighty hospital beds. "Israel Responds to Earthquake in Nepal," http://mfa.gov.il /MFA/PressRoom/2015/pages/Israel-Responds-to-earthquake-in-Nepal-25-Apr-2015.aspx, accessed March 29, 2018.

53 "Rescuers in Mexico Use Israeli 'See-Trough-Walls' Technology," http://www.israeldefense.co.il/en/node/31208, accessed March 29, 2018.

54 "Izrael jako pierwszy pomaga Zambii podczas epidemii cholery," http://epatmos.pl/szabat-szalom/item/izrael-jako-pierwszy-pomaga-zambii-podczas-epidemii-cholery, accessed March 29, 2018.

55 According to precise calculations of Elżbieta Kossewska, in 1955–1960 42,569 Polish Jews came to Israel, see Kossewska, "Ona jeszcze mówi po polsku, ale śmieje się po hebrajsku." However, Grzegorz Berendt reports that in the years 1956–1966 the number of immigrants from Poland to Israel amounted to 46,112 people, see Berendt, "Emigracja Żydów z Polski w latach 1960–1967," 308–309.

Many emigrants who came to Israel at that time played an important role in Israeli culture, science, economy, and politics. Among them is the already mentioned Dr. Karnit Flug, the first woman in the position of the President of the Bank of Israel, the writer Ida Fink, the popular musician and composer Svika Pick, the award-winning journalist Arie Golan, and the Israeli journalist and longtime Polish media correspondent Aleksander Klugman. It is also impossible to ignore Alex Danzig, who was a guide in the Yad Vashem Museum involved in the Polish-Israeli dialogue and one of the authors of the report on the image of Poland in the textbooks of Israeli high schools. Thanks to the Gomulka Aliyah, Polish-language culture was revived in Israel. The demand for Polish press and books increased. New Polish bookshops were opened, the most popular being founded in Tel Aviv by the then married couple Edmund and Ada Neustein. New press titles appeared, and those that had already been issued saw an increase in circulation. One could even say that the Polish-language press in Israel reached its heyday at that time.

It is worth mentioning that during the first few decades after Israel's proclamation of independence, the local press market was characterized by great diversity. Today, only three, up to four dailies count in Israel: the right-wing *Israel Hayom*, the left-wing *Haaretz*, and the central *Yedioth Ahronoth*. At that time, five or six titles were widely read, of which only *Haaretz* was not affiliated with any political party (it was Marcel's preferred newspaper). Others were published by political parties, such as *HaBoker*, the newspaper of general Zionists, and *Al HaMishmar* published by the extreme left wing of Zionists. In addition, there was a large number of titles published in the languages of the countries from which larger groups of Jews came. Polish newspapers were very popular; they were bought by, for example, Bianka's and Marcel's parents. In 1952, the daily *Nowiny Izraelskie* began to appear, which in the 1960s and 1970s reached a circulation of eighteen thousands copies on weekdays and twenty-six thousand in Friday editions. In 1956, the daily *Kurier* was founded, and after two years it merged with *Nowiny Izraelskie* under the common title *Nowiny Izraelskie-Kurier*, then renamed *Nowiny Kurier*, which was published until 1991.[56] This newspaper was sometimes called quite maliciously, *Kurwiny*.[57] An important place among

---

56 R. Löw, "Rozpoznanie. Rzecz o izraelskiej prasie w języku polskim," *Kontury* 6 (1995): 148–160.

57 A combination of the two titles, which also echoes the Polish swear word *kurwa*. Malicious comments were made about this newspaper because part of the journalistic community accused it of controversial journalistic practices, including making unmarked and uncopy-

weeklies was taken by *Przegląd* (1949–1982), *Opinia* (1950–1951), *Od Nowa* (1958–1965), *Po Prostu w Izraelu* (1959). In the years 1988–2006 the historical and literary magazine *Kontury* was issued. In the years 1991–1993 the literary yearbook *Akcenty* was also published. Beginning in the 1980s, interest in those newspapers began to gradually decline. The end of popularity of Polish-language titles seems to be the price for the rapid teaming up of Polish immigrants with the rest of Israeli society. Pressure from the Israeli authorities, who sought to accelerate the Hebraization of *olim chadashim*, had to play a role. Also, the Jews from Poland began themselves, of their own free will, to reach for the Hebrew press more and more often. They did so not only because they knew Hebrew better, but also because they wanted to learn it better and faster. In addition, newspapers published in languages other than Hebrew did not enjoy a good reputation. They were mainly based on reprints. Elżbieta Kossewska, the researcher of Israeli press, writes about this:

> The level of the foreign-language press aroused the opposition of journalists writing to the Hebrew press, they saw it as a margin of opinion regarding marginal matters, thus questioning its value and usefulness. For example, Azriel Karlebach, editor of *Ma'ariv*, writes about foreign-language journalism: "... You will probably ask: how can you make a living with Reb Ipcha Mistabra.[58] Between us, I can say: I don't know how, but he already knows. He takes scissors, cuts me out of the newspaper, translates me into Polish or into another language, prints, and sells, not caring about the fact that any other competitive Polish rag will do the same, steal the same article, and also sell it."[59]

Along with the Gomulka Aliyah, new people appeared in the life of the Goldmans, who would henceforth be their close friends. Marcel recalls:

> One day I heard the bell at the door to our apartment. After opening it, I saw two men. They looked like Pat and Patachon,[60] the first of them

---

righted translations from the Hebrew press. In addition, there were different circles around each of the newspapers, which did not hesitate to show their animosity.

58 The name of this imaginary character comes from a Talmudic phrase that means "on the contrary."

59 E. Kossewska, "'Ona jeszcze mówi po polsku, ale śmieje się po hebrajsku'—prasa polskojęzyczna i integracja językowa polskich Żydów w Izraelu," *Kultura i Społeczeństwo* 54, no. 4 (2010): 67.

60 Marcel Goldman refers here to the Danish comedic film duo, Carl Schenström and Harald Madsen, who played with their height difference. They were popular in Europe in the 1920s and 1930s.

short and stocky, the other slim and tall. They both introduced themselves. One of them was my future brother-in-law Henryk Grycendler, a shipbuilding engineer. The second was Abraham (most often called Abraszka) Aleksandrowicz, who specialized in high current research. He soon became a professor at the Electronics Department of the Technion in Haifa.[61]

The moment when they first crossed the threshold of the Goldmans' apartment was immortalised in Marcel's poem entitled *Urodziny Abraszki* (English: Abraszka's birthday). Here I quote its fragment:

W 1957 roku	**In 1957**
Znaleźli się na naszym progu,	They found themselves on our doorstep,
Pamiętam jak dzień dzisiejszy,	I remember as if it were today,
Jeden był czarny i duży	One was black-haired and big
A drugi „trochę" mniejszy.	And the other "a little" smaller.
Nie było wątpliwości	There was no doubt
Toż to polska kadra:	That's the Polish staff:
Jeden był profesorem,	One was a professor,
Drugi został za szwagra...	The second became my brother-in-law...
Wtedy się wszystko zaczęło,	Then it all began
Tańce, hulanka, swawola,	Let's eat, drink, be merry,
Abraszka w środku z gitarą	Abraszka in the middle with a guitar
Szefuniu kosim*—woła,	"Boss, glasses," he exclaims
Mój szwagier z drugą gitarą,	My brother-in-law with a second guitar
Spogląda mętnym wzrokiem,	Looking with fishy eyes
W rosyjski takt zaiwania	Playing in the Russian time
Z przymkniętym od dymu okiem.**	With an eye closed from smoke.

*   Kosot—"glasses" in Hebrew, mistakenly masculine here.
** Goldman, A *w nocy przychodzą myśli*, 38.

---

61 Interview with Marcel Goldman carried out on December 18, 2016.

Before the Gomulka Aliyah, the Goldmans mostly moved among members of their immediate family. Their circle of friends, as mentioned, was small, until the arrival of a new wave of emigrants significantly expanded it. In Marcel's assessment:

> We were born and raised in Poland, we did not attend school here, we did not belong to any societies, it was difficult without any foundation to suddenly build any friendships. In Gomułka's time, compact groups of people who knew each other well from Poland or made friendships here, on the spot—for example, in *ulpanim*, Hebrew language schools, arrived in Israel. Entering their environment, you immediately found yourself in a numerous and coherent community in terms of many life experiences and beliefs. For example, through Heniek Grycendler I immediately met his colleague Jurek Amir, who came with him and, like him, was an engineer in the shipyard. Later I came across Poldek Wasserman, who was my instructor in the Jewish scouting group Tzofim before the war. He was the oldest member of that organization who survived World War II. He came to Eretz Yisrael around 1946 and dealt with the illegal import of Jewish immigrants. On the ship he met Aviva, who later became his wife. We met them here as a couple. The meeting happened by accident, because—it turned out—we lived on the same street in Haifa as they did. Poldek was already a high Israeli naval officer. In turn, through him we made acquaintance with his closest friends, who were a Romanian navy colleague and his wife born in Vienna. Also by accident I met in Israel my distant cousin Rysiek Rechen. One day, I was going by taxi with Bianka in Haifa and the driver seemed suspiciously familiar to me. After a short conversation it turned out to be Rysiek.[62] During the Nazi occupation he was the driver of Oskar Schindler.[63]

---

62   Ryszard Rechen was born in 1921 in Wadowice, in the same house as Karol Wojtyła—later Pope John Paul II. In the early 1930s, his family moved to Krakow. They were wealthy, they had their own house in the first villa district of Krakow—Salwator. The father worked as a representative of European chemical concerns. There were car workshops near the Rechens' home that caught Rysiek's attention. He learned to fix various car models there. Before World War II he had yet to pass his final exams. When the war broke out, he escaped to Lviv, where his father also arrived. Later, his father was exiled to Siberia. Rysiek found employment as a mechanic in factories working for the needs of the Soviet army, which were later taken over by the Germans. During the war, he decided to return to Krakow, where his mother remained. With the consent of the superior in Lviv, he was transferred to a car mechanics factory in Krakow, and then found a job in Krakow's Emalia, which belonged to Oskar Schindler. He was in Grossrosen camp, and then was directed to Brünlitz to work there for Schindler. Goldman, *Iskierki życia*, 87–92.

63   Interview with Marcel Goldman carried out on December 20, 2016.

Marcel writes about Schindler in *Iskierki życia*:

> Jewish prisoners worked in the factory. They were deprived of their liberty, surrounded by SS guards headed by commander Leipold (former commander of the death camp in Majdanek), but they were not hungry because Schindler gave them food in addition to what K.L. delivered, and they did not risk death at the hands of the SS crew, because on Schindler's orders they were not allowed to enter the factory premises. They waited for liberation any day.[64]

In view of the impending fall of the Third Reich, the authorities issued an order to kill Schindler's Jewish crew. However, Schindler managed to save his employees. About 1,200 Jews survived thanks to him. At the end of the war, Jews repaid Schindler, saving his life. Thanks to the initiative of Dr. Hilfstein—a Zionist activist from Krakow who also found himself in Brünlitz—Schindler was able to escape from the impending Red Army.[65] In the event of his arrest by Red Army soldiers or Czech partisans, he would inevitably have been murdered before he could tell them about his merits. After the war, Schindler maintained lively contacts with the people he saved and even visited Israel. He died in 1974. Before his death he expressed his wish that he would be buried in the cemetery on Mount Zion in Jerusalem, and his request was fulfilled:

> Rysiek was asked to bring his body and arrange the funeral. Just like his other tasks, he did it properly, according to the circumstances. He gave a speech in honour of the deceased in the cathedral in Frankfurt, and thought out everything to the last detail to honour the memory of the deceased.[66]

The education and professional qualifications of Abraszka Aleksandrowicz and Henryk Grycendler reflect the great potential of Polish Jews who came to Israel with the Gomulka Aliyah. These were mostly young and well-educated people, who quickly acclimatized in Israel and successfully rearranged their

---

64 Goldman, *Iskierki życia*, 92–94.

65 First they escaped in a truck driven by Rysiek Rechen, then they travelled by rail and on foot (the story was described in detail in Goldman, *Iskierki życia*). They made it, Schindler survived. He emigrated to Argentina, where he tried to continue his business, but went bankrupt. In 1958 he returned to Germany, but he was not too lucky there, and several of his companies went bankrupt quite quickly. Ibid., 95–99.

66 Ibid., 99.

lives. They soon began using all the goods that their new homeland offered them. No one restricted their personal freedom—if they wanted to have fun, they could have fun until the morning. House parties were popular. At that time, people sang and danced to music played from gramophone records (sometimes imported from Poland) or played live using guitars, harmonies and other instruments. Alcohol was not avoided. Admittedly, it was Polish Jews who popularized the so-called boozy events. Earlier, alcohol was not popular (for Muslims it is banned, and Oriental Jews have adopted some of their habits). Henryk Palmon (Figielman), who was born in 1930 in Łódź and left for Israel in 1958, described the following story in his autobiographical novel *Powroty i wyjazdy Natana*:

> Every Saturday, residents of immigrant houses were invited by various political parties for sightseeing tours in Galilee. Each party wanted to win the hearts of new immigrants to gain votes in the Knesset elections. . . . Immigrants . . . willingly took part in those trips, because they were for free, and in kibbutzim, where they would stop to listen to the lecture, there was always a non-alcoholic refreshment. When the speaker asked if there were any questions, only Moses Zimnawoda raised his hand.
> "Yes?," the speaker said smiling.
> "Why do you consider us alcoholic impotents?"
> "I don't understand, please repeat."
> When Moses Zimnawoda repeated, the speaker understood.
> "Forgive me, I left Poland in 1920 and I forgot . . ."[67]

Traces of parties with alcohol can also be found in Marcel Goldman's poems, for example, in *Wesele (nie Wyspiańskiego)*—in English, *The Wedding (not Wyspiański's)*, and *Mesiba (Zabawa)*—in English, *The Party*.[68] I will cite a fragment of the second poem:

Przyszła kryska na Matyska—	What goes around comes around—
U Jasiów i Abraszków,	At Jaśes' and Abraszkas',
U Waltera i Jurka,	At Walter's and Jurek's
Piło się, tańcowało,	We drank, we danced,
Jadło, grało, śpiewało,	We ate, played, sang,
Trzeba wreszcie u siebie,	Finally it's my turn

---

67 H. Palmon, *Powroty i wyjazdy Natana*, Łódź 2000, 147.
68 Both poems can be found in Goldman. *A w nocy przychodzą myśli*, the first on 29–30, the second on 31–32.

Do swojego podwórka	At my patch
Też zaprosić.	To invite them
...	...
Marcel rolady taszczy, z rynku zakupy,	Marcel lugs roulades, groceries from the market,
Henek flaszki „soft drinki" zbiera do kupy	Henek piles up bottles of "soft drinks"
i na Hadar, z Hadaru	to Hadar, from Hadar
Na górę i znów do miasta.	Up and down to the city again.
Tu jeszcze czegoś brakuj...	There's always something missing...
W piecznikiu ciasta,	Cakes in the oven,
A na piecu barszcz kwaśny	Borscht on the stove, sour
Jak Bianki mina.	Like Bianka's face
Ona od nowa barszczyk robić zaczyna.*	She starts to do borscht once again.

* Both poems can be found in Goldman. *A w nocy przychodzą myśli*, 31–32.

The Polish culinary tradition maintained in the family is visible in *Mesiba*. In addition to the alcohol, we read about cakes and borscht. At the same time, a certain change in customs has obviously taken place in Israel: "Pork loin, bigos, or sausage—no longer in fashion"[69]. The abandonment of certain dishes resulted, for example, from the lack of ingredients. Besides, some warming dishes, which in Poland enjoy great recognition, especially in winter, are useless in Israel. Let's add that a frequent reason for social gatherings was to celebrate various holidays, anniversaries, and birthdays together. In addition to celebrations at home, the Goldmans and the new company willingly arranged round trips around Israel:

> After 1960, almost everyone in our company had cars. We were able to make an appointment spontaneously and in a group divided into several cars we set off to a fixed place or several in a row. After the Six-Day War, we gladly visited the Sinai Peninsula, which for a few years came under the rule of Israel. Besides, it was the Israelis that were the first to build resorts on the Red Sea there (such as Sharm El-Sheikh), on the basis of which Egypt created its tourist sector.[70]

---

69 M. Goldman, *Mesiba (Zabawa)*, in idem., *A w nocy przychodzą myśli...*, 31.
70 Interview with Marcel Goldman carried out on December 20, 2016.

Immigrants who arrived as part of the Gomulka Aliyah popularized the game of bridge in Israel. They were often professional players who later became the backbone of the Israeli team in that field of sport. Marcel mastered bridge rules in his childhood, and in a short time the game became his favorite hobby. He welcomed the arrival of new comrades (including the already mentioned Heniek and Abraszka) with undisguised joy. Social gatherings with games of bridge were generally held in private homes during weekend evenings. They kept the community together. They were saturated with passion, humour, and heated discussions on all possible topics. Here is the *Wieczór brydżowy* (Bridge Evening) according to Marcel:

Co za gwałty, co za krzyki,	What noises, what screams,
Niby w puszczach Ameryki.	As in the forests of America.
Co za rejwach! Pęka głowa.	What brouhaha! I've got a splitting headache.
Czy to z żoną jest „rozmowa"?	Is it a "conversation" with the wife?
Czy teściowej to tyrady	Or the tirades of the mother-in-law
Grzmią w powietrzu jak tornado?	Thundering in the air like a tornado?
Może się sąsiad rozwydrza?	Or maybe the neighbour is shouting?
To nasza czwórka gra w brydża.*	This is the four of us playing bridge.

* M. Goldman, *Wieczór brydżowy*, in idem., *A w nocy przychodzą myśli . . .*, 40.

Bridge evenings were primarily male entertainment. Bianka often joined the company, but more often looked after the children falling asleep. If the screams became unbearable in the bedroom, she began to whistle, which was a signal that the emotional men should calm down so as not to wake the children. She chose that way of communication, assuming that if she had screamed herself, the children would have waken up even more surely. That home tradition found its place in the quoted poem *Wieczór brydżowy*: "One and the other screams. / And you can't hear anything anymore— / just a scream, a commotion like in hell. / Bianka whistles furiously from the bedroom."[71] The love of bridge was common among Polish Jews. This is reflected in memoir literature, including texts written by women. I quote Ilona Dworak-Cousin, who arrived in Israel with her family in 1957:

---

71   M. Goldman, *Wieczór brydżowy*, in idem., *A w nocy przychodzą myśli*, 41.

We were always in a hurry—that is, my parents were always in a hurry. Bridge partners were already waiting for my dad. Later, my mother and her friends joined the game, who—having mastered the rules of the game with their husbands—completed their own bridge table on Friday afternoons. They played taking turns, every week with a different family. Two tables, male and female, played until late at night. They met in our house once a month.[72]

Social contacts in Israel are particularly respected and nurtured. The concern for maintaining deep family ties is rooted in Judaism, while close relationships with people outside the family are to some extent a legacy of the first years of Israeli statehood, in those difficult times people clung to each other. As a result of the Holocaust, many Jews reached Israel without relatives, or even without any soul mate—without anyone to whom they could entrust their worries, from whom they would hear words of encouragement and advice. With the developing economy, widespread contacts also made it easier to find a job or purchase the necessary products. Social life took place in private homes, but also in cafés or other places. Some of them were identified as "Polish," such as the Kocia[73] café described by Ilona Dworak-Cousin:

> The real life of the estate took place there. The owner was a pretty woman with fair hair arranged in line with the fashion of the sixties in a "big banana." Exactly the same hairstyles were worn by most regular female customers. Almost all the ladies, including Kocia [the owner of the place—Ł.T.S.], survived World War II, and in their opinion being blonde was synonymous with life. There were few brunettes.... In the late morning, when the house was cleaned and the men were still at work, the "liberated" ladies began to fill the café for a few hours, enjoying not only coffee, tea or cakes, but also gossip and interesting news that could only be heard there: who bought a new apartment, which student was the best in the class, which girl goes out with a new boyfriend and when the next wedding will take place in the estate, who is sick and what medicine they take. You could also hear, in a big secret, various spicy details from personal lives: who betrayed whom and why? How did the secret affair of the third-floor neighbour develop? And so on.[74]

---

72 Dworak-Cousin, *Podróż do krainy cieni*, 222.
73 The café was located in the shopping and entertainment complex in Ramat Aviv on a small square near the insurance company and the Orot cinema.
74 Dworak-Cousin, *Podróż do krainy cieni*, 224–226.

Another Polish café, called Piltza, occupied a beautiful location on the Tel Aviv promenade, at the height of the Frishman Beach. Its offer was much richer—next to the excellent cuisine, the owners took care of cultural events. They hosted artistic evenings, recitations of poems, and cabaret performances.

Current immigrants to Israel also know that it is worth having an extensive network of contacts, because it is more difficult living alone in a new land. There is a popular saying here: "If you have extensive contacts, you do not need protection."

Despite the profound changes brought by World War II, the formation of social networks is still strongly associated with the division into Ashkenazi and Sephardi Jews.[75] The Zionists recognized that the Sephardic Jewish culture retained the value of originality to the highest degree, while Ashkenazi Jews were seriously "contaminated" with the *galut* (Hebrew: expulsion of Jews from Israel and their lives abroad). Therefore, in Israel's public space, the Sephardic version of the Hebrew language, music, dances, and so forth was preferred, but Ashkenazi Jews occupied a larger number of positions in government, offices, and institutions of science and culture. This does not mean, however, that within these communities Ashkenazi or Sephardic people showed only solidarity and understanding. The fundamental division between Ashkenazi and Sephardic Jews coexisted with many other tensions. The country of origin was an important factor: integrating in some cases and exclusionary in others. For example, German Jews were not necessarily sympathetic to Polish or Russian Jews, and in this respect they could count on reciprocity. The Israeli-born Jews, *sabras*, were a distinct group. Another important criterion for the division was the date of arrival in Israel. For example, immigrants from Poland who came with the Gomulka Aliyah were distinctly separate from the groups of Polish Jews who had lived in Eretz Yisrael before World War II. Certain differences related to shared history and the use of specific cultural codes also separated the emigrants of the Gomulka Aliyah from those who arrived on the wave of March '68. In addition, due to historical and political factors, Jews emigrating to Israel were most often deprived of all property, so everyone had to start from the beginning. It is natural that representatives of the earlier *aliyot* were better off than newcomers—another reason for creating barriers between different social groups in Israel. People as ambitious and hardworking as the Goldmans had a chance to cross those barri-

---

75 The Ashkenazi Jews include primarily Jews from Western, Central, and Eastern Europe, and the Sephardi Jews mainly originate from Southern Europe (Spain, Portugal, southern France and Italy), North Africa, Asia Minor, Levant, Iraq, and Persia.

ers, but in doing so, they attracted the attention of people who at that time stood higher in the social hierarchy:

> A comic episode reflecting the attitude of "natives" to *olim*. Even though in the 1970s there were many more newcomers in Israel! We were invited to the villa of the general director of the bank in Tel Aviv [David Golan—Ł.T.S.] for a *garden party*. We felt foreign: all the guests were bigwigs from Jerusalem and Tel Aviv, and we came from the Haifa province. The lady of the house, from a family who had a long history of settlement in Jerusalem, noticed that and started a brief conversation. Who are we?
> "Well, I'm your husband's assistant in the bank's management and the head of the northern district."
> "But you are not born here, it is not a *sabra*'s Hebrew?"
> "No, I arrived in 1949."
> "Well, for a new *ole*, you've come far . . ."
> We had been living in Israel for almost thirty years then!⁷⁶

Fig. 102. Yohanan Bader (1901–1994), a Polish and Israeli lawyer, journalist, politician, influential member of the Knesset, member of the right-wing party Cherut, November 1, 1951, photo: Théodore Brauner, public domain

The antagonisms between the right and the left political wings and the profound differences between Orthodox and secular circles exert a destructive influence on Israel. A popular saying goes: "In Israel, everything is the same as elsewhere, only more." Everyone is familiar with the divisions between Republicans and Democrats in the United States or the sharp friction between

---

76   Goldman, *A w nocy przychodzą myśli*, 8–10.

Labourites and Conservatives in Great Britain. In Israel, the hostility between right and left camps has threatened the existence of the state at least once, and has repeatedly exposed it to serious trouble.

In 1948, David Ben-Gurion proclaimed the independence of the state and began to build its structures. On May 28, 1948, his government set up an army that took the name of the Israeli Defense Force (Hebrew: Tzava Hagana Le Yisrael, abbreviated TZAHAL), based on the Hagana paramilitary organisation from 1920–1948, which had a leftist profile. The right-wing formation Irgun (full name: Irgun Tzvai Leumi—National Military Organization) was left out. Undaunted, Irgun fighters ordered a large supply of weapons and ammunition, which was loaded onto the *Altalena* ship (the name of the ship was borrowed from the pseudonym of Jabotinsky).

It arrived at the shores of Israel in June 1948, but Ben-Gurion strongly opposed its docking, concerned about competition to the official army (he

i Menachem Begin was born on August 16, 1913 in Brest on the Bug as Mieczysław Biegun. In his youth, he joined the Zionist organisation HaShomer HaTzair (Hebrew: the young guard), then he joined Beitar (full name: Brit Josef Trumpeldor), in 1938 he became the leader of that organisation in Poland. He was a student and assistant to the world leader of revisionists Ze'ev Jabotinsky (1880–1940). He graduated with a degree in law from the University of Warsaw. After the outbreak of World War II, he managed to get to Vilnius. In 1940, he was arrested by the NKVD and, after a long investigation, sentenced to eight years in a Siberian labour camp.* In 1942, released from prison under the Sikorski-Mayski agreement, he joined the Polish Army formed by General Władysław Anders and left the Soviet Union at his side. After entering the British Mandate in Palestine, he left the Polish Army, most likely with the consent of its command. He joined the right-wing combat organisation Irgun, and soon became its head. In independent Israel, he founded the Cherut party (Hebrew: freedom), later transformed into Likud (Hebrew: consolidation). In 1949 he was elected to the first Knesset, where he also sat in subsequent terms. He worked mainly in parliamentary committees on foreign affairs and defense as well as the constitution, law, and justice. He became the leader of extreme opposition to the leftist government and the parliamentary majority. He was in sharp political conflict with David Ben-Gurion, who was so reluctant towards Begin that he never mentioned him publicly by name. For example, when Ben-Gurion had to refer to Begin during parliamentary debates, he said:

Fig. 103. Israeli Prime Minister Menachem Begin (in the foreground) exits the plane on arrival in the United States, accompanied by the then Israeli Minister of Foreign Affairs Moshe Dayan (in the back), 1978, public domain

"The man sitting next to the Knesset member Mr. Bader" (Dr. Jan Bader, mentioned earlier, was also a Cherut politician). Begin categorically opposed political negotiations with Germany and the acceptance of reparations from that country. In 1967 he accepted the position of minister without portfolio in the government of national unity of Levi Eshkol, and remained in the cabinet of Golda Meir. In 1977 he became the first right-wing prime minister in the history of Israel. He held that office until 1983. In 1981, he decided to bomb an Iraqi nuclear reactor in Osirak by the Israeli air force. He started peace negotiations with Egyptian President Anwar Sadat. For bringing peace to Israel and Egypt, both statesmen received the Nobel Peace Prize in 1978. With Begin, manners well known to Polish Jews appeared in the Israeli public space, which the Zionist left wanted to eliminate. Begin, to the surprise of many people, kissed women's hands and dressed like a European gentleman. It is well illustrated in Fig. 103, in which we can see him in a well-tailored three-piece suit and a perfectly ironed white shirt. Moshe Dayan, who is standing behind him, is dressed in a similar style, but, as a military man, he preferred loose clothes, closer to the ideals of the first leftist pioneers.

* See M. Begin, *Czas białych nocy. Opowieść o aresztowaniu i przesłuchaniach Menachema Begina, z załączeniem protokołów i dokumentów odtajnionych po upadku Związku Radzieckiego*, trans. M. Ornat, Krakow–Budapest 2010.

probably also took into account the predictable undermining of his political position in that situation). So he ordered to take over *Altalena* by force and, if necessary, sink it. A fight broke out, a dozen or so people were killed, mainly Irgun soldiers. Menachem Begin, the leader of Irgun, forbade his subordinates to counterattack. Thanks to that, further bloodshed, and perhaps even an outbreak of civil war, which in the face of the ongoing Arab-Israeli war could result in the immediate collapse of young Israeli statehood, was avoided.

It is interesting that those antagonisms and political divisions for a long time had a real impact on the private affairs and everyday life of Israelis. After 1948, Ben-Gurion pushed the right wing to the margins of political life, where it remained until the 1970s. In the current, already mature, Israeli democracy, political views do not have to affect everyday living conditions, but for almost thirty years after the creation of the state, the left had control over all of the most important spheres of life. One did not even have to be a right-wing politician to experience the unpleasant consequences—they also became part of Marcel's life. By not agreeing to the risky credit policy at the Halva'ah VeChisakhon Bank, Marcel came into conflict with his CEO. He then asked the trade union of Histadrut, to which he belonged, to defend him. He even made contact with Hesiek, an important official from the Haifa Histadrut and a graduate of the Hebrew Gymnasium in Krakow. After checking Marcel's files, Hesiek found an annotation "right-wing supporter" there, and said, "in this situation I cannot help you."[77] This annotation appeared because in the years 1955–1956 Marcel made friends with Johanan Bader, also born in Krakow, a graduate of the Jagiellonian University and a doctor of legal sciences, who was responsible for the political program of the right-wing Cherut party (Hebrew: freedom).

Although his friends, thinking about Marcel's good, advised him not to meet with Bader, he did not listen to them. They often talked about world and Israeli economics, which Marcel appreciated all the more because the content of the lectures at the university generally coincided with the policy and propaganda of the government, and he wanted to deepen his knowledge, approaching the essence of individual economic problems.

As far as economic issues were concerned, the differences between the Israeli left and the right were fundamental at the time. For example, the ruling left and Histadrut demanded fifty-one percent of shares from investors, which meant having power in the company. Marcel joined Bader in his serious criti-

---

77 Interview with Marcel Goldman carried out on September 21, 2018.

cism of such dependencies and promoted the free market.⁷⁸ In the end, in 1959, leaving the Halva'ah VeChisakhon Bank, he also left Histadrut, and sent his membership card back. He could allow himself such a gesture because he was already well-off and wealthy. The vast majority of Israelis did not have that option. Histadrut initially dominated not only social security, but also health insurance (Hebrew: Kupat Cholim). It had a monopoly on approximately eighty or eighty-five percent of medical services. After leaving Histadrut, Marcel had to buy private insurance, because leaving Histadrut meant leaving Kupat Cholim. Joining the private health insurance fund, Marcel found himself among the financial elite of Israel, although he was not as wealthy as its classical members: private entrepreneurs, factory owners, and large-scale buyers, who were not members of Histadrut.⁷⁹

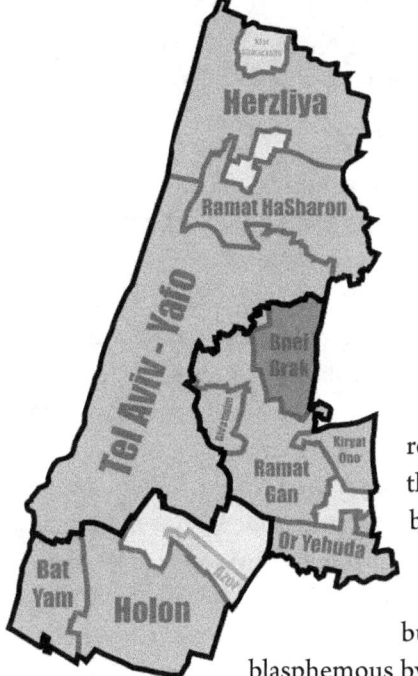

Fig. 104. Location of Bnei Brak in the Tel Aviv District, public domain

In addition to political antagonisms, religious discord was extremely strong in the country under construction. Frictions between Orthodox and secular Jews became apparent before independent Israel was established. The Zionist project to build an independent state was considered blasphemous by Orthodox Jews. They believed that only the messiah who would come into the world was competent to fully rebuild Jerusalem. Their resistance stood in the way of the Zionist project's success. The Jewish masses were religious, and without them the

---

78   Ibid.
79   Ibid.

Fig. 105. Shabbat in Bnei Brak, 2008,
photo: Kenyh Cevarom, public domain.
During the Sabbath in Bnei Brak (as well as in other Orthodox clusters)
there is a total ban on car traffic, which is why streets turn into promenades

resurrection of the state could not succeed. That is why the Zionists expressed their willingness to compromise. In the opinion of Marek Edelman, "Ben-Gurion made a deal that has survived to this day: you [religious Jews] will agree that the state will be created and we will succumb to you."[80] The problem was that this agreement was not accepted by everyone. A large group of secular Jews believe that the state should resist the Orthodox, exclude them from influencing the political system, and give them no say in determining social, political, and moral relations. Ultra-Orthodox Jews, a more severe Orthodox group, do not recognize the State of Israel at all. Among them, some people boycot conscription into the army. More moderate Orthodox Jews accept Israel's existence, but they want Israel to function on their terms. Under pressure from their side, the state has not yet adopted its own constitution (the Orthodox believe that the only and highest law flows from the Torah). This gap was filled by a number of basic laws that in fact replace the

---

80 Konstanty Gebert, "Kwestia moralności. Nie zawracaj mi głowy," interview with Marek Edelman, *Midrasz* 1 (1999): 8.

Fig. 106. Bnei Brak, Rabbi Akiva Street, 2010, public domain

constitution.[81] A formal registration of marriage can take place only after it has been sanctioned by the rabbi. The Jewish character of the state was actually defined in the 1948 Declaration of Independence. In 1950, the Knesset adopted the Law of Return, which was reiterated in 1952 as the Entry to Israel Law. It was, however, moderated by the amendment adopted in 1970 under the influence of Orthodox Jews, according to which a person born from a Jewish mother or a Judaism believer is considered a Jew. The official practice is that followers of other denominations were excluded from the law of return.

In addition to matters of the highest importance, there are also frictions and conflicts of a smaller format, which also cause agitation. An example is the constant tension with feminists at the Western Wall. To give another example: in places where the Orthodox live, owners of shops, restaurants, and all service points know that if they want to avoid trouble, they must observe the Sabbath. Therefore, they close the premises on Friday afternoon, and can open them only on Saturday evening. At the level of everyday interpersonal relations, most

---

81   *Konstytucja Państwa Izrael*, trans. and intro. K. Wojtyczek, Warsaw 2001, 10. See K. A. Wojtaszczyk, "System polityczny Izraela," in *Współczesny Izrael*, ed. K. A. Wojtaszczyk, Warsaw 2001, 9–19.

people try to avoid conflicts, which results in isolation of laymen from Orthodox Jews. The latter eagerly inhabit dense clusters like the Mea Shearim district in Jerusalem or the city of Bnei Brak, which was founded in 1924 by a group of Polish Hasidim led by Rabbi Icchak Gerstenkorn. Thanks to isolation, the Orthodox avoid shocking (in their view) attitudes and views. In addition, they provide themselves with access to religious schools and colleges, temples, and aid institutions (charity works occupy an important place in this community, because it is made up of large families, which often require material support). On the other hand, secular Jews keep their distance from the Orthodox settlements. Marcel's opinion is meaningful in this context: "I was both in Mea Shearim and Bnei Brak. I will never go there again and I do not recommend these places to anyone."[82] Indeed, looking at both places closely, one can get the impression that they are less interesting for their lay compatriots than for tourists from abroad, for whom visiting Orthodox communities is a kind of exotic adventure or a time travel, than for. Discretion is always to be kept during these visits, because the Orthodox do not want to be treated as museum objects.

It is worth emphasizing that kosher food is widely available in Israel, because most local producers and distributors make sure that their products have a kosher certificate granted by rabbis. They assume that this certificate does not bother secular customers, but without it they would lose the Orthodox clientele. They cannot afford it, especially since demography proves that the Orthodox community has greater growth dynamics. The reason is obvious—if the average secular family has two or three children, then the Orthodox has six or even seven. These proportions are very disturbing to the supporters of secularism of the state. In any case, the expansion of the Orthodox sphere of influence is visible, as diligent observance of the Sabbath has long been noticeable not only in Jerusalem and several other centers recognised as religious. To people like Marcel Goldman, the world of Orthodox people is alien, but it does not bother them until it interferes with their lives. The explanation for this ambivalence may be the fact that Marcel is a declared atheist, while the greatest disputes are taking place inside Judaism—they concern its shape and future. The competing models of Judaism are represented by its three main currents: Orthodox, conservative, and progressive (the latter is very weak in Israel, it is definitely stronger in the United States).

---

82 Interview with Marcel Goldman carried out on July 24, 2017.

When analyzing the Israeli political scene, one needs to take into account the fact that it exhibits dynamics unknown in many other countries. The reason is the overall volatility in the Middle East and in Israel (change of alliances with other countries, influx of new *aliyot*, demographic changes, and so forth). In the end of the twentieth century and the beginning of the twenty-first century, the Israeli right came closer to the Orthodox groups of Shas and Agudat Yisrael. The parties of Russian immigrants, Betheinu Israel and Israel BeAliyah, are closely associated with them. Uri Huppert, a religious critic of Israeli political life, is also of the opinion that there has been an agreement between Jews of African descent and Ashkenazi Orthodox Jews aimed against the secular Ashkenazi elites:

> In addition to the conflict between the secular and Orthodox vision of the state, there is a conflict in Israel between the secular Ashkenazi Jews who came from European democratic countries and immigrants from North Africa, who felt like second-class citizens for the first few decades of the state's existence. The alliance between the African and Ashkenazi Orthodox Jews, an alliance against Ashkenazi elites, was only a matter of time. A young generation of emigrants from North Africa created a new Ultra-Orthodox party Shas several years ago, which in the parliamentary election in 1998 won 17 seats in the 120-member Knesset, becoming the third political force of the country, necessary to form a stable government coalition. In that way, Shas joined the Hasidic party Agudat Yisrael, which in the Israeli parliament has always turned the scales, forcing—in exchange for supporting subsequent cabinets—numerous laws favourable only to Ultra-Orthodox Jews.[83]

Israel's main problem remains the unresolved Arab-Jewish conflict. It takes a bloody toll in the form of victims of Arab acts of terror, against which the Israeli army and special services cannot remain idle and take retaliatory actions that, despite the efforts of the Jewish side, also result in human losses. All Israel lives in danger, but it is not evenly distributed. First of all, people living in the immediate vicinity of the Arabs, of whom there are more than a million in Israel alone, are directly exposed to attacks. In a larger number they live, among others, in Nazareth, then Haifa and Jerusalem. The greater risk areas include most of the West Bank of the Jordan River. Residents of kibbutzim and cities located near the Gaza Strip, from which intentional shelling of Jewish housing estates

---

83 U. Huppert, *Izrael między kryzysem a konfliktem*, http://www.midrasz.home.pl/2000/lis/lis00_2.html, accessed July 24, 2017.

and other hostile acts, such as throwing incendiary materials, are carried out, are in a difficult situation. The security of Jewish settlements in the West Bank, for example, Hebron depends on the presence of thousands of Israeli soldiers. It is intriguing that this drama not only leads to the creation of a literal as well as a symbolical wall dividing Jews and Arabs, but also translates into intra-Jewish relations. Although the decision to live in the immediate vicinity of the Arabs is often made by people who are guided by ideological factors (such as the settlers in the West Bank), above all, they are motivated by economic reasons—fixed property prices are much lower here than in Tel Aviv. Meanwhile, the greater the geographical distance separates Jews from Arabs, the more the former are ready for a consensus. In this atmosphere, living (relatively) far away from the Arabs, residents of some kibbutzim and cities often face accusations from settlers and all other people living "door-to-door" with Arabs that they are selfish and naïve. Living in luxury and isolated neighbourhoods, they often forget about the threat of Palestinians. On the other hand, the settlers are accused of their uncompromising stance, fueling the anger of the Palestinian radicals, and being generally irresponsible. This second position is close to Marcel Goldman's opinion, who believes that all fundamentalism is evil, whether Arab, Jewish, or Christian. It is expressed in his poem entitled *Jerozolima Ir Szalom—Miasto Pokoju?!* (English: Jerusalem Yir Shalom—The City of Peace?!)

. . .	. . .
Trzy religie w tym mieście	Three religions in this city.
Razem się spotkały	They met together,
I łączą je niby wspólne ideały:	Connected by seemingly common ideals:
Wiara w jedynego Boga.	Faith in one God.
Tylko, że co je dzieli,	But what divides them,
Że do tego Boga	Is that to this God
Prowadzi w każdej wierze	In every faith
Całkiem inna droga.	A different road leads.
A ja skromniutko stoję	And I stand modestly
Przed plątaniną dróg	Before the tangled roads
I pytam się pokornie:	And I ask humbly:
Co ważniejsze?	What is more important?
Czy droga czy Bóg?	The road or God?

Mamy więc kościoły,	So we have churches,
Meczety, synagogi	Mosques, synagogues,
I przez nie prowadzą	And they lead through them,
Właśnie te oddzielne drogi.	These separate roads.
Jedni się modlą—klękają,	Some pray—they kneel down,
Drudzy się modlą—kiwają,	Others pray—they sway,
A jeszcze inni kucają	And others squat
Na modlitewnym kobiercu.	On a prayer rug.
A u większości	And the majority
Ich wszystkich	Of all of them
Jest miód na języku,	Have honey on the tongue
Ale nienawiść w sercu.	But hatred in the heart.
Miasto pokoju—	The city of peace—
Puste słowa:	Empty words:
Niby zjednoczone	Apparently united
A jednak podzielone.*	And yet divided.

* Goldman, *A w nocy przychodzą myśli*, 65–66.

These words correspond to the observations of Shimon Peres:

> In Jerusalem, more than anywhere else in the world, religion (or more precisely, a false interpretation of religion) creates invisible barriers between people—between Jews and non-Jews, between Christians and Muslims, between Jews and Jews, between Christians and Christians.... These barriers not only separate different communities, but try to draw boundaries between different sects or groups, whose followers, deriving often from the same religions, are ready to die for their beliefs.[84]

The accumulation of different religions and their factions in one (in addition, small) place naturally provokes conflicts. They are also strengthened by extremism that distorts orthodoxy. In this sense, it is easier to understand people

---

84 Peres, *Podróż sentymentalna*, 59.

who, knowing these realities, distance themselves from religion at all. It is hard to deny those who believe that indifference to religion protects against many problems.

On the basis of the presented facts, it can be said that Israel has joined the countries in which the political preferences of voters are in a strong relationship with their place of residence. In most countries of the world, political topography goes hand in hand with economic issues (salary, unemployment level, and so forth. The same regularities can be found in Israel. In addition to the universal factors that shape the political scene, each country has its own characteristics. For example, in Poland, the distribution of political forces is still related to the borders of former partitions (Prussian, Russian, and Austrian). In this context, the so-called Western Lands also stand out, that is, th territories annexed to Poland after World War II based on the agreement of the great powers. In Israel, as has already been mentioned, the proximity of Palestinians influences political views. The current situation makes it difficult for young Israelis to start their adult lives because they have to deal with political complications and extremely high real estate prices.

In his memoir book, *The Imaginary Voyage: With Theodor Herzl in Israel*, Shimon Peres mentions one of British students of that world leader of the Zionist movement, Sir Lewis Namier, who used to repeat: "Jews have always suffered from an excess of history and a shortage of geography."[85] In fact, Israel is one of the smallest countries in the world, occupying a territory of 22,072 square kilometers, which roughly corresponds to the size of the West Pomeranian Voivodeship in Poland with 22,896 square kilometers. When the first settlers arrived in Eretz Yisrael, they had to crowd on small scraps of land bought from the Arabs. Having no other choice, they paid dearly for extremely poor quality land: desert, semi-arid, and swampy areas. Before they yielded an abundant crop, they took a bloody harvest among the *chalutzim* who died due to malaria and other illnesses. Even today, climatic and geological conditions affect life in Israel. Currently, advanced technology allows to eliminate many inconveniences, but this has an obvious impact on the price of a square meter of buildings erected in such a place. Another factor that influences the prices is that wealthy Jews, who live in other countries, want to have property (also) in Israel for various reasons.

After 1959, Marcel Goldman's career gained momentum. His life attitude in that period is interesting, as, after a more accurate analysis, it allows to draw

---

85   Ibid., 7.

some important statements of a more general nature. Traditionally, historiography of Israel draws attention mainly to its founding fathers. We know the profiles of outstanding Israeli political and military leaders. In the book of Dan Senor and Saul Singer, cited earlier, the country's economic success was highlighted. It therefore seems that it is worth emphasizing the important role played by people of the Israeli middle and upper class, of whom we still know little. Indeed, Israel is a state that is unique by all means. It seems, however, that its political, economic, and military successes became possible due to the fact that the young state immediately gained a strong support in tens of thousands of people who began to build it with crazy determination. Many of them, including Marcel Goldman, "lost six years in their life story because of the war." After the war, consciously or not, they intended to prove something to themselves and to the world. They wanted to have children, to maintain the continuity of their families, against the intentions of the Nazis, who wanted to erase them from world history.

Polish Jews coming to Israel had the right to feel proud of their own education, achievements, social and professional competences. Behind them, there was the power of the tradition of their community—a centuries-old presence on Polish soil, with many achievements recorded in various fields, from science and culture to economy and politics. They stood out positively against the background of many other Jewish groups. The problem was that the events preceding their migration to Israel caused a deep crack in their private and group history. Their relatives, friends, and acquaintances perished in the Holocaust. The manifestations of antisemitism and the sense of danger associated with them, also recorded after the war, resulted in feelings of harm, humiliation, and bitterness. All that brought together a hubristic need to confirm one's own value. It lay at the root of their transgressive behaviors, which are understood here as creative problem solving, creative and progressive thinking, consent to go beyond known limits of activity, openness to new experiences, as well as a propensity for preemptive undertakings—strategy, from the survival strategy to the development strategy, is valued more than reactivity.[86] It is within the community of Polish Jews (though of course not only among them) that one can find sources of such features of Israeli society as emphasizing one's identity, which is related to

---

86 I am referring here to scientific findings concerning transgressive behaviours, see Z. Okraj, "Dlaczego działania transgresyjne intrygują i inspirują do badań (także) autobiograficznych," in *Biografie nieoczywiste. Przełom, kryzys, transgresja w perspektywie interdyscyplinarnej*, ed. M. Karkowska, Łódź 2018, 99–111.

the need to confirm one's own value, ambition, creativity, willingness to improve and develop, readiness for competition, and the emphasis on risk prevention.

Polish Jews faced the need to rebuild their family life and material status, because the war often took everything and everyone from them. Those who emigrated to Israel a little later, under the Gomulka Aliyah or after March '68, usually also arrived without property, because they came from an economically disturbed country. They willingly started families, regardless of the accompanying costs and sacrifices.

Fig. 107. Marcel Goldman during the Six-Day War in Al Qunaytirah, a city in southwestern Syria at the northern slopes of the Golan Heights, family collections of Marcel and Bianka Goldman (Tel Aviv)

They worked with passion and commitment. They went through a lot in their lives, which in a way strained their psyche. However, it also had positive effects. Accustomed to living in a state of permanent danger, they realised that each decision sooner or later brings certain effects. It made them feel responsible. The years of hunger motivated them to save. Awareness of the transience of life taught them to enjoy every moment (hence the passion for travel, which, after all, does not belong to cheap pleasures). Young people quickly acclimatized in Israel, older people had a bigger problem with it. Regardless of age, all Jews who lived in Israel had the right to feel at home at last. In numerous memories, we find accounts of a metaphysical feeling evoked by the fact that a bread seller from a nearby bakery, a waiter and a chef in a restaurant, a postman, an electrician, a cleaner, and, finally, all passersby were . At the same time, uncertainty did not disappear. From the first moments of its existence, Israel was in a state of constant threat: if not war, then terrorism. This danger had to have a mobilizing effect as well. From May 14, 1948, Jews knew there was no turning back. The Arabs threatened to "push the Jews into the sea," which in practice meant the threat of the Shoah being repeated. In that situation, almost all Israelis united for the sake of their country. They did not complain of high taxes, indispensable and difficult military service, and other hardships of everyday life. It can also be seen in Marcel's acts and statements. After completing military service, Israelis are transferred to the state of reserve. Men up to the age of fifty are later called to exercise monthly (the frequency and range depends on their military rank). Marcel also took part in such trainings several times. Obviously, a call to arms should be expected especially when an armed conflict breaks out.

In the spring of 1967, Marcel and Bianka spent their holidays in Switzerland. At the end of May that year they stopped in St. Moritz. The situation around Israel was becoming increasingly tense at that time. Therefore, their family in Israel received the postcards they sent, which depicted idyllic scenes and well-known European monuments, with little joy. The Swiss receptionist at the hotel, to whom Marcel said that he had to shorten his vacation and return to Israel, was not less amazed: "So from both sides of the Mediterranean it was thought that I was not all there. 'Are you going there now? And what for, after all, the war is imminent. Here you can live well, knowing languages and with your profession . . .' Try to explain this to a Swiss."[87] He also recalls:

> Only El-Al flights to Israel were available. Other airlines no longer flew there. The plane was quite empty, delayed Israelis returning, some volunteers. Reading Israeli newspapers, I realized for the first time how I underestimated the seriousness of the situation and how reckless I was. There was already a military mood at Lod Airport. Everywhere the army in full combat gear, sandbags, control.[88]

At the bank, the staff were surprised to see Marcel. All men in the prime of life were mobilized. Marcel had permission to leave his unit, but he realized that something was wrong and reconnected with it. During a telephone conversation he heard that he was looked for. He was assigned to the Thirty-Sixth Division

---

87   Goldman, *Iskierki życia*, 124.
88   Ibid.

located near Afula in the Jezreel Valley, near Jordan. He was appointed a supply officer in the staff of the division. Due to the fast moving front line, Marcel and his unit managed to reach Jordan, Syria, and the Golan Heights. The pace at which they moved (so fast that there was no time to sleep) reflects the scale of the Israeli success.

Fig. 108. A meeting with Ephraim Katzir, president of Israel in 1973–1978 (standing at the microphone) on the occasion of issuing the national loan, Marcel Goldman in the first row, third from the left, family collections of Marcel and Bianka Goldman (Tel Aviv)

Fig. 109. A meeting with Ephraim Katzir (first from the left), president of Israel in 1973–1978, on the occasion of issuing the national loan, Marcel Goldman second from the right, family collections of Marcel and Bianka Goldman (Tel Aviv)

During the Six-Day War, the fact that Israelis seized East Jerusalem caused a big stir. Marcel remembered two iconic themes associated with that event:

> At that time, a very popular singer, Naomi Shemer, performed the song "Jerusalem of Gold" [Hebrew title: *Yerushalayim shel zahav*. The performance of the song by a famous singer, Ofra Haza, was also unusual—Ł.T.S.]. This song immediately became an anthem. People sang with tears in their eyes, soldiers had small transistor receivers set up on Israeli stations that broadcast news from the fronts all the time. The Israeli army stood by the Suez Canal, Sinai and the Gaza Strip were occupied, there were tens or maybe hundreds of thousands of Egyptian prisoners. Jordan asks for a truce. And of course at all stations *Jerusalem of Gold* is played.... Something else stuck in my memory from that period—it is the photo that appeared in all newspapers. It showed three paratroopers in front of the Western Wall. One of them took his helmet off his head, holding it in his hand like a Polish peasant his cap in the church looking at the altar in religious delight. This was also the expression on the paratrooper's face. Soulful, as if he saw something beyond those archaic boulders, beyond that over two-thousand-year-old wall. He saw something we did not see.[89]

While Marcel was in the army, Bianka had to take care of the children and the home. She stocked up on water and food. She also bought black paper to cover the windows. On the night of the first day of the war, she experienced extreme stress when a phone call from the police station woke her up. She was expecting the worst news about her husband. However, she was reassured that nothing bad had happened. They asked about Marcel because a light came on in the bank he managed, and it had to be quickly turned off because of the blackout. After learning that Marcel was in the army, the policeman asked Bianka for the keys to the bank. Bianka could help, but she had only half a set of keys, and opening the bank required the presence of two authorized persons. A police car came for her, and Marcel's assistant already waited with the missing keys. On the way back, the police officer took Bianka to one of the command centers, where she learned that Israeli air forces had rapidly destroyed the Arab (mainly Egyptian) aviation, which had not even manage to rise in the air.[90]

Marcel was mobilized for the last time during the Yom Kippur War and served in anti-aircraft defense. In adulthood, military service has a destabilizing

---

89 Ibid., 134–135.
90 Ibid., 129–130.

effect on family and professional life. The Israelis, however, have learned to live with it. Such big sacrifices do not block their careers, they are not used to explain their passivity. The generally understood slow-paced creation of well-being leads to certain attitudes, among which we recognize frugality, rational and thoughtful behaviour, avoidance of unnecessary risk, thinking in historical categories (awareness of one's passing), and maintaining strong family and social ties. These features are all too evident in Marcel's private and professional life. His reluctance to be extremely risky certainly had a bearing on his banking policy, which will be discussed later. Subsequent promotions and the accompanying increase in income never caused a radical change in his lifestyle, excessive consumption, or other such phenomena often visible in people who earn extra money without much input of their own work and talents. Despite numerous external threats, subsequent Israeli governments have provided citizens with a sense of stability and responsibility in terms of economic policy. This stimulates investment activity, but also encourages people to accumulate savings that are not at risk. Unlike the so-called nouveau riches from countries with unstable political and economic situation, Israelis are not prone to manifest their possessions. Marcel's apartment is located in one of the most expensive districts in Israel, but its purchase can also be considered an investment. In addition, there is a guaranteed sense of security typical of so-called prestigious addresses. In terms of equipment, the interior does not differ significantly from what can be found in the houses of many other people who earn the Israeli national average salary. In 1972, the general manager (Hebrew: *menahel klali*, in short *mankal*) of the First International Bank of Israel appointed Marcel as the titular deputy director of the bank (Hebrew: *sgan mankal*), agreeing that he could remain in Haifa. At the time, he was probably the only deputy director of the Bank who did not work every day in Tel Aviv.[91]

Making a career required openness to the outside. Immigrants from Poland responded to that necessity differently, depending on their age, level of education, and knowledge of the Hebrew language and beliefs. Marcel spoke on this subject in beautiful and poignant words in the High Synagogue in Krakow in March 2007 during the promotion of his book *Iskierki życia*, against the background of the exhibition by Professor Aleksander B. Skotnicki, "Two Faces of Krakow Jews":

---

91   Correspondence with Marcel Goldman, January 4, 2019.

> My generation is a replanted generation. In the case of immigration of Polish Jews to Israel, that was a replanting from Polish soil to sandy Israeli land. Everyone tried to take roots. The results were of course individual. I know people who live there like a potted plant. In a Polish pot. They speak Polish, read Polish, if you enter their apartment—there is no doubt. Poles live there. People who tried to adapt to the environment, become Israelis, very often encountered difficulties.
>
> For many years, people did not talk about the Holocaust. People were hiding what they had been through. It wasn't until the seventies that the dam burst. What influenced that? It's hard to talk about one single event or one cause. Or maybe it was the fact that people just got old and did not want to take to their grave personal stories from the period of the Nazi hell. Returning to the issue of integration in Israel. Professor Skotnicki presented here beautifully "Two Faces of Krakow Jews."[92] Two worlds. It was much easier for Orthodox Jews in Israel. You can say about them that they carry their soil with them. They bring their world with them and integrate everywhere in this world. If it's not there, then they either create it or they just don't move there.

Among the newcomers, the most vulnerable were the middle-aged and older people who did not belong to any of the religious communities and did not speak Hebrew. In this context, the memories of Stanisław Wygodzki (1907–1992), prose writer, poet, literary critic, and translator are of interest. He settled in Israel in January 1967, when he was sixty years old. In an interview with Piotr Sarzyński, he admitted:

> At the beginning it was very difficult. Both financially and mentally. . . . I have practically never had the so-called social life. Two, three friends—Polish Jews, that's all. . . . My life is enclosed in four walls of the house—newspapers, books, classical music on the radio.[93]

Alexander Rozenfeld was also among the "maladjusted."[94] In Poland he proved to be a promising poet, in 1982 at the age of forty-one he emigrated to

---

92 I am talking here about the exhibition of Prof. Aleksander B. Skotnicki in the High Synagogue at Józefa Street in Krakow, which was admired by over 50,000 people from all over the world.

93 "Służyłem złej sprawie. Ze St. Wygodzkim rozmawia Piotr Sarzyński," in *Wygodzki. Zeszyt pamięci*, ed. K. Bernard, Tel Aviv 1992, 32.

94 Aleksander Rozenfeld was born in 1941 in Tambov, Russia (then the Soviet Union) in a family of Polish Jews. In 1946, his family settled in Wrocław. He began studying Polish at the Catholic University of Lublin, but did not complete the studies. He worked as a pur-

Israel. On the spot, not without difficulty, he learned the Hebrew language, the problem, however, was the lack of a specific profession—his position as a writer was not yet well-established enough to make him earn or receive a job related to it. He did not find himself as a labourer in a chocolate factory: "my job was that I carried a box of chocolate waste to the oven once every twenty minutes, but what to do for twenty minutes between the boxes?"[95] He decided to quit. At the adult vocational training center, he learned the profession of the plumber, without success. He eventually got employed as a cleaner at the Ashkelon bus station, which became the subject of media interest: "I didn't even notice that during work I became the object of someone's photographic activity, after a few days my photo appeared in the newspaper *Ma'ariv* with the caption: 'Polish Poet Sweeps the Bus Station in Ashkelon.' The immigration authorities could not stand it."[96] He was invited to a meeting at the headquarters of the government, where he was received by Mati Szmulewicz, then director of the office of Prime Minister Menachem Begin. However, Rozenfeld honestly admits that during the conversation he primarily expressed his desire to return to Poland, he could not receive the government's help in that matter, and he could not specify other expectations. After publicizing his situation in the Israeli media, he received a scholarship for newly arrived creators and artists. In 1986, a volume of his poems appeared in Tel Aviv in Polish, *Tam gdzie mnie nie ma, gdzie? Jestem*[97] (English: In the place where I am not, where? I am). With a volume of poems in his hand, he went to a meeting with the immigration minister:

> He receives me cordially with coffee and cognac, he explains that he was in Africa [the meeting took place three months after its announcement—Ł.T.S.]. "You know," he says (in Israel everyone is on first-name terms)—"We have problems with Jews from Abyssinia." I felt stupid, the guy has state affairs on his mind, and I'm talking crap, but after a while I shook off those thoughts, I began to explain to him that my case is not less important than the Jews from Ethiopia, that the image of Israel depends on how it is dealt with, not only in our eyes. I tell him about Jadwiga [his wife with whom he came to Israel—Ł.T.S.], that she has no job to this day, that this country cannot be normal, since my wife cannot get

---

chaser. In the years 1980–1981 he was active in the Solidarity movement, which became the leading anti-communist force in Poland.
95   A. Rozenfeld, *Podanie o prawo powrotu*, 42.
96   Ibid., 31.
97   Ibid., 47.

a job in her profession because she is not Jewish [she had a teacher's diploma—Ł.T.S.].

The minister referred to Rozenfeld's statement with understanding, declared that he would receive a special check as a gift from the president of the state, and that in two weeks he and his wife would be able to move to a new apartment. After that time, he was given an alleged allocation of the apartment, but it turned out to be a mistake. His cup of bitterness was filled to the brim, and Rozenfeld decided to return to Poland. He left Israel in 1986. His path to Poland led through France, Germany, and Italy, where he benefited from the help of Pope John Paul II. In March 1988 he received a document restoring his Polish citizenship.[98]

Marcel Goldman found himself in diametrically opposed life situations and had completely different problems than those worrying Stanisław Wygodzki and Aleksander Rozenfeld. He was young and creative, willing to take on new challenges and make new friends. He wanted to work on his own and did not expect anyone's help. Polishness survived in him and around him, but it no longer set a rhythm of everyday life for him. It was a subcutaneous cultural code; it remained important to him, but he did not cling to it. He was far from nostalgia, which was to be manifested in the later years of his life. He approached everything that surrounded him pragmatically. For example, he chose Polish or Hebrew language in specific situations. In Israel, he still reached for Polish literature, because it had fascinated him in his childhood, but he gave up the Polish-language press together with his first job. His then boss persuaded him to do so, explaining that in that way he would learn Hebrew faster and gain better insight into the affairs of the state. Marcel remembers that initially it was difficult to read the Hebrew press and admits that he did not understand everything, but he knew he had to be consistent. At home, Bianka and Marcel spoke Polish to each other, and with the birth of their daughter Orit, they decided to change to Hebrew. In practice, they could speak two languages simultaneously: Polish and Hebrew equally fluently, sometimes almost unconsciously switching from one to the other. The need of the moment was decisive when it turned out that expressing something in a particular language was better or easier, or proverbs and terms related to a particular language were useful. In Switzerland, a third language appeared in their home—German. Their daughter learned Polish, be-

---

98   Ibid., 46–104.

cause at the time of her birth both grandmothers lived and spoke to her in that language (in addition, Bianka's mother lived with them in one house). However, their son, born in 1959, did not speak Polish anymore. Marcel and Bianka did not teach their children Polish, because they did not think that they would need it. In their opinion, it was enough that the children knew Hebrew and English. Orit speaks French as well.[99]

In the early 1960s, the Goldmans were far ahead of other Israelis in financial terms. It is an interesting decade when it comes to observing important social and economic phenomena. From the end of the 1940s, through the 1950s, egalitarianism, promoted by the founding fathers of the Israeli state, gained popularity. It was, however, equality in poverty. Many Israelis lived modestly at the time, not necessarily by choice, but due to socio-economic conditions. A serious part of the nation were the newcomers who were trying to arrange their lives. For example, the last large migration wave came from Poland. It was the Gomulka Aliyah (the March Aliyah was important for the state, but not so numerous). At the end of the 1960s, the general development of the country became visible, emphasized by the euphoria after the brilliant victory in the Six-Day War. In the 1970s and 1980s, goods previously available only to the better-off people, such as refrigerators, washing machines, and electric stoves, became widely available. Also, the possession of a telephone or a car was no longer only the domain of the wealthiest people like the Goldmans. These items were now available to the newly created Israeli middle class. Those earning the largest amounts of money could afford even more, but with the Israeli model of successive earning based on one's own talents, it was not fashionable to manifest one's wealth. In addition, oligarchy and aristocracy assigned to land did not develop in Israel, hence no great latifundia and palaces appeared there. The richest preferred to invest and place the excess capital in the bank. At best, they bought spacious apartments and built villas with swimming pools, but these properties did not stand out excessively from the surroundings. They were built mainly in the luxurious districts of Tel Aviv, Herzliya, and Netanya.

The turn of the 1980s and 1990s brought social stratification, which was especially evident in the context of the next major *aliyot* that arrived from the countries of the former Soviet Union and Africa. The economic disparities and related social tensions intensified in the first decade of the twenty-first century.

---

99 Interview with Marcel and Bianka Goldman carried out on December 20, 2016; Correspondence with Marcel Goldman, February 8, 2019.

Israel used its potential and entered the path of rapid development, but not everyone became its beneficiary. The explosion of investment and entrepreneurship made a relatively narrow group of Israelis richer, while the others had to face the consequences arising from rising costs of living, primarily high prices of food, clothing, medicine, and housing. Even if the oligarchy has not yet developed, the Israelis have realized that the pace and directions of economic development of the state are set by a small, though influential group of businessmen with extensive political connections.

All that creates frustrations such as those that were the reason for the protests of young people on the streets of Tel Aviv in the summer of 2011. The Occupy Wall Street in the United States gave young people the impulse for action. In Israel, as in the United States, protesters demanded, in the realities of the free market economy, the possibility of living in conditions that create a chance for a dignified existence in material terms, allowing people to satisfy their basic needs such as owning a flat. Israeli youth, who for some time took over the Rothschild Boulevard located in the center of Tel Aviv, strongly criticized wage inequalities and demanded the restoration of elementary social justice.[100] The right-wing government of Israel entered into a dialogue with the protesters, but in general it did not bring about any real changes in social and economic relations.

In the article published on January 1, 2019 in the online issue of the journal *Haaretz* David Rosenberg questions the image of Israel resulting from the promotional materials of the local Ministry of Tourism or stereotypical carbon copy reproduced by the global media. For some, Israelis are scantily clad "high-tech wunderkinds" walking on the beaches, for others they are "fanatical settlers living on windswept hilltops."[101] Meanwhile, the picture of Israeli society is more diverse:

> Those kinds of Israelis certainly exist. But the reality is that only 8% or so of working Israelis are employed in high-tech and that number isn't growing. While the beaches are filled with people like the ones portrayed in tourism come-ons, the reality is that well over a third of Israelis are

---

100 "From the Protest Tents in Tel Aviv to Occupying Wall Street," https://www.haaretz.com/jewish/1.5191076, accessed November 12, 2018.

101 D. Rosenberg, "The Real Israel Isn't Startup Nation, It's Poverty Row," https://www.haaretz.com/israel-news/.premium-the-real-israel-isn-t-startup-nation-it-s-poverty-row-1.6803924?fbclid=IwAR2-Q8NRbMemjYq7R5eFtAngBAaB7Ynb7sBCcj2FNiLu-plqW-9w3q0ibddOI, accessed January 2, 2019.

religious Jews or Muslims whose women don't wear bikinis. The settlers account for about 5% of Israel's population.[102]

The problem of poverty in Israel is poignant and burning. Rosenberg continues:

> The other stark fact about Israel is about how poor many of its people are. As the government's National Insurance Institute showed again on Sunday [December 30, 2018—Ł.T.S.], Israeli poverty rates are high compared to other developed countries—and the years of economic growth have done little to fix the problem. Among the members of the Organization for Economic Cooperation and Development, Israel runs the highest rate of poverty (17.9% in 2016, the last year for which the organization has comparative figures).... It's even more distressing that a decade of uninterrupted economic growth has left far too many Israelis under the poverty line. Twenty years ago, the poverty rate for individuals was 17.5%; as of last year it was 21.2%, according to the latest NII data.[103]

A good punchline for Rosenberg's analysis is the title of his article: "The Real Israel Isn't Startup Nation, It's Poverty Row." It is difficult to argue with the hard data he quoted, although some space for polemics is opened. It is true, for example, that the high technology industry does not record such high employment growth as trade and gastronomy (where there are a lot of "simple" jobs like salesman or waiter). At the same time, Israeli high-tech revenues are seriously increasing[104]. In 2018, the unemployment rate in Israel was only 4.0%, with a slight decrease in comparison to the 4.2% recorded in 2017.[105] Israel is also very favourably assessed in the rankings relating to social and economic matters.[106]

---

102 Ibid.

103 Ibid.

104 In 2018, technology companies recorded (initially estimated at the beginning of 2019) a profit of USD 6.47 billion, an increase of seventeen percent compared to 2017. It is worth adding that this is the sixth consecutive year of uninterrupted revenue growth of Israeli industry, from approximately USD 1.88 billion in 2012, "Israeli Tech Companies Raised Preliminary $6.47 Billion Last Year, Up 17% from 2017," https://www.haaretz.com/israel-news/business/technation-israeli-tech-firms-raised-preliminary-6-47b-last-year-up-17-from-2017-1.6805700, accessed January 3, 2019.

105 *Raport Banku PKO BP: "Izrael. Analiza Międzynarodowa,"* https://supportamyeksport.pl/api/public/files/1559/Izrael_Analiza_Miedzacjonowa_2019_03.pdf, accessed March 29 2019.

106 For example: Doing Business 2019: 49/190, Index of Economic Freedom 2018: 31/180, Corruption Perceptions Index 2018: 34/180, Global Innovation Index 2018: 11/126, ibid.

The problem of poverty raised by Rosenberg has already ignited nationwide debates in Israel several times. However, it seems that such severe assessments of the state paradoxically result from its successes. At present, Israelis willingly compare their state and the conditions in it to the standards maintained by the richest countries in the world, which have often operated continuously for centuries. Meanwhile, Israel, which has ancient roots, in 2018 celebrated only its seventieth anniversary since it proclaimed its independence! Biographies of people like Marcel Goldman remind us that Israel is a state built from scratch by people who have started their lives again. Even now, when the situation seems stable, Israel is still accepting new immigrants.[107] Among them, of course, there are wealthy and educated people, such as Jews from Western European countries who migrate as a result of antisemitism there, but there are still many people deprived of their property, without education, and without knowledge of the Hebrew language. Rosenberg himself sees the causes of widespread poverty in the low professional activity of Arab and Ultra-Orthodox people—in total, one third of Israel's population. Both groups have a high poverty rate.[108] In addition, the country carries the burden of maintaining large supplies of weapons, constantly being in the state of military readiness, and developing the secret services and police. The overall effect of seven decades of building the state is impressive, but all weaknesses are especially visible in this context.

For a closer look at the formation of social and economic relations in Israel, two stories that happened in the Goldman family can be instructive. They concern diamond rings. In 1959, when leaving the Halva'ah VeChisakhon Bank, Marcel received a high compensation of about 5,000 Israeli pounds—approximately ten times his monthly salary—for which he bought a 1.5-carat diamond ring for Bianka.[109] He admits that it was a type of investment for him:

> In my memory I had family experiences from World War II, when my mother's diamond ring enabled us to escape from the ghetto and thus let us survive the occupation. Despite the years passed, I was still afraid that the moment might come that I would have to run away with my

---

[107] Only in 2018 there were 28,000 (with 185 thousand new births recorded in the state), Ministry of Foreign Affairs of Israel, https://mfa.gov.il/MFA/Pages/default.aspx, accessed January 2, 2019.

[108] This indicator was 47.1% for Arab families and 43.1% for Ultra-Orthodox. For comparison, among all Israeli Jews, the poverty rate for families was only 13.4%, D. Rosenberg, *The Real Israel Isn't a Startup Nation*.

[109] Correspondence with Marcel Goldman, February 8, 2019.

loved ones again. After all, Israel is in a constant state of danger, which was particularly felt in the first years of its existence. Some of my friends also shared the opinion that the existence of Israel could not be taken for granted.[110]

Marcel's statement confirms the thesis that in Israel, Polish Jews tended to repeat habits, attitudes, behaviours, and strategies developed in Poland. The most durable turned out to be those that had a basis in family traditions or in traumatic experiences, such as those from World War II.[111] In addition, it is clear that the constant threat Israel was in made the Holocaust survivors think in terms of real and potential danger. Constant information about border clashes, armed skirmishes, terrorist attacks and, finally, messages from subsequent wars probably did not facilitate mental relaxation. The Goldmans kept the above-mentioned ring almost always in the safe at the bank or at home. It was stolen from them along with the entire contents of the home safe after their return from Switzerland (their stay in Switzerland will be discussed later).[112]

For the second time Marcel decided to buy a diamond ring in the early 1980s. That time, the ring was "to be worn." This story is more complex. While still working at the Union Bank of Israel, he helped a woman who, according to what he remembers, was a modestly living Jewess from Romania. She worked in a bank, but not the same one as Marcel did. There she was responsible, among others, for letting customers into barred rooms with deposits. One day, a heavy metal door hit her and she was badly injured. She found herself in a legal conflict with her employer, who decided to fire her. As she was a single mother, she was looked after by a social worker, who, in turn, maintained close relations with Marcel and asked him for help. Marcel selflessly found a job for her. From what he remembers, it did not cause any unpleasant repercussions for the his bank, the woman turned out to be a reliable employee, she soon found another job, and Marcel forgot about her. At the beginning of the 1980s, when he received an anonymous phone call from a person well-versed in the realities of police work, he realized that, of all people he met and knew, the only one who had extensive contacts in the police (due to family ties) was that Romanian Jewess. It was confirmed by the course of the conversation with the anonymous interlocutor:

---

110 Interview with Marcel Goldman carried out on June 13, 2018
111 See E. Koźmińska-Frejlak, "Z tego się nigdy nie wyrasta," *Midrasz* 7–8 (2005): 11–14.
112 Correspondence with Marcel Goldman, February 8, 2019.

> One day, during the bank's working hours, the secretary came to me and said she had a woman on the line who did not want to introduce herself, but wanted to talk to me. I asked for connection. The lady said that she would not introduce herself, but she wanted to inform me that I should soon expect a call by the financial police based in Petah Tikva, which was investigating the allegedly illegal purchase of diamonds I made. Ending the conversation, she mentioned that she wanted to help me because I had once helped a person close to her.[113]

This case dates back to 1980 or 1981, when Marcel decided to buy the second diamond ring for his wife. It was supposed to be a gift. Marcel decided to ask one of the bank's regular clients for help in the purchase. He had a son who was a member of the jewelry market in Ramat Gan in the Tel Aviv agglomeration. By the way, it is worth noting that Israel is one of the world's largest diamond producers and exporters, currently competing in this field with Belgium, China, India, the United States, and Russia.[114] At the beginning of the 1980s, the grinding and jewelry industry seemed to be the most promising area of the Israeli economy. In any case, nobody talked about start-ups then. The state still practiced a restrictive policy regarding currency trading (for example, Israelis could not hold bank accounts and deposits abroad for a long time) and diamonds.

A few days after the above-mentioned conversation, Marcel actually received a phone call from the police, who summoned him for questioning. He was well prepared for that. From the anonymous woman he learned that he would probably hear two accusations: first, that he had not paid for the ring, and second, that he had bought diamonds without proper government consent, thereby violating the official procedure.[115] Marcel went to Petah Tikva with a receipt confirming that he had paid for the ring with his own money. It was a relatively small amount at the time, but the reason for the low price was that the two diamonds in the ring were damaged, although the defects were invisible without the jeweler's glass. In addition, Marcel did not buy the diamonds alone (which was prohibited by law), but a ring with those diamonds (which was allowed). He chose the diamonds separately, but bought them together with the ring. The

---

113 Interview with Marcel Goldman carried out on June 13, 2018.

114 The largest diamond trade and production centers in the world include Antwerp, Tel Aviv, and New York.

115 In short, the procedure consisted mainly in the fact that the Israeli government, constantly in need of foreign currency, promoted the export of diamonds, and at the same time prevented its own citizens from buying them.

police quickly dismissed the charge of accepting the ring without payment, but not the one regarding the purchase against the diamond law. The policemen argued that Marcel bought the diamonds first and only then ordered a ring for them. Marcel's bills confirmed, however, that only one transaction was carried out. The police were probably not sure of their accusations, because the officers applied a solution that could be interpreted as conciliatory—even an attempt to withdraw honourably from the case. Namely, a symbolic fine was imposed on Marcel corresponding to the price of a newspaper at the time. However, Marcel did not agree to it:

> I came back home and told Bianka about everything. She advised me to inform my supervisor at the bank, who at the time was Zadik Bino, about my case. The following day I told him about recent, unpleasant and undeserved events that had happened to me. Zadik Bino replied: "I was waiting when you come to tell me this." It turned out that he knew about the matter, because police officers talked to him about me. He told me that he absolutely shared my way of thinking, but decided that it was not worth disputing with the police, and advised me to close the case quickly by paying this symbolic fee. He even said that if I didn't do it, he would pay it for me.[116]

Marcel settled that payment and for a long time forgot about the events associated with it. He only remembered the circumstances of the gem's purchase when there was a burglary and theft in his apartment. Thieves, among other precious items, took the diamond ring just described.

In the 1970s, Marcel Goldman already had a high and established position in the banking sector. He enjoyed the reputation of a banker with extensive knowledge and experience, and, in addition, of a person independent in thinking and thoroughly honest. The range of his professional successes and subsequent promotions prove this. It was noticed by Dr Kashiv,[117] the president of the Association of Israeli Bankers and HR director of Bank Leumi. He entrusted Marcel with giving lectures on two-year courses for senior banking staff organized by the Association. They were proxies (employees with special attorney powers authorized to sign documents on behalf of the bank), some of whom were later promoted to branch managers and directors of branches.

---

116 Correspondence with Marcel Goldman, February 8, 2019.
117 Phonetic spelling of the name based on the interview with Marcel Goldman.

Marcel went to Tel Aviv once a month on average to give these lectures, for about five years.[118]

At the same time when Marcel Goldman was climbing to the top of the banking career, the Israeli economy already had a strong and stable position. This is proved by specific statistical data: in 1972, gross domestic product reached a level almost eighty percent higher than that recorded in 1966.[119] The indicators relating to individual segments of the economy and the progress recorded in areas close to the average citizen also deserve consideration. The development of the arms industry continued, which increased investment and employment. New ports in Ashdod and Eilat functioned successfully (later, the port in Ashkelon was also built). In 1965, the Israeli airlines El Al carried 300,000 passengers, which is six times more than it did in 1960.[120] At the end of that decade, El Al maintained regular connections with New York, London, Paris, Copenhagen, Amsterdam, Brussels, Frankfurt am Main, Munich, Zurich, Vienna, Rome, Athens, Istanbul, and Nicosia.[121] Israel had freight and passenger lines with the countries of Europe, North, Central and South America, Africa, and the Far East, as well as with the countries of the Mediterranean and the Black Sea.[122] The media, which became an important component of Israeli democracy, recorded impressive development and professionalization. An example of this is one of the most important Israeli newspapers, *Yedioth Ahronoth*, which was founded in Tel Aviv in 1939, during the period of the British Mandate. In 1950 the daily employed 16 reporters and editors, in 1969, already 104. In 1950, its weekly volume was 32 pages long, in 1969—228. In 1950, the editors of *Yedioth Ahronoth* had two printing machines with a printing capacity of 25,000 copies per hour, in 1969 it used the most modern printing equipment with the capacity of 280 thousand copies per hour. In 1950, advertisements published in the magazine covered 525 inches per week, in 1969—15,300.[123]

For the first thirty years of the existence of independent Israel, its socioeconomic relations had clear socialist accents. According to Amos Oz: "Israeli socialism was born... as an uneasy marriage between two different traditions—

---

118 Interview with Marcel Goldman carried out on October 19, 2018.
119 K. Chaczko, "Izraelskie państwo bezpieczeństwa socjalnego," in K. Chaczko, A. Srekrek, Ł.T. Sroka, *Demokracja izraelska*, preface by S. Weiss, Warsaw 2018, 219.
120 Ibid.
121 *Who's who in Israel...*, cover plate, 2.
122 *Robotniczy ruch spółdzielczy w Izraelu. Chewrat owdim*, Tel Aviv [n.d., circa 1956], 24.
123 *Who's Who in Israel*, 587.

the Jewish tradition of social justice and the Eastern European, and particularly Russian, social visions of the time."[124] Oz emphasized that the Israeli socialists started from scratch because: "Unlike any other socialist movement in the world, the early socialist Zionists had nothing to reform, seize, or conquer. They had a clean page before them, and so they created industries, settlements, and social and cultural institutions on a unique egalitarian basis."[125] The authorities made all possible efforts to ensure uniform development and distribution of goods, but still, the state that fought the victorious Six-Day War and entered a period of economic prosperity was not free from social inequalities and even poverty, which affected especially the lower social strata in the non-Ashkenazi group.[126] To counteract those phenomena, two special committees were established: the Committee on Income Distribution and Social Inequality, headed by the President of the Bank of Israel David Horowitz, and the Committee on Threats against Children and Youth, headed by Prime Minister Golda Meir. The existing social programs were extended. The amount of the child benefit was increased. In 1972, unemployment benefits were introduced for the first time. While in 1970 social expenditures accounted for thirteen percents of GDP, a decade later they increased to twenty percent.[127] We are talking about instruments that were also used by governments of other countries, especially in Western Europe, which provided protection for the lowest paid and those at risk of exclusion from the labour market in order to prevent the growing popularity of communist ideology and the Soviet Union. In this regard, we see that Israel, after all, was more like capitalist states than Eastern Bloc countries. Socialist postulates were introduced here selectively, without celebrating the ideology itself and resorting to violence (which marked socialism in Soviet fashion in Eastern Europe). Amos Oz asks why Israel, then, "didn't develop as the most egalitarian and creative social democratic society in the world?"[128] In his opinion, among the decisive factors there were:

> the mass immigration of Holocaust survivors, Middle Eastern Jews, and non-socialist and even anti-socialist Zionists who ached for "normaliza-

---

124 A. Oz, *Czarownik swojego plemienia. Eseje*, ed. D. Sękalska, afterword S. Bratkowski, Warsaw 2004, 84.

125 Ibid, 88–89.

126 Chaczko, *Izraelskie państwo bezpieczeństwa socjalnego*, 219.

127 Ibid., 221.

128 Oz, *Czarownik swojego plemienia*, 90.

tion." The Holocaust convinced many Jews that the cruel game of nations had to be played according to its cruel laws: statehood, a military establishment, and a pessimistic concept of the use of military power. At the same time, some of them wanted Israel to become a replica of prewar bourgeois Central Europe, with red-tiled roofs and good manners.... Then there were the masses of Orthodox Jews who wanted to create the replica of a Jewish ghetto and to whom socialism meant blasphemy and atheism.[129]

An important distinguishing feature of Israeli socio-economic relations was the principle of uniting and joining forces already known among Jews living in the diaspora. In Poland, before World War II, Jews favourably stood out in this way against the background of the Christian competition, which imitated those patterns to no avail.

Employee rights in Israel were protected by the strong trade unions affiliated to the Histadrut federation, which at the end of 1969 gathered 64.4% of the country's population.[130] Another active formation was Histadrut HaOvdim HaLeumit, or the National Labour Federation, founded in 1934. Branch organizations were thriving.[131] Organizations of kibbutzim and moshavim members also operated,[132] while their production was marketed through the Central Sales Cooperative Tnuva.[133] Already in the 1950s, industrial production developed in kibbutzim. It initially covered primarily building materials, plywood, veneers,

---

129 Ibid., 90–91.
130 *Who's Who in Israel*, 371.
131 For example: the Farmers' Federation in Israel (Hebrew: Hitachdut Ha'Ikarim LeYisrael, founded in 1903), the Engineers' Union (Hebrew: Histadrut HaMehandessim), the Association of Engineers and Architects in Israel (founded in 1921), Union of Craftsmen and Small Producers (at the end of 1969 it united 19,000 enterprises from 35 industries), the Association of Israeli Producers (founded in 1923), the Teachers' Union (founded in 1903 in Zikhron Ya'akov), the Federation of Building Contractors (founded in 1950, in 1969 it had 100 members representing 16 local organisations from all over the country), and Central Union of Industry, Transport, and Services.
132 For example, at the end of 1968, Hakibbutz Ha'Artzi had 17,807 members in 73 kibbutzim, which was 35.4% of all kibbutzim members in the state. A total of 32,061 people belonged to that movement. Established in 1921, the Moshav Movement in Israel at the end of 1969 connected 230 settlements throughout the country, which had a population of over 85,000. people. *Who's Who in Israel*, 371.
133 At the beginning of the 1950s, it united around 500 agricultural settlements from all over the country. In 1955 it had a seventy-three-percent share in the domestic market. It supplied mainly dairy products, poultry, fruit, fish, vegetables, and sugar beets. *Robotniczy ruch spółdzielczy w Izraelu*, 10.

canned goods, juices, and preserves. As part of the Histadrut movement, there appeared the cooperative Solel-Bone (Paving Roads-Builder), which united entrepreneurs performing construction and public works.[134] Production cooperatives in various industries also developed in the cities.[135] The first chamber of commerce operated in Jerusalem from 1908, it expressed the official voice of entrepreneurs during the existence of the Ottoman Empire. In 1919, it underwent a reorganization to adapt to the realities of the British Mandate. At the end of 1969 it brought together 312 import, export, and wholesale companies, as well as banks and financial corporations from Jerusalem and the district, and even industrial plants. The Tel Aviv chamber of commerce, established in 1919, had about a thousand members at the turn of 1969 and 1970. Chambers of commerce stimulated economic exchange with other countries, including England (from 1951), Italy (from 1955), Sweden, Canada, and the United States. The Israeli ministries of Finance and Trade and Industry set up the State Investment Office, which at the end of 1969 had offices in Tel Aviv, Jerusalem, New York, London, and Zurich.[136]

Political organizations also had an impact on economic development. The most important among them were the World Zionist Organization, the Jewish Agency, the World Jewish Congress, Keren Kayemet LeYisrael, Keren HaYesod and WIZO (Women's International Zionist Organization). They supported the aliyot and their members' adaptation to life in Israel.[137]

Serious remodeling of the Israeli economy took place when the right wing came to power. Menachem Begin took office as prime minister on June 20, 1977. He was the founder and leader of the Cherut party, which later became Likud. That political environment was interestingly but critically characterized by Anita Shapira:

---

134 The largest industrial enterprises of Solel Bone included iron and steel processing factories, plants that produced cement and electric motors, foundries, shipping and surveying factories, pipe factories, rubber footwear and galoshes factories, a battery box factory, glassworks, various metallurgical plants, and lime kilns. Ibid., 16, 18.

135 These included metallurgy, electromechanics, construction, woodworks, printing, artificial ice production, baking, textiles and clothing, leather, chemical, and pharmaceutical industries. Ibid., 20.

136 *Who's Who in Israel*, 318, 382–384.

137 For example, Keren Kayemet LeYisrael and Keren HaYesod financed the construction of new housing estates. WIZO ran kindergartens, vocational and agricultural schools, and published textbooks for women in various languages, helping them to run a household and enter the labor market. There were also handicrafts workshops at WIZO, which gave women an income. Their products were sold in WIZO shops in Jerusalem, Tel Aviv, and Haifa.

Cherut was a "family" party, whose leadership had been forged when the Etzel[138] was underground. There was an intimacy among the veterans, who accepted Begin's leadership unquestioningly. Most of the members came from Poland, and Begin's authoritarian style matched the conventional practice in the nationalist movements of that country between the two world wars.[139]

A certain paradox is that, although the Likud party was founded by Ashkenazi citizens, it found its so-called tough electorate among Sephardic Jews. In a special way, it was connected with Eastern Jews (Mizrachi). Although strictly religious parties operate on the Israeli political scene, Likud did not forget about Orthodox circles. This all-embracing strategy meant that the decisions taken by Begin had a clear political justification, but were economically inconsistent. His government pushed the Israeli economy on a path of liberal development, a clear signal was sent to the society that economic calculations had to be made more actively than before, and business was urged to be more competitive. Subsidies for kibbutzim, which were associated mainly with the left-wing Zionist movement, were heavily cut. At the same time, however, Begin was ready to make very expensive gestures for Orthodox circles. Examples are given by Anita Shapira:

> When the Ultra-Orthodox requested that El Al not fly on the Sabbath, he quickly acceded to this request as selfevident. He increased allocations to the yeshivas, resulting in the growth of the class of unemployed yeshiva students to a scale previously unknown in the history of Israel. He also cancelled the cap on the number of yeshiva students exempt from military service (which Ben-Gurion had set at 400 and Dayan increased to 1,500); since then the number has increased to tens of thousands.[140]

There was certainly an economic recovery, but a huge deficit in the state's balance of payments quickly appeared. Between 1977 and 1980, inflation increased from 42.8% to 132.9%.[141] In response to the economic crisis, the new finance minister Yigal Horowitz prepared an operation to replace the Israeli

---

138 It was an underground paramilitary organization whose purpose was to give Jews access to Eretz Yisrael and to make an effort to build their own state.
139 A. Shapira, *Historia Izraela*, trans. A. D. Kamińska, Warsaw 2018, 417.
140 Ibid., 419.
141 Ibid., 434.

lira, also known as the "Israeli pound" (the name borrowed from the British Mandate period), with a new currency called shekel.[142] While the name "lira" had a foreign origin, "shekel" was associated with the biblical history, so, next to the mercantile goal, it was also intended to pursue a political project. Shekel was introduced into circulation on February 24, 1980, the conversion factor was ten Israeli liras to one shekel. However, inflation could not be stopped and Yigal Horowitz resigned.[143] In January 1981, the portfolio of the Minister of Finance was given to Yoram Aridor, who abandoned the program of savings and limiting the amount of money in circulation. He focused on the development of internal consumption. The government removed customs duty and tax on consumer goods.[144] According to Anita Shapira: "An unparalleled consumer feast ensued. Middle- and lower-class families rushed to buy colour TV sets, VCRs, and cars."[145] That policy soon needed a major correction, as the inflation problem persisted. In 1984, the inflation rate exceeded the gigantic 400%.[146] Krzysztof Chaczko enumerates the following reasons for that state of affairs:

> On the one hand, it was the result of the Yom Kippur War and the oil crisis, when after the decisions of oil producers the prices of this raw material increased almost five times. On the other hand, defense spending increased, becoming a huge burden on the state budget, absorbing twenty-five to thirty percent of gross domestic product. In addition, in 1977 the rule of the social democratic option ended, and conservative forces came to power..., which were not interested in the development of universal social programs being the core of the state of social security.[147]

As a consequence of that difficult situation, on April 1, 1985, the old shekel was replaced by the new shekel (New Israeli Shekel, or NIS). At that stage, the following course was introduced: 1,000 old shekels equalled one "new shekel," that is, one "new shekel" (NIS) corresponded to 10,000 Israeli liras.[148] In addition, focus was placed on further economic liberalisation of the state.

---

142 In Hebrew the verb *shakal* means "to weigh."
143 Shapira, *Historia Izraela*, 435.
144 Ibid.
145 Ibid.
146 Chaczko, *Izraelskie państwo bezpieczeństwa socjalnego*, 221.
147 Ibid., 221–222.
148 Shapira, *Historia Izraela*, 435.

In the 1980s, social sentiment improved in Israel, which in turn was not without significance for the economy itself. Another impulse for economic growth came along with geopolitical changes. The turn of the 1980s and 1990s brought about the dismantling of the communist system in the countries of Central and Eastern Europe, which after World War II found themselves depending on the Soviet Union. The Soviet Union itself also underwent profound social, political, and economic changes. International trade revived. New markets emerged. In addition, Jews could finally leave the territories of the former Soviet Union. Over one million Russian-speaking Jews came to Israel. They naturally required state support, which was expensive. Their arrival, however, had many positive aspects: they increased the internal market, settled in places previously less popular, they joined scientific, health, or cultural institutions. Many of them had higher education, a relatively large group were doctors, musicians, and held degrees in exact and natural sciences. People with lower education filled less attractive jobs related mainly to trade and services. Young people were valuable new blood for the army.

The economic situation of Israel was also influenced by the work of earlier generations. Investments made in the area of education, services, and industry, as well as land, sea, and air transport began to bring profits. The defense industry is a good example. In the first years of Israel's existence, great expenses were incurred to create and maintain the army and defense industry. The costs of Israeli army and intelligence are still high, but the defense industry has begun to make profit. In addition, the development of sophisticated military technology, a strong army, and access to advanced intelligence have become a bargaining chip for Israeli governments in international negotiations on political and economic issues. The same applies to the absorption of subsequent *aliyot*. On the one hand, they were a real challenge for state institutions; on the other, they were a positive impulse for the economy. Under the then political and economic conditions of the world, Israel began to grow into a major exporter. Israeli citruses, olive oil, and other food industry products were very popular. At the time, diamonds occupied an important position among the exported goods. Then the time for other areas came. Progress in military technologies had a positive impact on almost all branches of the Israeli industry. For example, the quality of manufactured telecommunications and precision devices as well as medical equipment increased, they were now exported.

In the 1980s, no one talked about the "nation of start-ups." Despite that, Israel, built basically from scratch, rivalled then dozens of other countries that were at a higher level of development already in the decades of the 1940s and

1950s. In the 1950s, the newly arrived Polish Jews testified that they received with undisguised joy parcels sent by friends or relatives from Poland with sugar, flour, cereal, and products. In the 1980s, that situation was unthinkable, not because of the rupture of diplomatic relations between Poland and Israel, but because the economies of both countries went it two different directions. In Poland, until the democratic changes of 1989, central planning and state monopoly were in force in all areas. In Israel, the private sector—despite the strong position of the state and the main trade union Histadrut—had relatively large freedom of action. In Israel, when the right-wing government came to power, the process of privatization began, which in Poland started on a larger scale only after 1990.[149] Poland was in a strong dependence on the Soviet Union, which concerned politics, security, and the economy.

Israel quickly developed very good political and economic relations with the United States. American financial and military assistance, which began to flow to Israel from the beginning of the state's existence, was difficult to overestimate.[150] Military cooperation continues to be of great importance. In the beginning of the twenty-first century Israel still occupies a leading position among the beneficiaries of US military assistance.[151] From Israel, the United States receives research results that are applicable in the defense industry and invaluable intelligence data.

From the beginning, Israel's political ties with Western Europe were more loose, with the exception of the already mentioned "Operation Musketeer" carried out in 1956 jointly by Great Britain, France, and Israel. In any case, Israel's economic cooperation with France, Great Britain, Germany (then the Federal Republic of Germany), Italy, Switzerland, and the Benelux countries developed favourably. In the political dimension, Israel's relations with Western European

---

149 Pursuant to the Act on the Privatization of State Enterprises of July 13, 1990 and other legal acts.

150 In the 1990s, US financial assistance fluctuated around USD 1.2 billion a year. In the twenty-first century, it began to decrease, until it reached a level insignificant for the Israeli economy. "Sojusz amerykańsko-izraelski w perspektywie realistycznej," in *Teoria realizmu w nauce o stosunkach międzynarodowych*, ed. Edward Haliżak, Jacek Czaputowicz, Warsaw 2017, 280–281, http://ptsm.edu.pl/wp-content/uploads/publikacje/teoria-realizmu-w-nauce-o-stosunkach-miedzynarodowych/A.Skorek.pdf, accessed January 3, 2019.

151 For example, in 2009–2018, Israel received USD 30 billion in armaments from the United States. According to the agreement signed in 2016, the United States is obliged to provide Israel with a total of USD 38 billion for this purpose in 2019–2028. "Porozumienie atomowe z Iranem," https://www.tvn24.pl/wiadomosci-ze-swiata,2/amerykanska-pomoc-wojskowa-dla-izraela-miliardy-dolarow-pomocy,678272.html, accessed December 16, 2018.

countries got complicated with the emergence of the European Union (November 1, 1993), which distanced itself from the US policy, and independently pursued new, improved relations with Arab states.

For many, the greatest surprise came to life: Israel and West Germany had good and sometimes even close relations. After 1990, Israel continues its cooperation with the united Germany. Tom Segev writes about this matter as follows: "In the first months of Israel's existence, it seemed that the state would ban all contacts with Germany and introduce a boycott lasting for generations."[152] However, pragmatism, or the political and economic interests of the state, took the upper hand. The course on rapprochement with the United States and West Germany was personally set by David Ben-Gurion, and he put his authority at stake. It was accompanied by negotiations on reparations and German compensations for Israel. In addition to members of the Israeli government, also involved were the president of the Bank of Israel, David Horowitz, and the president of the World Jewish Congress, Nahum Goldmann. The Israeli right wing, with Menachem Begin, expressed fervent criticism of those negotiations. Begin called them "extermination," and identified the left-wing party Mapai with the NSDAP. The Cherut party believed that the Israeli government had no moral right to forgive Germany on behalf of millions of victims of the Holocaust, and "the money from reparations was stained with Jewish blood," therefore it should not be accepted.[153] The ceremonial signing of the Israeli-German agreement took place on September 10, 1952 in Luxembourg. Germany pledged to pay 3.4 billion marks, or approximately 820 million dollars. Of that amount, around seventy percent was allocated for the purchase of goods produced in Germany, and around thirty percent, for the purchase of fuels. In addition, Germany was to pay individual pensions to victims of the Nazi regime. The number of benefits provided by Germany and their amount increased over the following years; the total went from 6 million dollars in 1954 to 100 million in 1961.[154] For Israel, this was a serious support. After all, the state incurred large expenses related to social and health care over the population affected during World War II. Large amounts were also spent on absorbing subsequent waves of *aliyot* and on developing the state's defense. Thanks to funds obtained from Germany, the Israeli

---

152 Segev, *Siódmy milion. Izrael—piętno Zagłady*, 181.
153 Ibid., 201.
154 Ibid., 220–221.

Fig. 110. The establishment of the city of Tel Aviv, 1909,
photo: Abraham Suskin (Soskin), public domain

government was able to afford larger investments in municipal and communication infrastructure.

Due to their different development paths, Israel distanced itself from the Eastern Bloc countries. Countries such as Poland, which had been significantly ahead of Israel several dozen years earlier, were now overshadowed by it. It applied not only to macroeconomic indicators, but also to the general well-being of residents. This is very well portrayed by the scene from the life of Aleksander Rozenfeld, who, as described, did not find himself in the new reality and returned to Poland. In October 1989 he received a phone call from his sister who remained in Israel:

"You know that our mother is in the institution for the terminally ill?"

"I know," I answered.

"You know how much it costs me, eight hundred dollars a month. And you are my mother's son, just like I am her daughter, so you could help me a little bit."

"How?" I asked.

"Well, you could send me two hundred dollars a month."

"Helusia," I asked, "you know how much I earn?"

"How much?" asked my sister.

"Twenty dollars per month."[155]

---

155 Rozenfeld, *Podanie o prawo powrotu*, 109.

The story of Marcel Goldman also fits into this context. In 1990, he organized a party for his friends from school and university in a restaurant at the then well-known hotel Cracovia in Krakow. Today he recalls:

> Initially, I assumed that I would agree with the waiter about what to order for everyone. When I saw how low the prices were, I told everyone to order what they wanted. Now, when my thoughts come back to that situation, I feel a bit embarrassed, because, firstly, such behaviour is not my style, and secondly, I think that someone could perceive it as an unnecessary manifestation of wealth. Anyway, the whole party cost me just over ten dollars.[156]

1981 went down in the history of the world in various ways. On December 13, 1981, General Wojciech Jaruzelski, the head of the communist regime in Poland, announced the imposition of martial law. It did not affect the Goldmans in any way. At that time, they had too many other things on their minds to be interested in Poland's political position. It was not peaceful in Israel either. Menachem Begin used the international turmoil caused by the situation in Poland to sort out the situation on the Israeli-Syrian border. On December 14, 1981, the Israeli Parliament adopted a resolution to incorporate the Golan Heights into Israel. This operation was carried out at a convenient time from Israel's point of view with the precision of action appropriate for that country. Therefore, it did not have a direct impact on the current life of its inhabitants. From Marcel and Bianka's perspective, that year was primarily marked by moving to Tel Aviv. In Haifa, they had already settled in and helped found the local establishment, but only Tel Aviv or Jerusalem (due to its capital nature) are places where one's career should come to its culmination. The path of promotion, as already mentioned, leads from Haifa to Tel Aviv, and not the other way around. For years, many inhabitants of Haifa or smaller cities looked at Tel Aviv as "something better." It was the object of longing in underdeveloped rural settlements. Evidence of that can be found, for example, in the memories of Nili Amit. As a child, she sneaked off to Tel Aviv together with a group of children living in the same transit camp. They were fascinated by watching the café life on the seafront promenade. In the following years, she came there with her father to settle various errands, go shopping, or go to the cinema.[157]

---

156 Correspondence with Marcel Goldman, December 16, 2018.
157 Amit, *A miałam być księżniczką z bajki*, 112.

Fig. 111. Tel Aviv, Allenby St., British Mandate period, Itamar Atzmon's collection

In 1981, Tel Aviv was only seventy-two years old. In the place where it was laid out, there had been no municipal infrastructure before. There were only coastal dunes there, alongside a trail traversed by camel caravans travelling between Africa, the Middle East, Asia Minor, and Europe. Nearby, there was a port, which was beautiful but small and dangerous (due to reefs at the waterfront). The city was built from scratch: Fig. 110 shows a historical moment on April 11, 1909, the drawing of shells assigned to specific plots, where the first sixty houses were to be built. The future owners of the houses had previously paid up the appropriate capital, most often obtained in the form of preferential loans.

The initiators of the construction of Tel Aviv founded the cooperative Achuzat Beit, which can be easily translated as "homestead." The Hebrew word *achuzat* can be translated as "state," "property." *Beit* (*bait*) means "home." So the Jews wanted to build houses and the city in their own way: in their own land of Israel and also on their own ground. Building the city from scratch brought considerable effort. Activists of the Zionist movement, however, assumed that that effort was worth undertaking, because a completely new city would be created for the "new Jew." Unlike Jerusalem, Tel Aviv was not burdened with bad memories and was not dominated by places of religious worship. It was not far from the historic capital, and at the same time it was separated from it by a safe distance. Here,

Fig. 112. Tel Aviv, Dizengoff roundabout, 1940s,
public domain

Jews who broke up with the diaspora heritage were to live. They were expected to be strong and brave.

The hopes and aspirations associated with Tel Aviv are already expressed in its name, which means "Hill of Spring" in Hebrew. The word *tel*, however, means something more than just a hill (which in Hebrew is called *rama*). The word *tel* has a clear archaeological context related to antiquity and excavations (such as a mound, barrow, or hillfort). According to one interpretation, the name Tell Aviv can be read as "Hill of Rebirth" (typical of spring). It was to take place on the foundation of the ancient heritage. Going forward, for the better, the Jew was to remember his pedigree. This code is also inscribed in the Hebrew word *kadima* (Hebrew: forward), in which the term "distant past" (antiquity), which is expressed by the phrase *kdumim amanim*, is also embedded The name "Tel Aviv" was invented by Nahum (Natan) Sokołow,[158] as the title to the Hebrew translation of Theodor Herzl's book *The Old New Land*. Shimon Peres noted: "As my friend, former secretary of state of President Clinton, said to me a few

---

158 Nahum (Natan) Sokołow, born in 1859 in Wyszogród near Płock, died in 1936 in London. He was a Zionist activist, writer, and pioneer of Hebrew journalism.

years ago, Tel Aviv is undoubtedly the only city on the surface of the earth whose name comes from the title of the book written long before it appeared."[159] The agglomeration around Tel Aviv is called Arei Gush Dan (the Metropolitan Ring of Dan's Tribe). Marcel believes that is an example of the fact that "in Israel, the story described in the Bible is constantly affecting us, biblical characters are still involved in our lives. That is why the group of cities gathered around Tel Aviv like a bunch of grapes together is called Arei Gush Dan, because Dan's tribe lived here in ancient times."[160]

The first historical district of Tel Aviv adopted the suggestive name Neve Tzedek, which means "the Abode of Justice" (from the Hebrew words: *neve*—abode and *tzedek*—justice). In Polish, this name is often translated interpretively, but not literally, as the House of Justice. Here, the first buildings were erected, usually small and modest in all respects. They resembled the poor houses in Polish villages and shtetls. Only a few remain today. Most were demolished by developers implementing large-scale construction investments. Relatively late, the authorities of Tel Aviv decided to protect the remaining buildings, recognizing their historical value. Currently, the unique space of Neve Tzedek attracts artists and tourists. There are lots of small galleries, art studios, cafés, and restaurants. The pulse of this district beats in a different rhythm than the seaside promenade or the business part of the city.

During the first few decades of its existence, the city experienced rapid development. The influx of Polish Jews in 1924–1926 as part of the Grabski Aliyah largely contributed to that (in total, over 30,000 of them reached Eretz Yisrael at that time).[161] They were mostly townspeople and entrepreneurs. Some newcomers managed to bring some of the savings from Poland that they could use here. They proved to be hard-working and creative people. Very quickly, they regained confidence, set up their own businesses, and invested in real estate. The houses they built looked far more impressive than those of the first emigrants. They enjoyed great interest of the passersby, and soon they became known as "dream houses." In the following years, a large wave of wealthy and entrepreneurial immigrants from Germany, who left the country due to the spreading of brutal antisemitism, flowed into Tel Aviv. The emigration of German Jews intensified after Hitler came to power in 1933.

---

159 Peres, *Podróż sentymentalna*, 28.
160 Interview with Marcel Goldman carried out on December 27, 2016.
161 E. Mendelsohn, *Żydzi Europy Środkowo-Wschodniej w okresie międzywojennym*, trans. A. Tomaszewska, ed. J. Tomaszewski, Warsaw 1992, 93.

The Mature Age (1954–2019) | 317

Fig. 113. Espresso Roma Café in Tel Aviv, around 1957,
public domain

Fig. 114. Tel Aviv, Dizengoff St., February 28, 1965, photo: Dan Hadani,
public domain

Fig. 115. The Dan Tel Aviv Hotel (present view), photo: Łukasz Tomasz Sroka. The first hotel located on the beach in Tel Aviv, right next to the representative promenade (Hebrew: *tayelet*). The original building was erected in the 1930s as a small guesthouse, Kaete Dan. In mid-twentieth century it was thoroughly rebuilt and reorganized. At that time, it deserved to be called the first luxury hotel in the city. It was the first installment of the Dan Hotels chain

In that group there were architects who helped create the Bauhaus school in Dessau, dissolved by the Nazis because of the large percentage of Jews in its staff. Deprived of occupation, they quickly found employment in the flourishing Tel Aviv, there they could fully develop their talents. It should also be emphasized (which is often overlooked in literature) that among the most outstanding architects representing the Bauhaus style, Polish Jews took an important place.[162] The Bauhaus architecture corresponded well with Zionist ideology, because it preferred simple forms, without unnecessary stucco, and functionality. Its characteristic elements are symmetry, a large number of small windows, and ribboned balconies designed to protect residents against excessive sun exposure. White or

---

162 Among them were Abraham Markusfeld from Łódź, Dov Kutchinsky from Krakow, Pinchas Hutt from Lviv, Schlomo Bernstein from Vilnius, Lucjan Korngold from Warsaw, and Arieh Sharon from Jarosław. Ł. Wróbel, "Miasto dla ludzi bez ziemi. Tel Awiw," *Słowo Żydowskie* 7–8 (2008): 18.

cream facades are typical of these buildings, which gave the name of the White City to the central districts of Tel Aviv. In the climatic conditions prevailing in Israel, flat roofs were designed, where spacious terraces were arranged, used for rest or more practical purposes, such as hanging laundry. The first houses of the Bauhaus style appeared on the most representative streets: Allenby, Dizengoff, and Rothschild Boulevard (see Figs. 111 and 112). In 2003, the Tel Aviv White City, which is composed of nearly 4,000 Bauhaus-style buildings, was made part of the UNESCO World Heritage List.

The vast majority of the first inhabitants of Tel Aviv came from European bourgeois families. They started building a city that was to meet their aspirations, but also made a quite successful attempt to recreate there what they knew and considered valuable. As Shimon Peres writes: "People wanted to live and work in their dream city, they wanted it to be modelled on European cities, with wide cobbled streets, with detached houses. And that there would be public parks and government buildings, downtown commercial areas, tree-lined streets, and boulevards where urban youth could gather."[163]

A serious discussion ensued regarding the width of the main streets of Tel Aviv. The first idea was to model them on the streets of London. This seems natural because it was the time of the British Mandate. However, there were skeptical voices and counterproposals. It was finally decided to take an example from the representative streets of Warsaw, primarily from Marszałkowska Street. The residents' concern was the access of children and young people to good kindergartens and schools. Great importance was attached to libraries.[164]

Even before the outbreak of World War II, cafés, restaurants, hotels, shops, bookshops, theaters, service outlets, banks, and the stock exchange appeared in Tel Aviv. In 1923 a power plant was built. Only a few weeks after the outbreak of World War I, the first cinema theater called Paradise Cinema (Hebrew: Kolnoa Eden) was opened here. In a short time, the Turkish authorities ordered to close it claiming that it was possible to use the screening equipment for the purposes of enemy troops. It resumed activity during the British Mandate, until in 1974 Paradise was closed because it was replaced by more modern cinema halls. In 1930, a wealthy merchant, Yaakow Mograbi, founded the legendary Mograbi

---

163 Peres, *Podróż sentymentalna*, 30.
164 TAYMHA, collection 5132, file number 08–233; Letters and documents 1926, collection 5132, file number 08–230; Resolutions of the City Council 1938–1939, collection 5132, file number 8–231; Letters and documents—file number 1929, collection 5136, file number 08–254; Protocoles of groupings and communities 1926–1935.

Fig. 116. Migdal Shalom under construction, July 1964, photo: Rudi Weissenstein, public domain

Cinema. In the specially erected building, next to the cinema on the upper floor, the first Hebrew theaters (including Habima) and the opera house were located.

In the '70s, all rooms were adapted for the needs of the cinema. As a result of fire, the building was destroyed and demolished in 1989.[165] The establishment of the Israel Philharmonic Orchestra (previously known as the Palestine Orchestra), was initiated by the violinist Bronisław Huberman,[166] and its activity was inaugurated by a concert that took place on December 26, 1936 in Tel Aviv; the conductor was Arturo Toscanini.

As far as the greenery is concerned, the city owes a lot to thw Lviv-born Avraham Karavan (father of the outstanding sculptor Dani Karavan), the main gardener of Tel Aviv for its first forty years. Engineer Simcha Blass (born in 1897 in Warsaw), who came up with a simple and effective system of drip irrigation, also contributed to the greening of Tel Aviv and many other cities in Israel.

In 1924–1925 the area of Tel Aviv almost doubled—from 3,500 to 6,500 dunams.[167] At that time, the number of its inhabitants increased from 20 to

---

165 *Allenby and Mongrabi*, http://www.eretzmuseum.org.il/e/327/, accessed November 29, 2018.

166 Bronisław Huberman, born in 1882 in Częstochowa, died in 1947 in Switzerland. He was an excellent violinist, who studied with the most eminent virtuosos in various European centers and toured all over Europe. He also visited Tel Aviv many times.

167 1 dunam is equal to 1000 m^2.

Fig. 117. Migdal Shalom in the historic center of Tel Aviv (9 Ahad Ha'am Street), near Rothschild Boulevard, the tallest skyscraper in Israel until 1999, public domain

34 thousand, and in 1933–1936 it grew from 80 to 150 thousand.[168] Today, like decades ago, Tel Aviv attracts new residents, enjoying the opinion of a friendly and comfortable city, creating career opportunities and better earnings. It is teeming with life all day long. Its hallmark are cafés and restaurants filled to the brim, noisy streets, and the coastal shoreline full of amused public. The city has undergone far-reaching modernization. Some of the densely erected old buildings were demolished, and, in their place, Israel's first skyscrapers were built.

In 1958, the popular Herzliya Hebrew Gymnasium (Hebrew: HaGymnasia HaIvrit Herzliya), founded in 1905, which is considered the first Hebrew secondary school in the world, was moved to Jabotinsky Street, and the next year, its old building was demolished. Its old site became the building ground for Migdal Shalom (Hebrew: Peace Tower), which was opened in 1965. According to commonly available publications, it was the tallest building in Israel until 1999. In recent years, a lot of high-rise buildings have been constructed in Israel, in response to high land prices and the tastes of buyers who value tall and modern comprehensively equipped facilities. Despite such trends, quite a few elements of the original urban layout survive in Tel Aviv. In addition to the Bauhaus buildings already mentioned, it is possible to point out, for example, many narrow streets that cross perpendicularly with palm trees, adjacent parks, and gardens.

Tel Aviv became the center of social and cultural life of Polish Jews. Of course, they also lived in many other cities, they reached Acre and Nahariya

---

168 See the city's official website, http://www.tel-aviv.gov.il, accessed February 2, 2015.

in the north, and Beersheba and Eilat in the south of Israel, they made a significant contribution to the development of Haifa and Jerusalem, they created kibbutzim and moshavim, but they especially liked Tel Aviv. Here they created the largest and most operative community. Why Tel Aviv? Many factors caused its popularity. In terms of climate (literally and figuratively), architecture and infrastructure, this is the most European of all Israeli cities, so it is no wonder that the eyes of emigrants from the old continent were looking in this direction. The city's cosmopolitan character meant that it had a special power of attraction for secularized Jews, expressing democratic and liberal beliefs. The first enclaves of Polish culture were private salons, modelled on those known from prewar Krakow or Warsaw. Sinai Aleksandrowicz mentions them: "For twenty years, Róża Aleksandrowicz [1866–1973, in Israel from 1951—Ł.T.S.] hosted in her small apartment in Sirkin Street the daily cultural 'salon of Cracowians' who talked in Polish and borrowed books in that language from her huge collection."[169] Café Dalia, located by the beach, was a favorite among the Polish Jews. Chess players from Poland could also be found in the San Remo café.[170] In the years 1936–1961 at 41 Gruzenberg Street, Arie Rachum ran (most probably) the first Polish antiquarian bookshop in Israel.[171] The already mentioned Polish bookshop, founded in 1958, became legendary. It was commonly called the Neustein Bookshop after its founders Ada and Edmund Neustein. Located in the underground passage at Allenby Street, it existed until the end of the twentieth century. It enjoyed the opinion of the best-stocked and best-run bookshop with Polish-language literature operating outside Poland. Moreover, in the times of the Polish People's Republic many items forbidden by communists on the Vistula could be bought there. Although the place was not very big, it was visited every day not only by book and newspaper buyers, but also those who came to discuss politics and social issues, get acquainted with new titles, or simply maintain social contacts. The outstanding Polish-Israeli journalist, bibliographer, publisher, literature historian, and literary critic Ryszard Löw admits that he visited the Polish bookshop daily, sometimes even several times a day, only making an exception when he was outside Tel Aviv.[172] Marcel also bought books there: "I used to come here before I moved to Tel Aviv. Arriving from

---

169 S. Aleksandrowicz, "Wilek," in his *Polska i Palestyna*, 9.
170 Ibid., 61.
171 M. Lewińska, *Przechowane słowa*, Tel Aviv 2008, 46.
172 Interview with Ryszard Löw, carried out in Tel Aviv on November 22, 2016.

Haifa, I considered it a must to visit the Neusteins and purchase a book that interested me. It was all the more important to me as I could not bring any book from Poland."[173] Meetings with Polish and Israeli writers took place in the bookshop. Before 1989, members of the Polish anti-communist opposition visited the place, and later the Neusteins were eagerly visited by Polish diplomats and journalists. Allenby Street in Tel Aviv was called "Polish" because, in addition to the Neustein Bookshop, it housed Bank Pekao S.A. and Orbis Travel Agency. Today, there is no trace left of those institutions.

Tel Aviv enjoyed the interest not only of Polish Jews, but also of Poles. In 1934, the city was visited by Andrzej Strug (real name, Tadeusz Gałecki, 1871–1937), a writer, publicist, independence fighter, and co-founder of the Grand National Lodge of Poland, who headed the League for the Protection of Human and Citizen Rights. He was received by Arie Leib Yaffe, a famous Zionist writer and director-general of Keren HaYesod. The same year, Hanka Ordonówna (1902–1950), a famous singer, actress, and dancer, performed in Israel. While travelling around the land of Israel she also reached Jerusalem, accompanied by her husband, Count Michał Tyszkiewicz, consul general of the Republic of Poland in Jerusalem, Zdzisław Kurnikowski, and the director of the Bank Pekao Branch in Tel Aviv, Tadeusz Piech.

During World War II, a peculiar and unprecedented event in the history of Polish-Jewish relations took place in Eretz Yisrael: the Polish Army formed in the Soviet Union and commanded by General Władysław Anders arrived there.[174] It was accompanied by civilians evacuated from the Soviet Union, among them a large group of children—including a thousand Jewish children, mostly orphans. Their wandering trail led through Tehran, so these orphans were known in Israel as "Tehran's children." Poles and Jews who, along with General Władysław Anders, left the Soviet Union, miraculously avoided death threatening them because of the difficult living conditions and hard work in labour camps. After reaching Eretz Yisrael, some Jews, largely with the tacit consent of the commanders, left the ranks of the Polish Army. Others continued their route to Europe, as confirmed by Jewish gravestones at the Polish War Cemetery

---

173 Interview with Marcel Goldman carried out on December 21, 2016.
174 This army was comprised of 77 thousand soldiers. It included about 6,000 Jews: over 1,500 civilians, 146 officers, 416 non-commissioned officers, and 3,839 privates. D. Levin, "Alija 'waw'. Masowa dezercja żołnierzy żydowskich z Armii Polskiej w Palestynie w latach 1942–1943," in his *Żydzi wschodnioeuropejscy podczas II wojny światowej*, trans. E. Balcerek, Warsaw 2005, 122.

at Monte Cassino. Among those who stayed were Jews who later distinguished themselves in the history of Israel, including outstanding politicians, such as Menachem Begin, soldiers and national heroes, such as the general Avigdor "Yanush" Ben-Gal (born in 1936 in Łódź as Janusz Goldlust, died in Israel in 2016), and scientists, such as Prof. Zeev Schuss (born in 1937 in Poland), mathematician, pianist, and translator of Sławomir Mrożek's books. It is difficult to overestimate their social, cultural, and political activities that are counted among Israel's civilizational achievements. For Poles, staying in Eretz Yisrael was also an extraordinary, even metaphysical, experience. They found themselves here not of their own will, but as a result of the turmoil of war. However, they took the opportunity to visit places related to biblical history. Many of them lived in Tel Aviv. In Eretz Yisrael, the Poles met tens of thousands of Jews speaking their language, often their former neighbours.

The famous writer Marek Hłasko arrived in Israel in January 1959, and lived here for two years. He was not an anonymous figure in this country: a year before a volume of his stories published in Hebrew appeared on the local book market.[175] His observations are all the more valuable because, as maladjusted man, he visited places that exemplary fathers and husbands avoided. In port pubs and alleys he had contact with people who were at odds with the law, and also saw the so-called dull reality of Israel. He recorded his experiences in such works as *Nawrócony w Jaffie* (English: Converted in Yaffa), *Opowiem wam o Ester* (English: I will tell you about Esther) and *Wszyscy byli odwróceni* (English: Everybody was turned away).[176] The last novel was screened by West German television in 1969, and in 2013 became the basis for a play staged by Michał Zara in the Museum of History of Polish Jews in Warsaw.[177]

In June 2000, the Polish Institute in Tel Aviv was opened. It organizes literary meetings, Polish language courses, film and theater showings, culinary shows, exhibitions, and debates devoted to Polish-Jewish and Polish-Jewish-Israeli relations, as well as matters of science and culture. Thus, it is an important center through which Polish culture is imported to Israel. In 2004, two solemn author's evenings with the participation of the Polish Nobel Prize winner Wisława

---

175 W. Mrozek, *Co Hłasko zobaczył w Izraelu—nowy spektakl Zadary*, http://wyborcza.pl/1,75410,14326181,Co_Hlasko_zobaczyl_w_Izraelu_nowy_spektakl_Zadary.html, accessed September 2, 2017.

176 M. Lewińska, "Hłasko," *Kontury* 5 (1994): 50–53. See P. Weiser, *"To nie ja wymyśliłem ten kraj." Izrael Hłaski*, Krakow 2015.

177 Mrozek, *Co Hłasko zobaczył w Izraelu*.

Szymborska took place in Tel Aviv: first in the auditorium of the Museum of the Land of Israel, and second at the Beit Ariel Culture Center. A large audience gathered in both of them.[178]

The end of the 1970s and the 1980s brought a crisis of kibbutzim. As mentioned, the right wing in force since 1977 cut the kibbutzim off from numerous subsidies, which meant that they had to adapt to the conditions of the free market economy in a short time. In addition, a new generation grew up that felt overwhelmed with the monotonous kibbutz life. Tony Judt brilliantly summarized the problem: "Israel seemed a kind of prison at the time, and the kibbutz—a crowded cell."[179] Nili Amit, who was a teenager at the time, must have had similar thoughts, and she decided to make profound changes in her life. For a good start, she began looking for a man with a car:

> No, I didn't suddenly change into a greedy snob, but a boy without a means of transport has no chance to get to my village or leave it, and the only entertainment he can offer his partner is a walk in the fields. And I got bored with that topic. He walked in the fields, she walked in the fields, they walked in the fields... Damn, it is enough! I don't want to walk in the fields anymore! Basta! I want to parade in nylons and stilettos around city streets, sit in cafés, or have a romantic dinner by candlelight in some elegant restaurant.[180]

But life in a big city is not only about bustling cafés and restaurants, cinemas and theaters, elegant boutiques, representative routes, and promenades. It also means a necessity of finding job without outside help. It is a multitude of relationships, many of which are shallow or one-way. It is a burden of living with the high cost of renting or buying a property. Many of those who had been enthusiastic about Tel Aviv were disappointed, including Nili Amit:

> As you can see, I'm not created to be a member of high-society and "celebrity" society. Quite down to earth, I dream of a house with a garden, shared with someone who will be happy to see me twenty-four hours a day, and then all my life. So goodbye Tel Aviv, we'll meet again in the

---

178 M. Lewińska, "Wizyta laureatki Nagrody Nobla. 'Chciałabym żyć długo,'" *Biuletyn Izrael Polska* 2005, 24–25.

179 T. Judt, "Kibuc," *Gazeta Wyborcza*, January 30–31, 2010, 19.

180 Amit, *A miałam być księżniczką z bajki*, 116.

future, but only briefly, like distant friends bowing coldly from a safe distance.[181]

For Goldmans, Tel Aviv became a haven for the rest of their lives. They never experienced disappointment in this city, because they did not expect anything either. It appeared in their lives when they were successful people, it was the culmination, not the beginning of their careers. Soon they saw a number of advantages resulting from the move from Haifa to Tel Aviv: more places related to culture and entertainment, proximity to the seats of science and business institutions, easy access to the airport, and so forth. No differences separating Tel Aviv from Haifa are, however, as significant as those which distinguish life in any large city from that in kibbutzim and moshavim.

People distancing themselves from the elite, urban chic, and snobbery could have shunned Tel Aviv. Marcel is by nature a social person, and he has felt great in Tel Aviv. He does not feel embarrassed living in the most expensive district of this city, namely Ramat Aviv.[182] Later he got to know London and Zurich, cities that turned out to be made for him. Banquets, receptions, and speeches are nothing unusual for him. The superficiality of acquaintances and the high dynamics accompanying them are an inherent part of the banker's profession (same as with lawyers or doctors). This did not bother Marcel, who has found stability and a sense of security in the family. What undoubtedly cements his marriage is Bianka's great independence. She has always maintained her own opinion and provided criticism. Certainly, the innate sense of humor of both of them is also important. Marcel often reminds Bianka of the moment of their wedding and adds that "it had to happen in August, because it is the hottest period in Israel then, so people do not know what they are doing."[183]

The nomination of Zadik Bino, an experienced and skilful director of the accounting department, who was not a banker, for the FIBI Chief Executive in 1980 (he held that position until 1986) was the reason why the Goldmans moved to Tel Aviv. He offered to Marcel the position of his deputy (Hebrew: *mishne le-mankal*, the second person in the hierarchy of importance), and asked him to urgently come to Tel Aviv. That is why initially Marcel went there alone

---

181 Ibid., 132.
182 Ramat Aviv is located in the north of Tel Aviv, which is why its residents are sometimes referred to as *tzofim*, which in Hebrew means "northern."
183 Interview with Marcel Goldman carried out on December 18, 2016.

and lived in hotels for six months. Commuting every day from Haifa was out of the question because, in such a high position, he had to work until late afternoon and sometimes even evening. Prior to moving to Tel Aviv, Marcel worked as director of the bank's northern district and had eighteen branches from Netanya to Kiryat Shmona under control, in addition to being also the director of the main branch in Haifa. In that situation, he had to find a deputy and train him in his duties. By the way, he suggested dividing the northern district into two separate areas, because it was too large for one managing director.

At the FIBI headquarters in Tel Aviv, the following board structure was adopted: not counting the supervisory board and its president, all matters were managed by the CEO, Zadik Bino. Marcel Goldman became the head of the bank's administrative division (*agaf* in Hebrew). He was responsible for the personnel and training department, the bank's archives, and the management of Mataf—theoretically a separate company, but wholly owned by the bank, which dealt with IT and related issues, computer support, design, software, hardware, statistics, and so forth. In addition, he supervised the administration of approximately 100 branches of the Bank throughout the country. Apart from him, there were two more deputy CEOs: one headed the credit department, and the other, accounting.[184] Zadik Bino often repeated during conversations with his colleagues: "If I want to have something calculated up to the last cent, I give it to Mund [chief accountant], when I want to give a negative answer, I give it to Koren [credits], but if I want something to be done, I give it to Marcel."[185] In 1986, Jacques Nasser took control of the FIBI Holdings. The Safra brothers, well-known and respected in international banking, cooperated with him[186] and in 1990 they officially acquired the FIBI. In April 2003 they sold the Bank to the Bino-Lieberman Group, consisting of Zadik Bino's Bino Holdings and the Australian Lieberman family. This group has control over the Bank to this day (as of January 2019).[187]

---

184 Correspondence with Marcel Goldman, January 4, 2019.
185 Conversation with Marcel Goldman carried out on November 24, 2018.
186 The Safras come from the Syrian city of Aleppo, from where they emigrated to Brazil in 1952. In 2019, *Forbes* magazine stated that Joseph Safra, who was eighty-one years old then, was the richest banker in the world. Earlier he became the richest Brazilian. He was also awarded the thirty-first place on the list of the richest people in the world kept by Forbes, with assets valued at USD 25.2 billion. https://www.forbes.pl/rankingi/ranking-najbogatsi-ludzie-swiata-2019-lista-miliarderow/nbkd4g9, accessed April 13, 2019.
187 "Fibi History," https://online.fibi.co.il/wps/portal/FibiMenu/MarketingEN/AnInformation/AnInvestorRelations/AnAboutFibi/AnFibiHistory, accessed January 4, 2019.

Working in Tel Aviv brought Marcel many more challenges than he could have expected. In addition to those that naturally resulted from a change of residence and assuming new responsibilities, he had to face a serious crisis in the entire banking sector that occurred in Israel in the early 1980s. It began with the fact that banks, with the government's consent, lent large amounts to the diamond industry, which was providing the state with the foreign currency it needed. It turned out to be unfavourable for banks because the interest rate on loans was limited by the rate of interest set by the Bank of Israel. With the high inflation, real interest rates on loans to individuals were lower than inflation, even negative. Money taken from the bank was therefore a gift. Diamond manufacturers were in an even better position because their loans had half the interest rate of those granted to other customers. Therefore, many representatives of this industry, instead of dealing with the production of diamonds, focused on banking activities and money turnover on a large scale. They used cheap loans to invest the capital obtained, for example, in the real estate market and other projects that brought them profits much higher than the interest due to banks. In that way they began to earn extra money. Over time, that system collapsed, and a payment gridlock occurred. Banks should have collected claims from companies in the diamond industry, but they could not cope with it because they lost their liquidity themselves. Their investments, which were considered simple and profitable, ceased to be such. The crisis did not bypass the bank in which Marcel worked: "Zadik came to my hotel almost every evening. After swimming in the pool and a modest dinner, we sat up late and debated about the situation of the bank."[188] While preparing a recovery plan, they took advantage of the fact that their bank was of medium size and its debt was proportionally small. As a result, they began to effectively enforce their debts from companies that, in order to get rid of the problem, asked for loans in large banks that had greater capital resources and could afford to wait for loan repayment longer. Above all, however, the large banks were afraid of their clients' bankruptcy, as they owed them serious sums of money, which is why, as Marcel said, "they gnashed their teeth and repaid the loans taken from us."[189] Marcel mentions that the so-called diamond-dealers remembered that situation and later, when things returned to normal, they no longer wanted to cooperate with the bank that he represented: "They told me directly: in times of crisis, instead of helping us, you demanded

---

188 Correspondence with Marcel Goldman, February 8, 2019.
189 Ibid.

loan repayment from us. But no one explained to them that the bank had to demand repayment for its own and its clients' sake, because it was in an extremely difficult situation."[190]

The banks sought to change their unstable position. They decided to expand equity through a new issue of shares. In order to sell them successfully on the stock market, the banks had to increase demand, which is why bankers began to convince customers to buy the shares, promising profits. It was misleadingly explained that the banks' shares would always go up. In that mechanism, there was the germ of the next great crisis of the Israeli banking (the earlier crisis, already described, occurred in the second half of the 1950s and lasted until the Six-Day War).[191] Marcel Goldman thinks that:

> the first mistakes were made then, which brought the following ones, and finally made a cursed circle. On the stock exchange, banks were inevitably compared with companies that were highly profitable and brought relatively large and quick profits to their investors. The banks tried to repeat this success. They directed advertisements to their clients, which showed that their shares would only grow and that this would be a constant trend. To confirm this, they began to interfere in the price of their shares on the stock exchange. Every day, stock exchange quotations were observed and when it was noticed that the supply of shares of a bank was rising and the price of its shares was starting to decrease, the shares were bought up. In this situation, however, regulatory provisions had to be bypassed, because, according to the applicable law, if bank X bought its own shares, it had to reduce its own capital, which was not in its favor. That is why large banks formed illegal agreements and made mutual intervention purchases of shares. For example, if someone earmarked for sale a large number of bank X's shares, which could have resulted in a reduction in their price, then bank Y immediately joined the purchase of shares. The next day, the same operation could have been carried out by bank X in relation to bank Y. In this way artificial demand was launched, which was not based on the banks' real financial results. Later, this situation was accurately described by Ernest Jaffet, then the CEO of Bank Leumi: "I found myself in the position of a person who rushes to attack a tiger. I knew that I could not stop, because then this tiger would devour me."[192]

---

190 Interview with Marcel Goldman carried out on April 17, 2017.

191 Ibid.

192 Ibid.

That situation lasted for a year or two, after which the possibility of buying banks' shares by the same banks was over.[193]

In 1983, a great crisis broke out. It affected almost all banks, except for the one in which Marcel worked. Initially, a group of shareholders and their representatives tried to force him to follow the same policy as the competitors. The CEO came under enormous pressure, so that at some point he decided to step down and bought the shares of the bank he managed. Marcel thinks it was "the black day in the history of their bank," but notes that the other board members: he himself, the other deputy director responsible for the credit department, and the bank's chief accountant, gave the director a hard ultimatum. If their bank continued that and the CEO ordered the purchase of their bank's shares once again, they would demand his resignation, and if he did not give up, they would leave. The managing director needed an hour to think, but he agreed. Thanks to that, their bank spared itself the trouble that the entire sector later experienced.[194]

When in trouble, bankers asked the Bank of Israel to intervene. In Marcel's opinion, it was a rather ambiguous situation, because the central bank as the controller should have intervened much earlier, before the case was widely known on the market.[195] The Israeli government had a special meeting on that subject. The stock market was closed for several days. The government asked Zadik Bino for consultation, because he did not participate in that procedure (in fact, he did it only once), and so enjoyed a good reputation. A method of overcoming the crisis was developed, which consisted in the government gradually buying back the shares of banks in trouble from citizens. The process was spread over several years.[196] As Marcel notes:

> Almost all banks were nationalized except ours. However, the state did not interfere in the daily work of the banks, so they found themselves in a different situation than typical state-owned enterprises. Supervisory boards were still at the head of banks, although of course their staff composition changed, because those responsible for the situation had to leave.[197]

---

193 Ibid.
194 Ibid.
195 Ibid.
196 Ibid.
197 Ibid.

Not all banks could be saved, some had to be liquidated, sold, or merged with others. Most often it concerned the institutions with the biggest problems.[198] Marcel himself participated in such an event:

> One day, it was in 1983, around midnight I received a phone call from the chief executive officer of my bank, Zadik Bino, who informed me that he was in Jerusalem at a government meeting regarding the situation in the banking sector. He told me that the Bank of Israel got the government's decision to take one of the banks from its owners, dismiss its directors, dismiss the entire supervisory board and transfer its management to me. I had time until the following morning to select colleagues from our First International Bank of Israel employees. I was to take office in Tel Aviv and make general orders in the bank, and then close it. I informed Bianka of the situation. By eight o'clock in the morning I already gathered a set of twelve associates ready to work in branches of this bank in the country. These matters belonged to Bank Control. At that time, the Bank Controller was Galia Maor (later the general manager of Bank Leumi). I received direct guidance from her and she was responsible for the Parliament's permission to receive current loans from the Bank of Israel to repay the deposits, in short, so as not to go bankrupt. The shareholders of the bank entrusted to me included a group of politically minded people and a group of US businessmen. This company was very doubtful from the point of view of running a bank. After starting work at this bank, I had to quickly familiarize myself with its financial situation. I anticipated that after the announcement of the information about the controller's entry there in the media, creditors would come and demand that their deposits be paid to them. If I did not have the proper funds, the rumor would spread very quickly that the bank went bankrupt. The help of the Bank of Israel did not cover all needs. That's why I decided to cash what I could. The fact that a relatively small bank had so many cars in its possession drew my attention. Normally, banks, such as mine, had several cars, an average of two to four, for the general director and his deputies. There were about twelve to fifteen cars in this bank, which were given to various politicians. To make matters worse, the bank paid their maintenance costs. Officially, the cars were supposed to serve these politicians to find new customers, but nothing like that happened. It was also said that it was a kind of remuneration for them for various services rendered to the bank. In fact, it was just political corruption. I ordered the takeover of these cars from the hands of politicians and put them up for sale in the form of a transparent auction. In addition, I reviewed

---

198 Ibid.

the loans granted. The results of this audit chilled my blood. Among the suspicious loans I found one that was worth a million dollars, which was a very large sum at that time. It was given without interest to a certain politician, who was known at the time, although still climbing the career ladder in Israeli politics, and eventually found himself in prison. I remember giving him an ultimatum—forty-eight hours to pay back the loan. Otherwise, I threatened to make this situation public in the media. He repaid his debt through a loan he took out from another bank. I had many more such situations to straighten out in this bank . . . Over time, I informed the Bank of Israel that I wanted to quit my job in this corrupted bank. I did not want to be associated with it in my further career and I did not intend to appear as his liquidator. However, I did not leave the Bank of Israel without help. I knew one Israeli banker who did not have a job because his contract in London ended. I recommended him and promised that I would help him get to know his new duties. And so it happened. I returned to my home bank.[199]

At the time Marcel started working in Tel Aviv, his children were already adults. His daughter studied at the Hebrew University in Jerusalem, his son at the Haifa Technion. Bianka decided to return to professional activity. In Haifa she worked as a medical secretary in a hospital. After half a year she joined her husband in Tel Aviv, got a job in the Library of Tel Aviv University. Marcel mentions that in 1981 Tel Aviv had much of its prewar charm. Following the example of European cities, the city center was marked by main streets and squares, such the Dizengoff and Allenby Streets, which attracted residents going for walks or shopping. Much changed in the following years. Huge shopping centers were created, and swallowed some of the clientele. According to Marcel, in both Israel and Tel Aviv the local weather conditions contributed to it:

In our country, as the Polish Jews say, it either pours or heats up. Both variants create some discomfort. So it turned out that air-conditioned and spacious shopping centers fit perfectly into Israeli conditions. Unfortunately, it was at the expense of the partial collapse of the so-called shopping streets, which had to find a new way to attract customers. Unique cafés and restaurants, sophisticated boutiques, shops with unique souvenirs, art workshops, and shops with organic food turned out to have attractive values. In general, a lot has changed for the better. Sustained economic growth means that Tel Aviv authorities could allocate large sums of money to embellish the city. An example are the

---

199 Ibid.

roads connecting Tel Aviv with Jerusalem and Haifa. They used to be unattractive, full of fairly average buildings. Later they were planted with palm trees. Houses with modern architecture grew around them. Thanks to this, the first sights of Tel Aviv that welcome visitors look impressive. Then the Golda Center was erected, which includes a theater, a ballet, and an opera. An elegant shopping center appeared on Einstein Street. Tel Aviv University has undergone incredible expansion and development.[200]

It also took Marcel and Bianka some time to set up in Tel Aviv and build a circle of friends and acquaintances. The majority of people with whom they had close contacts remained in Haifa. Initially, it changed their way of spending free time. In Haifa, private parties, the already mentioned dances and bridge games were the main entertainment. In Tel Aviv, the Goldmans began to enjoy urban life more often, they willingly visited cinemas, theaters, the ballet, and opera. They quickly saw the differences between Haifa and Tel Aviv. Marcel declares: "Today I would not exchange Tel Aviv for Haifa. I think Haifa is more beautiful. However, in Tel Aviv I am enchanted with the metropolitan style and impressive development, which is much faster than in Haifa."[201]

Writing Marcel's biography, it is difficult not to refer to the relations prevailing in his immediate family. Getting to know them will help to better understand not only the Goldman family, but social relations in past and present Israel in general. Undoubtedly, both Marcel and his wife transferred to Israel bourgeois cultural models acquired in Poland, which they also enriched with new experiences. It is interesting because in Israel it is common to emphasise its multiculturalism. This is confirmed by the image of the Israeli street—due to the specific customs and expressive clothing, Orthodox Jews and the Arab population stand out, and an important complement to this mosaic are people shunning religion or even declared atheists. In addition to people with conservative views, there is no lack even of supporters of extreme liberalism in interpersonal relations (we associate this community with Tel Aviv in particular).

The rather traditional and patriarchal Goldman family found their place in the multicultural and cosmopolitan Tel Aviv. The arrangement prevailing in their family, however, was not imposed by force, but resulted from a series of different situations that Bianka accepted.

---

200 Interview with Marcel Goldman carried out on December 27, 2016.
201 Ibid.

Fig. 118. Tel Aviv panorama visible from the Yitzhak Rabin Center, July 6, 2017, LaMèreVeille, public domain

The thing is that Marcel got higher education and qualifications that led him to the top of Israeli banking. It gave the family overall well-being. Thanks to the father, the family lived at a level exceeding the average Israeli standard (which is important because the Israeli standard is already among the highest in the world). Bianka quit her job and devoted herself to raising children and running a home. Her decision basically conditioned the continuation of the marriage, because it is difficult to imagine a situation in which the family would continue to function if Marcel worked in Zurich, and Bianka, in Tel Aviv. The Goldmans' children grew up in an atmosphere of respect for human choices, and at the same time they were strongly influenced by the pattern of the relationship between their father and mother. Their daughter, entering adult life, made a correction of that pattern and decided to build a more equal relationship, which allowed her to realize not only family, but also professional aspirations. However, she did not resign from the role traditionally assigned to the woman—that of a mother and a homemaker.

Character traits and values presented by Polish Jews for a long time exerted a strong influence on the functioning of Israeli society. Israel's builders especially valued diligence, dedication, courage, straightforwardness, resourcefulness, and responsibility. It is difficult not to ask to which extent these features are still present and valued in Israel. From the beginning of the twentieth century, the social and cultural mosaic of Eretz Yisrael and then of Israel has undergone significant transformations several times.

Fig. 119. Azrieli business and shopping center in Tel Aviv, May 7, 2010, Rastaman3000, photo: public domain.

The Azrieli Center consists of three luxury skyscrapers, which were built in 1996–2007. Each of the skyscrapers has a different geometric shape: a cylinder, a triangular prism, and a cuboid. This cluster became a symbol of Tel Aviv's modernity and its international aspirations. Inside, there are offices, a hotel, cinema halls, theater, fitness club, several dozen cafés and restaurants, and shops. This is one of the largest and most recognizable facilities of this type in the Middle East. Its architect and developer was David Azrieli, who was born on May 10, 1922 in Maków Mazowiecki (he died on July 9, 2014). During World War II he escaped to Eretz Yisrael. In 1954 he emigrated to Canada. He was one of the giants of the Israeli and Canadian construction market, and a great philanthropist

Let us remind: in the years 1924–1928 Polish Jews who came to Eretz Yisrael as part of the Grabski Aliyah were strongly distinguished; in the 1930s, German Jews who came there fleeing the Nazis began to play an important role; another larger wave of Polish Jews came just after the end of World War II; later, Polish Jews became again more visible after the Gomulka Aliyah in the years 1956–1960; the emigration of Polish Jews on the wave of March '68 was not so numerous, but it was made up of people with high social status, level of education and professional competences.²⁰² The events of March '68 can be treated as a kind of cut-off date, because after them no larger and organized migration wave of Polish Jews was recorded in Israel. In fact, only a handful of Jews remained in Poland then.²⁰³ In Israel, in the following decades, there was an increase in numbers and an overall increase in the importance of the Sabras. In addition, groups of tens of thousands Jewish immigrants from the Middle East and Africa came. At the turn of the 1980s and 1990s, there was an *aliyah* of Jews from the countries of the former Soviet Union involving about a million people. Clearly, Israel has experienced profound transformations, some of which resulted from successive *aliyot*, others were closely related to economic development, and these matters were bound up. However, they did not lead to questioning the basic principles that accompanied the beginnings of Israeli statehood.

For Israelis, the family and the circle of close friends still remain very important, children also play a significant role. Looking at families in their private homes and in public places, one acquires the belief that children are valued, understood, pampered, and treated as partners. In public spaces, it is easy to see many facilities for the youngest citizens. Social gatherings at home or, more often, in cafés and restaurants (the latter especially in the evenings, when it is not so hot) are still in vogue. The army and special services still enjoy great prestige. Israeli shops are full of clothing with graphic signs and slogans promoting TZAHAL and Mosad, Israel's main civilian intelligence service. As in the United States, the army and special services permanently established themselves in mass culture in Israel. Military service, although long and arduous, is treated as an honour and a challenge, evading it is publically disapproved. Just like in interwar Poland veterans proudly remembered serving in the Legions alongside Józef Piłsudski, today in Israel politicians and public figures eagerly exhibit their service in military formations such as Sayeret Matkal, the Golani Brigade, the Duvdevan Unit, and others. This trend is discreetly reinforced by a well-designed state policy, thanks to which people previously employed in front units are pre-

---

202 Based on Grzegorz Berendt's calculations, we assume that in the years 1945–1955 41,839 people emigrated from Poland to Israel; in the years 1956–1966 the number of immigrants from Poland amounted to 46,112 people; between 1967 and 1969, 3,397 Polish Jews reached Israel. Berendt, *Emigracja Żydów z Polski*, 308–309.

203 According to the results of the census carried out in Poland in 2002, out of the population of 38.2 million people only 1,133 people declared Jewish nationality and ethnicity. In 2011 1,636 people declared homogeneous (single) Jewish national and ethnic identification, and 5,871 people, complex Polish-Jewish identification. *Ludność. Stan i struktura demograficzno-społeczna. Narodowy Spis Powszechny Ludności i Mieszkań 2011*, Warsaw 2013, 92.

ferred candidates for positions in the security sector. In this way, young people not only go to the army, but often volunteer to more demanding and, in fact, less secure elite units. It is not surprising these units see ten times more volunteers than there are places available. It was not different in the case of the Goldman family. The children and grandchildren of Marcel and Bianka also took military service seriously and did it with full commitment. Marcel talks about it with undisguised pride ... The photo of his daughter Orit in TZAHAL uniform was the first family picture that he allowed the author of this book to see. Taking it from the album, he did not hide his pride and emotion...

Fig. 120. Orit Goldman during basic military service in the Israeli army (1974–1976), family collections of Marcel and Bianka Goldman (Tel Aviv)

For young Israelis, military conscription happens in an important time—after graduating from high school and before starting university or vocational studies. This is an important period in the life of every young person, in which their character, personality, vocabulary, and other features are ultimately shaped. At this age, people are critical but open to learning and new experiences. The TZAHAL service teaches ingenuity and the use of non-standard solutions. The army operates in extremely difficult conditions; its soldiers must live in a hostile environment, exposed to attacks by the regular armies of enemy troops as well as the most sophisticated terrorists. There is also a problem (typical for the Middle East) of densely located buildings, such as in Jerusalem, where houses of friends and foes are adjacent. This situation has an impact on the work of military laboratories in which weapons as precise as possible are constructed, but this is not enough.

In some situations they have to resort to mystification and improvisation. Some special forces have polygons at their disposal, which include simulations of Arab villages and cities. Israeli soldiers are diligently learning the rules of navigation and movement without leaving a trace. They practice moving on an Arab street, take Arabic lessons combined with learning Arabic culture, habits, and

Fig. 121. A soldier of the elite Golani Brigade during field exercises, November 2005, photo: Israel Defense Forces

Fig. 122. Apache helicopters of the Israeli and Greek air forces fly together over Greece as part of a joint flight exercise, June 21, 2011, photo: Israel Defense Forces. These types of exercises result from the close military cooperation of Israel and Greece

Fig. 123. Exercises of the Israel Defense Forces 319th Armor Division, also known as the HaMapatz (English: bang) Formation, April 29, 2013, photo: Ariel Khermoni, public domain. This armored infantry unit was founded in 1954. It played am important role during the Suez campaign (1956), the Six-Day War (1967), and the Yom Kippur War (1973)

Fig. 124. Installation of the Israeli "Iron Dome" presented at the Israeli Air Force exhibition in Ramat David on the occasion of the Sixty-Ninth Israeli Independence Day Celebration, May 2017, photo: Oren Rozen, public domain

gestures. The disguises they have in stock could impress the world's most professional theaters. All this means that young people from the army take a lesson that they would not receive anywhere else. Experience gained in the army is also useful in business, where the winner should also be able to confuse the competition and find solutions that break the routine.

Due to the unique training system, numbers, experience, and technologically advanced equipment, the Israeli army is considered one of the strongest in the world. In 2019, Israel took the sixteenth position (out of 137) in the annual Military Strength Ranking report by Global Firepower.[204]

The widespread threat of war and terrorism and demanding military service mean that Israeli youth, though they are considered spoiled with all its consequences, develop a sense of responsibility, resourcefulness, and creativity. Also, the weight of education and work ethos have not lost their relevance. The Israeli labour market and the economy in general are both competitive and demanding. In all types of analyses regarding the phenomenon of the Israeli economy, attention is paid to its favorable circumstances: a strong army that creates a modern defense industry, well-organized intelligence that provides the state with a variety of information (including, naturally, the economic data), highly developed education at all levels. In addition, the lack of natural resources (only recently did Israelis discover more serious deposits of natural gas off the Mediterranean coast) and harsh climatic conditions encourage the search for alternative, unobvious, and pioneering solutions. Paradoxically, the constant threat also brings positive effects. All government services must be fully alert, stagnation and relaxation could lead to serious security problems. The historical, cultural, and religious context of Israel's success is rightly pointed out. The oldest key to understanding it can be found in the Talmudic treatises. In Pirkei Avot we read: "An unlearned person cannot be scrupulously pious." Self-study of religious texts, criticism, and bold questions are the domain of Judaism.

In my opinion, this list should also be supplemented with the information that, like the United States, Israel is a country built by immigrants and their descendants. Naturally, the historical context is completely different, because Jews who migrate to Israel in fact return to their homeland. Nevertheless, the mechanisms that accompany migration are essentially similar: healthy, determined, brave, and creative people do it most often. These are the people who want

---

204 "2021 Israel Military Strength," https://www.globalfirepower.com/country-military-strength-detail.asp?country_id=israel, accessed April 27, 2019.

to improve their fate. The contribution of immigrants to building the United States is obvious to everyone. With regard to Israel, one may get the impression that more recognition is attributed to the state itself than to immigrants, as it is broadly commented how, despite being young and endangered from all sides, Israel managed to absorb more people than it had had at the time of proclaiming independence.

This is all true, but it should also be emphasized that immigrants created the economic situation, especially on the food, clothing, education, construction, and household appliances markets. An important advantage of the Israeli immigration movement is its diversity: among the immigrants are both educated people with specialized skills as well as people with only elementary education, who fill the lower-paid jobs, mainly in trade and services, which are also important for the economy.

The problem is the large social stratification. Less wealthy immigrants have little chance of competing with representatives of the Israeli establishment. In subsequent generations, this situation is not so obvious, because in Israel (as almost everywhere in the world) immigrant children are more ambitious and determined. The army offers great development opportunities. First of all, it provides a career that does not depend on connections, besides, it gives young people a chance to establish lasting friendships, sometimes with representatives of the higher-ranking social strata, on which they could not count in other countries. In many countries around the world, children from the poorest and richest families generally do not meet directly. In Israel, this kind of contact occurs in the army and is creative for both sides. It is assumed that the army is a place where the diverse Israeli society merges into one whole. Here, the rich, the poor, residents of kibbutzim, moshavim, and cities, *sabras* and newcomers use and create common cultural codes and establish understanding.

In Israel, great importance is attached to education and, as a result, to school and university diplomas. People (especially newcomers) find employment mainly in positions strictly corresponding to their competences and qualifications confirmed by these documents, or positions to which they can adapt relatively quickly. A good example is the professional career of the late Oleś Szonberg, who obtained the diploma of mining engineer at the AGH University of Science and Technology in Krakow. He was a long-time friend of the Goldman family and had known Bianka since childhood. In Israel, he worked in the Timna Valley, where he mined copper. But then he retrained and started building a road from Beit Shemesh to Jerusalem. While breaking a rock to build the highway, a cavern was discovered, which is now known as Me'arat HaNetifim—

a natural wonder full of stalactites and stalagmites that became a tourist attraction. A plaque commemorating the cave explorer, a Polish Jew, Oleś Szonberg, an engineer, graduate of the AGH University of Science and Technology in Krakow was placed at the entrance.[205] Szonberg paved the path of professional development for other miners, whose skills were used in the construction of roads, bridges, and viaducts.

The problem of employing people in accordance with their competencies manifested itself with full power at the turn of the 1980s and 1990s, when a great *aliyah* of Jews from the former USSR countries reached Israel, including a large group of doctors, musicians. and engineers. The first group were quickly absorbed by hospitals and health centers—doctors are almost always needed everywhere. Musicians had more trouble: some found work in various types of orchestras and music groups, theaters, operas and philharmonics, but it soon turned out that these institutions had exhausted the possibility of further employment. Therefore, many musicians, even titled ones, had to be content with giving private lessons or playing in squares and streets. Some completely abandoned the profession.

In addition to the lack of natural resources, the Israeli economy's major difficulty is the relatively low absorption of its internal market and strained relations with neighbouring countries, which could be natural trading partners in a normal situation. Currently, the Israeli internal market creates over eight million consumers. This is definitely not enough to maintain, for example, the profitability of the new technology industry. The development and implementation of inventions for production involves great costs that can be paid back only if they find the largest possible market (preferably with hundreds of millions of consumers). For this reason, the Israeli economy quickly orientated itself to exports to more distant countries. Activity on foreign markets requires great flexibility and competitiveness, but in the long run it brings significant benefits. Today, it is difficult to find a larger Israeli industry or company that would not be active on international markets. Therefore, it is not surprising that Marcel Goldman has also been engaged in such activities.

In the early 1980s, the authorities of the First International Bank of Israel decided to open representative offices abroad, thus establishing the FIBI London (1981) and the FIBI Zurich (1984). The London branch specialized in commercial banking for entrepreneurs, the Bank in Zurich focused on private

---

205 Correspondence with Marcel Goldman, March 24, 2018.

banking. In 1986, Shalom Singer became the CEO of the First International Bank of Israel (he held that position until 1990). It was an awkward situation for everyone, because in the 1970s Singer was taken as a young and ambitious employee by . . . Goldman. The natural order of things indicated that the CEO position should have been taken by Marcel or the other deputy director. It did not happen, however, because Zadik Bino, who became the president of the supervisory board (1986–1987), preferred to introduce someone from the outside of the top management of the Bank, who would owe him such a big promotion. Singer quickly climbed up and became the head of the department in one of the branches in Krayot (suburbs of Haifa), and then the head of the entire branch. After Marcel assumed the position of deputy CEO and settled in Tel Aviv, Singer also moved to that city and became the head of the central district.[206] Our protagonist accepted that situation and even expressed his positive opinion on Singer's candidacy, however, he noted that he wanted to work independently, without dependence on his immediate superior. In addition, Marcel developed an international career: in 1981 he was appointed a member of the supervisory board and a member of the Credit Committee of the FIBI London, whose president was the local owner of a shoe factory, not a banker. In the bank's London structures he was responsible for granting loans, in the course of which gained even more international experience and new contacts. He lived permanently in Tel Aviv, and flew to London every three months on average. His on-site duties took several days, he usually booked a room at the same hotel, with good location and proven quality of service.[207]

In 1987, Marcel was offered the director's position at FIBI Zurich. From the beginning, this branch brought losses of around two million francs a year. In the opinion of the management in Tel Aviv, its CEO, a Swiss, did not show particular commitment to work, while the deputy, an Israeli, was not a good fit for that position and sent repeated letters to Tel Aviv in which he insisted that the bank had to be closed. After two years of losses, the management in Tel Aviv decided to liquidate the branch. This task was entrusted to Marcel, who at the headed the administration department of the bank. The owners asked Marcel to ensure an uneventful closing of the Swiss branch. Preparations for the closure of the FIBI Zurich started immediately, although they met with severe criticism of the Banking Commission in Bern, which, as Marcel notes, "was right to state

---

206 Correspondence with Marcel Goldman, July 26, 2018.
207 Interview with Marcel Goldman carried out on December 27, 2016.

that it was not responsible to open the bank in 1984 and close it in 1986."[208] At the end of 1986, the direction of activities carried out in Switzerland changed rapidly. Marcel recalls:

> The First International Bank of Israel was actually bought by the Safra brothers. One day, in the morning, I got a call from Edmund Safra from Geneva, whom I didn't know personally at that time. He asked for my immediate arrival in Geneva, and of course I agreed. I informed Zadik about it and was on the plane the next day. During the meeting, I reported on the bank's closure in Zurich, convinced that this was the reason for the meeting. Safra listened calmly until I finished talking. His reaction was: "We're not closing, you'll be the general manager from the beginning of 1987." I was dumbstruck. Mr. Safra, there is nothing to manage. We gave notice to the employees (at that time there were 10,000 vacancies in banks in Zurich), we informed clients, even the building owner was informed that we were leaving the office and ending the rent . . . In response, Safra said: "I rely on you, you have thirty years of banking practice behind you, you will manage . . ." Already at the door, I heard Safra's words: "And decide what your salary will be!!!"[209]

Marcel decided on the salary after conversations with the directors of Leumi, Haapali, and Mizrachi, banks with Israeli roots operating in Zurich, whom he knew personally. He determined the amount of their monthly salary and on that basis calculated his own salary approved by Edmund Safra.[210] His work in Zurich was to last a maximum of three years, but he stayed there for ten years (the Safra brothers convinced him personally to extend his stay). During the first few months he managed to take control of personnel and organizational matters. He stopped the outflow of employees, rebuilt the structure of the bank, and, above all, thoroughly familiarized himself with the state of its finances and began the process of healing it. The contacts he made in London, one of the most important financial centers in the world, were very helpful, because there he met, among others, clients who held accounts not only at the FIBI London, but also at various Swiss banks. It often happened that people taking a business loan in London kept their private savings in Switzerland. He held talks to convince them to transfer money from other Swiss banks to accounts and deposits at the

---

208 Correspondence with Marcel Goldman, February 8, 2019.
209 Ibid.
210 Ibid.

FIBI Zurich. Those negotiations were not easy, but Marcel's advantage was the trust he had gained from his interlocutors during their cooperation in London. He managed to convince some of them. With time, as the bank's development became visible, it began to attract completely new customers. In addition, under the leadership of Marcel, the FIBI Zurich became responsible for the economic exchange between the United States and Western Europe and the so-called Eastern Bloc, limiting itself to transactions from the civil sector (mainly related to food products, clothes, and cosmetics). Many other banks refused to do it for a variety of reasons, but those transactions proved to be a very profitable segment of the FIBI bank's operations. In the first year of Marcel's work, the FIBI Zurich began to cover its expenses itself, and in the second year it brought income. Over time, the annual profits of the bank reached twelve percent of capital clear.[211]

After ten years of managing the bank in Zurich, Marcel decided to invest part of the accumulated profits in its own headquaters. It was a good investment because it was expected that real estate prices in Zurich would rise, which actually happened. Thanks to that solution, the bank also made large savings, as it did not have to pay high rent.

The first headquarters of the FIBI Zurich was at Bahnhofstrasse, the second at Bleicherweg. Now, Marcel was looking for a building of a convenient size, its location was less important because the local Swiss were not the bank's customers. In addition, the bank was not looking to attract the so-called street customers, who could fall in love with a logo or an attractive website. Nevertheless, the building at 61 Seestrasse, which Marcel found, had a convenient location, close to the city center. However, it required renovation at the time of purchase. A century-old object, it was included in the register of architectural monuments, so construction works were carried out under the conservator's supervision. The bank had no problems with that; on the contrary, the local residents were thankful for restoring the splendour of the historic building and its surroundings. Marcel received telephone calls and letters with these sentiments, which were sent to the bank's address or to the architectural bureau that worked on the project.[212]

Marcel worked in a select company at the FIBI Zurich. The Swiss law required that the majority of the supervisory board of the bank acting under Swiss

---

211 Interview with Marcel Goldman carried out on December 28, 2018.
212 Family collections of Marcel and Bianka Goldman (Tel Aviv): collections, documents and correspondence; Correspondence with Marcel Goldman, July 26, 2018.

Fig. 125. The building at Seestrasse in Zurich purchased by the FIBI, view from the beginning of the twentieth century, a horse tram in the lower left-hand corner, family collections of Marcel and Bianka Goldman (Tel Aviv)

Fig. 126. The building at Seestrasse in Zurich purchased by the FIBI, view (most likely) from 1997, after restoration and adjustment to the needs of the bank, family collections of Marcel and Bianka Goldman (Tel Aviv)

jurisdiction be Swiss. The first composition of the FIBI supervisory board consisted of two Israelis and four Swiss, its president was Peter von Muralt, a widely known and respected Swiss baron.[213] A very important place was occupied by a doctor of law, Jagmetti, who was a member of the supervisory board and legal adviser of the Bank. He had Italian roots associated with the famous Jacometti family in Italy. In addition, he held the rank of an artillery captain, which was highly valued in Switzerland. The management board also included the CEO of the FIBI Bank in Tel Aviv and the director of the FIBI London. Similarly, Marcel belonged to the management board of the FIBI London.[214] While working in Zurich, Goldman was in touch with his previous boss, Shalom Singer, who was also a member of the FIBI Zurich supervisory board on behalf of the FIBI headquarters in Zurich. However, Marcel was not dependent on him in any way. The gentlemen met so often that they managed to build close and friendly relations. Shalom Singer today believes that "his relationship with Marcel Goldman, both professional and private, was based on the respect and esteem he had for him."[215]

Marcel was alone in Zurich for the first six months. In June 1987, Bianka joined him. Their stay in Switzerland was an excellent opportunity to observe a society with a different mentality than that of Poland or Israel. For example, they made note of Switzerland's principled attachment to the broadly understood order, both in terms of cleanliness, and in terms of acting in compliance with generally applicable rules and regulations in that country. In his book *A w nocy przychodzą myśli* Marcel recalls:

> ... in a large car park of the Migros company (a state within a state in Switzerland). A long queue before the entrance. Everyone is standing motionless. The disciplined Swiss are standing still, they aren't hooting. They know: if it isn't moving, there is a reason for this. But I am an Israeli, so I get out of the car, go to the head of the column. There is a desperate Swiss standing. His car door is open, he is holding a receipt in his hand, which should be inserted into the hole in the gate. "What's happening?" "The receipt does not enter, the ramp is broken!" "Sir, the ramp is open, go on!"—I shout.—"But what will I do with the receipt?!"[216]

---

213 His family was knighted by the German Emperor Frederick Barbarossa (c. 1122–1190) for the bravery of his ancestor during the battle of Muralto (hence the surname).
214 Interview with Marcel Goldman carried out on December 28, 2018.
215 Correspondence of Shalom Singer, November 16, 2017.
216 Goldman, *A w nocy przychodzą myśli*, 11.

In Swiss cities, they noticed the inhabitants' unimaginable concern for keeping the quiet, even in the early evening. For example, if the waste sorting buckets were close to the houses, there was often a plate with information that bottles, glass, and metal, which are known to make noise, can only be thrown away until a certain time (for example, until 6pm), so as not to interrupt the peace of the inhabitants. In one of the villages, every evening, even the course of a mountain river was changed so that its noise did not disturb anyone. For that purpose, a capacity regulator was installed on a nearby dam. During the day, the river was directed to its regular channel that led through the city, but in the evening a lever was twisted and the river flowed into a special canal around the city.

Living in Switzerland, Marcel and Bianka travelled a lot around Europe. They visited Italy, Austria, the Czech Republic, and other countries. In Switzerland, their lives were facilitated by their good command of German, according to Marcel: "In the German-speaking part of Switzerland (about sixty percent of the population), if you know German, the Swiss consider you their own. You can even speak with an accent, then they will think that you are from some German land. They regard the Germans as their own anyway."[217]

Working in London and Zurich, Marcel made not only professional contacts, but also many new friendships, which, as a norm in his case, proved to be cordial and long-standing. In the supervisory board of the FIBI London he worked, for instance, with Hersch Rieck, with whom he quickly found the so-called common language and interests. They were friends for many years. When Rieck became seriously ill, he instructed his daughter to transfer all her banking matters with which he had dealt so far under the care of Marcel Goldman. Marcel not only agreed to run her finances, but also, with Bianka, established friendly relations with her, which, despite the significant age difference (Rieck's daughter is younger than Marcel by over thirty years), have continued to this day. An intense friendship united Marcel with Peter von Muralt, who personally organized a farewell party when Marcel finished his work in Zurich. Peter von Muralt said then that "with the departure of Marcel Goldman, Swiss banking is losing a lot." After he learned about the preparation of Marcel's biography, he sent the following letter:

> I got to know Marcel when I was asked to join the board of the newly founded Swiss subsidiary of First International Bank of Israel in Zurich, Switzerland. He was new in Zurich but being "a man of the world" he

---

217 Interview with Marcel Goldman carried out on June 13, 2018.

found his way here very quickly and also made friends in no time. I guess that his passion for bridge made it easy for him to introduce himself in bridge circles.

I got to know Marcel—at that time Mr. Goldman according to Swiss formal rules—as a person of great integrity. He used his business sense extensively but wisely, never went for a quick deal but always used his vast know-how with caution. I specifically appreciated the fact that there was never cause to doubt his presentation of a transaction to be discussed. He was absolutely reliable with the facts presented, never omitted anything which might have had some importance in making a decision.

He managed the bank carefully and was able to purchase the bank-building and organise its premises in a stately but affordable way, no bling bling but solid presentation. He also had a good hand in hiring good staff and managed it in a friendly but effective way.

Over the years we became good friends, Mr. Goldman was now Marcel to me and we saw each other also outside the business hours. It was then that I got to know his sense of humour which made spending time together with him always a pleasure ... When he returned to Israel it was a loss for our finance community and my wife and I are happy that we never lost contact with Marcel and Bianka. It is not long ago that we met again during their stay in Interlaken.

I also like to mention that his comments about his country, as well as his introductions to the Jewish habits with which I was not very familiar, have widened my horizon and my understanding of Israel and its people.

Marcel Goldman [is] a gentleman for whom I have the highest regards and respect as a personality as well as a businessman.[218]

In 1997, Marcel retired, but for several years he sat as a director on supervisory boards of the FIBI London and the FIBI Zurich. Previously, he had not belonged to the supervisory board of the FIBI Zurich, because the local law did not allow him to sit on the bank's executive and supervisory boards at the same time. After leaving the chair of the director of this institution, Marcel could get an engagement in its supervisory board. In 1998, he became a member of the supervisory board of Bank Pekao S.A. in Tel Aviv, for which he received a special permission of the Bank of Israel to confirm that his work on the supervisory boards in London and Zurich did not interfere with sitting on the supervisory board of Bank Pekao S.A.[219] As he recalls: "Together with Bianka, we had a very nice period of approximately five years of frequent visits, four times a year,

---

218 Correspondence of Peter von Muralt, July 2018.
219 Correspondence with Marcel Goldman, July 26, 2018.

Fig. 127. During the Polish President Aleksander Kwasniewski's visit to Israel in 1999, a meeting with the management and supervisory board of Bank Pekao S.A. at the headquarters at Allenby Street in Tel Aviv, family collections of Marcel and Bianka Goldman (Tel Aviv). In the foreground, Aleksander Kwaśniewski and Marcel Goldman

to Poland. Namely, quarterly meetings of the supervisory board took place in Warsaw."[220] Work for Bank Pekao S.A., however, meant not only regular trips to Poland. The Bank's management board expected Marcel to use his knowledge of economy and extensive international experience to organize its finances and focus it on development. He also had a lot of diplomatic responsibilities. The Polish authorities treated this bank as an extension of the embassy, so it was often visited by diplomats and politicians from Poland (see Fig. 127). They looked for contacts and ways of understanding with Israeli entrepreneurs there.

In 2003, Bank Pekao S.A. in Tel Aviv was sold by Italian owners to one of the Israeli banks, which ended its seventy-year long (it was opened on May 15, 1933) history in Tel Aviv. It is worth noting that the First International Bank of Israel, which Marcel helped manage for forty years, since its creation, is in very good economic condition today. It is among the five largest banks in Israel, and

---

220 Goldman, *A w nocy przychodzą myśli*, 11.

its headquarters is located in the imposing, more than 130-meter-tall International Tower at Rothschild Boulevard in Tel Aviv.

The indisputable successes of the State of Israel, built practically from scratch, has been discussed quite thoroughly, but its unsolved problems should also be mentioned. First of all, it is necessary to point out the gap between Orthodox and Ultra-Orthodox Jews and the secularized part of society. The founding fathers of the Israeli state made some concessions to religious circles in the name of national consensus. At the dawn of Israel's independence, the numbers of Orthodox and Ultra-Orthodox Jews were estimated at around 30,000 to 40,000, but today this community has over a million people and shows high growth dynamics. Demography played a key role here: in the average Ultra-Orthodox family there are seven children, in others—two or three.[221] Already today, a real problem for the state is the fact that *charedim*[222] do not function fully in its bloodstream. The clusters they create are often enclaves of poverty, avoiding modern technologies and contacts with other social groups. Inhabited by Orthodox Jews, the city of Bnei Brak is one of the poorest in Israel. As the Polish *Gazeta Wyborcza* from Jerusalem, April 3, 2018, shows, every second Ultra-Orthodox man and thirty-six percent of Ultra-Orthodox women do not work. To integrate them in the Israeli society, practical and educational projects are launched, for instance, by Kivun (Hebrew: direction), a vocational training center in Jerusalem.

Its representative, Itzik Colbi, cited by *Gazeta Wyborcza*, notes that: "*Charedim* spend time in the yeshivot. They don't know English, they don't know mathematics. Even if they want to work, they have no qualifications. Besides, many of them have no idea what work is all about."[223] Thanks to institutions such as Kivun, *charedim* can receive secular education, learn teamwork and basic computer literacy, and then receive help finding a job. Kivun alone works with 573 companies and over the past five years has helped 7,000 people find jobs.[224] Manufactures established by the Orthodox are noteworthy. Some of them specialize in jewelry and tailoring and create exclusive products, largely intended for export, for example, to the United States.

---

221 B.T. Wieliński, "Izrael oswaja ortodoksów z kapitalizmem," *Gazeta Wyborcza*, April 3, 8.
222 *Charedim*, a Hebrew term for Orthodox Jews.
223 Wieliński, "Izrael oswaja ortodoksów z kapitalizmem."
224 Ibid.

Fig. 128. Current headquarters of The First International Bank of Israel in Tel Aviv, March 31, 2009, photo: Gellerj, public domain

Some *charedim* show an appalling lack of loyalty to the state. For example, representatives of Neturei Karta have visited Iran, a state hostile to Israel, to meet with its leaders. A systemic solution for their evasion of military service has not been implemented yet. The TZAHAL command has long established a compromise with the more conciliatory Orthodox—solutions have been introduced to adapt the rhythm of their functioning in the army to the calendar of holidays and religious duties. Special battalions and platoons were created for them. For the time being, a large proportion of the Ultra-Orthodox are rejecting all proposals because they question not so much the army itself or the specific rules associated with it, but the legitimacy of the existence of the Jewish state as such, which they call the product of the Zionist movement. For them, a consensus from the times of Ben-Gurion, according to which Ultra-Orthodox studies at religious universities are considered as alternative to enlisting in the army, is convenient. Currently, tens of thousands of people use this solution. This has a depressing effect on those who, despite various objections, join the army. Moreover, if this community continues to grow, the lack of its representatives in the ranks of the army will become increasingly problematic for subsequent governments. And above all, in 2017, the Supreme Court of Israel recognised the dismissal of the Ultra-Orthodox from military service as contrary to Israeli legislation and ordered the authorities to pass a law that would regulate the matter. It was the basis for the self-dissolution of the coalition led by Prime Minister Netanyahu on December 24, 2018 and the announcement of new elections for April 2019.

Felicia Schwartz and Dov Lieber from the *Wall Street Journal* see the symptoms of changes taking place within the Ultra-Orthodox community itself. This community has grown considerably, and different views and positions have emerged within it. In fact, these changes began much earlier. Artur Skorek notes that the complicity of the Agudat Yisrael party in the 1970s and 1980s allowed a stream of money to be directed to the *charedim* community. It accelerated the growth of this community, which began to build its settlements in new cities throughout the country. As a result, whether they wanted to or not, the *charedim* were exposed to constant contact with secular Jews. In addition, the dispersion of the *charedim* also weakened their own social control mechanisms.[225] In the opinion of Artur Skorek: "Since the mid-1990s, rabbis have been increasingly favouring the vocational training of community members. A breakthrough was the establishment of a technical university for *charedim* in 1996."[226]

Schwartz and Lieber point out that: "In the years 2009–2017, the number of Ultra-Orthodox Jews in the army more than doubled and amounted to 3.7 thousand. However, this is still only a fraction of nearly 60 thousand young men who qualify for military service as members of the community of about one million people." Because a large proportion of the Ultra-Orthodox are still poor, military service is, for them, a chance for a career and social advancement. They hope that after the army they will find a well-paid job, for example in the technology industry.[227] Not only economic factors but also their Zionisation may bring about a further increase in the percentage of *charedim* in the ranks of the army. This is illustrated by their involvement in the development of Jewish settlements in the West Bank, which has ideological as well as financial reasons. The rapprochement of conservative Zionist Jews and ultra-religious Jews gave rise to the ideology of *chardalim*—nationalist *charedim*.[228]

One must note a certain regularity regarding the deep division into secular and religious Jews in Israel. Namely, despite the disturbing increase in the importance of religious and ultra-religious circles, it was their own statehood that elevated the importance of secular attributes on a scale unknown in the diaspora era. At the time when Jews were deprived of their own state, religion was a factor that conditioned their identity and prevented them from melting into the sea

---

225 A. Skorek, *Żydowskie ugrupowania religijne w Państwie Izrael. Polityczna rola ortodoksyjnego judaizmu*, Krakow 2015, 208.

226 Ibid., 209.

227 F. Schwartz, D. Lieber, "Ultraorodoksyjni Żydzi idą do armii, rząd upada," *Gazeta Wyborcza*, January 12–13, 2019, supplement: *Wall Street Journal* 2 (2019): 5. At the beginning of 2019, the *charedim* population was estimated, according to the local Central Statistical Office, at twelve percent of Israeli society, by 2065 they will account for one third of the total population of the state. See Skorek, *Żydowskie ugrupowania religijne*, 209.

228 Skorek, *Żydowskie ugrupowania religijne*, 212.

of other nationalities. Today, the State of Israel, with its own legal, political, and defense system, guarantees the separateness, integrity, and security of the Jewish people.

Unfortunately, the skill developed by Israelis to take advantage of the effects of war and terrorism also has unambiguously negative consequences. Mental pressure is stimulating and motivating, but if it lasts constantly, it eventually has to bring unpleasant results. In Israel, compared to world standards, there is an increase in sales of antidepressants and other pharmacological agents to help deal with psychological ailments. Trauma, a sense of alienation, physical and mental convalescence after terrorist attacks, mourning after losing loved ones and fear of such an eventuality have become a permanent element of Israeli everyday life, so strong that it is inscribed in high and mass culture.

The tourism sector is very important for Israel, including what we call "Heritage Tours." Statistics on the tourist traffic in Israel reveal that in general terms it is doing quite well.[229] The data, however, show a holistic picture that does not reflect the scale of problems and challenges associated with the turmoil accompanying Palestinian wars and uprisings. They are particularly severe for small hotels, which, unlike their network competitors, are much worse at dealing with suddenly cancelled reservations.

The emigration of Jews from Israel, which has been recorded for years, has not yet reached an alarmist level, but it is difficult to hide that this problem exists. It is not known in what direction it will evolve. To make matters worse, from the point of view of Israel's interest, the structure of the emigration movement is extremely unfavorable. This phenomenon occurs all over the world, but usually demographic surpluses, less educated or unemployed people, are pushed out of their homeland. In Israel, the opposite is the case—the most educated and most mobile inhabitants emigrate. It is not about people who are content with any occupation, but about competent, open, and creative people who want

---

229 In 1969, Israel was visited by 410,000 tourists. In 2017, there were already 3,600,000, which was the largest number in history (an increase of twenty-five percent compared to the previous year). According to the data of the Israeli Ministry of Tourism, tourists spent twenty billion shekels in this country in 2017, and 200,000 Israelis worked in the tourism industry. The five main countries from which tourists came were the United States, Russia, France, Germany, and the United Kingdom. Fifty-four percent of these tourists were Christians and only about twenty-five percent were Jews. Others belonged to other denominations or were not affiliated. "More Tourists Visit Israel in 2017 than Ever Before," https://www.jpost.com/Israel-News/More-tourists-visit-Israel-in-2017-than-ever-before-522665, accessed December 23, 2018; *Who's Who in Israel*, 317.

to find better (maybe safer?) living conditions. Ironically, the development of antisemitism in highly developed countries can help to stop this emigration. Today (often due to immigrants from African and Middle East countries) it is also spreading to countries that seemed to have learned that lesson long ago. Suffice it to mention the sudden increase in the emigration of Jews from France to Israel, which was most likely caused by the apparent intensity of aggression directed against Jews and their institutions. Although in France there was an increase in the activity of far-right organisations, the overwhelming majority of attacks and crimes against Jews were carried out by persons of the Arab origin.[230] Jews living in other Western countries react much more moderately. For example, in 2015, 774 British Jews and only 150 German Jews decided on an *aliyah*, which does not mean that the scale of antisemitic attacks is smaller in these countries.[231]

At the time of writing this book, the immediate family of Marcel and Bianka, living in Israel, looks at the situation of Jews in Europe from a distance. Until the turn of the 1980s and 1990s, they were not too much interested in the situation in Poland. Thanks to democratic changes, round table deliberations, and the fall of communism, the world heard about Poland again, and the news also reached the Goldmans. In Israel, there was a certain stir, because during the times of communism, the iron curtain separated the Polish Jews living in Israel from their former homeland. Even emigrants from Poland living in the United States already for some time could feel the positive effects of the crumbling communist system in Poland and its gradual opening up to the world. In the case of Poland and Israel, the diplomatic relations were broken in 1967, and Polish Jews living in Israel felt deeply affected. Many left friends, acquaintances, and sometimes relatives in Poland, but because of the decision of the communist authorities they could not freely maintain contact with them. They were denied the right to travel to Poland. Marcel remembers that his brother-in-law, who wanted to visit his seriously ill brother, could not get a visa. He submitted his application through the Dutch embassy, which represented Poland in Israel

---

230 From the beginning of the 1970s to the year 2012, the emigration of Jews from France to Israel maintained more or less constant dynamics (one or two thousand people a year). In subsequent years, there was a rapid acceleration: in 2013, nearly 3,300 people decided to take such a step, in 2014 over 7,200, in 2015 almost 8,000. "Francuscy Żydzi masowo emigrują do Izraela. Uciekają przed islamistami," http://forsal.pl/artykuly/920720,francuscy-zydzi-uciekaja-przed-islamistami-do-izraela.html, accessed April 2, 2018.

231 In 2014, there were 1596 of them in Germany, which is the largest number in the European Union. The same year in Great Britain there were 1168 (which was the worst result in the history of this country!). Ibid.

under a special agreement. He got an answer that, if his brother died, he would get a visa for the funeral.[232]

Polish Jews once again felt repelled by their former homeland. The fact that Poland was in political and military dependence on the Soviet Union was of little importance in that context. Their hearts were deeply wounded. The resumption of diplomatic relations between Poland and Israel turned out to be easier than healing this wound. In 1986, the Representation of Israeli Interests was opened in Warsaw, Poland set up a similar branch in Tel Aviv. On February 13, 1990, the Israel-Poland Chamber of Commerce was registered in Israel, which opened its office in Tel Aviv on 66 Rothschild Boulevard. The protocol on the resumption of diplomatic relations between the Republic of Poland and the State of Israel was signed on February 27, 1990.

Marcel admits that the new information about Poland gave him an impulse to think:

> During the first forty years of my life in Israel, from 1949 to 1989, although I stayed here in a Polish community, I was so busy with myself, my family, and career, building the foundations of our existence, that I had no time to ponder on Poland and what connected me with it. At the very beginning I was only in correspondence with the girl I left in Poland. Before I emigrated, I managed to fall in love with her, but, as it happens with young people, it passes. Let me explain this situation with a little "spicy" joke: "During World War II, American soldiers stationing in Italy wrote to homes in the United States that Italian women were very beautiful. American women who felt aggrieved asked in their letters: what do Italians have that we don't have? The soldiers answered them: they have it here." For young people, direct contact is crucial. That is why my exchange of correspondence with the girl in Poland ceased after some time.[233]

Until 1989, Polish Jews in Israel cherished the image of Poland preserved like an insect in an amber. They remembered it as it had been years ago. Those who left as children or adolescents often kept it in their minds like a dreamlike fairytale land. Adult immigrants saw a more complex picture of the country on the Vistula. Some of them have not yet healed the wounds caused by unpleasant relationships with Polish neighbours. The year 1989 brought a new opening.

---

232 Interview with Marcel Goldman carried out on December 21, 2016.
233 Ibid.

Marcel and Bianka observed everything that happened then from Switzerland, where they had been living for two years:

> One day I received a call from Tel Aviv with information that a bankers' meeting is being prepared in Warsaw in connection with the jubilee of Bank Pekao and Israeli bankers are invited to this meeting. Because in Tel Aviv they knew that I came from Poland and I knew Polish, I was offered to go straight from Zurich and join the Israeli delegation, which will soon reach Warsaw. I accepted this offer right away, and said that I would come with my wife. In this way, it can be said that suddenly I found myself in Poland after forty years of separation.[234]

In Warsaw, each guest was assigned a guardian, who was someone from the management of Bank Pekao S.A.:

> I found myself paired with Mr. Cieśla. First, he was very surprised by how beautiful my Polish was, because I spoke without accent. Mr. Cieśla also took care of us on Sunday. We ate dinner at his house. Later, I asked him to take us to Żelazowa Wola for Chopin concerts. On the way back, after a day spent together, he turned to me and said: "Mr. Goldman, you are panting with Polishness." I thought about it for a long time and came to the conclusion that it was so, indeed . . . Despite forty years of separation and thousands of kilometers of distance, I retained Polish roots.[235]

Under the influence of the emotions accompanying his travel to Poland, Marcel announced to his wife that next year they would go to Poland privately. While in Poland in 1990, he decided to bring together his friends from school and academic benches. However, he mainly reached his colleagues from high school, because, as he admits, he attended classes at the Krakow School of Economics (today's Krakow University of Economics) rarely, too busy earning his living. From the group of students he managed to meet only a few people who helped him get stamps for a given subject in his student's book. The party he organized in the restaurant of the Cracovia Hotel became an opportunity for discussion and memories. After that meeting, Marcel's interest in Poland was revived and he decided to look for traces of his own past there. Later, he met with friends from school and university benches several more times.[236]

---

234 Ibid.
235 Ibid.
236 Ibid.

In 1997, the Goldmans returned from Switzerland to Israel. In social terms, they had to rearrange their lives:

> The move from Haifa to Tel Aviv already resulted in major changes in our social situation. The friends from our youth stayed in Haifa, in Tel Aviv we began to make new contacts, but they were also interrupted for a long time as a result of our stay in Switzerland. When we returned to Tel Aviv in 1997, I was seventy-one and Bianka was sixty-seven years old. At this age, it is difficult to form new friendships. Biology brutally impacted these matters: most of my peers are simply dead. For example, I will tell you about a situation that I once found myself in. One of my friends, with whom I worked at the bank, much younger than us (she emigrated from Poland to Israel as part of the March '68 Aliyah), invited me to a party with our mutual friends. As it turned out, I was the only man there. In addition to me, there were six women, each of whom was a widow. In this situation, Bianka and I had to look for new friends in Tel Aviv, but our time now is filled mainly with contacts with family, in addition, we continue to travel actively. We play bridge quite often, it is not uncommon for us to go to international competitions to various countries of the world; recently we have been to Montenegro and Austria. In our immediate vicinity there is a sports and recreation center and a swimming pool, which we use on average a few times a week. We try to go to the cinema at least once a week. We read a lot of books in several languages. I also took over my wife's musical interests. I admit that, when I met Bianka, I knew that she and her parents attended classical music concerts. Before World War II, Bianka's father was a lawyer, and her mother was a housewife. Going out to concerts was their favorite form of joint entertainment, which they continued while living in Israel. I didn't like it because I was raised listening to popular music. With my dad, I attended the Krakow operetta, but not for classical music concerts. Beautiful but popular songs were played in the operetta. One time I found out that a boy, a friend of Bianka, who was interested in music, went to the concert with them for a few times in a row. I took it as a form of competition and a threat. I told Bianka that it couldn't go on and I started going to concerts with her. The first and second time—jokingly—I suffered a little. Later I found myself in these musical environment. To this day, when driving a car, I always turn on classical music. For several decades, we have been purchasing an annual subscription for concerts of the Israel Philharmonic Orchestra, which is one of the best in the world. We value the artistry of Zubin Mehta [born on April 29, 1936 in Mumbai—Ł.T.S.], a world-famous conductor, who is the music director of this institution.[237]

---

237 Conversations with Marcel Goldman carried out on December 21, 2016 and May 26, 2019.

Fig. 129. Marcel Goldman accompanied by his wife Bianka and (most likely) Mr. Cieśla from Bank Pekao S.A. during a flight from Warsaw to Krakow on a plane chartered by Bank Pekao S.A., 1989, family collections of Marcel and Bianka Goldman (Tel Aviv)

Fig. 130. One of Marcel's (under the window on the right) meetings with friends from high school and university, Krakow, June 1995, family collections of Marcel and Bianka Goldman (Tel Aviv)

In Tel Aviv, Marcel learned about the establishment of the Polish-Israeli Friendship Society. He joined it and became a member of its board. Through this organization, he gained many contacts in Poland. In 2000, the publishing house Arcana published his autobiographical book *Iskierki życia* (English: Sparks of life), which caused a wide response and became a bestseller. The publication was accompanied by promotional activities in various Polish cities. A meeting was held in Krakow at the Palace of Fine Arts. In Ustroń, the Protestant community arranged for Marcel to speak at the local cinema. People of all ages came to hear him, in particular, students from the last form of the local high school who had read the book and asked a lot of important questions. That gave Marcel the impetus to participate in subsequent meetings with school and college students. He was also urged to do so by Mrs. Emilia Goryczka, then head of the Protestant community in Ustroń. She organized a series of meetings between Marcel and high school youth from Silesia. To this time, Marcel has held several dozen of such meetings throughout Poland. In 2015, he gave a special lecture for students of history at the Pedagogical University in Krakow and participated in a debate with them.

It took Marcel three years to prepare *Iskierki życia*. He wrote the book mainly at night, just as the majority of his other texts. The influx of thoughts was so great that he would wake up in the middle of the night to write down his memories. In consequence, one of the volumes of his works was entitled *A w nocy przychodzą myśli* (English: And thoughts come at night, Krakow 2012).

Starting with the turn of the 1990s and the first decade of the twenty-first century, Marcel and Bianka have often come to Poland. They travel in their relatives' footsteps (hence their frequent visits to Krakow, Bielsko-Biała, and the Żywiec region) and visit friends and acquaintances. They participated many times in the Krakow Marches of the Living, which are organized annually to commemorate the liquidation of the ghetto in Podgórze. Their route reflects the path which, on March 13 and 14, 1943, was taken by Jews imprisoned in the ghetto, leading from today's Bohaterów Getta Square (then Zgody Square), via Lwowska Street, then along Wielicka and Jerozolimska Streets to the area of the former Płaszów concentration camp.

On March 17, 2008, Marcel Goldman was the guest of honour during the thirty-seventh solemn session of the Krakow City Council, convened on the sixty-fifth anniversary of the liquidation of the Krakow ghetto. There were also Lili Pohlmann from London, Edward Mosberg from New York, Bronisława Horowitz-Karakulska from Krakow, Aleksander Allerhand from Haifa, Yossef Levy, vice ambassador and political adviser at the Israeli embassy Bishop Albin

Małysiak (holder of the Righteous Among the Nations Medal), Prof. Aleksander Skotnicki, the president of Professor Julian Aleksandrowicz's Foundation, Prof. Jacek Majchrowski, the mayor of the city of Krakow, Andrzej Sztorc, chairman of the Lesser Poland regional council, and Cardinal Franciszek Macharski. Marcel Goldman told the story of his escape with his family from the Krakow ghetto and the first days spent on Aryan papers in Radom.[238] In the following years, Marcel and Bianka travelled to Poland with their daughter Orit, as well as their son-in-law and grandchildren. They were also joined by friends, acquaintances, and neighbours from Tel Aviv, whom Marcel encouraged to come to Poland.[239]

By acting as a banker and economic advisor, Marcel Goldman contributed to the development of economic ties between Poland and Israel. He points out that Israelis are currently the most active investors in Poland. He distinguishes three main areas in which the largest inflow of Israeli capital to Poland is noted. The first of them is the construction sector—in almost every large Polish city there are shopping centers and residential buildings built by Israelis. The second field is the industry, especially food and pharmaceutical. Cinemas, often located in shopping malls, rank third. The full scale of previous and current investments is difficult to estimate, as many Israeli companies operate through funds already established in third countries. Cooperation in the field of security and defense is also developing successfully, accompanied by the export of Israeli armaments to Poland. Currently, Poland and Israel are not the most important trade partners for each other, but there is a clear upward trend.[240] In 2017, imports of goods

---

238 The transcript of the thirty-seventh solemn session of the Krakow City Council, March 17, 2008.

239 Marcel Goldman initiates discussions about Poland and provides various materials (such as information folders) about the country in many places, including the district club of Ramat Aviv.

240 According to data from the israel.trade.gov.pl portal, which refers to the calculations of the Israeli Central Statistical Office: "the main goods exported from Poland to Israel in 2015 were: food preserves, beverages, tobacco (USD 67.7 million), machines and mechanical devices (USD 55.9 million), live animals; animal products ($ 33.8 million), chemical industry products (USD 30.7 million), vehicles, aircraft, and accessories (USD 16.5 million) and base metals; metal products (USD 10.6 million). It should be taken into account that these are data by country of purchase, not by country of manufacture, and actual deliveries of Polish products to Israel are higher. According to CSO data, the total value of Israeli imports from Poland in 2015 was USD 269 million (an increase of USD 24.4 million compared to 2014)." On the other hand, in the same year, that is, in 2015, Polish imports from Israel were mainly composed of: "products of the chemical and related industries (USD 75.4 million), machines, electrical equipment and parts (USD 47 million), plastics, rubber and products (USD 20.9 million), base metals and products (USD 19.6 million), mineral products (USD

Fig. 131. Marcel Goldman with his daughter Orit during a trip to Zakopane, exact date unknown, most likely the end of the 1990s or the beginning of the twenty-first century, family collections of Marcel and Bianka Goldman (Tel Aviv)

to Israel totalled EUR 61.7 billion, including from Poland EUR 518.6 million (0.8%). In industry analyses it is possible to trace the trade exchange between Israel and other countries[241] and what products it covers.[242]

18.7 million), optical devices, photographic, measuring, control, and medical instruments (USD 17.4 million), textiles and textile products (USD 13.5 million). According to CSO data, the total value of Israeli exports to Poland in 2015 was USD 231.2 million (a decrease of USD 14.7 million compared to 2014)." "Co kupić, a co sprzedać," https://israel.trade.gov.pl/pl/izrael/wymiana-handlowa/524,co-kupic-a-co-sprzedac.html, accessed March 29, 2019.

241 The largest exporters sending their goods to Israel include China (EUR 8.1 billion), the United States (EUR 7.3 billion), Germany (EUR 4.4 billion), Belgium (EUR 3 billion), Italy (EUR 2.9 billion), Turkey (EUR 2.6 billion), and Japan (EUR 2.1 billion). Total Israel exports in 2017 reached EUR 47.6 billion, including EUR 209.6 million (0.4%) to Poland. The largest recipients of Israeli exports were the United States (EUR 12.9 billion), the United Kingdom (EUR 4 billion), Hong Kong (EUR 2.8 billion), China (EUR 2.6 billion), Belgium (EUR 1.9 billion), and India (EUR 1.5 billion). Platforma wsparcia eksportu, https://wspieramyeksport.pl/znajdz-rynki-eksportowe/il/izrael, accessed March 29, 2019.

242 The groups of goods exported by Israel with the fastest growth are, among others: aluminum and aluminum products, chemical products, essential oils, perfumery, cosmetics and toiletries, plastics and their products, aircrafts, spacecrafts, and parts thereof. In imports to Israel, the highest growth dynamics was recorded for mineral fuels, mineral oils, bituminous

In Marcel Goldman's opinion, the prospects for economic cooperation between Poland and Israel are promising, which is positively influenced by private contacts between Poles and Israelis. According to him, entrepreneurs from both countries easily establish friendly relations because they have a similar mentality and approach to business. He also believes that, although due to the inexorable passage of time today there are fewer people directly originating from Poland in Israel, it turns out that the second or even the third generation has adopted the Polish mentality and some elements of Polish culture.[243]

It is also worth noting the friendship of Marcel Goldman and Professor Aleksander B. Skotnicki, an outstanding doctor, hematologist, transplantologist, and specialist in internal medicine.[244] The commemoration of the Jewish heritage in Poland and Polish-Jewish and Polish-Israeli dialogue became an important area of his activity. He made himself known to the general public as the "professor who builds bridges."[245] He wrote dozens of works about Polish Jews, and Krakow Jews in particular. In a series of publications and exhibitions, he commemorated Oskar Schindler and those who survived World War II thanks to him. On his initiative, the Stradom Center for Dialogue was created, of which he became the president. Marcel recalls:

> I learned that a very important person involved in the Polish-Jewish and Polish-Israeli dialogue is the well-known and respected Polish scientist Professor Aleksander B. Skotnicki. I wanted to meet him personally. The first meeting allowed me to conclude that he is a wonderful man, open and extremely creative. I had the opportunity to visit an exhibition at the High Synagogue in Krakow, which was organised by Professor Skotnicki. He gave it the title: "Two Faces of Krakow Jews." One of these faces was shaped by Orthodox Jews, the other by progressive and assimilated Jews. Soon Professor Skotnicki visited me in Israel.[246]

---

substances, fish, crustaceans, molluscs, cast iron and steel, furniture, bedding, mattresses, frames, and pillows (data for 2017 in comparison to 2016). *Raport Banku PKO BP*.

243 Interview with Marcel Goldman carried out on March 16, 2019.
244 Prof. Aleksander Skotnicki is a student and successor of Prof. Julian Aleksandrowicz, a respected physician and social worker. He was the chair of Hematology Department at the Collegium Medicum of the Jagiellonian University and was the head of the Hematology Clinic at the University Hospital in Krakow (1993–2018). Krakow owes to Prof. Skotnicki the creation of a modern center for the treatment of blood cancer and bone marrow transplantation.
245 K. Kachel, "Aleksander Skotnicki: Profesor, który buduje mosty," http://www.dziennikpolski24.pl/region/ wiadomosci-krakow/a/aleksander-skotnicki-profesor-ktory-buduje-mosty,11499731, accessed July 20, 2018.
246 Interview with Marcel Goldman carried out on December 21, 2016.

In the following years, Goldman and Skotnicki continued friendly meetings. Together, they also joined together numerous educational and cultural projects that propagated knowledge about the common past of Poles and Jews and facilitated the dialogue between the two nations. Marcel and Bianka received a special invitation to the celebrations related to Professor Skotnicki's seventieth birthday and his retirement, which took place in Krakow on June 28, 2018. The celebrations were organized at the Collegium Maius Hall of the Jagiellonian University, and the event was attended by the city mayor Prof. Jacek Majchrowski. Marcel Goldman was asked to speak, and he said the following words:

> Ladies and Gentlemen,
> I am honoured that a true friendship was established between us, my wife and me, and Professor Skotnicki, which has lasted nearly twenty years. Let me read a poem that I wrote to him, impressed by the exhibition "Two Faces of Krakow Jews." The exhibition took place at the High Synagogue and there, to my great surprise, I found a photo of my mother from 1938 with my sister and me in the Planty Park in Krakow.
> They are telling me that Prof. Skotnicki is retiring. What a nonsense. A man who used every spare moment for readings, travels, and activities among the Polish and Jewish communities. You will ask: why? Because Prof. Skotnicki took to heart, also because of the history of his family, what is written in the third book of the Old Testament, translated from Hebrew: "Ve-achavta reecha kamocha"—"Love your neighbour as yourself"!!! He has dedicated his time to it, his incredible talent, and intelligence, his extraordinary level of knowledge and memory, and sometimes a lot of money. He has fought the hatred of those who are different, the philistinism of antisemitism, everything that divides, not unites. He has tried to bring closer the hearts of two nations who lived next to each other, but not always together. People who survived the hell of concentration camps and lost their faith in the man asked: "'The man,' does it sound proud?" with a question mark. People like Professor Skotnicki gave the answer.
> "The man" sounds proud!!!
> Thank you.[247]

The poem mentioned above is entitled *Do profesora Skotnickiego* (English: To Professor Skotnicki) and it says a lot about its author and addressee both. Marcel expresses in it his respect and appreciation for his friend, who is valued for his erudition, passion, and commitment to recreating the world of Polish

---

247 Correspondence with Marcel Goldman, July 20, 2018.

Jews. However, he clearly feels doubt about the possibility of the revival of Jewish life in Poland:

Profesorze! Polskich Żydów już nie ma	Professor! There are no more Polish Jews
i też ich nie będzie,	and they will not be there either,
próżne Twoje wysiłki,	your efforts are vain when you
gdy szukasz ich wszędzie,	look for them everywhere,
bo ci co są, nie trzeba tłumaczyć,	because those who are left,
bo przecie	needless to say, because
to tylko niedobitki, rzucone po świecie,	they are just survivors, dispersed in the world,
są Żydzi polscy, lecz nie w Polsce,	there are Polish Jews, but not in Poland,
tylko na obczyźnie	abroad
albo w Izraelu, swej własnej ojczyźnie.	or in Israel, their own homeland.
A ten świat, który istniał,	And this world that existed,
który tętnił życiem,	which was full of life,
Mój Boże! Nawet Ty go nie wskrzesisz,	My God! Even you won't bring it back
Panie Profesorze.	Professor.*

* Tel Aviv, August 9, 2008. Cited in Goldman, *A w nocy przychodzą myśli*, 84.

Elements visible in this poem are characteristic of many testimonies written by Polish Jews and their descendants, who recognize and respect the contemporary manifestations of Jewish life in Krakow and Poland, but do not see in them a simple continuation of what was before World War II. Marcel believes that no one can resurrect what was destroyed by the war. One can even observe his growing skepticism towards actions to commemorate and popularize Jewish history and culture in Krakow. He undoubtedly respects those who undertake this effort, but considers it futile and naïve. This is expressed in the poem that he wrote on October 8, 2018 in Tel Aviv, and because it has not yet appeared in print in Poland, I quote it in full as a remarkable word of a thinker and a witness to history. This text is an interesting assessment of Krakow, a story about it and an account of a visit there, written by a keen observer, a Krakovian, who now permanently lives 3.5 thousand kilometers away.

Kraków 2018	Krakow 2018
Inaczej wyglądasz w moich oczach,	You look different in my eyes.
Krakowie stary.	Old Krakow.
Stary? Bo to taki posąg narodowy?	Old? Because it's such a national statue?
Ale w moim sercu	But in my heart
Za każdym razem nowy.	You are new every time.
Fotografuję Planty, mury, bramy,	I photograph the Planty, walls, gates,
Czy jest tu coś	Is there anything here
Czego jeszcze nie znamy?	We do not know yet?
Więc się na Plantach o to	So in the Planty we ask
Jednej sympatycznej pary pytamy.	A nice couple about that.
O tak, tu za plecami	"Oh yes, here behind
Teatru Słowackiego	the Słowacki Theater
Jest kościół...	There is a church..."
No cóż w nim dziwnego?"	"Well, what's special about it?"
Otóż w środku głównej nawy	"In the middle of the main nave
Postawili kolumnę,	They put up a column,
bardzo dziwny montaż	a very strange place
Bo komuś kto za nią stoi	Because to someone standing
zasłania mu ołtarz!	behind it covers the altar!"
Stare miasto a jednak zmienione	The old town, but changed
Niby na nowo po wojnie stworzone.	Apparently created again after the war.
Na Sukiennice patrzę, no tak	I am looking at the Cloth Hall, yes,
Przecież znam,	I know a church
kościół z różnymi wieżami,	with the different towers,
Na cokole Mickiewicz otoczony	On the pedestal Mickiewicz surrounded
Turystów chmarami.	By crowds of tourists.
Ale dlaczego wszystko we mgle?	But why is everything in the mist?
Siedzę na krakowskim Rynku	I am sitting
	on the Krakow Market Square
I patrzę, nie ma mgły.	I am looking, there is no mist.
Cały widok się przede mną otwiera,	The whole view opens up to me,
A ta mgła to na mych oczach się zbiera.	These are my eses misted over.
Na podrapanych bramach	On the scratched gates
Lwy otwierają swe pyski	Lions are opening their mouths

Łasi się Dama z Łasiczką	The lady with an ermine is fawning
W Muzeum Czartoryskich.	At the Czartoryski Museum.
Na placu Zgody, dziś Bohaterów Getta	On Concord Square, today Ghetto Heroes
Krzesła stoją dalej puste, opuszczone	The chairs are still empty, abandoned
Tu i tam kwiatki przez ludzi rzucone.	Here and there flowers thrown by people.
Jeździliśmy tutaj do Podgórza do babci	We used to come here to Podgórze to grandma
W niedziele i święta.	On Sundays and holidays.
Kto to dzisiaj jeszcze w ogóle pamięta?	Who still remembers that today?
Plac Bohaterów Getta.	Ghetto Heroes Square.
A ja się pytam, jakich bohaterów?	And I ask, what heroes?
O czym wy ludzie mówicie?	What are you people talking about?
Czy tam walczyli?	Were they fighting there?
Czy tam się bronili?	Were they defending themselves there?
Kto tam miał bronić, kto walczyć?	Who was to defend there, who was to fight?
Czy ci starzy ludzie, czy kobiety i dzieci?	Those old people or women and children?
Czy rodziny, które jeszcze wlekły swoje mienie	Or families dragging their property
Nie wiedząc, że ta droga wiedzie na stracenie!	Not knowing that this path leads to death?!
Niemcy strzelali i bili.	The Germans shot and beat.
Krew zabitych i rannych ludzi niewinnych	The blood of killed and wounded innocent people
płynie do rynsztoku po ulicy.	flows into the gutter down the street.
Nie, to nie bohaterzy, ale męczennicy!	No, they are not heroes, they are martyrs!
Kazimierza zapomnieć nie można.	You cannot forget Kazimierz.
Dziś turystyczny biznes tu panuje	Today, tourist business rules here
Tam gdzie się Żydzi modlili	Where the Jews prayed
Sprzedaje się	People sell
I kupuje,	And buy,

A na końcu ulicy nawet jakiś malarz maluje.	And at the end of the street even a painter works.
Tu wystawa, tam cmentarz	Here an exhibition, there a cemetery
Jakiś przewodnik grupę turystów prowadzi,	A guide is leading a group of tourists,
Coś tam im tłumaczy i radzi	Explaining and advising them
W jakimś korytarzu...	In some corridor...
A ja myślę, czy oni wiedzą	And I think if they know
Że się znajdują	That they are
Na olbrzymim cmentarzu...?	At a huge cemetery...?
Na muzea przerobione bożnice	Synagogues converted into museums
Pokazują pamiątki, albo	Show mementoes, or
Z nich pozostałe szczątki.	Their remains.
Dla ludzi którzy się tutaj	For people who used to
W tałesach nad Torą modlili	Pray over the Torah in *tallitot* here
To nie były pamiątki, gdy oni tu żyli!	They were not mementoes when they lived here!
Są dziś marzyciele naiwni,	There are naïve dreamers today,
Naprawdę trochę dziwni,	Really a bit weird,
Myślą, że im się uda	They think they will succeed
Wskrzesić do życia Kazimierz żydowski.	In bringing the Jewish Kazimierz back to life.
Chcą podlać te martwe korzonki.	They want to water those dead roots.
Nie zdając sobie sprawy,	Not realizing
Że to sen.	It is a dream.
Że to puste mrzonki.	That it is an empty fantasy.

A long-standing friendship connects Marcel and Bianka Goldman with Gabriela Haratyk from Bielsko-Biała, an entrepreneur and social activist. A meeting with her is always included in the program of their arrival in this city. Together, they travel to the region of Podbeskidzie and Żywiec. Wisła has become their favorite place for joint trips. Gabriela Haratyk speaks extremely warmly and positively about their relationship:

> I met Marcel and Bianka Goldman through my aunt, my father's sister. My aunt (unfortunately already deceased) kept in touch with them, largely due to the fact that both my aunt and Bianka's family came from Bielsko. After World War II, the inhabitants of Bielsko-Biała, regardless of where they their fate led them, maintained bonds of friendship. What undoubtedly distinguishes Marcel is the incredible brilliance of mind and his fantastic sense of humor—combined with a great distance to himself. We often visit each other. I stay with them in Israel, they come to me in Bielsko. Moreover, on average, once a year I go with Marcel to various schools in Podbeskidzie, where he meets with students, telling them about our experiences from World War II. These are very informative and emotional meetings. I admire that, despite many hardships they faced, Bianka and Marcel have stayed together for so many years, maintaining serenity, a lot of spontaneity and warmth in their relationship. They enjoy every day of life, but also enjoy themselves. Undoubtedly, they set a constructive example for others. Marcel's Polish is wonderful, it's amazing, especially when you consider how many years they have been living in Israel.[248]

With his retirement, Marcel began to speak more widely on matters relating to history, politics, economy, religion, and interpersonal relations. *Haaretz* published several of his memoirs related to World War II and a number of letters in which he criticized the rule of the right-wing Prime Minister Benjamin Netanyahu. For example, in a letter that appeared on November 24, 2018, he spoke about government policy towards refugees:

> Are we already totally stupid? We are bringing Thai people to work in agriculture, Filipinos to look after old people, Chinese, Romanians, and Bulgarians to work on construction sites, but a few thousand Africans bother us? Instead of sending them to jobs all over the country and giving them work, the state is ready to pay millions of shekels to send them to Rwanda.[249]

Marcel proudly talks about the achievements of his country, but he also points out that a lot of things remain unsettled. Much depends not only on Israel itself, but also on more complex international agreements. For example, providing residents with access to water intended for direct consumption as well as

---

248 Interview with G. Haratyk on July 21, 2017.
249 M. Goldman's letter, *Haaretz*, November 24, 2018, trans. M. Goldman.

for the needs of agricultural crops and industrial activities will be of paramount importance for Israel and all countries in the Middle East. The first major hydrological projects regarding Eretz Yisrael date back to the interwar period (which was discussed in the first chapter). In the second half of the twentieth century, Israeli politicians and scientists returned to this matter. In the book *The New Middle East*, published for the first time in 1993, Shimon Peres reported an increase in social tensions related to water and food shortage in Syria, Egypt, Iraq, and Jordan, and he also expressed concern about dealing with the problem of water supply in relation to Israel. Soon, Peres's words were confirmed by real political events, including the effects of prolonged drought, which are considered to be the cause of the outbreak of the social revolt in Syria in 2011. All the more, it is worth noting that Peres also saw an opportunity in the same thing that today is the main source of the problem: "If roads lead to civilization, then water leads to peace."[250] Peres formulated this lofty thought based on very mundane premises—further wars will not solve the hydrological problems of any state, but many countries and nations that express their will to cooperate may gain a lot. In the case of Israel, the Jordan River provides an opportunity for international cooperation. In the history of this country it played a special role. According to biblical tradition, God stopped its waters so that the Israelites returning from Egyptian slavery could pass:

> So when the people broke camp to cross the Jordan, the priests carrying the Ark of the Covenant went ahead of them. Now the Jordan is at flood stage all during harvest. Yet as soon as the priests who carried the ark reached the Jordan and their feet touched the water's edge, the water from upstream stopped flowing. It piled up in a heap a great distance away, at a town called Adam in the vicinity of Zarethan, while the water flowing down to the Sea of the Arabah [that is, the Dead Sea] was completely cut off. So the people crossed over opposite Jericho. The priests who carried the Ark of the Covenant of the Lord stopped in the middle of the Jordan and stood on dry ground, while all Israel passed by until the whole nation had completed the crossing on dry ground. (Joshua 3:14–17).

After immersing his hands in Jordan seven times, Naaman was cured of leprosy (2 Kings 5:10–14). Christians associate Jordan mainly with the figures of John the Baptist and Jesus. The river originates in Lebanon, then it flows through

---

250 S. Peres, *Nowy Bliski Wschód*, trans. K. Wojciechowski, Warsaw 1995, 124.

Israel, Syria, and Jordan, it crosses Lake Hula and Lake Tiberias, and at the end it flows into the Dead Sea. The Dead Sea is a unique publicly accessible reservoir of the most saline water in the world, which pushes man to the surface, so you can float on it without swimming. In total, the Jordan is 251 kilometers long. In the past, many political disputes were fought over this river, today the main problem is its intensive exploitation by Israel and Jordan due to irrigation and energy reasons. In the 1930s Jordan poured 1.3 billion cubic meters of water into the Dead Sea annually, but in recent years it was no more than 400 million. At the same time, during the year, 1050 tons of water disappeared from the basin of the Dead Sea as consequence of evaporation.[251] In this way, the surface of the Dead Sea lowered by twenty-two meters between 1970 and 2015. If this trend continues, it will mean the complete destruction of the Dead Sea, which in turn will bring a biological disaster and serious social, political, and economic effects. For Israel and Jordan, this is a matter of great importance, since both countries have developed tourist services and industries around the Dead Sea that use its rich resources, for example, for cosmetics. Even the most rational management of water resources is not able to heal this situation. That is why the possibility of building a 200-kilometer channel that would pump water from the Red Sea to the Dead Sea has been discussed for years (pumping water from the Mediterranean Sea into Israel is also considered). Specific tasks for the planned investment were formulated by Shimon Peres:

> The future channel will have many uses. It will be used to transfer water from the Red Sea to the Dead Sea to replenish water from Jordan and Yarmouk, which Israel and Jordan will allocate for irrigation. Water will also be used for research and fish farming, tourism development in the Israeli and Jordanian Arabah, and infrastructure for future economic growth in the Arabah Depression. Water will flow from the rocks to the Dead Sea in cascades. The energy generated due to the difference in height will be used to produce electricity.[252]

The electricity production mentioned by Peres is quite realistic, because the Dead Sea water table is currently 419 meters below sea level—this is the difference between this reservoir and the Red Sea shore. In 2008 the inżynieria.

---

[251] A. Sumara, "Czy kanał uratuje Morze Martwe?," https://inzynieria.com/wpis-branzy/projekty/3/9266,czy-kanal-uratuje-morze-martwe, accessed April 14, 2018.

[252] Peres, *Nowy Bliski Wschód*, 132.

com portal announced that Israeli, British, and French scholars and experts began working on the "Red—Dead" project. The cost of this investment was estimated at around USD 5 billion (funding was offered, among others, by the World Bank), and its duration, nearly a decade.[253] The research and experiments were to concern not only engineering. The possible consequences of mixing the waters of the Red Sea and the Dead Sea required scrupulous verification. In addition, the project also required agreement between Israel, Jordan, and the government of the Palestinian Authority (through which the channel would partly run). In 2015, an agreement on this matter was signed by the Israeli and Jordanian authorities. Both states assumed that the project would solve their water supply problems (not excluding Palestinians). A special water pumping station was expected to be built around the resort of Aqaba. The more salty water would be transported to the Dead Sea, and the less saline water would be used for utility purposes. The pipeline would transport 300 million cubic meters of water from the Red Sea to the Dead Sea each year. A joint Israeli-Jordanian company, created for this purpose, would be responsible for its service.[254] In addition, Israel is already seeing great results in the field of modern water use and treatment technology.

If the peace process were to proceed, the tourism sector would be the first to feel it. It is enough to mention that routes connecting different countries are the still unused opportunity to develop tourism in this region of the world. Today, for example, routes connecting European countries are popular. The prospect of success could also be possible a route that would connect the greatest attractions of the Middle East. Unfortunately, today round trips through Israel and Jordan (where most tourists go to Petra) are the peak of possibilities. Recently, Saudi Arabia also gave signals of joining the countries that make money from tourist services, along with the relative liberalization of some laws. However, the question is to what extent these trends will prove permanent, what their fate will be. Peace would also give an opportunity to other sectors of the economy. The many speculations about the peace process seem as interesting as (unfortunately) devoid of scientific qualities, it is pure guesswork, for which there is no place for it in this book. I only wanted to point out that despite the already known and the

---

253 Sumara, "Czy kanał uratuje Morze Martwe?"

254 "Izrael i Jordania z umową wodną. Ratunek dla Morza Martwego," https://www.polskieradio.pl/42/273/Artykul/1387754,Izrael-i-Jordania-z-umowa-wodna-Ratunek-dla-Morza-Martwego, accessed April 15, 2018.

emerging problems on the horizon in Israel and in its immediate surroundings, there is still a large and untapped potential for socio-economic development.

In spite of still unresolved internal and external conflicts and high prices, especially on food and housing, which are troublesome for the average people, the beginning of the twenty-first century brought further strengthening of the Israeli economy. A clear sign of this are the high ratings given by international experts for the Bank of Israel's policy and the position of the shekel. In 2013, the Israeli currency propped up against the dollar by 7.5%, which was the best result among thirty-one major currencies in the world. The indicator of the second currency, the Danish krone, was twice as low. The reason for that was the start of gas production by Israel, which produced a growing surplus. However, such good shekel performance was problematic for Israeli industrial exporters who pointed out that a strong currency reduced their competitiveness in global markets.[255] Remaining on the subject of exports, it is worth emphasizing the fact that since the declaration of independence of the state, changes have started in this area,[256] which brought about a profound transformation in 2017.[257] Earlier export products, which belonged to the agricultural sector, were replaced by products of the manufacturing industry.[258]

The relatively high demographic growth of Jews in Israel is of great population and political significance. In 2018 it reached 2% and was for the first time

---

255 M. Wierciszewski, "Izrael nie przegra wojny walutowej," https://www.pb.pl/izrael-nie-przegra-wojny-walutowej-749732, accessed December 16, 2018.

256 Already in the first years of the country's existence there was a clear increase in export, but its structure did not change significantly. Between 1961 and 1970, the value of goods exported from Israel increased from USD 237.8 to USD 714.1 million. During this time, the value of exported services increased from USD 178.6 to 650.4 million, respectively. In the group of exported goods, agricultural products still had an important position: citrus—17% in 1961, 11.6% in 1970, citrus products—3.3% in 1961 and 4.9% in 1970, other products produced in the agricultural sector—9.5% in 1961, 6.1% in 1970. Horowitz, *The Enigma of Economic Growth*, 124.

257 In 2017, exports of goods totaled USD 61.2 billion, an increase of 1.0% compared to 2016. In 2017, the products of the agricultural, forestry and fishery industries accounted for only 2.0% (a year earlier, 1,9%) of total exports, while the majority—exactly 93.7% of total exports—was taken by the manufacturing industry,with 92.8% a year earlier. Central Bureau of Statistics, http://www.cbs.gov.il/reader/?MIval=cw_usr_view_SHTML&ID=461, accessed December 14, 2018.

258 In 2017, the leading industries were: diamond (USD 12.3 billion, 20.1% of total exports), computer, electronic, and optical (USD 10.5 billion, 17.2%), chemical (USD 7.8 billion, 12.7%), and pharmaceutical (USD 7.5 billion, 12.3%). Ibid.

higher than the increase of the Arab population. At the beginning of 2019, Israel had 8,972,000 inhabitants.[259]

The cultural and creative industries are an important factor that determines Israel's international position. To explain this phenomenon, it is worth referring to the example of Great Britain. After World War II, the British failed to defend their superpower status, but they still play an important role in the world, greater than would result from their military or economic strength. This is influenced by, among others, the opinion-forming British media. It suffices to mention the BBC (British Broadcasting Corporation) established in 1922—the main public radio and television broadcaster, or the world's leading economic-oriented newspaper *Financial Times*, published since 1888. Israel also strongly influences the international public opinion through high-quality cinematography, theater, and literature. For a long time, an Israeli author, Amos Oz (1939–2018), belonged to the most frequently translated and cited writers. The young historian Yuval Noah Harari (born in 1976 in Kiryat Ata), professor of the Hebrew University in Jerusalem, also gained international fame. A book he wrote, *Sapiens. A Brief History of Humankind*, became a world bestseller. In the first half of 2019, it was already translated into nearly fifty languages (the original edition was published in 2011 in Hebrew). The following writers enjoy readers' interest: Leore Dayan, Etgar Keret, Yishai Sarid, and Meir Shalev. The works of Israeli performers, designers, graphic designers, and architects are also popular around the world.

The social and economic issues raised above have never ceased to interest Marcel Goldman. After retiring, he decided to continue operating as an international banking and financial advisor. In addition, he became a representative of one of the American companies on the Israeli market. For many people, including Israeli and foreign entrepreneurs, he became a mentor and a treasury of valuable advice. Also, the community of residents functioning in his apartment building in the Ramat Aviv district decided to use his knowledge and experience and entrusted him with the function of treasurer. Although the rank of this role obviously cannot match what Marcel was responsible for earlier, it shows that he always approaches his tasks with full seriousness and professionalism. In a short time, under his care, the community had a considerable amount of money on its bank account, which made it possible carry out a major renovation of the entire building. Naturally, it was not without adequate contributions from

---

259 Data from the Israeli Ministry of Foreign Affairs, https://mfa.gov.il/MFA/Pages/default.aspx, accessed January 2, 2019.

the residents themselves, but the thing was that Marcel managed to organize them, and then use them in a favourable way.

It may seem surprising that a man who deserved to retire after years of hard work and secured economic safety for himself and his loved ones, did not want to rest on his laurels. To explain his constant need for activity, it is not enough to state that he is a transgressive personality. It is necessary to strongly emphasize his two main features: diligence and modesty. Work has always been a passion for him, not a chore. Striving for professional development, he was able to derive satisfaction from what he owned at a given moment, and enjoy life: "One man, when he has something to eat, somewhere to live, and can send his children to school, considers himself wealthy, and the other wants more, no matter how much he has. In the Hebrew language there is such a wise saying: *ashrei ha-sameach bechelko*, that is, happy is the man who is pleased with what he has."[260] Marcel is reluctant to discuss his possessions. He assesses this matter accurately and calmly: "I am aware that some will assess me as a wealthy man, others will say that I have little. It all depends on who makes the assessment. That is why it is an issue to which I pay no attention to at all."[261] After retiring, instead of cashing in on his achievements, he preferred to focus on social work and helping others, while continuing to do business.

In the past, he did not have time to meet with school and university students, but after his retirement he began to take part in such meetings in Poland and Israel. Marcel became a participant in the Zikaron BaSalon (Hebrew: memory [or: memories] in the living room) program, which organizes every year, in the week of the Holocaust Remembrance Day (Hebrew: Yom HaShoah),[262] meetings with Holocaust survivors in private homes. In addition to the hosts, such meetings include family members, friends, and special guests. People interested in history join the meetings and receive contact details of a witness of history who had previously registered in this program. Then they agree on the details of the appointment, collect the witness, and drive home. Marcel, who has a car at his disposal, comes to the agreed place himself. During the meeting, the witnesses share their memories and talk with the hosts, sometimes there are debates and joint singing. The initiative was born because of the decreasing contact of today's society with memories of the Holocaust in Israel. According to data of

---

260 Correspondence with Marcel Goldman, February 8, 2019.
261 Interview with Marcel Goldman carried out on February 7, 2019.
262 The full name of this holiday in Hebrew: Yom Hazikaron laShoah ve-laG'vurah, which literally means "Holocaust and Heroism Remembrance Day."

Zikaron BaSalon, since the beginning of 2019, the program has brought together half a million hosts and participants. The interest in the initiative is growing and currently it takes place not only throughout Israel, but also abroad. So far, they have reached Germany, the United States, India, the Netherlands, Canada, China, South Africa, Great Britain, Spain, and Argentina.[263]

With his retirement, literary activity and poetry took an important place in Marcel Goldman's life. There are serious reasons to believe that this type of activity is more than an attempt to manage excess time. His numerous family, social, and business responsibilities do not let him get bored. For Marcel, reaching the age of retirement was an impulse for a retrospection. Previously, he lived at full speed, but now he slowed down a bit and realized that the time had come to reflect on what he had experienced and what he had done. Undoubtedly, he was influenced by the awareness of the passing of time and the inevitably approaching end of life. We can find traces of these thoughts in his poems from the collection *A w nocy przychodzą myśli*, such as *Oda do siebie samego* (Ode to myself, November 7, 2006, 45–46), *Dzień i godzina* (Day and hour, Tel Aviv, November 9, 2008, 58), and *Smutno* (It's sad, Tel Aviv, February 28, 2009, 59). The second of these poems begins with words addressed to his wife:

Kiedy przyjdzie ten dzień i godzina,	When this day and hour comes,
A przyjść ona musi,	And it must come,
Kiedy dłoń niewidzialna ostatni dech zdusi,	When the invisible hand stifles the last breath,
To zasadnicze pytanie kołacze się po głowie:	This crucial question is spinning in the head:
Czy Ty będziesz przy mnie?	Will you be with me?
Czy ja będę przy Tobie?	Will I be with you?*

* Goldman, *A w nocy przychodzą myśli*, 58.

With his witing activity, Marcel did the same as many Polish Jews who wrote memoirs based on personal experience. For people who experienced traumatic and groundbreaking events, writing an autobiography is a type of therapy—

---

263 "How do You Commemorate the Holocaust?," https://www.zikaronbasalon.org, accessed February 13, 2019.

a phenomenon well recognised in science.²⁶⁴ It is no accident that the works of Polish Jews in Israel focused mainly on their own experiences and thoughts. This type of writing not only has a therapeutic value, but also provides an opportunity for self-discourse, an attempt to understand what happened and to testify about it.²⁶⁵ It is in these categories that Marcel's literary output should be read, as well as that of other Polish writers who continued or started writing in Israel. In this way, talented artists who gained international fame appeared naturally.

Ida Fink (1921–2011), a writer, pianist, and author of highly acclaimed novels, short stories, and autobiographical books, should be mentioned here. She emigrated to Israel in 1957, taking her several early stories with her. She published her first literary work in the late 1940s in the Swiss press, translated into French. In 1974, she published a collection of short stories in Israel, entitled *Peset zman*, for which she received the Dutch Anne Frank Prize in 1975. She was on the list of the one hundred major Jewish writers published by the National Jewish Book Center in New York. So far, several films inspired by her life and work have been made in Israel and France.²⁶⁶ Alona Frankel (born in 1937), a writer and illustrator of several dozen publications for children, gained great popularity. For her first book for adults, *Girl* (2005), which described her own fate during the Holocaust, she was awarded the Sapir Prize, a prestigious Israeli literary distinction, and the Buchman Prize. Among most outstanding artists of Polish origin is Irit Amiel (born in 1931), a translator, poet, and prose writer. Her parents died in Treblinka in 1942, but they had managed to hide her and she survived the war on Aryan papers. The experience of war became the leitmotif of her work. She made her debut with a volume of poems entitled *Test in the Holocaust*. Her prose and poetry have been translated many times. Works of other writers, such as Marek Hłasko, Henryk Grynberg, Leo Lipski, Hanna Krall, and Wisława Szymborska, were also translated from Polish into Hebrew.²⁶⁷ Miriam Akavia, who was born in Krakow in 1927 and died in 2015 in Tel Aviv, is another one of the most respected writers. She debuted relatively late, only in 1975, with the Hebrew novel *Neurim be-shalechet*, which had several Polish editions. In Polish translation it was titled *Jesień młodości* (English: Autumn of

---

264 See D. Demetrio, *Autobiografia. Terapeutyczny wymiar pisania o sobie*, trans. A. Skolimowska, Krakow 2000.

265 See M. Czermińska, *Autobiograficzny trójkąt: świadectwo, wyznanie i wyzwanie*, Krakow 2000.

266 K. Famulska-Ciesielska, S. J. Żurek, *Literatura polska w Izraelu. Leksykon*, Krakow–Budapest 2012, 52–54.

267 Ibid., 17–19.

youth).[268] Roman Frister (1928–2015) was a successful writer and journalist. In the years 1965–1990 he worked in the daily *Haaretz*. He was also the rector of the Journalism College in Tel Aviv, cooperated with Radio Free Europe and the Polish section of the BBC. He published several high-profile books, and received the greatest recognition from readers and professional literary critics with his autobiography *Diokan atzmi im tzaleket* (English: Self-portrait with a scar), which was published in 1993 in Tel Aviv and translated into many languages. Eli Barbur (born in 1948) is one of leading Polish and Israeli journalists. He emigrated from Poland following the March '68 antisemitic campaign. His autobiographical novel *Grupy na wolnym powietrzu* (English: Outdoor groups)[269] is an original portrait of the March '68 generation. This long list of names is by no means a complete one, but only a subjective choice of the author. In 1986, the Association of Polish Writers was established in Israel. Between 1988 and 2006 it published the historical and literary magazine *Kontury* in Tel Aviv.

Marcel Goldman never competed with the most successful writers, he never aspired to awards, distinctions, and decorations. In his writing he focused on attention to detail and faithful reflection of his own experiences and observations, rather than form. Family stories related to the period of World War II became the main motif of his work. In 2002, *Iskierki życia*, a collection of his short stories, appeared. This publication perfectly reflects the dynamics of the growing terror against the Jews, with thoughtful and cynical antisemitic policy of the Nazi occupiers. Before the mass extermination began, the Jews had been subjected to degrading procedures, then the foundations of their economic existence were undercut, their property was taken, and they were deprived of their sources of income. Finally, they were forced into ghettos, which were a trap with no way out. Theoretically, they could try to escape from the ghetto, but people who did that would be in danger from the Germans as well as blackmailers, the lowest part of the Polish society. Any survival strategies chosen by the Jews could prove wrong. *Iskierki życia* also reveals Marcel's talent for building an extremely vivid narrative, which undoubtedly has a positive effect on the readers' perception of his work.

As I mentioned in the introduction, Marcel writes in Polish, and the intertextuality of his work, located on the crossroads of Polish and Jewish cultures, is also characteristic. The influences of the leading Polish writers are clearly visible

---

268 Ibid., 15.
269 E. Barbur, *Grupy na wolnym powietrzu*, Warsaw 1995.

through quotes and borrowings, first of all the Polish national bard Adam Mickiewicz and the Nobel laureate Henryk Sienkiewicz. In his works, Marcel reveals himself as a rational, responsible, cordial, warm, caring, and humorous person for whom his family is very important.

In 2012, he published a collection of stories, poems, and epigrams entitled *A w nocy przychodzą myśli* (ninety-six pages). Most of the works contained in this volume refer to his life in Israel or to the latest moments spent in Poland. The text *Talit* (Tallit) chronologically describes mainly the events of World War II, but it is focused on Marcel's life in Israel. Some of the works in this collection are addressed directly to Marcel's Polish and Israeli friends, such as *Do Profesora Skotnickiego* (To Professor Skotnicki, 84). This volume is a kind of a social chronicle of the generation of Polish Jews newly arrived in Israel. First of all, the adaptation process and the first years of life in Israel are described, for example, in the stories *Pogaduszki i wierszydła* (Talks and poems, 5–12) and *Polak—Żyd? 100%?* (A Pole—a Jew? 100%?, 13–18). Next, close relations between Marcel and Bianka with the participants of the so-called Gomulka Aliyah are visible, for example, in the poems *Wesele (Nie Wyspiańskiego)* (The wedding [not Wyspiański's], February 1971, 29–30), *Mesiba (Zabawa)* (The party, November 7, 1969, 31–33), *Oda do Heniusia, na jego 50 urodziny* (Ode to Henius, on his fiftieth birthday, Haifa, October 31, 1977, 34–35), *Urodziny Abraszki* (Abraszka's birthday, Tel Aviv, January 23, 2009, 38–39), *Wieczór brydżowy* (A bridge evening, 40–42), and *Do Heniusia w 84 urodziny* (To Henius on his eighty-fourth birthday, Tel Aviv, October 2011, 47–48). Marcel dedicated two works to his wife on the occasion of their wedding anniversaries, which is visible in the titles: *25-lecie* (The twenty-fifth anniversary, Haifa, August 12, 1979) and *55 rocznica ślubu* (The fifty-fifth wedding anniversary, Tel Aviv, August 8, 2009). Both are not only declarations of love, but also collections of comments on the marriage of Marcel and Bianka. It is significant that (especially in the second poem), in addition to love, he emphasizes his deep attachment to his wife and the desire to live with her in the years to come:

Ale wracam do sprawy—	Coming back to the point—
Tak to przeleciało	It passed so fast,
To życie i już poza nami,	That life, and it is already behind us
A wciąż by się chciało	And you would still want
I to i tamto,	This and that,
Tego jeszcze mało . . .	This is still not enough . . .

Jedną prośbę mam,	I have one request,
Do kogo—nie wiadomo—	To whom—no one knows—
Ażebyśmy lata,	To spend the years
Które nam jeszcze przyznali	Still granted us
Razem spędzali!	Together!*

* Goldman, *A w nocy przychodzą myśli*, 36–37.

Grandchildren have an important place in Marcel Goldman's life. He devotes a lot of attention and care to them. On July 19, 2008, he wrote a poem dedicated to one of his granddaughters, entitled *Taniec* (English: Dance):

Tańcz, moja wnuczko, tańcz,	Dance, my grandchild, dance,
W melodii dźwiękach, piękna, smukła, młoda,	In the melody of the sounds, beautiful, slim, young,
Takt na estradzie wybijają nogi.	Your legs are beating time on the stage.
Ja na widowni…	Me in the audience…
Dokąd i jak daleko doszły moje drogi?	Where and how far have my roads come?
A serce pełne miłości, nadziei i… trwogi.	And the heart full of love, hope and… fear.
Ty, nieświadoma tego, co się we mnie dzieje,	You, unaware of what is going on inside me,
Do Ciebie świat należy,	The world belongs to you,
Do Ciebie się śmieje.	It is laughing for you.
Piękne Twe ciałko na scenie pręży się i wygina…	Your beautiful body on the stage flexes and bends…
A mogło się to skończyć kamieniem w Treblince.	And it could have ended with a stone in Treblinka.
Lub dymem z auschwitzkiego komina.	Or with smoke from the Auschwitz chimney.
A może nawet z rąk sowieckich zbirów	And maybe even at the hands of Soviet thugs

Mogłaś zginąć na stepach Sybiru.	You could have died in the Siberian steppes.

My, cudem uratowani,
           tu nam życie płynie,
Dlatego Ty tańczyć możesz—
           tu w Jerozolimie
	We, miraculously saved,
	           passing our lives here,
	That is why you can dance—
	           here in Jerusalem

Savta i Saba,* w tych słowach moc treści:
I miłość i troska i duma i szczęście—
	Savta and Saba, in these words lies
	           the power:
	And love and care and pride
	           and happiness—

Wszystko się w nich mieści.	Everything is in them.

Tak by się chciało chronić,
Skrzydła opieki roztoczyć,
Pilnować, aby nic złego, nic złego się
           nie stało,
Ale cóż, ile jeszcze,
           bo już czasu mało. . . .
	I would like to protect you,
	Spread the wings of care,
	Make sure that nothing bad, nothing
	           bad happens,
	But how long,
	           because time is short. . . .**

  * In Hebrew: grandmother and grandfather.
** Goldman, *A w nocy przychodzą myśli*, 51.

    The language of this poem is literal: the author, without reaching for rhetorical figures or other literary means of expression, writes directly that he cares about the fate of his granddaughter. At the same time, he feels a certain helplessness, because he would like to always protect her, while his "time is short." The emphasis is on making sure that "nothing bad happens" to his granddaughter, the expression "nothing bad" is repeated twice. The motif of evil often plays an important role in the writing of those who survived the Shoah. The attitude that the author presents is largely due to his own fears, deeply embedded in him and resulting from traumatic experiences of World War II. The omitted part of the poem also talks about contemporary threats, mainly from Iran. The poem's focus is not on current and already defined threats, but on what is only waiting to happen. In the background, there is hope that his granddaughter would never be exposed to the threats that he and his wife had to face.

    In 2018, Marcel Goldman decided on the second edition of the book *A w nocy przychodzą myśli* because the first one sold well and disappeared from the book shelves. On January 25, 2019, in the main building of the Pedagogical

University in Krakow, an event was held to celebrate the publication of the second edition of this volume. The meeting was hosted by Prof. Aleksander B. Skotnicki, who talked about the author and read a few of his works, and Paweł Lachowski, a friend of Marcel, who helped make this publishing project successful. It was attended by the rector of the Pedagogical University of Krakow, as well as over a hundred other guests, most of whom were students.

Marcel Goldman became an active participant in the debate on social, political, and economic relations in Israel as well as Polish-Jewish and Polish-Israeli relations. He is particularly interested in the history of World War II and the Holocaust. On these matters, he speaks most often. His thoughts are expressed in poems and letters, his position is always firm but prudent. He usually refers to his own experience, because he does not act as a politician, but rather formulates statements as a witness to history. Being an eyewitness or even a participant of the past events, he does not accept that today they are instrumentalized and politicized. He critically reacted to antisemitic rhetoric, which resounded in Poland at the beginning of the twenty-first century, when the right-wing circles strengthened their position. Admittedly, Marcel does not hide his dislike of the right wing and ultra-religious circles (regardless of the religion), but in this case he strongly criticised the reappearance of attitudes, behaviours, accents, and vocabulary that were characteristic of prewar Polish extreme right, especially of the National Radical Camp (ONR).[270] In response to these events, on April 5, 2012, Marcel Goldman wrote a poem entitled *Do moich polskich przyjaciół* (English: To my Polish friends). Below I quote it in full:

Proszę uprzejmie mi podać	Please kindly tell me
Do jakiej się zgłosić komisji,	Which committee to report to,
Bo mianowicie, po latach	Because after many years
Podaję się do dymisji.	I resign.
Przecież nawet za najcięższe winy	Even for the most serious faults
Kara ma swoje terminy.	Punishment has its deadlines.
I jeśli przyjmujemy tę powyższą zasadę,	And if we accept this principle,
To ja moją prośbę przed Życia	I put my request before
Trybunałem kładę.	the Life Tribunal.

---

270 On ONR, see S. Rudnicki, *Obóz Narodowo-Radykalny. Geneza i działalność*, Warsaw 1985.

Jako Żyd żyję już ponad 8 lat dziesiątek.	I have lived for over eighty years as a Jew.
I czy to dzień tygodnia,	No matter whether it is a weekday,
Czy świątek, czy piątek,	Or weekend, or Friday,
Zawsze muszę pamiętać swój życia początek:	I always have to remember the beginning of my life:
Ż y d z i a k	A J e w
Niemiec mnie bił i uśmiercał,	The German beat me and killed me,
Ukrainiec się nade mną znęcał,	The Ukrainian abused me,
Rosjanin-Własowiec śpiewając pomagał,	The Russian member of Vlasov's Army helped, singing,
A Polak szmalcował,	And the Pole blackmailed,
A Polak wydawał.	And the Pole revealed.
W tym czasie w Europie	At that time in Europe
To rożnie bywało, ale większość narodów	It could be different, but most nations
Też przyklaskiwało.	Also applauded.
A co najbardziej bolało?	And what hurt the most?
To tutejsze, własne, domowej roboty.	The local, own, homemade.
Kiedy pochód starych i kobiet, i dzieci	When the march of the old, women and children
Ku Zagładzie kroczy	Walking towards the Holocaust
To go odprowadzają spojrzenia sąsiadów,	Is followed by the neighbours' eyes,
Przyciemnione nienawiścią oczy.	Hate-tinted eyes.
Ja wiem!	I know!
Zabiłem Chrystusa!	I killed Christ!
Wprawdzie mojego Króla, bo On Król Żydowski	Who was indeed my King, as He was King of the Jews
Syn Maryi z Nazaretu, Żydówką z Galilei była.	The son of Mary of Nazareth, a Jewess from Galilee.
Czy to wie ten oszołom, gdzie gwiazda świeciła?	Does this fool know where the star shone?

Prawdę trzeba powiedzieć,	The truth must be told,
Choć niemiło będzie.	It will not be nice though.
Ale wtedy nienawiść panowała wszędzie.	But then hatred was everywhere.
W mniejszości się znalazły	They found themselves in a minority,
Uczucia ludzkie i chrześcijańskie miłosierdzie!	Human feelings and Christian mercy!
Przeskakujemy teraz, co za gracja!	We are hopping now, what a grace!
No niby demokracja, Zachód i cywilizacja.	Well, democracy, the West, and civilization,
Ale tak naprawdę to te oenerowskie korzonki	But in fact these are nationalist roots.
Znowu coś tam rodzą,	They are growing again,
No i z tej polskiej gleby	And from this Polish soil
Jakieś chwasty wychodzą.	Some weeds are coming out.
Sam się tu przekonałem:	I found out here myself:
Coś się w państwie psuje,	Something is rotting in the state,
I duch czarnosecinny	And the spirit of the Black Hundreds,
Znowu tu panuje.	It reigns here again.
Bo po 63 latach usłyszałem znów „Żyd" jako obelgę!	Because after sixty-three years I heard "Jew" as an insult again!
Wracam więc do początku.	So I am going back to the start.
Mam dość tego w klubie bycia,	I am sick of being in that club
W którym już siedzę	In which I am already
Od początku życia.	From the beginning of my life.
Ale jak się to robi?	But how is it done?
Choć byś się ruszał w prawo	Although you would move right
Lub w lewo z ostrożna,	Or left with caution,
To i tak z tego klubu	From this club
Się wypisać nie można!	You cannot resign anyway!
Nie wiem, czy tegoście chcieli	I do not know if that is what you wanted
Czy tego żądali,	What you demanded:

Ale macie Polskę bez Żydów...	You have Poland without Jews...
Z antysemitami!	But with antisemites!
Pragnę zaproponować:	I would like to propose:
Zaniechanie mitów,	To give up myths,
Aby choć troszkę oświecić	To enlighten a little bit
Tych	These
Antysemitów!	Antisemites!*

* The poem, sent in a letter from Marcel Goldman of July 21, 2018, has not been published yet.

Marcel's position expressed in *Haaretz*, regarding the joint statement by the prime ministers of Poland and Israel concerning the often tragic Polish-Jewish relations during World War II, evoked a great response. That declaration is treated as a consequence of the diplomatic dispute that broke out internationally after the Polish authorities adopted the amendment to the Act on the Institute of National Remembrance (IPN) at the beginning of 2018. Great controversy was caused mainly by Article 55 a.1:

> Whoever claims, publicly and contrary to the facts, that the Polish Nation or the Republic of Poland is responsible or partially responsible for Nazi crimes committed by the Third Reich, as specified in Article 6 of the Charter of the International Military Tribunal enclosed to the International Agreement for the Prosecution and Punishment of the Major War Criminals of the European Axis, signed in London on August 8, 1945 (Polish Journal of Laws of 1947, item 367), or for other felonies that constitute crimes against peace, crimes against humanity, or war crimes, or whoever otherwise grossly diminishes the responsibility of the true perpetrators of said crimes, shall be liable to a fine or imprisonment for up to three years. The sentence shall be made public.[271]

In Israel, and in many other countries, that legal act was perceived as a threat to the freedom of expression and scientific research concerning the shameful attitudes of some Poles towards Jews during World War II. On the other hand,

---

271 "Nowelizacja ustawy o Instytucie Pamięci Narodowej," http://trybunal.gov.pl/postepowanie-i-orzeczenia/komunikaty-prasowe/komunikaty-przed/art/10459-nowelizacja-ustawy-o-instytucie-pamieci-narodowej, accessed January 11, 2022.

the government of the Republic of Poland argued that the only intention behind the amendment to the Act on the Institute of National Remembrance was to protect the nation and the Polish state against assigning to it the responsibility for the crimes of the Third Reich. Regardless of our assessments related to the amendment itself, it must be admitted that international public opinion and global political centers important for Poland (mainly American authorities) did not accept the actions and interpretation provided by the Polish government. In June 2018 the Polish parliament quickly withdrew the disputed amendment. This was accompanied by the aforementioned joint declaration of the prime ministers of Poland and Israel—Mateusz Morawiecki and Benjamin Netanyahu—which states:

> We acknowledge and condemn every single case of cruelty against Jews perpetrated by Poles during World War II.We are honored to remember heroic acts of numerous Poles, especially the Righteous Among the Nations, who risked their lives to save Jewish people. We reject the actions aimed at blaming Poland or the Polish nation as a whole for the atrocities committed by the Nazis and their collaborators of different nations. Unfortunately, the sad fact is that some people—regardless of their origin, religion, or worldview—revealed their darkest side at that time. We acknowledge the fact that structures of the Polish Underground State supervised by the Polish Government-in-Exile created a mechanism of systematic help and support to Jewish people, and its courts sentenced Poles for their collaboration with the German occupation authorities, including denounciations of Jews.[272]

In response to that declaration, Marcel Goldman presented his own point of view in a special letter that appeared in the Israeli daily *Haaretz* on August 22, 2018. Primarily, he voices opposition to politicians who wish to settle historical disputes in any form. He recalls the research carried out by historians, which can be read as a clear message that explaining the events of the past should belong to scientists who, in their studies, take into account the experience of witnesses to history. Marcel also protests against simplifying and generalising Poles' attitudes during the war. On the one hand, he refuses to assign collective responsibility to all Poles, but on the other he does not consent to "exaggerating the participation of Poles in saving Jews." He admits that his family survived thanks to the

---

272 Joint Declaration of the Prime Ministers of the State of Israel and the Republic of Poland, https://www.premier.gov.pl/wydarzenia/aktualnosci/wspolna-deklaracja-premierow-pan-stacja-izrael-i-Rzeczypospolitej-Polskiej.html, accessed July 18, 2018.

help of a friend from Poland, but he also reminds "with sadness" that "the help of Poles was a drop in the sea" in the face of many atrocities that Jews suffered from them.[273]

Closing this chapter, I would like to quote Marcel Goldman's words:

> I am not uncritical of Israel. I am aware that this country faces numerous problems and does not always do it skillfully. Since I came here, my sense of dignity has increased, because I feel that I am here at home and no one has the right to question it. The sense of equality, that I live in my own country, that everyone around me was Jewish gave me a lot. In *Hatikvah* there is such a phrase: "Lihyot 'am chofshi be'artzenu," which means: "To be a free nation in our land" [you can also translate more literally: "in our country"—Ł.T.S.]. When I sing our anthem and I come to this verse, I cry ... This emotion can be understood only by other Jews who survived a certain period of their life in the diaspora and dreamed of building their own state sometime.[274]

Does Marcel Goldman regret that he emigrated from Poland in 1949 despite his strong bond with Israel? According to his assurances, no, because leaving at that stage of life enabled a relatively smooth acculturation into the mainstream of Israeli society. In addition, he is afraid that if he had not left soon after the war, he would have been forced to emigrate, if not in 1956, then in 1968. To make matters worse, later emigration could have complicated his life, because he was in love with a girl who was Polish, without any Jewish roots. It is possible that then he would have been her husband, and it is not certain if she would have got permission to leave the country, let alone whether she would have decided to do so.[275]

Tracing Marcel Goldman's biography allows me to formulate some statements important from the perspective of Israel's history. This country was built to a large extent by people accustomed to problems, challenges, and sacrifices, who were often forced to make important decisions. Most of its inhabitants have roots outside their current place of residence, so it is a country heavily influenced by immigrants, and they are generally distinguished by high mobility, courage, creativity, and diligence. It is these qualities of immigrants that are considered

---

273 Here, I am quoting a translation of the original letter made by M. Goldman for the needs of the book.
274 Interview with Marcel Goldman carried out on December 21, 2016.
275 Interview with Marcel Goldman carried out on March 16, 2019.

i The poem *Hatikvah* (Hebrew: the hope) was written in 1878 by the Hebrew poet Naftali Herz Imber, a Polish Jew born in 1856 in Zolochiv in Galicia. In 1897, Zionist activists meeting at the First Zionist Congress in Basel adopted *Hatikvah* as their anthem. In 1948, along with the proclamation of Israel's independence, it became the national anthem. Its text combines the heritage of antiquity with the recent history of Jews. External influences can also be found in the poem. Naftali Herz Imber, as a Polish Jew, probably knew *Mazurek Dąbrowskiego*, written in 1797 by Józef Wybicki, which in 1927 became the official national anthem of the Republic of Poland. *Mazurek Dąbrowskiego* begins with the words: "Poland has not yet perished. . . ." Similarly, in *Hatikvah* there is a clear reference to memory and the desire to live in a free homeland: "Our hope is not yet lost . . ."

> *Hatikvah*—**Hope**
> As long as in the heart, within,
> A Jewish soul still yearns,
> And onward, towards the ends of the east,
> An eye still gazes toward Zion;
>
> Our hope is not yet lost,
> The two-thousand-year-old hope,
> To be a free nation in our land,
> The land of Zion and Jerusalem.

the source of success for the largest modern power, namely the United States, but there is a clear difference between the United States and Israel.

The United States often "tempted" new residents with richness and the possible "career from rags to riches," while Israel by the end of the twentieth century could hardly appear as a place where most potential immigrants from Europe could count on a staggering career. It should be assumed that the optics of emigrants from the Middle East and North Africa were different. From their point of view, Israel quickly became a highly developed country in terms of civilisation and economy. However, Polish Jews had deep fears as to their material and professional future in Israel. Reading dozens of accounts written by emigrants from the interwar period, the postwar period, during the rule of Gomułka, and after March '68, it is hard to see the belief thay would have the opportunity to

Fig. 132. Bianka and Marcel Goldman at the Arcaffé café in Ramat Aviv, November 2016, photo: Łukasz Tomasz Sroka

earn big money and live in better conditions than before. The Second *Aliyah* (1904–1914) was largely made up of poor people, but there were many ideologically motivated individuals among them. It is enough to mention that David Ben-Gurion came to Israel as part of this immigration wave. Also in subsequent migration waves to Eretz Yisrael before World War II, the financial stimulus was visible, but the driving force was mainly the Zionist inspiration and the fear of antisemitism growing in Poland and Europe. In the postwar period, fear of antisemitism, a sense of alienation after losing loved ones, and recognition of the need to build an independent Jewish state prevailed. As for the Gomulka and March '68 *aliyot*, despite their obvious differences they had one common denominator—their participants were not so much attracted by Israel as repulsed by from Poland. Among them were social pauperization, having to deal with the consequences of the Stalinist period (after October '56), antisemitic propaganda (which reached a critical moment in March '68), degradation or loss of job, hostile reactions from some people and institutions, fear of the worst-case scenarios of the past being repeated (including physical extermination).

Marcel Goldman's biography makes it possible to take into account factors that, although important, are difficult to grasp using scientific instruments and statistics. It is about decisions that have personal motives, such as the desire to support loved ones and reunite with the family. Emphasizing that Israel was built by immigrants, it should be added right away that it was a special group of immigrants. Many of them left not because they wanted to, but because they had to. They often experienced the drama of separation from Poland, which had been their home for a significant part of their lives. In their position, re-emigration was not possible (after 1945 such applications were mostly rejected by the authorities of the Polish People's Republic) or did not solve the problem because they missed Poland, but they also identified with Israel, and they were torn apart. Such situations took place even before World War II.

Until the Zionist idea was born, two elements, Polish and Jewish, would often tear the Polish Jews apart. The end of the nineteenth century brought a third one element, the Israeli one (first associated with Eretz Yisrael, then Israel). The complicated and mostly dramatic history of Poland and Israel meant that, far more often than any valuables, Jewish emigrants only took with them an excess of impressions and experiences, and they were usually bad ones, although good ones were also there. The good ones were probably connected with their old customs and traditions, but the bad ones were the burden of memories and habits dictated by their negative experience. To put it simply, many Jews had no way back, so they were determined to survive in Israel. That proved beneficial for the very concept of the state of Israel, because it gained builders ready to work with the greatest effort. And that effort had to finally bring the desired fruit for the state and its builders . . .

Conclusion

What is unique in the history of Jews is the fact that by explaining their collective, and sometimes individual fates from recent times, we reach not hundreds, but thousands of years back. The conquest of Jerusalem by the Romans turned out to be fraught with consequences. In 66 CE riots against the Romans led to the siege of Jerusalem and the destruction of the Second Temple. The Masada fortress located in a mountain massif on the Dead Sea defended itself the longest. It was not defeated until 73 CE, which is considered the actual end of the so-called Jewish war. The Bar Kokhba revolt, which took place in 135 CE, ended tragically. After its suppression, the Romans banned Jews from entering Jerusalem. Currently, some historians interpret that event as the actual beginning of the diaspora (Greek: dispersion).

Jews never forgot about Jerusalem. The most beautiful greeting they addressed each other with was: "Next year in Jerusalem!" (Hebrew: L'Shana Haba'ah B'Yerushalayim). Masada became an iconic place for Jewish culture and identity, here Israeli soldiers swear that: "Masada will never be conquered again." Here, the bar mitzvah of Gai, Marcel Goldman's grandson took place. During the ceremony, he donned the *tallit*, which earlier belonged to his father and survived World War II with his family. The participants of the ceremony were strongly impressed by the combination of stories about the unique fate of the hidden *tallit*, about risking life, and about the history of the place where Jewish insurgents defended themselves, ready for heroic death. "And so, after 'the priestly blessing' (my son-in-law and therefore my grandson come from a priests' line), the two thousand-year-old stones of the synagogue destroyed by the Romans listened to the story of one Jewish *tallit* from Poland. A small addition to the myth of Masada?"[1]

Staying in the diaspora, the Jews were looking wistfully towards Zion. Mourning their fate, they reflected on what was happening in their old homeland, recalled its historical places, landscape, nature . . . A perfect example of this is the poem *El ha-tzipor* (*To the Bird*) by Chaim Nahman Bialik, the future

---

1 Goldman, *A w nocy przychodzą myśli*, 26.

national poet of Israel.[2] This work was his literary debut. In it, he describes the beauty of "the wonders of the distant land," which he contrasts with his own tragic fate in the "cold corner of the earth":

> Greetings to you, kind bird, upon your return
> From the hot lands back to my window.
> Back to your pleasing voice, my soul perishes
> In the winter when you leave.
>
> Sing, tell me, my beautiful bird,
> About the wonders of the distant land.
> Is it full of evils and hardships also
> There in the hot beautiful land?
>
> Will you bring me regards from my brothers in Zion,
> From my brothers far and near?
> O happy they are! Do they know
> How I suffer, O suffer, from grief?
>
> Do they know how many accusers I have here,
> How many, so many, rise up against me?
> Sing, my bird, of the wonders of the land
> The spring is coming, but to stay forever.
>
> Will you bring me from the bounty of the land,
> From the valleys and ravines, from the mountaintops?
> Has God had compassion, has he comforted Zion,
> Or is she still left to the graves?
>
> Have the valley of the rose and the hill of frankincense
> Produced their myrrh and spikenard?
> Has the old man in the woods, the sleeping Lebanon,
> Awaken from his slumber?
>
> Does the dew drip like pearls on Mount Hermon,
> Does it drip and fall like tears?
> And how fares the Jordan and its clear waters?
> And how about all the mountains, the hills?

---

2   Chaim Nahman Bialik, born in 1873 in the town of Rady (today's Ukraine), died in 1934. He settled in Eretz Yisrael in 1924.

Has the heavy cloud, which spreads gloom
and the shadow of death, departed?
Sing, my bird, of the land in which
My fathers found life and death!

Have the flowers, which I planted,
Not yet withered, as I have withered?
I recall days when I blossomed like they,
Now I have aged and my strength is no more.

Tell me, my bird, the secret of all secrets
And what did they whisper of their prey?
Did they offer comfort or hope for days
When its fruit like the Lebanon will roar?

And my brothers the workers who sow with tears,
Have they harvested the omer with joy?
O that I had wings to fly to the land
Where the almond and date-palm blossom!

What shall I tell you, good bird?
What do you expect to hear from my mouth?
From this cold corner of the earth you will not hear songs,
Only dirges and sighs and wailing.

Shall I tell you about the hardships,
Which are known in the land of the living?
O who will count the number of passing sorrows,
The approaching and raging troubles?

Fly, my bird, to your mountain, your desert.
You are happy for you have left my tent.
Were you to live with me, O wing of song,
You too would cry bitter tears at my fate.

But weeping and tears will bring no cure
These cannot heal my wounds.
My eyes have grown dim; a sack filled with tears,
My heart has been struck like a weed.

Now the tears and the bruises have stopped,
But the end of my sorrow has not yet come.

> Greetings, my dear bird, upon your return
> Oh please cry aloud for joy!³

For a long time, the Land of Israel was a reference point for Jews scattered all over the world. It had the power of attraction, although not everyone could or wanted to migrate there. Its memory had an integrating and mobilizing power, in difficult moments it raised the spirits of the Jews and allowed them to dream of improving their fate, of a chance for a better life there . . . The thing was that the mythical "land flowing with milk and honey" (Hebrew: *eretz zavat chalav u-dvash*) was not free from problems and threats. However, it did not cease to fascinate Jews. Therefore, especially when the Zionist movement was born, the Jewish soul was torn apart by three elements: the attachment to the diaspora (the current place of residence, treated most often as the homeland), Jewish culture and Judaism, and the Land of Israel, later the State of Israel. Living in the diaspora, the Jews missed Israel. Living in Israel, they could not easily get rid of ties connecting them to their abandoned homes. Aleksander Rozenfeld, a writer, aptly put it: "the curse of being in several places at once, in several forms at the same time is my fate, my Jewish fate. And it doesn't matter what feelings bind me to Israel or Poland, the only important thing is that you are in both places at once, this is the curse of a Polish Jew, this is the curse of a Russian Jew!"⁴

Marcel Goldman claims that, after moving to Israel, the Polish element did not enslave him. However, he does not deny that he never broke the deep spiritual bond that connected him with Poland. It was there even when formally he had no contact with it. His connection with the Polish culture, in which he grew up, turned out to be very strong.

The first generations of Israel's builders, as I emphasized many times in this book, were mainly immigrants. Being rooted in foreign cultures could be problematic for them and tear them apart internally, but at the same time it enriched Israel. Each of them had a different point of view on various cultural issues and traditions, rich and often unique experiences, knowledge and skills. In addition, many of them possessed natural predispositions and advantages, such as courage, creativity, openness, and determination in pursuing the goal. These qualities laid the foundation for Israel's success.

---

3   Ch. Bialik, *To the Bird*, trans. Jonathan A. Lipnick, https://blog.israelbiblicalstudies.com/holy-land-studies/bialiks-to-the-bird/, accessed 19/02/2020.
4   Rozenfeld, *Podanie o prawo powrotu*, 95.

Of course, there were many problems. A nation built by people of different cultural backgrounds had to face various tensions and conflicts. Most often, Jews did not bring larger property with them, their belongings were usually packed in one or several suitcases. The most valuable was what they had in their heads, although those heads were also burdened with a sense of fear and sad stories from their childhood. In the new, and at the same time old, homeland they had to find a new life not only in material but also in spiritual terms.

The dispersion of Jews over the centuries did not prevent the great development of their culture. Scattered around the world, they have achieved impressive successes in many areas. However, life in the diaspora (Hebrew: *galut*) was disastrous due to the numerous pogroms and persecutions of Jews that occurred in various countries throughout all eras only because they remained faithful to their religion and customs. The Holocaust of the Jews during World War II was an unprecedented drama in the history of the world.

The emigration of Jews to Eretz Yisrael and then to Israel was determined by attracting (related to memory, identity, and hope) and pushing factors (antisemitism), which sometimes were combined. After 1948, individual human dreams had a chance to come true, because Theodor Herzl's prediction that "The Jews who will try it shall achieve their State; and they will deserve it"[5] had been fulfilled. One can look at that matter in a different way—the success of the Jews living in Israel was conditioned by the generally understood prosperity of their state, and at the same time Israel's success is the sum of the successes of its citizens. This is well documented by the history of Marcel Goldman, who not only benefited from living in a free, lawful, and democratic state, but also made a great contribution so that it could be so. It is hard to imagine the emergence of independent Israel without eminent statesmen such as Theodor Herzl, Leon Pinsker, David Ben-Gurion, Vladimir Ze'ev Jabotinsky, Chaim Weizmann, and Nahum Sokolow. They took on the burden of inventing and implementing the political concept. However, the daily effort of building the state rested on the shoulders of its inhabitants, among which there were well-educated, competent, determined, hard-working, and creative people, such as Marcel Goldman. Dreams, ambitions, and aspirations played a significant role here. Marcel willingly emphasizes his pragmatism and realism. He presents himself as a "professional banker, realist and materialist who spent a lot of time in his life reading

---

5   Herzl, *Państwo żydowskie*, 46.

balance sheets—'debits and credits.'"⁶ A person with this type of personality is a perfect candidate (however high-flown these words may sound) for the builder of Israel. We can probably assume that Herzl, Ben-Gurion, or Weizmann, when talking about dreamers, did not mean people "walking with their heads in the clouds," who were carefree, reckless, or naïve. Above all, they wanted people who skillfully combined courage and prudence, had high ambitions, but at the same time critically assessed their capabilities. We see these predispositions in Marcel Goldman. In many ways, he is an exceptional man, but his life also includes experiences that have become part of thousands of other Jewish stories. World War II took six precious years of his life, even robbed him of his youth.⁷ However, unlike six million European Jews, he was able to survive the war. Moreover, his parents and siblings also survived. They were rescued thanks to their escape from the Krakow ghetto, and later they used false documents issued for the name Galas. In his touching story *Spowiedź starego człowieka* (English: Confession of an old man), Marcel summarizes his relationship with his father in the following words: "My father gave me life twice. The second time was when he managed to save his family from the furnaces in Bełżec."⁸

Many Polish Jews in Israel were professionally successful, but not all to the same extent as Marcel Goldman. Starting from the lowest level, he reached top management positions in Israeli banking. At that time he was the youngest founder and director of a private bank branch. Certainly, the fact that he did not have to change his profession, as many Polish Jews, reaching Israel, were forced to do, helped him achieve success. Other immigrants, for example, journalists, lawyers, or teachers who did not know Hebrew well enough could not continue employment in these positions in Israel, so they found other jobs and often stayed with them. At first, Marcel was not fluent in Hebrew, but he was determined to learn it quickly. Undoubtedly, his young age spoke in his favour. The measure of his success are not so much the positions he held but his specific achievements. Under his management, the Haifa branch of his bank became the most prosperous one among all other branches; its splendor was restored. Later, Marcel led an Israeli bank in Switzerland to new paths of development, although it had previously been intended for liquidation due to management errors and adverse economic conditions. He developed his reputation as a wise, honest,

---

6   Goldman, *A w nocy przychodzą myśli*, cover.
7   I am referring to the title of the film by Teresa Olearczyk *Zrabowana młodość* (English: Stolen youth), which is dedicated to Marcel Goldman.
8   Goldman, *Spowiedź starego człowieka*.

hard-working, inventive, and discreet man. As a result, he was repeatedly asked to carry out complex financial operations, or to prepare and implement recovery plans for other banks.

Marcel Goldman's achievements help us better understand how Israel's economic miracle happened. In the studies of economics in the world's leading universities, the case of this country is considered unique, because its birth was accompanied by war and the inflow of many times more people than had lived there before the proclamation of independence. This state must command respect due to the fact it was built basically from scratch, in a backward area, and has now become a model of economic prosperity, good governance, and modernity in the broad sense. Once it has its own sovereign and strong state, the nation persecuted and deprived of its own state became a nation of start-ups.[9] Israel's strength results not only from its defense technologies, but also from its economic potential.

Today, it is very clear that already in the first years of its existence, in Israeli society there was a division into four distinct groups related to the following fields: defense and intelligence, science, agriculture (kibbutzim and moshavim), and economy concentrated in urban centers (industry, high technologies, banking, and so forth). They were connected because they all served one state, most people had the same religion with similar cultural traditions and education, they had almost all been in the army, and all shared a a sense of danger. In Israel, Judaism is absolutely dominant: even Jews who distance themselves from religion are usually brought up according to the rules of the religious tradition. Every Jew living in Israel must perform military service. Young people from different social and geographical backgrounds serve side by side in the army for two (women) or three years (men). In conditions of great effort and danger, they learn to take responsibility for themselves and find out more about habits and customs of various communities. In a sense, their language and cultural codes are unified. Science has a strong position, as it has been valued by the Jewish people since antiquity. This is confirmed by numerous passages of the Talmud, for example: "If you have acquired knowledge, what do you lack? If you lack knowledge, what have you acquired?" (Leviticus Rabbah 1:6); "The world exists only through the breathing of school children"; "We must not stop teaching our children, even to rebuild the Temple"; "A city without school children will be annihilated"

---

[9] I am referring to the well-known, already cited book, Senor, Singer, *Naród start-upów*, Warsaw 2013.

(Shabbath 119 b)[10]. In Israel, science is permanently rooted in every area of life. Its achievements are used in all sectors of the economy. It was science that gave Israeli agriculture its innovative character. There is a noticeable synergy between Israeli science and the army and special services. Marcel Goldman also showed his understanding of the value of science: after all, only an internal order to acquire knowledge helped him show the willpower required to complete economic studies in unfavourable living conditions.

Undoubtedly, all these life experiences shaped Marcel's fortitude, diligence, and reliability. "An uncompromising will to succeed"[11] is another of his traits, which was inherited by his daughter Orit. I identify Marcel Goldman as a transgressive man for whom success does not mean the end of a creative path. Zofia Okraj defines this type of personality as a man "who does not agree to 'stand still,' who remains 'on the wave of success,' sets new goals to be achieved and new limits to change or exceed."[12] He received his first lesson on this topic before the war from his parents who ran a profitable haberdashery shop in Krakow. As a watchful observer, he probably noticed and remembered that only persistent work, moderation, reliability, and consistency are the path to professional success. That lesson turned out to be very useful, because, he had to follow a similar path to the one his parents had taken before World War II, although in different realities. Like them, he started from scratch, as he had to work out his professional position, social network, and savings. From the first days spent in Israel he gained momentum, and later he did not stop. His daughter writes that he "galloped forward on the fuel of crazy ambition."[13] Although he was a man "devoted to his family, warm and tender,"[14] there was a clear dissonance between him and his children. They did not want or could not keep up with him. They grew up in different conditions, they needed not only a father who would be a mentor and a guide, but also a companion for play, an understanding interlocutor—this was lacking ...

---

10 A. Cohen, *Talmud. Syntetyczny wykład na temat "Talmudu" i nauk rabinów dotyczących religii, etyki I prawodawstwa*, trans. R. Gromacka, Warsaw 1999, 185.
11 Goldman, "Congratulations to My Father on His Ninetieth Birthday."
12 Z. Okraj, "Dlaczego działania transgresyjne intrygują i inspirują do badań (także) autobiograficznych," in *Biografie nierzeczywiste. Przełom, kryzys, transgresja w perspektywie interdyscyplinarnej*, ed. M. Karkowska, Łódź 2018, 105.
13 Goldman, "Congratulations to My Father on His Ninetieth Birthday."
14 Ibid.

Marcel Goldman's biography confirms that the state is not only the sum of its public, but also a community consisting of specific individuals. Although the protagonist of this book is an extraordinary character, and many of his experiences are unique, it is clear that his life reflects the dynamic development of Israel. Marcel Goldman is almost equal to Israel. He came to this country about a year after its independence had been proclaimed. He devoted the first stage of his life in Israel to finding sustenance for himself and his parents. Then he thought about his personal development. He resumed his studies, which had been interrupted as a result of leaving Poland. He planned his strategy on the labour market. He started a family. He climbed the career ladder. He finally achieved impressive prosperity in private and professional life. The first association between Marcel's life path and Israel's development path is quite simple and obvious: just as the entire state apparatus, he began from scratch. No less important is another statement. Marcel Goldman's career is impressive, but it was not born from one spectacular idea, it results from his diligence, wisdom, courage, and ingenuity. It developed relatively fast, but there is not one decisive turning point in it. Instead, a number of decisions and events influenced it. The subsequent stages of his life are closely related. His successes were not free from dilemmas, problems, and hesitations—with difficult moments in his memory, he behaved prudently and sparingly. The history of Israel can be read in a similar way. This country did not become rich quickly based on natural resources or risky speculative decisions. The Israeli economy is firmly anchored in solid foundations. It was built by generations of kibbutzniks, moshavim workers, merchants, craftsmen, road and factory workers, dockers, and representatives of many other professions. The current shape of the Israeli economy results from the accumulation of their successes and experiences.

Also, Marcel Goldman's success is the result of successful teamwork. Undoubtedly, he became the leader of his family, but it is difficult to overstate how much he owes to his parents and his wife Bianka. He also met many people of good will on his life path who gave him advice and specific help. The personality profile of Marcel Goldman and the genetic code of Israeli statehood have one more important common feature—a strong attachment to history manifested in the memory of their own roots, ancestors, remembering what happened, and attempts to draw conclusions from it. In Marcel's statements, similarly to what has been said by Israeli statesmen, politicians, military and business people, the past is intertwined with the present. Sometimes, listening to or reading their words, it is difficult to know whether they are talking or writing about something that has already happened, is happening now, or will happen in the future...

At least one other similarity deserves to be noted between Marcel Goldman's attitude and the policy of the State of Israel. In the first period of the state's existence, several governments practiced breaking with the diaspora heritage (exceptions include relations with Jewish communities in the United States, which the Israelis treated with great care), while cultivating the memory of ancient times. In recent years, this course of action has clearly been corrected, which is confirmed, for instance, by the court battle of the Israeli authorities to take over the legacy of Franz Kafka, to which I referred in this book. The Israeli governments are still calling on Jews from all over the world to come to this country, but they no longer require them to abandon their identity. For example, pressure is not exerted on immigrants to change their names to Hebrew ones. Marcel has never cut his cultural connection with Poland, but for a few decades he broke off direct contact with it. The lack of visits to Poland can be briefly explained by formal reasons. After breaking off diplomatic relations with Israel, the authorities of the People's Polish Republic generally forbade Israelis to cross the country's borders. Some Polish Jews made such attempts, but they were usually unsuccessful. Only after the fall of communism the governments in Poland started to liberalize the border-crossing procedures. Marcel did not make such attempts. He also did not maintain correspondence contacts with friends left in Poland. He claims that he did not feel such a need. We can also assume that he was absorbed in everyday affairs. It is impossible to rule out some unconscious grudge and a desire to cut off bad memories related to Poland. In any case, the situation changed with his first arrival in Poland after emigration in 1989. At that time, his lively contact with Poland, especially with his native Krakow, was revived. Travelling to Poland did not cause any disturbance to Marcel Goldman's identity. He puts Israel first because he has managed to take root there, his relatives live there, his greatest private and professional achievements, developed with great dedication, are associated with it.

The Israelis achieved their success with effort and toil. Their own success and that of the state they were building was paid for with sacrifice. That is why the mood of joy is so often mixed with reflection and sadness in Israel. Even on the most joyous holidays, such as Israel's Independence Day, the inhabitants do not lose the thoughts of those who paid the highest price for this independence. In Israel, Yom HaShoah (the full name is Yom HaZikaron LaShoah Ve-LaG'vurah, Holocaust and Heroism Remembrance Day) and Yom HaZikaron (Hebrew: Yom HaZikaron LeChaialei Ma'arakhot Yisrael U-L'Nifge'ei, the Memorial Day for the Fallen Soldiers of Israel and Victims of Terrorism) are celebrated with great deference. On these days, at designated times, the alarm sirens are turned on and the traffic stops. This combination of the pride of widely known achievements and the bitterness of unparalleled tragic experiences is reflected in Marcel Goldman's poem entitled *Wiosna w Izraelu* (English: Spring in Israel):

W judejskich górach kwitną już migdały.	In the Judean mountains almonds are already blooming.
Otulił się świątecznie w wiatr wiosenny,	He wrapped himself festively in a spring wind,
Kolorowy, wspaniały	Colorful, wonderful,
Izrael cały.	All Israel.
Na czerwono, różowo, niebiesko i biało	In red, pink, blue, and white,
I wspomina historie,	And he remembers stories
Jak to dawniej bywało.	Of what used to be.
Mamy więc Pesach—z egipskiej niewoli	So we have Pesach— from Egyptian captivity
Do wolności,	To freedom,
A krótko po tym— Acmaut, Święto Niepodległości.	And shortly after— Atzmaut, the Independence Day.
Mimo że jest tyle przyczyn do radości,	Although there are so many reasons to be happy,
To w tymże czasie cień żałoby i smutku	At that time a shadow of mourning and sadness
Też w naszych sercach gości.	Is also present in our hearts.
Tak się to u nas splata	This is how they interweave,
I radość i żal	Both joy and regret,
W dniach nie bardzo od siebie odległych:	On days not very distant:
Bo z jednej strony niepodległość,	On the one hand, independence,
A z drugiej wielu poległych.	On the other, many fallen.
Na cmentarzach wojskowych	At military cemeteries
W całym naszym kraju	In our whole country
Ceremonie żałobne	Mourning ceremonies
W tym miesiącu, maju.	In this month of May.

I w tym miesiącu także	And this month also
Gdy powietrze majowe	When you breathe in
Wdychasz pełnym haustem	The May air at a gulp
Przychodzi dzień smutny,	A sad day comes,
Dzień Holocaustu.	The Holocaust Day.
Za pamięć tych co zginęli ot tak	For the memory of those who died just like that
Bez powodu,	For no reason,
Zamordowani, zagazowani, spaleni,	Murdered, gassed, burned,
Czy zmarli od zimna i głodu.	Or dead of cold and hunger.
W kalendarzu historii	In the calendar of history
Na karcie honorowej	On the honour card
Zapiszcie:	Write down:
Wiosna w Izraelu	Spring in Israel
Liczy dni 6 milionów	Has 6 million days
Żałoby bezgrobowej.	Of graveless mourning.
A wiatr?	And the wind?
Wiatr sobie hula zgodnie,	The wind is raging in peace,
Raz się śmieje, raz płacze,	Once it laughs, once it cries,
Wszystko po kolei	Everything in turn
W górach jerozolimskich,	In the Jerusalem mountains,
W górach Judei...	In the mountains of Judea...*

* M. Goldman, "Wiosna w Izraelu," Tel Aviv, spring 2011, typescript.

Modern Israel was built by immigrants from various countries and continents. There are a lot of Polish accents there. For years, Polish Jews set the tone for social, political, scientific, cultural, and economic life, and dominated numerically in the highest organs of power. Most of them quickly merged with the general Israeli society. Today their children and grandchildren take the floor. Polish aliyot have become a more historical than political topic. Immediately after them, numerous waves of migration arrived from the Middle East, Africa, and the former Soviet Union. Naturally, Polish bookshops were replaced, for example, with Russian ones. For obvious reasons, all government agencies controlling the absorption have lost interest in Polish Jews. This is not only a natural course of things, but also a sign of strength and success of the latter. The fact that they exerted an overwhelming influence on the shape of today's Israel is much more important. The values they instilled there turned out to be durable and attractive also to immigrants from other countries. The middle-class culture and work ethos they represented became a point of reference for the whole of society. The government, scientific, cultural and economic institutions they once co-created stood the test of time. They have been modified and improved many times but never denied. The passage of time did not break ties with Poland, not only of those who were born there, but also their descendants. It was expected that the latter would no longer show any interest in Poland. However, it did not happen. Of course, the *sabras* do not have and will not have such a sentimental relationship with Poland as their parents or grandparents, but while building their family trees, at some stage they will write there the names of Polish cities and towns, where their ancestors were born.

In recent years, the number of young Israelis who travel to Poland not only to traverse the Holocaust trail has been systematically increasing. There are also those who want to know their roots and reach the places where their family members lived. The pilgrimages of pious Jews to the graves of famous rabbis and *tzaddikim* continue (they visit Krakow, Leżajsk, Łańcut, and other places). There are more and more people interested in tourist and cultural values of Poland. For example, the POLIN Museum of the History of Polish Jews, opened on April 19, 2013, is attractive for them.[15] Marcel and Bianka's daughter and grandchildren have already travelled in Poland in their footsteps, it is very likely that one day they will also come here with their own children. Business contacts between Poles and Israelis are developing successfully. It is too early to consider the story described in this book as completed. I am not placing a full stop here, life will write the rest . . .

---

15 The permanent exhibition of the POLIN Museum was opened on October 28, 2014.

Afterword

My friendship with Marcel Goldman goes back to the prewar Krakow. We were both students of elementary school at the renowned Hebrew Gymnasium in Krakow. The level of teaching at that school was very high. Teachers, however, were focused on something more than just that we learn hard. They wanted to raise us as decent citizens. Of course, the school had a Zionist profile, but the school headmasters made sure to stay away from politics. Through the extensive learning curriculum emphasizing the Hebrew language, and the history and culture of Eretz Yisrael, our love for the former homeland from which our ancestors had derived was stimulated. At the same time, we were raised as exemplary Polish citizens who know, understand, and love their country. That is why so much importance was attached to Polish history and literature. It was all harmoniously arranged with my after-school life, which took place only in the traditional Jewish community. Together with my parents and my elder brother (I knew my sister only from my parents' stories, because she died in 1915 during World War I) we lived in Krakow. We formed a traditional family, but not a religious one. Naturally, we celebrated the Sabbath and other Jewish holidays. The duty to support the family rested with the father, who worked as a sales representative. He supplied various delicatessen in Lesser Poland with goods that were considered luxury at the time, such as Hungarian salami, sardines, dried fruit, and delicious sweets. My mother was a housewife and raised children. One can say about my parents that they lived according to the principle propagated by Moses Mendelssohn (he lived in the years 1729–1786 and was a leading figure of the Enlightenment): "to be a Jew at home and a citizen on the street." We cried a lot in my family home after the death of Józef Piłsudski. I attended his funeral. Then, as a sign of mourning, I wore a black armband for a year.

In everyday life, my parents used the Polish language. Their Polish was very good. They also knew Esperanto and often spoke that language. The years of their youth fall at the peak of fashion for that artificial language created by Ludwik Zamenhof, a Jewish doctor born in Białystok (1859–1917). My parents met at an Esperanto language course.

Jews loved Krakow! Here, for centuries, despite various adversities, Jewish life had been successful. Krakow became a place of Jewish culture unique in Europe and even in the world. Krakow Jews had eight major synagogues and dozens of smaller prayer rooms at their disposal. In addition, there were Jewish religious and secular schools. The Jewish religious community in Krakow had its own hospital, which was located at Skawińska Street. Many Krakow Jews had significant achievements in various fields of culture, science and economy. All that did not bother us to dream of building a Jewish state in Eretz Yisrael.

I was slowly becoming ready for Zionist ideas. First, my elder brother instilled in me an interest in those matters. He took me to various meetings where Zionist activists gathered. For example, I attended an evening meeting with Ze'ev Jabotinsky. Since I was the youngest person in the room, I was called to shake his hand, I treated it as a great honour. Shortly after that I was asked to help in the election campaign of Zionist groups that applied to join the Sejm of the Republic of Poland. For instance, my role was to hand out leaflets in various places in Krakow. Inspired by my brother, I joined the Zionist Jewish scout organisation Tzofim, which was affiliated at the Hebrew Gymnasium in Krakow. In one of the following years I became its instructor, maybe even the youngest in the whole organisation. I was less than fifteen years old. Today, I think that my rapid rise in the ranks of Tzofim came from the fact that a colleague who had previously performed that function emigrated to Eretz Yisrael. Marcel Goldman joined that organisation. In that way he became my subordinate, although I know that it was not like that. I admit that I was a very young person at the time and before each meeting I was under a lot of stress, and I had serious concerns if everything would go well. Our meetings, in which Marcel participated, were usually held in the school's common room, which was at our disposal. In addition, we had various classes and trainings in the field. We gladly set off on scout trips. We devoted a lot of time to learning the Hebrew language, we read the Torah in Hebrew, we also learned Hebrew songs. A lot of information about Eretz Yisrael was given to us by a teacher who spent some time there and returned to Krakow. His lectures were very popular. A question may be asked: why did I not emigrate to Eretz Yisrael? Well, I really wanted to go to Eretz Yisrael, but my parents stopped me. They thought that my elder brother should go there first. It wasn't until later that I was to emigrate. I did not want to oppose my parents' will. The outbreak of World War II found us in that situation.

World War II abruptly and brutally interrupted our, in my opinion, cheerful and happy years of youth. All that was accompanied by enormous chaos, pain and suffering. At the first stage of the war, we stopped organizational activity. Soon I had the opportunity to meet Marcel again. It was a friendly meeting, organizational dependency ceased to exist between us. To put it simply... Just after the outbreak of war, I found myself in Łagiewniki with my family. Marcel lived in Borek Fałęcki. So we were close to each other. In the farmer's barn where I lived, there was a table on which, together with Marcel, we played table tennis. The farmer used that barn to kill rabbits and to remove and dry their skins. That's why the whole place stank, but we somehow managed to bear it. That's why we were able to play many matches. Later, my family, just like Marcel's family, found itself in the Krakow ghetto. I was asked to participate in an underground organization Akiba and I joined it without hesitation. That conspiracy was created by people who had no illusions about how tragic the situation of Jews in Europe was. We fought not so much to save our lives, but for dignity. We thought our sacrifice made sense, even if one day it would all come down to a few sentences in historical books: "Jewish youth took up arms . . ." I was only a teenager. At first, I was too young to act as a fighter. So I was assigned the function of a liaison, observer and purchaser. In that role, I often left the ghetto, performing various actions on the so-called Aryan side. Over time, my responsibilities increased. On the night of December 24–25, 1942, my formation took part in an action led by the famous Jewish Combat Organisation (ŻOB) against German soldiers spending time in the café Cyganeria (then *nur für Deutsche*) in Krakow at Szpitalna Street. Several grenades were thrown inside, which killed a dozen and wounded a dozen or so German soldiers.[1] It was one of the largest actions of this type in Europe, and which is important, it occurred at a time when German troops were still a power. Because our organisation did not have enough money for activities, we were forced to conduct robbery actions—I know it doesn't sound elegant. During one of such actions, which took place in Bochnia, I was arrested. It was 1943. For a month, I was brutally interrogated in a Krakow prison at Montelupich Street. I didn't reveal any organisational secrets. Then I was sent to Auschwitz. I fell seriously ill in the camp. I was in hospital. One day I received information that by selecting my camp number, I was assigned to gas the following day. When a paramedic came to me, I asked him to sit down next to me. I decided to tell him a little about myself and what I had done before so that any trace of me would remain. Among other things, I briefly summarised for him what I was doing in the underground. It turned out that my listener was also a member of the underground. He belonged to secret camp structures, which were managed by, among others, a socialist activist Józef Cyrankiewicz (1911–1989). He informed him of what he had heard from me. Cyrankiewicz

---

1 According to the accounts of some people living at the time, only one German soldier was killed, while a dozen others were injured.

instructed him to exchange my camp number. I received the identity of a man who died the day before. His corpse was put into the gas chamber in my place. In that way I was saved from certain death! I joined the group led by Cyrankiewicz, although I told him that I would not be convinced to the socialist idea, let alone the communist one. I suffered a lot, but I managed to survive. In January 1945, I found myself in the "death march" that left Auschwitz. In the face of the approaching fronts of the Allies, and above all due to the impending Red Army, Germany began to liquidate concentration and extermination camps and blur the traces of its criminal activities. Germans took hungry, sick, and generally emaciated prisoners westwards into the Third Reich to continue using them as free labour. At the same time, it was a way to annihilate a large proportion of prisoners who were dying of cold, hunger, and disease along the way. Along the way, we were quartered in different places. In one of the barracks where we were accommodated for the night, I met my brother who survived the war in the Płaszów Camp. A peculiar situation occurred. I went to one of the beds and asked the boy lying there to move a little and make place for me. Because it was dark, he asked, "Who are you?" That's how we recognized each other. I decided to escape, to which I also tried to persuade my brother. However, I did not succeed. So I escaped with a few other companions. Shortly afterwards, World War II ended. Together with a group of Jewish conspirators, I got to Germany to retaliate for all our suffering during the war, and especially for the deaths of millions of Jews. We were going to poison the drinking water tanks. We even managed to poison the water that German soldiers were drinking in the camp in Nuremberg. However, we decided to stop our further activities in that direction. In 1946 I emigrated to Eretz Yisrael. In 1948, my brother arrived in Israel.

In independent Israel I served in the navy. I came to the rank of lieutenant colonel. I lived in Haifa for a while, in a cooperative block occupied by Israeli army officers. It turned out that Marcel Goldman and his wife Bianka live on the same street (on its corner). My wife Aviva was a nurse in a maternity hospital. I remember that she helped Bianka with the first baths of her newborn daughter Orit. Here I have to point out that I met personally not only Marcel and Bianka, but also their loved ones. I knew Marcel's mother well, whom I remembered as a wonderful and affectionate person. Marcel's family survived World War II in an extraordinary way. I believe that Marcel's mother played a key role in this respect, she turned out to be not only a brave and inventive woman, but also a generous one—I would like to remind you that during the war she took in and took care of her sister's little daughter, who was murdered by the Germans. Marcel's mother did something that few people were ready for at the time. I also know how wonderful the family of Marcel's wife, Bianka, was. To this day I am very impressed by Bianka's father, who was a doctor of law, a man of exceptional wisdom, an erudite, and a great interlocutor. I have a great affection for Bianka, who in my opinion, thanks to the fact that she is a wonderful and wise mother and wife, undoubtedly contributed to her husband's professional success. I value our friendship, which has lasted for several dozen years. It seems to me that the period of our most intense relationship are the years lived in Haifa. There were very often home parties to which we invited each other. Initially, we lived very modestly, even poorly. Nevertheless, we enjoyed life, we had a great time with bridge, good music and alcohol. Parties were held on a contributory basis: everyone bought something and prepared something to eat. I must admit that Polish Jews popularized the so-called boozy events in Israel. They also contributed to the popularization of the bridge, in this regard the members of the Gomulka Aliyah played a special role. Apparently, we were partying very loudly, because one day even the police came to Marcel's apartment, called by one of the neighbours, who was disturbed by the music and shouts coming from us. The policemen knew, however, that it was the apartment of Marcel Goldman, who was already an important and known person in Haifa. They were not eager to intervene. After drinking a few glasses of vodka with us, they left . . .

Dance parties and bridge games cannot, however, obscure the fact that Marcel Goldman was above all a man of action. His main features include wisdom, diligence, prudence and goodness—openness to the needs of other people. In my opinion, his unusual ambition to be the best in his profession became his trademark. He prepared himself carefully for it, obtaining economic education and specialising in banking. He climbed the career ladder, which should not be interpreted as a coincidence, but a simple consequence of the fact that he was able to perfectly organise the work of subordinate bank outlets, and above all he was the highest-level banker. He just knew that job like hardly anyone; this is not only my assessment, it was and still remains a common opinion about Marcel Goldman, which I have come across in many places. Everyone I knew trusted Marcel. There was agreement that he could be given uncounted money and he would not lack a penny. He fully deserved to hold one of the highest positions in Israeli banking.

I have welcomed the idea of writing a book that is a biography of Marcel Goldman and presenting Israel from the perspective of his life and achievements with joy. I think that he is an excellent model to show and follow. His life teaches us how much a person can do if he is determined to succeed. Marcel is a representative of that generation of Jews who suffered the disaster of World War II.

He reached Israel, just like me, with absolutely nothing. He did not receive the "silver spoon" as a gift. He did not become the heir to a large fortune to multiply it peacefully. He had to start on his own from the beginning. I could watch closely how it all looked. I know that after years of war he forgot a lot from the Hebrew language and basically had to learn it from scratch. In a short time he not only learned the Hebrew language, but also improved his German language skills and learned English very well. He graduated in economics in Israel. He started with a one-room flat that didn't even have heating. However, he soon earned for a lot of material goods, bought a car, a large and elegant apartment, and so forth. I believe that in our group of friends he went the farthest, in terms of private and professional life his achievements seem to me the most impressive among all that I could observe. He achieved everything with his own strength, today he can undoubtedly serve as a model for young people.

In my opinion, everyone who will get to know the biography of Marcel Goldman has a great opportunity to learn lessons for himself, how to live wisely for yourself and for others . . .

Leopold "Poldek" Wasserman,[2]
or Yehuda Maimon

Tel Aviv, July 29, 2018

---

[2] Leopold "Poldek" Wasserman (real name Yehuda Maimon) was born in 1924 in Krakow. He died in 2020 and was buried in the Moshava Nir Zvi cemetery. Before World War II, he was an instructor in the Jewish scout organisation HaTzofim. During World War II, he was a member of the underground formation Akiba, which in 1942 became famous for participating in the attack by the Jewish Combat Organisation on the café Cyganeria in Krakow, during which several German soldiers were killed and wounded. He was also member of underground organizations in the German Auschwitz-Birkenau Nazi Concentration Camp. In 1946 he emigrated to Eretz Yisrael. After 1948, he served in the Israeli navy, he became a lieutenant colonel (Hebrew: *sgan aluf*), two ranks lower than the general.

Bibliography

I Archival Sources

1. The Municipal Historical Archives of Tel Aviv-Yafo
Collection 5132, file number 08–233, Letters and documents 1926.
Collection 5132, file number 08–230, Resolutions of the City Council 1938–1939.
Collection 5132, file number 08–231, Letters and documents, file number 1929.
Collection 5136, file number 08–254, Reports on groupings and communes 1926–1935.

2. The National Archives in Krakow
Reference number 29/1473/110, Civil registry files of the Klasno-Podgórze Israeli Metrical District, Marriage certificate of Maksymilian Goldman and Sara Goldberger.
Reference number 29/218/867, Krakow District Office, Applications for an ID card: Sara Goldman, Maksymilian Goldman.
Reference number 29/33/SMKr 582 (folder "c"), Department of applications of Jews from areas connected to Krakow, Files of the city of Krakow, Marceli and Maks's applications for Kennkarte.
Reference number 29/83/393, Health Office in Krakow, Marcel Goldman's birth certificate.

3. The Central Zionist Archives in Jerusalem
Reference number KH4/10023, Documents of Keren Hayesod.
Reference number S6/2937, Documents concerning Keren Kayemet LeYisrael and other Zionist organisations.

4. The Central State Archives of Ukraine in Lviv
Fond 335, description 1, Society for the Reconstruction of Palestine Keren Hayesod [1921–1939].
Case 36: Information of the Central Office in Jerusalem regarding the publication of propaganda literature.
Case 177: Correspondence with the Central Office in Jerusalem, regarding organisational matters [1927].
Fond 338, description 1, National Zionist Organisation in Lviv.
Case 736: Lectures on Zionism and Palestine, the first lecture: Palestine's absorption capacity, Lviv–Warsaw 1939.
Case 759: Report on the activities of the Polish-Palestinian Chamber of Commerce for 1935, Warsaw 1936.

5. Private Archives

Family collections of Marcel and Bianka Goldman (Tel Aviv).
Family collections of Prof. Stanisław Grzybowski (Krakow).
Collections of manuscripts, typescripts, prints, books, and magazines of Ryszard Löw (Tel Aviv).
Collections of postcards, cards, and postage stamps of Prof. Aleksander B. Skotnicki (Krakow).

II Printed Sources

Almanach żydowski, edited by Herman Stachel, Lviv–Warsaw–Poznań 1937.
Borzymińska Zofia, *Dzieje Żydów w Polsce. Wybór tekstów źródłowych. XIX wiek*, Warsaw 1994.
Corpus studiosorum Universitatis Iagellonicae in saeculis, vol. 3: *1850/51–1917/18, E–D*, edited by Krzysztof Stopka, Krakow 2006.
Dokumenty polityki syjonistycznej. Od programu Bazylejskiego do enuncjacyj MacDonalda i Weizmanna. 1897–1931, Krakow [n.d.].
Dzieje Żydów w Polsce 1944–1968. Teksty źródłowe, edited by Alina Cała i Helena Datner-Śpiewak, Warsaw 1997.
Fijałkowski Paweł, *Dzieje Żydów w Polsce. Wybór tekstów źródłowych. XI–XVIII wiek*, Warsaw [n.d.].
Herzl Teodor, *Mowy ze Zjazdów Bazylejskich*, Warsaw 1900.
———, *Państwo żydowskie. Próba nowoczesnego rozwiązania kwestii żydowskiej*, translated by Jacek Surzyn, Krakow 2006.
Konstytucja Państwa Izrael, translated and introduction by Krzysztof Wojtyczek, Warsaw 2001.
Kronika Szkolna uczennic żydowskich z lat 1933–1939 Miejskiej Szkoły Powszechnej nr 15 im. Klementyny Tańskiej-Hoffmanowej przy ul. Miodowej w Krakowie, introduction by Aleksander B. Skotnicki, Krakow 2006.
Kuncewiczowa Maria, *Miasto Heroda. Notatki palestyńskie (1938 r.)*, Warsaw 1982.
Łętocha Barbara, Messer Aleksander, Cała Alina, Jabłońska Izabela, *Palestyna w żydowskich drukach ulotnych wydanych w II Rzeczypospolitej. Dokumenty ze zbiorów Biblioteki Narodowej*, Warsaw 2009.
Stosunki polsko-izraelskie (1945–1967). Wybór dokumentów, selected and edited by Szymon Rudnicki and Marcos Silber, Warsaw 2009.
Żebrowski Rafał, *Dzieje Żydów w Polsce. Wybór tekstów źródłowych. 1918–1939*, Warsaw 1993.

III Conversations and Correspondence

Goldman Bianka—conversations and correspondence 2014–2019
Goldman Marcel—conversations and correspondence 2014–2019
Haratyk Gabriela—conversations and correspondence July 20–21, 2017
Löw Ryszard—conversations November 22, 2016, May 17, 2019
Muralt Peter—correspondence July 2018
Singer Shalom—correspondence November 16, 2017

IV Diaries, Memories, Studies Based on Personal Experience

Aleksandrowicz Sinai, "Wilek," in *Polska i Palestyna—dwie ziemie i dwa nieba. Żydzi krakowscy w obiektywie Ze'eva Aleksandrowicza*, idea by Sinai Aleksandrowicz, text by Edyta Gawron, Tomasz Strug, Krakow 2012, 5–10.

Amit Nili, *A miałam być księżniczką z bajki...*, translated by Katka Mazurczak, Krakow–Budapest 2009.

Barbur Eli, *Grupy na wolnym powietrzu*, Warsaw 1995.

Begin Menachem, *Czas białych nocy. Opowieść o aresztowaniu i przesłuchaniach Menachema Begina, z załączeniem protokołów i dokumentów odtajnionych po upadku Związku Radzieckiego*, translated by Małgorzata Ornat, Krakow–Budapest 2010.

Ben-Zion Gold, *Cisza przed burzą. Życie polskich Żydów przed Holokaustem*, translated, edited, and footnotes by Joanna Preizner, Krakow–Budapest 2011.

Canin Mordechaj, *Przez ruiny i zgliszcza. Podróż po stu zgładzonych gminach żydowskich w Polsce*, translated by Monika Adamczyk-Garbowska, Warsaw 2018.

Cukierman Icchak ["Antek"], *Nadmiar pamięci (Siedem owych lat). Wspomnienia 1939–1946*, edited and preface by Marian Turski, afterword by Władysław Bartoszewski, Warsaw 2000.

Dworak-Cousin Ilona, *Dybuk wspomnień*, Krakow–Budapest 2008.

———, *Podróż do krainy cieni*, translated by Henryk Szafir, Krakow–Budapest–Siracuse 2018.

Frankel Alona, "Rozdwojona," interview by Katarzyna Bielas, *Wysokie Obcasy* 25 (2007): 10–17.

Friedman Ryszard, *Jeden spośród wielu*, translated by Justyn Hunia, Krakow 2017.

Goldman Marcel, *A w nocy przychodzą myśli*, Krakow 2012.

———, *Iskierki życia*, 3rd ed., Krakow 2014.

———, "Spowiedź starego człowieka," *Haaretz*, February 21, 2014, supplement: *Culture and Literature*.

———, "W małym pokoju w Ramat Ha-Szaron" (manuscript), Tel Aviv, August 2018.

Gross Natan, *Kim pan jest, panie Grymek?*, Krakow 1991.

———, *Przygody Grymka w Ziemi Świętej*, Krakow 2006.

———, *Rękopis znaleziony w piwnicy*, in *To była hebrajska szkoła w Krakowie. Historia i wspomnienia*, edited by Natan Gross, Tel Aviv 1989, 52–61.

Grynberg Henryk, *Uchodźcy*, Warsaw 2004.

Hartglas Apolinary, *Na pograniczu dwóch światów*, introduction and edited by Jolanta Żyndul, Warsaw 1996.

Keret Orna, "Byłam sroga, łagodny był mąż," interview by Agata Tuszyńska, *Wysokie Obcasy* 50 (2014): 11–15.

Klepfish Heshel, *Przedwojenny świat przez pryzmat młodego Żyda polskiego. Eseje 1931–1937*, Tel Aviv 1937.

Kornblum Josef, *Ziemia przeobiecana*, Krakow 1993.

———[Kornblum Józef], *Miłość i szarańcza na tle Ziemi Obiecanej*, Bielsko-Biała 1999.

Lewińska Maria, *Analfabeci z wyższym wykształceniem*, Krakow–Budapest 2016.

———, *Emigracji dzień pierwszy*, Warsaw 1999.

———, *Posuń się*, Warsaw 2000.

———, *Przechowane słowa*, Tel Aviv 2008.
Lubetkin Cywia, *Zagłada i powstanie*, translated by Maria Krych, Warsaw 1999.
Meir Golda, *My Life*, Jerusalem–Tel Aviv 1975.
Ostatnie pokolenie. Autobiografie polskiej młodzieży żydowskiej okresu międzywojennego ze zbiorów YIVO Institute for Jewish Research w Nowym Jorku, edited and introduction by Alina Cała, Warsaw 2003.
Oz Amos, "Opowieść o miłości i mroku," translated by Leszek Kwiatkowski, *Literatura na Świecie* 11–12 (2004): 209–233.
Peres Shimon, *Podróż sentymentalna z Teodorem Herzlem*, translated by Bohdan Drozdowski, Warsaw 2002.
Pruszyński Ksawery, *Palestyna po raz trzeci*, Warsaw 1996.
———, *Sarajewo 1914, Szanghaj 1932, Gdańsk?*, Warsaw 1932.
Ritterman-Abir Henryk, *Nie od razu Kraków zapomniano*, [Tel Aviv] 1984.
Rozenfeld Aleksander, *Podanie o prawo powrotu*, Poznań 1990.
Sylwin Anatol, *Śnieżyca*, Warsaw 1986.
To była hebrajska szkoła w Krakowie. Historia i wspomnienia, edited by Natan Gross, Tel Aviv 1989.
Weiss Szewach, *Cherezińska Elżbieta, Z jednej strony, z drugiej strony*, Warsaw 2005.
———, *Czas ambasadora*, edited and compiled by Joanna Szwedowska, Krakow 2003.
———, *Ludzie i miejsca*, Krakow 2013.
———, *Pamiętam...*, a conversation with Kamila Drecka, Krakow 2018.

V Albums, Atlases, Encyclopedias, Reference Books, Dictionaries

Cała Alina, Węgrzynek Hanna, Zalewska Gabriela, *Historia i kultura Żydów polskich. Słownik*, Warsaw 2000.
Famulska-Ciesielska Karolina, Żurek Sławomir Jacek, *Literatura polska w Izraelu. Leksykon*, Krakow–Budapest 2012.
Gilbert Martin, *Atlas historii Żydów*, Kryspinów [n.d.].
Israel. The Chosen Land, Tel Aviv 1961.
Klugman Aleksander, *Nowy słownik polsko-hebrajski, hebrajsko-polski*, Tel Aviv 1993.
Nowy leksykon judaistyczny, edited by Julius H. Schoeps, Warsaw 2007.
Polski słownik judaistyczny. Dzieje. Kultura. Religia. Ludzie, vols. 1–2, edited by Zofia Borzymińska and Rafał Żebrowski, Warsaw 2003.
Unterman Alan, *Encyklopedia tradycji i legend żydowskich*, translated by Olga Zienkiewicz, Warsaw 1994.
Urbański Krzysztof, *Leksykon dziejów ludności żydowskiej Kielc 1789–1999*, Krakow 2000.
Wigoder Geoffrey, *Słownik biograficzny Żydów*, translated by Andrzej Jaraczewski, Irena Kałużyńska, Piotr Łomnicki, Anna Maria Nowak, Bożena Stokłosa, Warsaw 1998.
Żydzi w Polsce. Dzieje i kultura. Leksykon, edited by Jerzy Tomaszewski, Andrzej Żbikowski, Warsaw 2001.

VI Press

Biuletyn Izrael–Polska, 2005–2013.
Chidusz, 2018–2019.

Dialog, 2002, no. 60.
Gazeta Wyborcza, 1991–2019.
Haaretz, 1919–2019.
Jidełe, Spring 2000.
Kontury, 1988–2006.
Kultura (Paris), 1948–1989.
Midrasz, 1997–2019.
Polityka, 1991–2019.
Rzeczpospolita, 1989–2019.
Słowo Żydowskie (*Das Yiddishe Vort*), 1992–2019
Tygodnik Powszechny, 1989–2019.
Yedioth Achronoth, 1948–2019.
Yisrael Hayom, 2008–2019.

VII Literature

Adamczyk, Kazimierz, *Doświadczenia polsko-żydowskie w literaturze emigracyjnej (1939–1980)*, Krakow 2008.
Aleksiun-Mądrzak, Natalia, "Stosunek żydowskich partii politycznych w Polsce do emigracji," *Polska 1944/45–1989. Studia i Materiały* 2 (1996): 123–150.
Aleksiun, Natalia, *Dokąd dalej? Ruch syjonistyczny w Polsce (1944–1950)*, Warsaw 2002.
———, "Stosunki polsko-żydowskie w piśmiennictwie historyków żydowskich w Polsce w latach trzydziestych XX wieku," *Studia Judaica* 1 (2006): 47–67.
———, "Nielegalna emigracja Żydów z Polski w latach 1945–1947," part 1, *Biuletyn Żydowskiego Instytutu Historycznego* 3, no. 2 (1995/96): 67–99; part 2, *Biuletyn Żydowskiego Instytutu Historycznego* 3 (1996): 33–49; part 3, *Biuletyn Żydowskiego Instytutu Historycznego* 4 (1996): 35–48.
Arendt, Hannah, *Pisma żydowskie*, translated by Mieczysław Godyń, Piotr Nowak, Ewa Rzanna, Piotr Nowak, introduction by Piotr Nowak, Warsaw 2012.
Armstrong, Karen, *Jerozolima: miasto trzech religii*, translated by Barbara Cendrowska, Warsaw 2000.
Avineri, Shlomo, "Dzienniki Teodora Herzla jako Bildungsroman," translated by Piotr Paziński, *Midrasz* 9 (2004): 10–17.
———, *Herzl's vision. Theodor Herzl and the Foundation of the Jewish State*, translated by Haim Watzman, Katonah, NY 2014.
Avner, Yehuda, *The Prime Ministers: An Intimate Narrative of Israeli Leadership*, 2nd ed., Jerusalem 2017.
———, *The Young Inheritors: A Portrait of Israel's Children*, photographs by Gemma Levine, with an introduction by Herman Wouk, New York 1982.
Balint, Benjamin, "Czyje gołębie powinien karmić Kafka," interview by Michał Nogaś, *Gazeta Wyborcza*, March 23–24, 2019, 20–21.
———, *Ostatni proces Kafki*, translated by Krzysztof Kurek, Warsaw 2019.
Banet-Fornal Zofia, "Hatikwa znaczy nadzieja," *Midrasz* 6 (2007): 30–31.
Bania, Radosław, "Status Jerozolimy a konflikt bliskowschodni," in *Międzynarodowe studia polityczne i kulturowe wobec wyzwań współczesności*, edited by Tomasz Domański,

Łódź 2016, 309–323, http://dspace.uni.lodz.pl:8080/xmlui/bitstream/handle/11089/17627/17-309_323-Bania.pdf?-sequence=3&isAllowed=y, accessed March 17, 2018.
Barbur, Eli, Urbański Krzysztof, *Właśnie Izrael. „Gadany" przewodnik po teraźniejszości i historii Izraela*, Warsaw 2006.
Bar-Zohar, Michael, *Ben Gurion: Biografia*, Jerusalem 1980.
———, *Ben Gurion: Biografia medinit*, 3 vols., Tel Aviv 1975.
———, *Ben Gurion: Ha-yish me-achorei ha-agadah*, Tel Aviv 1987.
———, *Kitzur toldot Yisrael*, Rishon LeZion 2018.
Bar-Zohar, Michael, Mishal Nissim, *Mossad. Najważniejsze misje izraelskich tajnych służb*, translated by Katarzyna Bażyńska-Chojnacka and Piotr Chojnacki, Poznań 2013.
Bauer, Yehuda, *Flight and Rescue: Brichah, the Organized Escape of Jewish Survivors of Eastern Europe 1944–1948*, New York 1970.
Ben-Artzi, Josi, *Haifa—historia mekomit*, Haifa 1998.
Bensimon, Doris, Errera Eglal, *Żydzi i Arabowie. Historia współczesnego Izraela*, translated by Regina Gromacka, Krzysztof Pruski, Warsaw 2000.
Benson, Michael T., *Harry S. Truman and the Founding of Israel*, foreword by Stan A. Taylor, Westport, CT 1997.
Berendt, Grzegorz, "Emigracja Żydów z Polski w latach 1960–1967, in *Z przeszłości Żydów polskich. Polityka—gospodarka—kultura—społeczeństwo*, edited by Jacek Wijaczka and Grzegorz Miernik, Krakow 2005, 297–309.
———, "O walce z 'nacjonalizmem żydowskim' w Polsce Ludowej (1950–1955)," *Midrasz* 5 (2006): 33–36.
Bergman, Ronen, *Powstań i zabij pierwszy. Tajna historia skrytobójczych akcji izraelskich służb specjalnych*, translated by Piotr Grzegorzewski and Jerzy Wołk-Łaniewski, Katowice 2019.
Bieleń, Stanisław, "Stosunki izraelsko-polskie," in *Współczesny Izrael*, edited by Konstanty Adam Wojtaszczyk, Warsaw 2001, 80–105.
Biografistyka we współczesnych badaniach historycznych. Teoria i praktyka, edited by Jolanta Kolbuszewska, Rafał Stobiecki, Łódź 2017.
Bojko, Krzysztof, *Izrael a aspiracje Palestyńczyków 1987–2006*, Warsaw 2006.
Bożyk, Stanisław, *System konstytucyjny Izraela*, Warsaw 2002.
Brandstaetter, Roman, "Jerozolima światła i mroku," *Midrasz* 10 (2009): 10–11.
Briks, Piotr, "Ślady żeglugi po Morzu Martwym w starożytności (VII w. przed Chr.–II w. po Chr.): stan i perspektywy badań," part 1, *Klio. Czasopismo poświęcone dziejom Polski i powszechnym* 36, no. 1 (2016): 3–16.
Chaczko, Krzysztof, "Ewolucja systemu partyjnego Izraela w perspektywie społecznych determinantów zmiany," in *Medinat Israel. Państwo i tożsamość*, edited by Joanna Krauze andi Konrad Zieliński, Lublin 2013, 127–140.
———, "Od konfiguracji unipolarnej do konfiguracji trójpolarnej? Próba typologizacji izraelskiego systemu partyjnego," *Studia Judaica* 1 (2011): 87–105.
———, *System partyjny Izraela w perspektywie struktury podziałów socjopolitycznych*, Wrocław 2011.

Chaczko, Krzysztof, Skorek Artur, Sroka Łukasz Tomasz, *Demokracja izraelska*, preface by Szewach Weiss, Warsaw 2018.
Chojnowski, Andrzej, Tomaszewski Jerzy, *Izrael*, Warsaw 2001.
Chwalba, Andrzej, *Dzieje Krakowa*, vol. 5: *Kraków w latach 1939–1945*, Krakow 2002.
———, *Okupacyjny Kraków w latach 1939–1945*, 2nd ed., Krakow 2011.
Cichopek, Anna, *Pogrom Żydów w Krakowie 11 sierpnia 1945*, Warsaw 2000.
Cohn-Sherbok, Dan, El-Alami Dawoud, *Konflikt palestyńsko-izraelski*, translated by Janusz Danecki and Maciej Tomal, Warsaw 2002.
Czermińska, Małgorzata, *Autobiograficzny trójkąt: świadectwo, wyznanie i wyzwanie*, Krakow 2000.
Demetrio, Duccio, *Autobiografia. Terapeutyczny wymiar pisania o sobie*, Krakow 2000.
Dobroszycki, Lucjan, *Survivors of the Holocaust in Poland. A Portrait Based on Jewish Community Records, 1944–47*, Armonk–London 1994.
Dowgiałło, Jan, "Stosunki z Izraelem," *Roczniki Polskiej Polityki Zagranicznej* 1995, 139–146.
Dyduch, Joanna, "Dyplomacja kulturalna w służbie polityki zagranicznej państwa. Nowe formy promocji kraju za granicą na przykładzie 'Roku Polskiego w Izraelu,'" in *Historia—polityka—dyplomacja. Studia z nauk społecznych i humanistycznych. Księga pamiątkowa dedykowana Profesorowi Marianowi S. Wolańskiemu w siedemdziesiątą rocznicę urodzin*, edited by Maciej Mróz, Elżbieta Stadtmüller, Toruń 2010, 605–619.
———, "Percepcja Polski i Polaków przez Izraelczyków," in *Uwarunkowania i kierunki polskiej polityki zagranicznej w pierwszej dekadzie XXI wieku*, edited by Marian S. Wolański, Wrocław 2004, 364–393.
———, *Stosunki polsko-izraelskie. Próba analizy czynników je kształtujących*, https://www.academia.edu/5193057/Joanna_Dyduch_Stosunki_polsko-izraelskie._Pr%C3%B3ba_analizy_czynnik%C3%B3w_kszta%C5%82tuj%C4%85cych, accessed August 8, 2014.
———, *Stosunki polsko-izraelskie w latach 1990–2009. Od normalizacji do strategicznego partnerstwa*, Warsaw 2010.
Eisler, Jerzy, *Marzec 1968. Geneza. Przebieg. Konsekwencje*, Warsaw 1991.
———, "Rok 1968: Żydzi, antysemityzm, emigracja," in *Z przeszłości Żydów polskich. Polityka—gospodarka—kultura—społeczeństwo*, edited by Jacek Wijaczka and Grzegorz Miernik, Krakow 2005, 327–358.
———, *Zarys dziejów politycznych Polski 1944–1989*, Warsaw 1992.
Eilam, Igal, *Ha-Hagana—ha-derech ha-tzionit el ha-koach*, Tel Aviv 1979.
Essen, Andrzej, "Znaczek pocztowy jako źródło ikonograficzne," *Studia Środkowoeuropejskie i Bałkanistyczne* 25 (2017): 191–206.
Famulska-Ciesielska, Karolina, "Ida Fink (1921–2011)," *Archiwum Emigracji. Studia—Szkice—Dokumenty* 1–2 (2011): 369–371.
———, *Polacy, Żydzi, Izraelczycy. Tożsamość w literaturze polskiej w Izraelu*, Toruń 2008.
Fałowski, Janusz, *Mniejszość żydowska w Parlamencie II Rzeczypospolitej (1922– 1939)*, Krakow 2006.

———, *Posłowie żydowscy w Sejmie Ustawodawczym 1919–1922*, Częstochowa 2000.

———, "Prasa syjonistyczna w Polsce 1918–1939," *Biuletyn Zespołu Badań Dziejów, Oświaty i Kultury Grup Etnicznych i Polonijnych Wyższej Szkoły Pedagogicznej w Częstochowie* 1 (1992).

———, "Udział posłów mniejszości narodowych parlamentu I kadencji 1922–1927 w debacie nad regulaminem obrad Sejmu," *Biuletyn Instytutu Filozoficzno-Historycznego Wyższej Szkoły Pedagogicznej w Częstochowie* 10 (1998).

Feldman, Wilhelm, *Asymilatorzy, syjoniści i Polacy. Z powodu przełomu w stosunkach żydowskich w Galicyi*, Krakow 1893.

Figiela, Piotr, "Działalność ŻTS Jutrzenka Kraków i ŻKS Makkabi Kraków," in *Machabeusze sportu. Sport żydowski w Krakowie*, by Maciej Władysław Belda, Piotr Figiela, Anna Hałambiec, Michał Luberda, Krzysztof Śmiechowski, Krakow 2012, 69–107.

———, "Losy i kariery uczniów Gimnazjum Hebrajskiego," in *To była hebrajska szkoła w Krakowie. Historia i wspomnienia*, edited by Natan Gross, Tel Aviv 1989, 187–239.

Fuks, Marian, *Żydzi w Warszawie. Życie codzienne. Wydarzenia. Literatura*, Poznań–Daszewice 1992.

Gawron, Edyta, "Matka Izraela," translated by Iwona Reichardt, *Herito. Dziedzictwo, Kultura, Współczesność* 4 (2015): 48–57.

Gąsowski, Tomasz, "Galicja—'żydowski matecznik,'" in *Galicja i jej dziedzictwo*, vol. 2: *Społeczeństwo i gospodarka*, edited by Jerzy Chłopecki, Helena Madurowicz-Urbańska, Rzeszów 1995, 125–135.

———, *Między gettem a światem. Dylematy ideowe Żydów galicyjskich na przełomie XIX i XX wieku*, 2nd ed., Krakow 1997.

———, *Pod sztandarami Orła Białego. Kwestia żydowska w Polskich Siłach Zbrojnych w czasie II wojny światowej*, Krakow 2002.

———, "Polscy Żydzi w sowieckiej Rosji," in *Historyk i historia. Studia dedykowane pamięci Prof. Mirosława Frančicia*, edited by Adam Walaszek, Krzysztof Zamorski, Krakow 2005, 223–236.

Gebert, Konstanty, "Całkiem inny Izrael. Syjonizm Teodora Herzla," *Midrasz* 9 (2004): 28–37.

———, *Miejsce pod słońcem. Wojny Izraela*, Warsaw 2008.

———, *Wojna czterdziestoletnia*, Warsaw 2004.

Gervassi, Frank, *The Life and Times of Menahem Begin: Rebel to Statesman*, New York 1979.

Goldsztejn, Josef, *Golda: Biografia*, Beersheba 2012.

Gordis, Daniel, *Menachem Begin: Ha-maabak al nishmatah shel Yisrael*, Jerusalem 2015.

Gorny, Joseph, *The British Labour Movement and Zionism. 1917–1948*, London 1983.

———, "The Ethos of Holocaust and State and its Impact on the Contemporary Image of the Jewish people," in *Major Changes within the Jewish People in the Wake of the Holocaust*, proceedings of the Ninth Yad Vashem International Historical Conference, edited by Israel Gutman, Jerusalem 1996, 709–731.

Gotzen-Dold, Maria, *Mojżesz Schorr und Majer Bałaban. Polnisch-jüdische Historiker der Zwischenkriegszeit*, Göttingen 2014.

Grabski, August, Berendt Grzegorz, *Między emigracją a trwaniem. Syjoniści i komuniści żydowscy w Polsce po Holocauście*, Warsaw 2003.
Grosbard, Ofer, *Menachem Begin: Diyukano shel manhyig—Biografia*, Tel Aviv 2006.
Grynberg, Henryk, *Dzieci Syjonu*, historical footnotes by Daniel Boćkowski, Warsaw 1994.
Grynberg, Michał, *Żydowska spółdzielczość pracy w Polsce w latach 1945-1949*, Warsaw 1986.
Haber, Eitan, *Menahem Begin. The Legend and the Man*, translated by Louis Williams, New York 1978.
Hazleton, Lesley, *Israeli Women. The Reality behind the Myths*, New York 1977.
Hertz, Aleksander, *Żydzi w kulturze polskiej*, introduction by Czesław Miłosz, 2nd ed., Warsaw 2003.
Hoffmann, Krzysztof, "Rana i staranność. Wokół 'Spóźnionej' Irit Amiel," *Miasteczko Poznań* 2 (2016): 150-155.
Holokaust—lekcja historii. Zagłada Żydów w edukacji szkolnej, edited by Jacek Chrobaczyński and Piotr Trojański, Krakow 2004.
Holtzman, Awner, "Chaim Nachman Bialik—Zarys biografii," in *Literackie spotkania w międzywojennej Polsce: Chaim Nachman Bialik i Salomon Dykman. Studia nad hebrajskim "poetą narodowym" i jego polskim tłumaczem*, edited by Marzena Zawanowska and Regina Gromacka, Krakow–Budapest 2012, 117–140.
Horowitz, David, *The Economics of Israel*, Oxford 1967.
———, *The Enigma of Economics Growth. A Case Study of Israel*, New York 1972.
Huppert, Uri, *Izrael. Rabini i heretycy*, Łódź 1994.
———, *Izrael na rozdrożu*, Łódź 2001.
Izydorczyk, Monika, "Polityka bezpieczeństwa i zagraniczna Izraela," in *Współczesny Izrael*, edited by Konstanty Adam Wojtaszczyk, Warsaw 2001, 34–56.
Jasina, Łukasz, "Biedne kino w kraju z bogatą historią. Uwagi o kinematografii w Izraelu," in *Medinat Israel. Państwo i tożsamość*, edited by Joanna Krauze and Konrad Zieliński, Lublin 2013, 141–144.
Jaworski, Wojciech, *Struktura i wpływy syjonistycznych organizacji politycznych w Polsce w latach 1918-1939*, Warsaw 1996.
———, *Syjoniści wobec Rządu Polskiego w okresie międzywojennym*, Sosnowiec 2002.
Katz, Shmuel, *Zhabo: biografia shel Zeev Zhabotinski*, Tel Aviv 1993.
Kamczycki, Artur, "Syjonizm i sztuka. Analiza ikony Teodora Herzla w kontekście aszkenazyjskiego kręgu kulturowego," *Studia Judaica* 1 (2006): 33–46.
Karczewska, Agnieszka, "Kształtowanie tożsamości kulturowej czytelników 'Chwilki Dzieci i Młodzieży' (1925–1937)," in *Naruszone granice kulturowe. O kondycji ludzkiej w dwóch przestrzeniach: polskiej i żydowskiej XX wieku*, edited by Monika Szabłowska-Zaremba, Beata Walęciuk-Dejneka, Lublin 2013, 203–222.
———, "'Stary-nowy' kraj—obraz Erec Israel w 'Chwilce Dzieci i Młodzieży' (1925–1937)," in *"Stare" i "nowe"—czasopisma dla dzieci i młodzieży*, edited by Bożena Olszewska and Elżbieta Łucka-Zając, Opole 2013, 303– 320.
———, "'Wieczór cudów.' O twórczości Maurycego Szymla dla dzieci," in *Żydowskie dziecko*, edited by Anna Jeziorkowska-Polakowska, Agnieszka Karczewska, Lublin 2013, 111–125.

———, "Źródła topiczne dziecięcej literatury polsko-żydowskiej publikowanej w 'Chwilce Dzieci i Młodzieży' (1925–1937)," in *Nowe opisanie świata. Literatura dla dzieci i młodzieży w kręgach oddziaływań*, edited by Bernadeta Niesporek-Szamburska, Małgorzata Wójcik-Dudek, Katowice 2013, 359–372.

Kark, Rut, *Jafo: tzemichata shel ir 1799–1917*, Jerusalem 1984.

Karkowska, Magda, "Tajemnice i ich biograficzne znaczenia a proces kształtowania tożsamości," in *Biografie nieoczywiste. Przełom, kryzys, transgresja w perspektywie interdyscyplinarnej*, edited by Magda Karkowska, Łódź 2018, 113–137.

Katz, Yaakov, Bohbot Amir, *Czarodzieje broni. Izrael—tajne laboratorium technologii militarnych*, translated by Norbert Radomski, Poznań 2018.

Kaye, Ephraim, *The Image of Polish Jewry Between the Two World Wars, 1919–1939. Jewish Political Parties and Movements: Zionists—Haredim—The Bund*, Jerusalem 2009.

Kącki, Czesław, *Izrael. Informator*, Warsaw 1999.

Klugman, Aleksander, *Izrael. Ziemia świecka*, Warsaw 2001.

———, "Ostatnie nowiny," http://tygodnik.onet.pl/ostatnie-nowiny/bk4lx, accessed January 1, 2014.

———, *Polonica w Ziemi Świętej*, Krakow 1994.

———, "Pomoc Polski dla żydowskiego ruchu narodowego w Palestynie," *Więź* 5 (1997): 133–151.

———, *Psiakrew, znowu Żydzi...*, Warsaw 1991.

Kossewska, Elżbieta, "'Ona jeszcze mówi po polsku, ale śmieje się po hebrajsku'— prasa polskojęzyczna i integracja językowa polskich Żydów w Izraelu," *Kultura i Społeczeństwo* 54, no. 4 (2010): 59–76.

———, "Ona jeszcze mówi po polsku, ale śmieje się po hebrajsku." *Partyjna prasa polskojęzyczna i integracja kulturowa polskich Żydów w Izraelu (1948–1970)*, Warsaw 2015.

Koźmińska-Frejlak, Ewa, "Z tego się nigdy nie wyrasta...," *Midrasz* 7–8 (2005): 11–14.

Krakovsky, Shmuel, "Yehudim be-tzava ha-polani be-maarekhet september 1939," in *Studies on Polish Jewry. Paul Glikson Memorial Volume*, edited by E. Mendelsohn and Ch. Shmeruk, Jerusalem 1987, 149–171

Laqueur, Walter, *A History of Zionism*, London 1972.

Lapierre, Dominique, Collins Larry, *O Jeruzalem! Dramatyczna opowieść o powstaniu Państwa Izrael*, translated by Bogusław Panek, [s.l.] 1998.

Legeżyńska, Anna, "Wystarczy mocno i wytrwale zastanawiać się nad jednym życiem... Biografistyka jako hermeneutyczne wyzwanie," *Teksty Drugie* 1 (2019): 13–27.

Lejeune, Philippe, *Napisać swoje życie. Droga od paktu autobiograficznego do dziedzictwa autobiograficznego*, translated by Aneta Słowik, Małgorzata Sakwerda, Wrocław 2017.

Levin, Dov, "Alija 'waw.' Masowa dezercja żołnierzy żydowskich z Armii Polskiej w Palestynie w latach 1942–1943," in his *Żydzi wschodnioeuropejscy podczas II wojny światowej*, translated by Ewa Balcerek, Warsaw 2005, 117–140.

Lewińska, Maria, "Wizyta laureatki Nagrody Nobla. 'Chciałabym żyć długo,'" *Biuletyn Izrael Polska* 2005, 24–25.

Literatura polsko-żydowska. Studia i szkice, edited by Eugenia Prokop-Janiec and Sławomir J. Żurek, Krakow 2011.
Löw [Loew], Ryszard, "Druki polskie w Izraelu. Bibliografia 1948–1990," *Biuletyn Żydowskiego Instytutu Historycznego w Polsce* 3 (1991): 71–81.
———, "Kontury," in *Przechowane słowa*, by Maria Lewińska, Tel Aviv 2008, 68–93.
———, *Literackie podsumowania polsko-hebrajskie i polsko-izraelskie*, edited by Michał Siedlecki and Jarosław Ławski, afterword by Barbara Olech, Białystok 2014.
Łazor, Jerzy, *Brama na Bliski Wschód. Polsko-palestyńskie stosunki gospodarcze w okresie międzywojennym*, Warsaw 2016.
Medzini, Miron, *Ha-yehudiah ha-geah: Golda Meir ve-chazon Yisrael. Biografia politit*, Tel Aviv 1990.
Marcel Goldman. Krakowianin i Izraelczyk, edited by A. B. Skotnicki with M. Ostoja-Wilamowska, [s.l.] 2008.
Mendelsohn, Ezra, *Zionism in Poland. The Formative Years. 1915–1926*, New Haven–London 1981.
———, *Żydzi Europy Środkowo-Wschodniej w okresie międzywojennym*, translated by Agata Tomaszewska, edited by Jerzy Tomaszewski, Warsaw 1992.
Mendelsohn, Szlomo [Szloyme], *Polscy Żydzi za murami nazistowskich gett*, introduction by Marek Skwara, translated by Marta Skwara, Szczecin 2017.
Meraw, Gideon, Kartun-Blum Ruth, "Wstępne uwagi o literaturze nowohebrajskiej i jej tle historycznym," *Literatura na Świecie* 5–6 (1992): 335–344.
Meus, Konrad, "Anti-Jewish Riots in the Cities of West Galicia in 1918: an Outline of the Problem," in *Veľká doba v malom priestore: zlomové zmeny v mestách stredoeurópskeho priestoru a ich dôsledky (1918–1929)*, edited by Peter Švorc and Harald Heppner, Prešov–Graz 2012, 376–389.
Montefiore, Simon Sebag, *Jerozolima. Biografia*, translated by Maciej Antosiewicz, Władysław Jeżewski, Warsaw 2011.
Mrozek, Witold, "Co Hłasko zobaczył w Izraelu—nowy spektakl Zadary," http://wyborcza.pl/1,75410,14326181,Co_Hlasko_zobaczyl_w_Izraelu_nowy_spektakl_Zadary.html, accessed September 2, 2017.
Near, Henry, *The Kibbutz Movement. A History*, vol. 1: *Origins and Growth, 1909–1939*, vol. 2: *Crisis and Achievement, 1939–1995*, Oxford 2008.
Nowak, Artur, "Wędrowiec: Leo Lipski (1917–1997)," *Archiwum Emigracji. Studia—Szkice—Dokumenty* 1 (1998): 195–197.
Okraj, Zofia, "Dlaczego działania transgresyjne intrygują i inspirują do badań (także) autobiograficznych," in *Biografie nieoczywiste. Przełom, kryzys, transgresja w perspektywie interdyscyplinarnej*, edited by Magda Karkowska, Łódź 2018, 99–111.
Oz, Amos, *Czarownik swojego plemienia. Eseje*, selected and translated by Danuta Sękalska, afterword by Stefan Bratkowski, Warsaw 2004.
———, *Do fanatyków. Trzy refleksje*, translated by Leszek Kwiatkowski, Poznań 2018.
Padva, Gilad, "Mocking the 'Polaniyah': Marginalization and Demonization of Israeli Women of Jewish-Polish Origins in Israeli Cinema and Popular Culture," in *Polish-*

Israeli Cooperation Experience, from Zionism to Israel, Collection of Studies, edited by Łukasz Tomasz Sroka, Batya Brutin, Krakow 2017, 206–222.
Panas, Władysław, "Topika judajska," in *Słownik literatury polskiej XX wieku*, edited by Alina Brodzka, Mirosława Puchalska, Małgorzata Semczuk, Anna Sobolewska, Ewa Szary-Matywiecka, Wrocław 1992, 1095–1104.
Patek, Artur, *Birobidżan. Sowiecka ziemia obiecana? Żydowski Obwód Autonomiczny w ZSRR*, Krakow 1997.
———, *Polski cmentarz w Jerozolimie. Polacy pochowani na cmentarzu katolickim na górze Syjon*, Krakow 2009.
———, *Wielka Brytania wobec Izraela w okresie pierwszej wojny arabsko-izraelskiej maj 1948–styczeń 1949*, Krakow 2002.
———, *Żydzi w drodze do Palestyny 1934–1944. Szkice z dziejów aliji bet, nielegalnej imigracji żydowskiej*, Krakow 2009.
Paziński, Piotr, "Palestyna światła i mroku," *Midrasz* 10 (2009): 8–9.
———, "Państwowiec," *Midrasz* 4 (2000): 18–21.
Peres, Szymon, *Nowy Bliski Wschód*, translated by Krzysztof Wojciechowski, Warsaw 1995.
Pillersdorf, Esty, *Celina*, translated by Michał Sobelman, Joanna Stöcker-Sobelman, Krakow–Budapest 2012.
Pisarski, Maciej, "Emigracja Żydów z Polski w latach 1945–1951," in *Studia z dziejów i kultury Żydów w Polsce po 1945 roku*, by August Grabski, Maciej Pisarski, Albert Stankowski, edited by Jerzy Tomaszewski, Warsaw 1997, 13–81.
Pod klątwą. Społeczny portret pogromu kieleckiego, vol. 2: *Dokumenty*, edited by Joanna Tokarska-Bakir, Warsaw 2018.
Polonsky, Antony, *Dzieje Żydów w Polsce i Rosji*, translated by Mateusz Wilk, Warsaw 2014.
———, *Stosunki polsko-żydowskie od 1984 roku: Refleksje uczestnika*, Krakow–Budapest 2009.
Prokop-Janiec, Eugenia, "Literatura polska w Izraelu: pomiędzy pamięcią Europy a nowym życiem," *Roczniki Humanistyczne* 64, no. 1 (2016): 63–74.
Przewrocka-Adert, Karolina, *Polonim. Z Polski do Izraela*, Wołowiec 2019.
Radosh, Alice, Radosh Ronald, *A Safe Haven. Harry S. Truman and Founding of Israel*, New York 2009.
Raport Banku PKOBP: "Izrael. Analiza Międzynarodowa," https://wspieramyeksport.pl/api/public/files/1559/Izrael_Analiza_Miedzynarodowa_2019_03. pdf, accessed March 29, 2019.
Rodak, Paweł, "Od biblioteki do archiwów. Droga badawcza 'papieża autobiografii,'" *Teksty Drugie* 1 (2019): 128–137.
Rosenberg, David, "The Real Israel Isn't Startup Nation, It's Poverty Row," https://www.haaretz.com/israel-news/.premium-the-real-israel-isn-t-startup-nation-it-s-poverty-row-1.6803924?fbclid=IwAR2-Q8NRbMemjYq7R5eF-tAngBAaB7Ynb7sBCcj2FNiLuplqW9w3q0ibddOI, accessed January 2, 2019.
Rudnicki, Szymon, *Obóz Narodowo Radykalny. Geneza i działalność*, Warsaw 1985.
———, *Żydzi w parlamencie II Rzeczypospolitej*, Warsaw 2004.

———, Wójcicki Maciej, "'Polska' alija," *Kwartalnik Historii Żydów* 1 (2008): 20–34.
Schoenbaum, David, *The United States and the State of Israel*, New York 1993.
Schwartz, Felicia, Lieber Dov, "Ultraortodoksyjni Żydzi idą do armii, rząd upada," *Gazeta Wyborcza*, January 12–13, 2019, supplement: *Wall Street Journal* 2 (2019): 5.
Segev, Tom, *Siódmy milion. Izrael—piętno Zagłady*, translated by Barbara Gadomska, Warsaw 2012.
Shmeruk, Chone, *Historia literatury jidysz. Zarys*, 2nd ed., edited by Monika Adamczyk-Garbowska, Eugenia Prokop-Janiec, Wrocław 2007.
Sherwin, Byron L., *Duchowe dziedzictwo Żydów polskich*, Warsaw 1995.
Shipler, David, *Arabowie i Żydzi w Ziemi Obiecanej*, translated by Jerzy Jan Górski, Jan Kabat, Witold Nowakowski, Warsaw 2003.
Silber, Marcos, "'Immigrants from Poland Want to Go Back.' The Politics of Return Migration and Nation Building in 1950s Israel," *Journal of Israeli History* 27 (2008): 201–219.
Silber Marcos, "Swoi i obcy—Izrael, Polska i Żydzi w Polsce (1948–1967): zwięzłe prolegomena do stałego problemu," in *Brzemię pamięci. Współczesne stosunki polsko-izraelskie*, edited by Elżbieta Kossewska, Warsaw 2009, 31–53.
Simoni, Janusz, "Polscy Żydzi w Izraelu," *Więź* 4 (1992): 67–80.
Skorek, Artur, "Sojusz amerykańsko-izraelski w perspektywie realistycznej," in *Teoria realizmu w nauce o stosunkach międzynarodowych*, edited by Edward Haliżak, Jacek Czaputowicz, Warsaw 2017, 279–294, http://ptsm.edu.pl/wp-content/uploads/publikacje/teoria-realizmu-w-nauce-o-stosunkach-miedzynarodowych/A.Skorek.pdf, accessed January 3, 2019.
———, *Żydowskie ugrupowania religijne w Państwie Izrael. Polityczna rola ortodoksyjnego judaizmu*, Krakow 2015.
Skotnicki, Aleksander B., *Juliusz Feldhorn. Poeta, pisarz, tłumacz, wybitny polonista Gimnazjum Hebrajskiego w Krakowie*, Krakow 2011.
———, *Oskar Schindler w oczach uratowanych przez siebie krakowskich Żydów*, Krakow 2007.
———, *Polsko-izraelskie losy Tulo Schenirera i jego rodziny*, Krakow 2009.
———, *Pożegnanie Oskara Schindlera*, Krakow 2014.
Skotnicki, Aleksander B., Klimczak Władysław, *Społeczność żydowska w Polsce. Zwyczaje i udział w walce o Niepodległość: Dwa oblicza krakowskich Żydów*, Krakow 2006.
Slezkine, Yuri, *Wiek Żydów*, translated by Sergiusz Kowalski, Warsaw 2006.
Smith, Sidonie, Watson Julia, "Archiwa zapisów życia: czym i gdzie są?," translated by Dorota Boni Menezes, *Teksty Drugie* 6 (2018): 174–199.
Sommer, Schneider Anna, *Sze'erit hapleta. Ocaleni z Zagłady. Działalność American Jewish Joint Distribution Committee w Polsce w latach 1945–1989*, Krakow 2014.
Sosnowski, Remigiusz, *Polityka imigracyjna Izraela*, Warsaw 2014.
Sroka, Łukasz Tomasz, "Izrael w relacjach międzynarodowych. Tradycje i współczesność," in *Społeczne, gospodarcze i polityczne relacje we współczesnych stosunkach międzynarodowych*, edited by Bogusława Bednarczyk and Marcin Lasoń, Krakow 2007, 85–97.

———, "Israel and its Friends: Selected International Relations Issues in the Nineteenth and the Twentieth Centuries," in *Poles and Jews: History—Culture—Education*, edited by Mariusz Misztal and Piotr Trojański, Krakow 2011, 29–44.
———, "Migracja Żydów polskich do Izraela. Aspekt antropologiczno-historyczny," in *Nietypowe migracje Polaków w XIX–XXI wieku*, edited by Anna M. Kargol and Władysław Masiarz, Krakow 2011, 65–86.
Sroka, Mateusz, "Emigracja Żydów polskich w latach 1918–1939. Zarys problematyki," *Państwo i Społeczeństwo* 10, no. 2 (2010): 109–121.
Stola, Dariusz, *Emigracja pomarcowa*, Warsaw 2000.
———, *Kampania antysyjonistyczna w Polsce 1967–1968*, Warsaw 2000.
———, *Kraj bez wyjścia? Migracje z Polski 1949–1989*, Warsaw 2012.
Surzyn, Jacek, *Antysemityzm, emancypacja, syjonizm. Narodziny ideologii syjonistycznej*, Katowice 2014.
Studies on Polish Jewry. Paul Glikson Memorial Volume, edited by Ezra Mendelsohn and Chone Shilon Avi, Begin, Tel Aviv 2007.
Styrna, Natasza, "Juliusz Feldhorn (Jan Las)," in *Krakowianie. Wybitni Żydzi krakowscy XIV–XX w.*, edited by Agnieszka Kutylak, Krakow 2006, 168–170.
Szałagan, Alicja, "Maria Kuncewiczowa w podróży," *Pamiętnik Literacki: czasopismo kwartalne poświęcone historii i krytyce literatury polskiej* 3 (2014): 223–237.
Szaynok, Bożena, *Ludność żydowska na Dolnym Śląsku 1945–1950*, Wrocław 2000.
———, *Pogrom Żydów w Kielcach 4 lipca 1946*, introduction by Krystyna Kersten, Warsaw 1992.
———, "Stosunki polsko-izraelskie w latach 1948–1967," in *Państwo Izrael. Analiza politologiczno-prawna*, edited by Ewa Rudnik, Warsaw 2006, 101–111.
———, *Z historią i Moskwą w tle. Polska a Izrael 1944–1968*, Warsaw–Wrocław 2007.
Szczepański, Władysław, *Palestyna po wojnie światowej. Światła i cienie*, Krakow 1923.
Szir [Wolman-Sieraczkowa], Miriam, Szir Dawid, *Słownik polsko-hebrajski*, Tel Aviv 1976.
Tański, Paweł, "'Kontury'—izraelskie pismo literackie," *Archiwum Emigracji. Studia—Szkice—Dokumenty* 3 (2000): 301–307.
Tokarska-Bakir, Joanna, *Pod klątwą. Społeczny portret pogromu kieleckiego*, vol. 1, Warsaw 2018.
Waligóra, Janusz, "Nikomu się nie udało . . . O prozie Irit Amiel," in *Lęk, ból, cierpienie. Analizy i interpretacje*, edited by Grażyna Różańska, Słupsk 2015, 17–27.
Weinberg, Robert, *Stalin's Forgotten Zion. Birobidzhan and the Making of a Soviet Jewish Homeland. An Illustrated History. 1928–1996*, Berkeley 1998.
Węgrzyn, Ewa, "Emigracja ludności żydowskiej z Polski do Izraela w latach 1956–1959. Przyczyny, przebieg wyjazdu, proces adaptacji w nowej ojczyźnie," *Zeszyty Naukowe Uniwersytetu Jagiellońskiego* 1312, *Prace Historyczne* 137 (2010): 137–151.
———, *Wyjeżdżamy! Wyjeżdżamy?! Alija gomułkowska 1956–1960*, Krakow–Budapest 2016.
Wieliński, Bartosz T., "Izrael oswaja ortodoksów z kapitalizmem," *Gazeta Wyborcza*, April 3, 2018, 8.

Wierzbieniec, Wacław, "Udział posłów żydowskich w pierwszej sesji Sejmu Ustawodawczego w 1919 roku," *Zeszyty Naukowe Wyższej Szkoły Pedagogicznej w Rzeszowie, Seria społeczno-pedagogiczna i historyczna, historia* 4 (1994): 89–101.
Wojtaszczyk, Konstanty Adam, "System polityczny Izraela," in *Współczesny Izrael*, edited by Konstanty Adam Wojtaszczyk, Warsaw 2001, 9–19.
Wróbel, Józef, *Tematy żydowskie w prozie polskiej 1939–1987*, Krakow 1991.
Wróbel, Łukasz, "Miasto dla ludzi bez ziemi. Tel Awiw," *Słowo Żydowskie* 7–8 (2008): 16–19.
Żółciński, Tadeusz J., "Dobrze, że przypomniane," *Słowo Żydowskie* 4 (2001): 15–26.
Żurek, Sławomir Jacek, "Krytyka literacka na łamach izraelskiego dziennika 'Nowiny Kurier' po roku 1968: wyimki z dyskursu," in *Prasa Żydów polskich: od przeszłości do teraźniejszości*, edited by Agnieszka Karczewska, Sławomir Jacek Żurek, Lublin 2016, 139–159.
———, "Polish literature in Israel: A Reconaissance," *Roczniki Humanistyczne* 64, no. 1 (2016): 125–137.
———, "Polska i Polacy w poezji autorów piszących po polsku w Izraelu," *Postscriptum Polonistyczne: pismo krajowych i zagranicznych polonistów poświęcone zagadnieniom związanym z nauczaniem kultury polskiej i języka polskiego jako obcego* 2 (2016): 59–75.

VIII Religious Literature

Dessler, Elijahu E., *Pożądaj prawdy. Eseje o księgach Wajikra, Bambidar i Dewarim oraz Rozważania o wolnej woli*, edited by Rabbi Sacha Pecaric, translated by Katarzyna Czerwińska, Krakow 2003.
Hagada na Pesach i Pieśń nad Pieśniami, edited by Rabbi Sacha Pecaric, Krakow 2002.
Jak modlą się Żydzi. Antologia modlitw, wybór, introduction and footnotes by Maciej Tomal, Warsaw 2000.
Kameraz-Kos, Ninel, *Święta i obyczaje żydowskie*, 2nd ed., Warsaw 2000.
Krajewski, Stanisław, *54 komentarze do Tory dla nawet najmniej religijnych spośród nas*, Krakow 2004.
Papieska Komisja Biblijna, *Naród żydowski i jego święte pisma w Biblii chrześcijańskiej*, translated by Ryszard Rubinkiewicz SDB, Kielce 2002.
Tarjag micwot (613 przykazań judaizmu) oraz Szewa micwot derabanan (Siedem przykazań rabinicznych). Szewa micwot bne Noach Siedem (Siedem przykazań dla nie-Żydów), translated by Ewa Gordon, Krakow 2000.
Tora. Pięcioksiąg Mojżesza, translated by Izaak Cylkow, Krakow 1895 [reprint: Krakow 2006].
Unterman, Alan, *Żydzi. Wiara i życie*, translated by Janusz Zabierowski, Łódź 1989.

Index

A
Abimelech, 137, 217
Abraham, 137, 216–17, 225
Abyssinia, 294
Achuza, 186
Achuzat Beit, 314
Acre, 226, 321
Adam, 369
Adoni, 137
Africa, 20, 52, 147, 149, 180, 211, 215, 217–18, 220–21, 263, 274, 283, 294, 296, 303, 314, 336, 375, 387, 401
Afula, 145, 201, 290
AGH University of Science and Technology, 85, 340–41
Agricultural University of Dubliany, 150
Agudat Yisrael, 283, 352
Ain Buweirde, 145
Akavia, Miriam, 23, 376
Akiba, 405
Al HaMishmar, 265
Al-Aqsa mosque, 225, 228
Al-Arish, 242
Al-Kantara, 141
Albin, Bishop, 359
Aleksandrowicz, Abraszka, 267, 269, 272
Aleksandrowicz, Julian, 360, 362n244
Aleksandrowicz, Róża, 322
Aleksandrowicz, Sinai, 322
Aleksiun, Natalia, 30
Aleppo, 144, 327n186
Alexandria, 142
Algeria, 156
Allenby, Edmund Henry, 140n30
Allerhand, Aleksander, 359
Altalena, 276, 278
Alterman, Natan, 214, 240
Amalekites, 216
America, 14n21, 52, 140, 147, 263, 272, 303
Ameryka, 144
Amichai, Rachel, 214
Amiel, Irit, 23, 376
Amir, Jurek, 268
Amit, Nili, 34, 152, 186, 313, 325
Amsterdam, 303
Anders, Władysław, 112–13, 276, 323

Anglo-Palestine Bank, 17, 145–147
Anielewicz, Mordechai, 120
Anne Frank Prize, 376
Antwerp, 2 38
Aqaba, 145, 237, 371
Arab-Israeli War, 15, 21, 278
Arab-Jewish War, 173, 180, 250, 283
Arabah, 369–70
Arad, 221
Argentina, 140, 375
Aridor, Yoram, 308
Ariel University, 27, 254
Armstrong, Karen, 14
Ashdod, 170, 303
Ashkelon, 170, 294, 303
Asia, 147, 149, 180, 217, 274, 314
Asia Minor, 217, 274, 314
Athens, 303
Atlas mountains, 156
Atlit, 116
Atlit Detainee camp, 175
Atzmaut Mortgage and Development Bank, 245
Auschwitz, 95, 99, 379, 405–6
Auschwitz-Birkenau, 90, 126
Australia, 147
Austria, 347, 357
Austria-Hungary, 51, 67, 73, 142
Aviva, 268, 406
Avner, Yehuda, 13
Azriel, 266

B
Bader, Yohanan, 277–78
Baha'i, 175
Balint, Benjamin, 194
Balzac, Honoré de, 41
Banco di Roma, 145
Bangkok, 261
Bank Polska Kasa Opieki S.A. (Pekao), 145, 323, 348–49, 356
Bar-El, Yair, 234
Bar-Zohar, Michael, 12, 14
Barbarossa, 111, 346n213
Barbur, Eli, 3 77
Basel, 52, 146, 387

Index   425

Bat Galim, 209
Bat Yam, 186, 222
Bata factory, 97–99, 101–3, 115
Bauer, Ludwig, 75
BBC, 373, 377
BeAliyah, Israel, 283
Beer Sheva, 141
Beersheba, 141, 168, 217–18, 220, 236, 322
Begin, Menachem, 13, 20, 76, 151, 178, 192, 196, 215, 257, 276–78, 294, 306–7, 311, 313, 324. *See also* Biegun, Mieczysław.
Beirut, 142, 146
Beisan, 141
Beit Berl College, 27, 143
Beit Rahel Friedman, 143
Beit Rahel Friedmann, 143
Beit She'an, 141, 145
Beit Shemesh, 221, 340
Beit Zera, 149
Beitar, 276
Belarus, 70
Belgium, 256, 301
Bełżec, 93, 395
Ben-Gal, Avigdor, 324
Ben-Gurion, David, 14n21, 20, 116, 137, 162, 164–66, 168–69, 179, 192, 215, 218, 220–22, 234, 249, 253, 276, 278, 280, 307, 311, 351, 388, 394–95
Ben-Tzvi, 192
Ben-Yehuda, Eliezer, 191
Ben-Yehuda, Israel, 191
Benelux, 310
Berendt, Grzegorz, 31, 264
Berger, Róża, 126
Bergman, Ronen, 14
Berlin, 52, 88, 114, 236
Berman, Jakub, 124
Bern, 342
Bessarabia, 164n79
Beta Israel, 180
Betheinu Israel, 283
Bethlehem, 141
Biała, 73
Bialik, Nahman, 56, 390
Białystok, 79, 139, 403
Bianka, passim
Bible, 16, 201, 316
Bibliographic Laboratory, 24
Biegun, Mieczysław, 192, 276. *See also* Begin, Menachem.
Bielsko, 68, 73, 108, 129–30, 368
Bielsko-Biała, 73, 359, 367–68
Bierut, Boleslaw, 124

BILU, 137
Bino-Lieberman Group, 327
Bino, Zadik, 302, 326–27, 330–31, 342
Birkat Shehecheyanu, 164
Birnbaum, Natan, 52
Biro-Bidzhan, 114
Birobidzhan, 114
Blachut, 102
Blass, Simcha, 150, 320
Bloomberg Index, 256
Bnei Brak, 222, 282, 350
Bochnia, 405
Bohbot, Amir, 14
Bohemia, 199
Bosak, Meir, 56
Boston, 3
Bratislava, 154
Bremen, 145
Brest, 276
Britain, 15, 67–68, 108, 112, 140, 146, 166, 241, 256, 276, 310, 354, 373, 375
Brod, Max, 194
Bronowice, 85
Brünlitz, 268n62
Brussels, 303
Buchenwald, 153
Buchman Prize, 376
Buchweitz, Menachem, 114
Budapest, 22
Bug, 109, 276
Bulgaria, 117, 221
Burma, 262
Burmel, 179n94
Bytom, 194
Byzantine, 216

C
Cairo, 142
Cambodia, 262
Canaan, 16, 137, 216
Canada, 256, 306, 375
Caramel, 144
Catholics, 73, 79
Central Bureau of Statistics Statistics, 27
Central Sales Cooperative Tnuva, 305
Chaczko, Krzysztof, 12, 308
Chan Junus, 141
Chełm, 85
Cherut party, 276–78, 306–7, 311
Chidusz, 35
China, 263, 301, 375
Chojnowski, Andrzej, 12
Chopin, Frédéric, 356

Chovevei Zion, 168
Christ, Jesus, 16, 225, 382
Christian-Jewish, 50, 229
Christianity, 225
Christians, 16, 47, 58, 135, 138–39, 173, 225, 227, 285, 369
Christmas, 48
Church of the Holy Sepulchre, 225, 229, 233
Cichopek, Anna, 128n8
Cieśla, 356
Cieszyn, 37, 154
Clandestine Immigration and Naval Museum, 119
Clinton, Bill, 315
Colbi, Itzik, 350
Constanta, 144
Copenhagen, 303
Cracovia hotel, 313, 356
Crédit Lyonnais, 145
Cyprus, 52, 247, 249
Cyrankiewicz, Józef, 405–6
Czechia, 73
Czechoslovakia, 129
Częstochowa, 320n166

D
Dachau, 86
Dagon, 175
Dahab, 237
Damari, Shoshana, 203
Damascus, 216, 225
Daniel Sieff Institute, 167
Danzig, Alex, 265
Dara, 141
Dayan, Leore, 373
Dayan, Moshe, 20, 226–27, 277, 307, 373
Dead Sea, 9, 66, 77, 95, 129, 132, 143, 170n85, 217, 240, 357, 367, 369–71, 390, 401
Decalogue plaques, 91
Degania, 148
Degania Alef, 143, 148, 226
Degania Bet, 148
Delhi, 262
Denver, 188
Dessau, 318
Dimona, 218, 242
Dizengoff, Meir, 157, 162, 169, 253n30, 319, 332
Dnipropetrovsk, 109
Dobrzyńska, Marysia, 132
Dome of the Rock, 225, 228
DP camp, 155

Dreyfus, Alfred, 51
Drohobych, 193
Duvdevan Unit, 336
Dworak-Cousin, Ilona, 23, 214, 238, 272–73
Dyduch, Joanna, 30

E
Eastern Bloc, 129, 179, 227, 264, 304, 312, 344
Ebersohn, Bianka, 19, 68, 70, 73, 108, 111–12, 130–31, 202
Ebersohn, Edward, 108n57
Ebersohns, 69, 73, 108, 110–112, 114–15, 129–31, 136, 140, 203
Edelman, Marek, 280
Edomites, 216
Egypt, 113, 137, 141–142, 144, 168, 216, 227, 241–42, 271, 277, 369
Egyptians, 241
Eichmann, Adolf, 116, 121
Eilat, 9, 170, 220, 236–37, 303, 322
Eisenhower, Dwight, 114
El-Al, 257, 289
El-Dedeide, 143
El-Kantara, 141
Elbit, 172
Emilia, 359
Emirate of Transjordan, 17
England, 14n21, 141–42, 144–45, 306
Enlightenment, 403
Equipped, 99, 110, 247, 321
Eretz Yizrael, passim
Eshkol, Levi, 13, 226, 228, 277
Esperanto, 403
Esther (Ilse), 194
Ethiopia, 180, 294
Etzel, 307
Etzion Immigrant Home, 195
Europe, passim
Ezra and Nehemia, 180

F
Falash Mura, 180, 220
Famulska-Ciesielska, Karolina, 25, 29
Feldblum, Ester, 140
Feldblum, Michał Teodor, 140
Feldhorn, Juliusz, 54–55
FIBI (First International Bank of Israel), 245–46, 326–27, 341–44, 346–48
Fink, Ida, 23, 265, 376
First Israeli-Arab War, 186, 217
Flug, Karnit, 207, 265
Follprecht, Kamila, 34
Foxley, 113

France, 14n21, 68, 108, 114, 139, 142, 156, 241, 256, 274, 295, 310, 354, 376
Frank, Hans, 85, 87–88, 106
Frankel, Alona, 193, 376
Frankfurt, 269, 303
Friedman, Ryszard, 78, 88
Frischer, 83–84
Frishman Beach, 274
Frister, Roman, 377

G
Galas, 49, 82, 91, 98, 101–2, 107, 126, 395
Galas, Marceli,126
Gałecki, Tadeusz. *See* Strug, Andrzej
Galicia, 29, 34–35, 47–48, 149–50, 387
Galil, 131
Galilee, 143–144, 168, 270, 382
Garti, Avram, 195
Gąsowski, Tomasz, 109
Gaza, 21, 141, 146, 241–42, 283, 291
Gaza Strip. *See* Gaza
Gazeta Wyborcza, 350
Gdańsk, 76
Gdynia, 144
Geddes, Patrick, 157
Genesis, 16, 137, 216–17
Geneva, 244, 245n9, 343
Gerar, 137
German police (Schupo), 103
Germany, 12, 21, 61, 65–66, 68, 78, 85, 102, 106, 108, 116, 123, 139, 142, 186–87, 206, 236, 277, 295, 310–311, 316, 354, 375, 406
Gestapo, 95, 97, 193
Ghana, 258, 262–63
Gieniusia, 95
Gierad, Janek, 98–99, 125
Givatayim, 222
Glinice, 99, 101
Goh Keng Swee, 262
Golan, Arie, 265
Golan, David, 245–46, 262, 275
Golan Heights, 288, 290, 313
Golan, Jehuda, 262
Golani Brigade, 199, 336
Goldberg, Lea, 214
Goldberger, Jakub, 36, 39, 49
Goldbergers, 39
Goldlust, Janusz. *See* Ben-Gal, Avigdor
Goldman-Galas, 29
Goldman, Maksymilian, 36–37, 39, 41, 46, 63–66, 68, 84, 96–99, 101, 115, 126, 129, 186, 188, 190, 199, 210

Goldman, Mania, 99
Goldman, Marcel, passim
Goldman, Sara, 39, 41, 63–64, 96–97, 99, 101, 115, 126, 129, 199, 210
Goldmann, Nahum, 311
Goldmans, passim
Goldstein, Janka, 32
Gomulka Aliyah, 22, 26, 30, 152–153, 183, 186, 197, 264–66, 268–69, 272, 274, 288, 296, 335, 378, 388, 407
Gomułka, Władysław, 264, 268, 387
Google, 172
Górka Narodowa, 85
Goryczka, Emilia, 359
Grabowski, 97–98
Grabski Aliyah, 316, 335
Grabski, Władysław, 138
Grand National Lodge of Poland, 323
Great Britain, 14n21, 15, 67-68, 108, 112, 140, 146, 166, 241, 256, 276, 310, 354n231, 373, 375
Grin, Irek, 29
Grodziski, Stanisław, 48
Gross, Natan, 54–55, 58
Grossrosen camp, 268n62
Grün, David, 168, 192
Grünberg, 65
Grycendler, Henryk, 197, 257, 267–69
Grynberg, Henryk, 69, 376
Gush Dan, 222, 316
Gymnasia Rechavia, 142

H
Haapali, 343
Haaretz, 26–27, 29, 190, 239, 265, 297, 368, 377, 384–85
HaAtzmaut, 131, 155
HaBank HaBeinleumi HaRishon LeYisrael. *See* FIBI
Haber, Lili, 34
Habima, 160, 320
HaBoker, 265
Habsburgs, 67, 85
Hadar, 173, 201, 258, 271
Hadassa Hospital,198
Hadassim, 187
Hadera, 149
Hagana, 117n74, 120, 154, 168, 226, 276
HaGymnasia HaIvrit Herzliya, 321
HaHistadrut HaKlalit shel HaOvdim B'Eretz Yisrael, 168
Haifa, passim

Halva'ah VeChisakhon Bank, 243, 245, 278–79, 299
Hanka, 323
Hanukkah, 205
Harari, Yuval Noah, 373
Haratyk, Gabriela, 34, 367
Hartglas, Apolinary, 187, 192
Hasbun, 143
HaShachar, 137
HaShomer HaTzair, 11n1, 137, 236
Hasidim, 215, 282
Hatikvah, 160, 162, 164, 386–87
Hatzerim, 150
HaTzofeh, 56
Hawaii, 262
Haza, Ofra, 291
Hebrew Pen Club, 159
Hebrew Reali School, 210
Hebron, 141, 146, 284
Hecht, 175
HeHalutz, 137
Herzl, Theodor, 51–52, 145–46, 162, 191, 286, 315, 394–95
Herzliya Hebrew Gymnasium, 142, 222, 296, 321
Hilfstein, Chaim, 54n34, 56, 269
Histadrut (Histadrut HaOvdim HaLeumit), 168, 188, 190, 198, 244, 259, 278–79, 305–6, 310
Hitler, Adolf, 65–66, 83, 87, 108–9, 122, 316
Hłasko, Marek, 324, 376
Hoff, Eva, 193
Holocaust, 9, 12, 21, 87, 106, 115–16, 119–21, 123, 133, 139, 161, 220, 233, 273, 287, 293, 300, 304–5, 311, 374, 376, 381–82, 394, 399, 401–2
Holon, 222, 254
Hong Kong, 261
Honolulu, 262
Horowitz-Karakulska, Bronisława, 359
Horowitz, David, 11, 207, 304, 307–8, 311
Horowitz, Yigal, 307–8
Horowitz's, 248
Huberman, Bronisław, 320
Hubert, 86
Hula, Lake, 370
Hungary, 99
Huppert, Uri, 283

I
IBM, 172
ICT company, 211, 222
Idumeans, 216
Igud Bank, 206
Imber, Naftali Herz, 387
Imperial Ottoman Bank, 145
India, 261, 263, 301, 375
Indonesia, 262
Intel, 172
Interlaken, 348
Intifada, 21, 228
Ipcha, 266
IPN (Institute of National Remembrance), 384
Iran, 220–21, 261–62, 351, 380
Iraq, 113, 142, 220–21, 241, 274, 369
Irgun (Irgun Tzvai Leumi, National Military Organization), 139, 276, 278
Iron Curtain, 129, 136, 155, 354
Isaac, 137, 216–17, 225
Isaiah, 137
Ishmael, 216
Iskierki życia (Sparkles of life), 25–26, 38, 89, 153, 269, 292, 359, 377
Islam, 225, 228
Israel Hayom, 27, 265
Istanbul, 144, 168, 303
Italian Renaissance, 55
Italy, 23n36, 113, 139, 142, 155–56, 188, 256, 274, 295, 306, 310, 346–47, 355
Izaak, 64

J
Jabotinsky, Vladimir Ze'ev, 60, 76, 276, 321, 394, 404
Jacob, 16, 137
Jacometti, 346
Jadwiga, 294
Jaes, 270
Jaffa, 141–142, 144, 146, 156–57, 160, 170, 225
Jaffet, Ernest, 206, 329
Jaffie, 324
Jagiellonian, 10, 71, 86, 89, 278, 363
Jagmetti, 346
Jakimyszyn-Gadocha, Anna, 34
Jakub, 39, 124
Jalal-Abad, 26, 112–13
Janin, 141
Japan, 256–58, 261–63
Jarosław, 70, 220n173
Jaruzelski, Wojciech, 313
Jenin, 141
Jericho, 141, 369
Jerusalem, passim
Jewish Agency, 12n1, 27, 179, 261, 306, 323

Jewishness, 50, 82
Jewry, 114
Jezreel Valley, 148, 290
Jibril, 225
Johanan, 278
John Paul II, Pope, 295, 268n62
John the Baptist, 295, 369
Jordan, 16–17, 144, 241, 283, 290–91, 369–71, 391
Joshua, 369
Judah, 216
Judaism, 71, 90, 180, 225, 228, 273, 281–82, 339, 393, 396
Judea, 16, 241, 401
Judei, 401
Judenfrage, 52
Judeo-Spanish, 191
Judgment Day. *See* Yom Kippur
Judt, Tony, 325
Julius Meinl, 98

K
Kabri, 185
Kadesh, 241
Kafka, Franz, 194, 399
Karavan, Dani, 320
Karlebach, Azriel, 266
Karmiel, 172
Kashiv, 302
Katarzyna, 103
Kathmandu, 263
Katowice, 52, 130
Katz, Bencjon (Bentzion), 14, 56
Katz, Yaakov, 14
Kazakhstan, 19, 109
Kazia, 132
Kazimierz, 45–47, 60, 66, 366–67
Keren Hayesod, 28, 306, 323
Keren Kayemet LeYisrael, 28, 306
Keret, Etgar, 373
Kfar Saba, 246n15
Kfar Stand, 149
KGB, 112
Kharkiv, 109
Khmelnytsky Uprising, 60
Khrushchev, Nikita, 264
Kielce, 99, 124–25, 128, 139
Kiev, 188
Kingdom of Jordan, 241
Kiryat Ata, 176n92, 373
Kivun, 350
Klarwein, Józef, 233
Kleparz, 45, 50

Klepfish, Heshel, 22, 75
Klimecki, 85
Klugman, Aleksander, 32, 265
Knesset, 192, 226, 233, 270, 276–77, 281, 283
Kobe, 262–63
Kochanowski, 55
Kokhba, 16, 390
Koło Ligi Obrony Powietrznej i Przeciwgazowej (LOPP, Group of the Air and Gas Defense League), 57
Kontury, 24, 32, 266, 377
Korczak, Janusz, 233
Koren, 327
Kornblum, Józef, 23
Kossewska, Elżbieta, 31, 195, 264, 266
Kozłowski, Eligiusz, 48
Krakauer Zeitung, 97
Kraków, passim
Krall, Hanna, 376
Krasnouralsk, 110–113
Krayot, 342
Kremlin, 19
Krzemionki Podgórskie, 63
Kuncewiczowa, Maria, 159
Kurier, 265
Kurnikowski, Zdzisław, 323
Kurwiny, 265
Kwutzat Shiller, 149
Kyrgyzstan, 19, 26, 112, 129

L
Lachowski, Paweł, 381
Ladino, 191
Landau, Felix, 193
Łańcut, 402
Łazor, Jerzy, 12, 30
League of Nations, 17, 57, 61, 140n30, 323
Lebanon, 21, 185n101, 205, 226, 241, 369, 391–92
Leipold, 269
Lejeune, Philippe, 33
Les Nouvelles Litteraires, 75
LeSahar Hutz Bank, 245
LeSahar Hutz Bank (Foreign Trade Bank), 245
Lesser Poland, 73, 360, 403
Levanon, Chaim, 253n30
Levant, 274
Levine, G., 13
Levinsky College of Education, 27, 147, 252, 359, 377
Levinsky, Elhanan Leib, 27, 147, 252

Levontin, Zalman David, 146
Levy, Yossef, 359
Lewińska, Maria, 23, 192
Leżajsk, 402
Libya, 180
Lieber, Dov, 351–52
Liga Morska (Marine League), 57
Likud, 228, 276, 306–7
Lipski, Leo, 23, 376
Lithuania, 70, 149
Lochamei, 120
Lod, 141, 168, 289
Loew, Chaim, 55
London, 112, 144–145, 198, 211, 303, 306, 315n158, 319, 326, 332, 341–44, 346–48, 359, 384
Los Angeles, 262
Löw, Ryszard, 24, 27, 34, 60, 169, 322
Lubetkin, Zivia, 121
Lublin, 293n94
Lubyanka, 112
Luxembourg, 86, 311
Łużki, 192n115
Lviv, 28, 70, 72, 78–79, 84, 108–110, 144, 149

M
Ma'ariv, 266, 294
Mabovitch, Golda, 188
Maccabees, 120, 205
Macharski, Franciszek, 360
Madatech-Israel (National Museum of Science), 175
Magic Carpet, 180
Mahane Israel, 195, 203
Maier, F. A., 145
Maimon, Yehuda Leib HaCohen, 5, 164, 408
Majchrowski, Jacek, 360, 363
Majdanek, 269
Malay Peninsula, 262
Malaysia, 262
Małysiak, Albin, 360
Mameluks, 16
Mané-Katz Museum, 175
Manougian, Nourhan, 229
Maor, Galia, 331
Mapai (Social-Democratic Workers Party of Israel), 168, 188, 198, 311
Mary of Nazareth, 382
Masada fortress, 390
Massachusetts, 2
Matam Industrial Center, 172
Mauritius, 117n74

Mayski, Ivan, 112
Mazurek Dąbrowskiego, 387
Me'arat HaNetifim, 340
Mea Shearim, 282
Mecca, 141, 225
Medinat, 16
Mediterranean, 16, 144, 156, 161, 170, 174, 222, 256, 289, 303, 339, 370
Mehta, Zubin, 357
Meir, Golda, 13, 20, 56, 157, 162, 188–89, 192, 227, 277, 304, 373
Mendelsohn, Szlomo, 32
Mendelssohn, Moses, 403
Merhavia, 188
Meus, Konrad, 35
Mexico, 264
Meyerson, Golda. *See* Meir, Golda
Meyerson, Morris, 188
Mezraa, 143
Mickiewicz, Adam, 26, 41, 69, 365, 378
Microsoft, 172
Midrasz, 32
Mifelew, Nachman, 56
Migdal HaEmek, 221
Migdal Shalom, 321
Migros company, 346
Miki (Michael), 210–211
Milówka, 37n3
Minc, Hilary, 124
Mishal, Nissim, 14
Mistabra, Ipcha, 266
Mitzpe Ramon, 221
Mizrachi, 307, 343
Mograbi, Yaakow, 319
Momentowicz, 101
Monte Cassino, 324
Montefiore, Simon Sebag, 14
Montenegro, 357
Moravia, 199
Morawiecki, Mateusz, 385
Moriah, 225
Morocco, 156
Mosad, 116, 188, 336
Mosberg, Edward, 359
Mościcki, Ignacy, 61
Moscow, 112, 183
Moses, 180
Moshav Movement, 176n92, 305n132
Moshav Nahalal, 148
Mossad, 14
Motzkin, 204–5
Mount Carmel, 120, 156, 172–74, 185–186, 209, 225, 227–28, 238, 269, 391

Mount Hermon, 391
Mrożek, Sławomir, 324
Muhammad, 225
Müller, Bruno, 86
Mumbai, 145, 262, 357
Mund, 327
Munich, 86, 188–89, 303
Munweis, Paula, 168
Muralt, Peter, 34, 346–47
Muslim, 16, 180, 227–28
Muslims, 216, 225, 228, 270, 285, 298

N
Naaman, 369
Nabataeans, 216
Nablus, 141
Nahalal, 148, 226
Nahariya, 205, 321
Nakba, 162
Namier, Lewis, 286
Narew, 109
Nasser, Jacques, 327
National Defense Fund, 61, 279
National Library of Israel, 194
National Radical Camp (ONR), 381
NATO, 21
Naval Museum, 119, 268
Nazareth, 141, 283, 382
Nazi, 19–20, 32, 68, 78, 86, 108–9, 114, 116, 122, 161, 180, 238, 268, 293, 311, 377, 384
Nazis, 36, 78, 86–87, 91, 93, 96, 106, 114, 122, 287, 318, 335, 385
Near, Henry, 13
Neeman, Jael, 151
Negev, 169, 179, 215–18, 220, 236, 242, 253
Nela, 65, 96–97, 101, 185–86, 197
Nepal, 263–64
Nesher, 176
Netafim, 150
Netanya, 172, 187, 204, 222, 260, 296, 327
Netanyahu, Benjamin, 351, 368, 385
Netherlands, 256, 375
Neturei Karta, 351
Neustein, Ada and Edmund, 265, 322
Neusteins, 323
Neve Tzedek, 316
New York, 12, 153, 168, 262, 303, 306, 359, 376
Nicosia, 303
Nir Gad, Ram, 140
NIS (New Israeli Shekel), 308
Nisk, 84
NKVD, 78, 112, 276

Nobel Prize, 26, 277, 324, 378
Nordau, 169
Nourhan, 229
Nouvelles, 75
Nowiny Izraelskie-Kurier, 265
Nowiny Kurier, 24, 265
Nowiny Poranne, 24
Nowy Dziennik, 24n40, 39, 365
NSDAP, 103, 311
Nuremberg, 86, 406

O
Odessa, 50, 144
Okraj, Zofia, 397
Old Testament, 217, 363
Olearczyk, Teresa, 29, 395n7
Olympics, 188
Orbis Travel Agency, 323
Ordonówna, Hanka, 323
Orient, 200, 212
Oriental Jews, 20, 213, 270
Orit, 196, 205–6, 209–210, 213–14, 238–39, 295–96, 337, 360, 397, 406
Orphaned, 37
Orthodox Jews, 54, 88, 191, 205, 229–31, 236, 275, 279–83, 293, 305, 307, 333, 350, 362
Ortner (Shatil), Celina, 116–17, 120, 140
Ortner, Celina, 116
Osirak, 277
Ottoman, 16, 141, 145, 149, 168, 306
Oz, Amos, 14n21, 303–304, 373

P
PAGI Bank, 246
Pahlawi, Mohammad Reza, 262
Palace under the Rams, 85
Palestine, 16–17, 30, 76, 159–60, 162, 166, 189, 191, 239, 241, 276, 320
Palestinians, 17, 228, 284, 286, 371
Palmon, Henryk, 23, 270
Pan, 25, 41
Panas, Władysław, 138n25
Paradise Cinema, 319
Paris, 51, 303
Pat and Patachon, 266
Patek, Artur, 15
Patria, 117
Patton, Francesco, 229
Paving, 306
Pecaric, Sacha, 137
Pedagogical University of Krakow, 8, 34, 253, 359, 380–81

Penderecki, Krzysztof, 223
Pennsylvania, 245
Perec, 190
Peres, Shimon, 13, 20, 143, 192, 285–86, 315, 319, 369–70
Persia, 274
Peru, 140
Pesachz, 400
Petah Tikva, 301
Petersburg, 51
Petra, 371
Philistines, 16, 137
Piastowska, 73
Pick, Svika, 265
Piech, Tadeusz, 323
Pilate, 225
Piłsudski, Józef, 50, 61, 84, 336, 403
Pinsker, Leon, 52, 394
Pirkei Avot, 339
Planty Dietlowskie, 57
Płaszów, 95, 359, 406
Płońsk, 168, 192
Poalei Zion (Workers of Zion), 168
Podbrodzie, 147
Podemska, Justyna, 15
Podgórze, 62, 64, 88, 91, 93, 96, 186, 359, 366
Podhale Rifles, 37–39, 199
pogrom, 78, 124–26, 128
Pohlmann, Lili, 359
Polajner, 202
Poldek. *See* Wasserman, Leopold
Police, 95, 97, 102–3, 124, 154, 230, 291, 299–302, 407
POLIN Museum of the History of Polish Jews, 402
Polish Government-in-Exile, 112, 385
Polish United Workers' Party (PZPR), 124
Polish Workers' Party (PPR), 124
Polish-Israeli Friendship Society, 9, 21, 30, 35, 265, 322, 359, 362, 381
Polonia, 144
Polonsky, Antony, 34
Pomeranz, Moses, 76
Portugal, 274
Potoks, 130
Poznań, 24
Prague, 129, 133
Protestant, 73, 359
Prussia, 67
Pruszyński, Ksawery, 76
Przegląd, 24, 266
Przemyśl, 110

Purchla, Jacek, 86

R
Raanana, 254
Rabin, Yitzhak, 13, 20
Rachel, 214
Rachum, Arie, 322
Radom, 19, 29, 97–99, 101, 106–7, 115, 125, 360
Rady, 391n2
Rafah, 141, 242
Rajcza, 37
Rakowice-Czyżyny airport, 86
Ramat Aviv, 238, 326, 373
Ramat Gan, 222, 253, 301
Ramat HaSharon, 26, 222
Rambam Medical Center, 176
Ramla, 141
Rashi, 137
Rechen, Rysiek, 268, 269n65
Rechtman, Pola, 70
Rehovot, 167
Reims, 114
Representation, 355
Republicans, 275
Reymont, Władysław, 41
Ribbentrop-Molotov pact, 109
Rieck, Hersch, 347
Rishon LeZion, 150
Ritter, Hubert, 86
Ritterman-Abir, Henryk, 24
Robinson's Arch, 231
Romania, 117, 221, 300
Romans, 16, 216, 390
Rome, 303
Rosenberg, David, 297–99
Rosh Hashanah (Jewish New Year), 39, 90
Rosman, Moshe, 32
Rothschild, 150, 155, 162, 258, 297, 319, 350, 355
Róża, 126, 197, 322
Rozenfeld, Alexander, 293–95, 312, 393
Rózia, 96–97, 101, 107
Rudnicki, Szymon, 30
Russia, 14n21, 19, 110, 142, 263, 301
Rutenberg, Pinkus, 144–45
Ruzik, 107
Rwanda, 368
Rywkind, Abraham, 257

S
Sabbath, 45–46, 126, 162, 164, 174, 177, 231, 281–82, 307, 403

Sable, David, 13
Sachsenhausen, 86
Sadat, Anwar, 277
Safed, 141, 146
Safra, Joseph, 327n186
Safras, 327, 343
Saint Adalbert, 51
Salah al-Din, 116
Salzburg, 155
Samaria, 241
Samuel, Herbert, 140n30
San, 109
San Francisco, 174, 262
Sando, 197
Sapir Prize, 376
Sapir, Pinchas, 245–46
Sarajevo, 76
Sarid, Yishai, 373
Sarzyński, Piotr, 293
Saudi Arabia, 371
Sayeret Matkal, 336
Scandinavia, 215
Scharf, Rafael F., 76, 196
Schenirer, Tulo, 9
Schindler, Oskar, 268–69, 362
Schori, Ilan, 14
Schulz, Bruno, 193
Schuss, Zeev, 324
Schwartz, Felicia, 351–32
Sde Boker Kibbutz, 169
Sderot, 221
Segev, Tom, 12, 311
Sejm of the Republic of Poland, 404
Seleucids, 205
Seljuk, 16
Senor, Dan, 11, 262–63, 287
Sephardi, 191, 274
Sèvres, 242
Shalev, Meir, 373
Shanghai, 76, 255
Shapira, Anita, 12, 306–8
Sharett. *See* Shertok
Sharm el-Sheikh, 237, 271
Sharon, Ariel, 20, 220–21, 228
Shas, 283
Shatil. *See* Ortner, Celina
Shaye, Uncle, 187
Shefayim, 189
Shemen company, 176
Shemer, Naomi, 291
Shertok, 116
Shiller, 149
Shindler, Colin, 12

Shmona, 221, 260, 327
Shoah, 12, 120, 181, 184, 249, 289, 380
Siberia, 109
Sienkiewicz, Henryk, 26, 41, 60, 69, 378
Sikorski-Mayski agreement, 112, 276
Silber, Marcos, 30–31
Siberia, 268n62
Silberg, Halinka, 65
Silbergs, 65
Silesia, 36–37, 49, 73, 102, 123, 133–35, 359
Simeon, 216
Sinai, 216, 291
Sinai Peninsula, 271
Singapore, 262
Singaporean, 262
Singer, Saul, 11, 262–63, 287, 342
Six-Day War, 21, 183, 208, 220, 223, 226–27, 271, 291, 296, 304, 329
Skorek, Artur, 12, 352
Skotnicki, Aleksander B., 5, 10, 27, 29, 34, 54, 292–93, 360, 362–363, 378, 381
Skwara, Marek, 32
Slovakia, 133
Słowacki, Juliusz, 41, 87, 365
Sokołów, Nahum (Natan), 311, 315, 394
Solel-Bone, 306
Solidarity movement, 294n94
Solomon, 180
Sonderaktion Krakau, 86
Soroka University Medical Center, 218
Soviet Union, 19–20, 78–79, 83, 108–115, 123, 129–131, 139, 145, 153, 155, 173, 179–81, 218, 220, 264, 276, 296, 304, 309–310, 323, 336, 355, 379, 402
Spain, 256, 274, 375
Spielberg, Steven, 189
Square, 45, 57, 64–65, 87, 92–93, 135, 160, 233, 238, 286, 359, 365–66
St. Mary's Church, 85
St. Moritz, 289
Staatstheater des Generalgouvernements, 87
Stalin, Joseph, 19, 108–09, 114, 264
Stalinist, 124, 388
Star of David, 88
Stefa, aunt, 238
Stein, Menachem, 56
Stendig, Samuel, 56, 70
Stola, Dariusz, 31
Stoss,Veit, 85
Stradom, 45, 362
Strait of Tirana, 241–42
Strasbourg, 86
Strug, Andrzej, 323

Suez campaign, 21, 186
Suez Canal, 141, 145, 241–42, 291
Sukiennice, 365
Supreme Court of Israel, 193, 230, 351
Suwałki, 246n15
Sverdlovsk Oblast, 110
Sweden, 306
Switzerland, 8–9, 215, 289, 295, 300, 310, 320n166, 343, 346–347, 356–57, 395
Swoszowice, 39, 132
Sylwin, Anatol, 133
Sylwins, 134–35
Syria, 21, 144, 226, 241, 290, 369–70
Szir (Wolman-Sieraczkowa), Miriam, 33
Szmulewicz, Mati, 294
Szonberg, Oleś, 340–41
Sztorc, 360
Sztybel, 60–61
Szymborska, Wisława, 325, 376
Szyszko-Bohusz, Adolf, 86

T
Taba, 237
Talmud, 396
Tanakh, 16, 201
Tańska-Hoffmanowa, Klementyna, 61
Tashkent, 112
Technion, 147, 172, 211, 222, 252, 255, 267, 332
Tehran, 261–62, 323
Tel Aviv School of Law and Economics (Beit Sefer Gavoha LeMishpat VeKalkala), 201
Tel-Aviv, passim
Temple, 52, 175, 205, 225, 227–28, 390, 396
Thai, 368
Thailand, 262
Thatcher, Margaret, 188
Theophilos III, 229
Third Reich, 78, 85, 87, 99, 109, 111, 114, 199, 269, 384–85, 406
Thirty-Sixth Division, 289
Thomas Cook company, 261
Tiberias, 141, 143, 146, 148–49, 370
Tikotin Museum of Japanese Art, 175
Timna Valley, 340
Tokyo, 262
Tomaszewski, Jerzy, 12
Torah, 137, 229, 280, 367, 404
Toscanini, Arturo, 320
Transjordan, 241
Trawers construction company, 133–35
Treblinka, 376, 379

Trump, Donald, 223
Tsanin, Mordechai, 125n5
Tulkarm, 141
Tyszkiewicz, Michał, 323
TZAHAL (Israeli Defense Force, Tzava Hagana LeYisrael), 276, 336–37, 351
Tzofim, 268, 404
Tzvai, 276

U
UK, 113
Ukraine, 28, 70
Ultra, 264
Ultra-Orthodox Jews, 229–31, 236, 246, 280, 283, 299, 307, 350–52
UN, 76, 117, 239
UN General Assembly Resolution, 117, 162, 241, 313
UNESCO, 35, 175, 319
United States, passim
Urals, 110
USA, 15, 144
USSR, 19n26, 109, 112–13, 166, 180, 242, 341
Uzbekistan, 112

V
Vashemthe, 121
Via Dolorosa, 225
Vichy, 226
Vienna, 52, 72, 154–55, 262, 268, 303
Vietnam, 226
Vilnius, 70, 76, 147, 276
Vision, 55, 283
Vistula, 5 8, 86, 152, 322, 355

W
Wächter, Otto, 86, 90
Wadowice, 139, 268n62
Wailing Wall, 223, 229
Walkowski, Szewach, 55
Wall Street Journal Journal, 75, 297, 351, 384
Wannsee, 78
Waqf, 227–228
War of Attrition (Israeli-Egyptian clashes), 21
Warsaw, 22n29, 36, 55, 60, 70, 73, 79, 85, 106, 120–22, 139, 144, 150, 168, 233, 240, 276, 319–20, 322, 324, 349, 355–56
Warsaw Uprising, 60, 120–22, 228
Wasserman, Leopold (Poldek), 5, 9, 34, 56, 209, 268, 408

Wawel, 85–86
Wehrmacht, 110
Weiss, Shevah, 12, 187, 249
Weitz, Joseph, 179
Weizmann, Chaim, 165–67
Weizmann, David, 239–40, 253, 255, 394–95
West Pomeranian Voivodeship, 286
Wichner, Uncle, 39, 90
Wisła, 367
Wittgenstein, Ludwig, 70
WIZO (Women's International Zionist Organization), 198, 205, 306
Wohlfeiler, Rena, 9
Wojtyła, Karol, 268n62. *See also* John Paul II, Pope
Wola Justowska, 85
Wolffsohn, David, 146
World War II, passim
Wrocław, 23n36, 186, 293n94
Wybicki, Józef, 387
Wygodzki, Stanisław, 293, 295
Wyszogród, 315n158
Wyżlińska, Zofia, 34

Y
Yad Vashem, 27, 106, 193, 233, 265
Yaffa, 324
Yafo, 28, 243
Yahoo, 172
Yarkon River,1 59, 161
Yarmouk, 370
Yedioth Achronoth, 27, 265, 303
Yemen, 203n139
Yiddish, 185, 191–192, 194–96
Yokneam, 172
Yom Ha-Atzmaut, 162
Yom HaShoah, 374, 399
Yom HaZikaron, 399
Yom Kippur, 21, 38–39, 90, 189, 227, 291, 308
Yugoslavia, 160

Z
Żabotyński, Włodzimierz. *See* Jabotinsky, Vladimir Ze'ev
Zamenhof, Ludwik, 403
Zamość, 114
Zaolzie, 98
Zarethan, 369
Zbaraż, 23n33
Zbydniowice, 39, 62, 64, 90
Żelazowa Wola, 356
Zhovti Vody, 60
Zhukov, Georgy, 114
Zikaron BaSalon, 374–75
Zikhron Ya'akov, 150
Zimmerer, Katarzyna, 31–32
Zimnawoda, Moses ,270
Zion, 52, 144, 146, 168, 225, 269, 387, 390–91
Zionism, 13, 52, 151, 227, 243
Zionists, 19n26, 39, 56, 67, 137, 185, 227, 265, 274, 280, 304
ŻOB (Jewish Combat Organisation), 405
Zolochiv, 387
Zuckerman, Yitzhak, 121
Żurek, Sławomir Jacek, 25, 29, 34, 324
Zurich, 16, 303, 306, 326, 334, 341–44, 346–48, 356
Zweig, Stefan, 75
Żyrardów, 22n29
Żywiec Beskids, 37